ICSEA 2020

The Fifteenth International Conference on Software Engineering Advances

October 18 -22, 2020

ICSEA 2020 Editors

Luigi Lavazza, Università degli Studi dell'Insubria, Italy

Roy Oberhauser, Aalen University, Germany

Mannaert Herwig, University of Antwerp, Belgium

Krishna Kavi, University of North Texas, USA

Printed from e-media with permission by:

Curran Associates, Inc.
57 Morehouse Lane
Red Hook, NY 12571

Some format issues inherent in the e-media version may also appear in this print version.

Printed with permission by Curran Associates, Inc. (2020)

International Academy, Research, and Industry Association (IARIA)
412 Derby Way
Wilmington, DE 19810

Phone: (408) 893-6407
Fax: (408) 527-6351

petre@iaria.org

Additional copies of this publication are available from:

Curran Associates, Inc.
57 Morehouse Lane
Red Hook, NY 12571 USA
Phone: 845-758-0400
Fax: 845-758-2633
Email: curran@proceedings.com
Web: www.proceedings.com

Table of Contents

ICSEA 2020

Forward

The Fifteenth International Conference on Software Engineering Advances (ICSEA 2020), held on October 18 - 22, 2020, continued a series of events covering a broad spectrum of software-related topics.

The conference covered fundamentals on designing, implementing, testing, validating and maintaining various kinds of software. The tracks treated the topics from theory to practice, in terms of methodologies, design, implementation, testing, use cases, tools, and lessons learnt. The conference topics covered classical and advanced methodologies, open source, agile software, as well as software deployment and software economics and education.

The conference had the following tracks:

- Advances in fundamentals for software development
- Advanced mechanisms for software development
- Advanced design tools for developing software
- Software engineering for service computing (SOA and Cloud)
- Advanced facilities for accessing software
- Software performance
- Software security, privacy, safeness
- Advances in software testing
- Specialized software advanced applications
- Web Accessibility
- Open source software
- Agile and Lean approaches in software engineering
- Software deployment and maintenance
- Software engineering techniques, metrics, and formalisms
- Software economics, adoption, and education
- Business technology
- Improving productivity in research on software engineering
- Trends and achievements

Similar to the previous edition, this event continued to be very competitive in its selection process and very well perceived by the international software engineering community. As such, it is attracting excellent contributions and active participation from all over the world. We were very pleased to receive a large amount of top quality contributions.

We take here the opportunity to warmly thank all the members of the ICSEA 2020 technical program committee as well as the numerous reviewers. The creation of such a broad and high quality conference program would not have been possible without their involvement. We also kindly thank all the authors that dedicated much of their time and efforts to contribute to the ICSEA 2020. We truly believe that thanks to all these efforts, the final conference program consists of top quality contributions.

This event could also not have been a reality without the support of many individuals, organizations and sponsors. We also gratefully thank the members of the ICSEA 2020 organizing committee for their help in handling the logistics and for their work that is making this professional meeting a success.

We hope the ICSEA 2020 was a successful international forum for the exchange of ideas and results between academia and industry and to promote further progress in software engineering research.

ICSEA 2020 Publicity Chair

Lorena Parra, Universitat Politecnica de Valencia, Spain

ICSEA 2020

Committee

ICSEA 2020 Publicity Chair

Lorena Parra, Universitat Politecnica de Valencia, Spain

ICSEA 2020 Technical Program Committee

Shahliza Abd Halim, UniversityTeknologi Malaysia, Malaysia
Tamer Abdou, Ryerson University, Canada
Eman Abdullah Alomar, Rochester Institute of Technology, USA
Ammar Kareem Obayes Alazzawi, Universiti Teknologi PETRONAS, Malaysia
Talat Ambreen, International Islamic University, Islamabad, Pakistan
Daniel Andresen, Kansas State University, USA
Jean-Paul Arcangeli, UPS - IRIT, France
Takuya Azumi, Saitama University, Japan
Gilbert Babin, HEC Montréal, Canada
Jorge Barreiros, ISEC - Polytechnic of Coimbra / NOVA LINCS, Portugal
Ateet Bhalla, Independent Consultant, India
Mina Boström Nakicenovic, Paradox Interactive, Sweden
Uwe Breitenbücher, University of Stuttgart, Germany
José Carlos Bregieiro Ribeiro, Polytechnic Institute of Leiria, Portugal
Carlos A. Casanova Pietroboni, National Technological University - Concepción del Uruguay Regional Faculty (UTN-FRCU), Argentina
Fuxiang Chen, DeepSearch Inc., Korea
Rebeca Cortazar, University of Deusto, Spain
Mónica Costa, Polytechnic Institute of Castelo Branco, Portugal
Yania Crespo, University of Valladolid, Spain
Luis Cruz, TU Delft, Netherlands
Beata Czarnacka-Chrobot, Warsaw School of Economics, Poland
Giovanni Daián Róttoli, Universidad Tecnológica Nacional (UTN-FRCU), Argentina
Darren Dalcher, Lancaster University, UK
Thiago C. de Sousa, State University of Piauí, Brazil
Lin Deng, Towson University, USA
Diogo Domingues Regateiro, Instituto de Telecomunicações | Universidade de Aveiro, Portugal
Imke Helene Drave, RWTH Aachen University, Germany
Holger Eichelberger, University of Hildesheim | Software Systems Engineering, Germany
Ridha Ejbali, National Engineering School of Gabes (ENIS) / University of Gabes, Tunisia
Gledson Elias, Federal University of Paraíba (UFPB), Brazil
Thelma Elita Colanzi, State University of Maringa (UEM), Brazil
Diana ElRabih, Monty Holding, Beirut, Lebanon
Christoph Elsner, Siemens AG, Germany
Romina Eramo, Universityof L'Aquila, Italy

Alexandre Marcos Lins de Vasconcelos, Universidade Federal de Pernambuco, Recife, Brazil
Célia Martinie, Université Paul Sabatier Toulouse III, France
Rohit Mehra, Accenture Labs, India
Kristof Meixner, Christian Doppler Lab CDL-SQI | Institute for Information Systems Engineering | Technische Universität Wien, Vienna, Austria
Vojtech Merunka, Czech University of Life Sciences in Prague / Czech Technical University in Prague, Czech Republic
José Carlos M. M. Metrolho, Polytechnic Institute of Castelo Branco, Portugal
Sanjay Misra, Covenant University, Nigeria
Mohamed Wiem Mkaouer, Rochester Institute of Technology, USA
Miguel P. Monteiro, Universidade NOVA de Lisboa, Portugal
Óscar Mortágua Pereira, University of Aveiro, Portugal
Kmimech Mourad, Higher Institute for Computer Science and Mathematics of Monastir, Tunisia
Kazi Muheymin-Us-Sakib, Institute of Information Technology (IIT) | University of Dhaka, Bangladesh
Marcellin Nkenlifack, University of Dschang, Cameroon
Marc Novakouski, Carnegie Mellon Software Engineering Institute, USA
Roy Oberhauser, Aalen University, Germany
Shinpei Ogata, Shinshu University, Japan
Thomas Olsson, RISE Research Institutes of Sweden, Sweden
Safa Omri, Daimler AG / Karlsruhe Institute of Technology, Germany
Flavio Oquendo, IRISA (UMR CNRS) - University of South Brittany, France
Marcos Palacios, University of Oviedo, Spain
Beatriz Pérez Valle, University of La Rioja, Spain
Monica Pinto, University of Málaga, Spain
Aneta Poniszewska-Maranda, Institute of Information Technology | Lodz University of Technology, Poland
Pasqualina Potena, RISE Research Institutes of Sweden AB, Sweden
Evgeny Pyshkin, University of Aizu, Japan
Claudia Raibulet, University of Milano-Bicocca, Italy
Muthu Ramachandran, Leeds Beckett University, UK
Raman Ramsin, Sharif University of Technology, Iran
Fernando Reinaldo Ribeiro, Polytechnic Institute of Castelo Branco, Portugal
Catarina I. Reis, School of Technology and Management | Polytechnic of Leiria, Portugal
Michele Risi, University of Salerno, Italy
Renaud Rwemalika, SnT - University of Luxembourg, Luxembourg
Nyyti Saarimäki, Tampere University, Finland
Bilal Abu Salih, The University of Jordan, Jordan
Hiroyuki Sato, University of Tokyo, Japan
Salva Sébastien, University of Clermont Auvergne | LIMOS Laboratory | CNRS, France
Vesna Šešum-Čavić, TU Wien, Austria
István Siket, University of Szeged, Hungary
Karolj Skala, Hungarian Academy of Sciences, Hungary / Ruđer Bošković Institute Zagreb, Croatia
Maria Spichkova, RMIT University, Australia
Fausto Spoto, Università di Verona, Italy
Sidra Sultana, National University of Sciences and Technology, Pakistan
Yingcheng Sun, Columbia University in New York City, USA
Mahbubur Syed, Minnesota State University Mankato, USA
Christos Troussas, University of West Attica, Greece

Copyright Information

A Systematic Literature Review on Misconceptions in Software Engineering

Carolin Gold-Veerkamp
University of Applied Sciences Aschaffenburg
Aschaffenburg, Germany
Email: carolin.gold-veerkamp@th-ab.de

Nermin Saray
University of Applied Sciences Coburg
Coburg, Germany
Email: nermin.saray@stud.hs-coburg.de

***Abstract*—From a constructivist perspective, learning is an active, cognitive process in which individuals construct their own knowledge by connecting new concepts with previous knowledge, skills, and experience that serve as points of departure. The purpose of this study is to identify and analyse known evidence-based misconceptions in Software Engineering to use these insights for higher education. We used a systematic literature review as a secondary data accumulation, searching 10 databases automatically using predefined search queries and selection criteria. Out of 2,158 publications found, 18 could be identified as appropriate for the selection criteria. These contain over 100 statements which the authors of these publications refer to as misconceptions/beliefs/myths. Yet, only a fraction of these are based on evidence; namely 20 items from 3 papers. Currently, evidence-based research on misconceptions in Software Engineering is limited. We, therefore, deduce that evidence-based primary data acquisition and analysis should be the research desideratum.**

***Keywords*–Software Engineering, Higher Education, Misconceptions, Systematic Literature Review.**

I. Introduction

From a constructivist point of view, learning is to be understood as an active, individual, situated, social, and cognitive psychological process. Each individual has to build up their own knowledge by combining new concepts based on previous knowledge, existing competencies, previous experience, as well as conceptions and putting it into a network-like relationship. This means, learners form conceptions and models to explain phenomena, processes, and artifacts before they are confronted with them in institutional learning. These possibly alternative – from scientific or expert perspective – conceptions have a twofold significant impact on the learning process. On one hand, they can serve as the basis for learning, on the other, they can also contradict the educational content and thus hinder the learning process.

In order to be able to achieve sustainable learning (in higher education), a purely technical structuring of the learning content is therefore insufficient. Furthermore, didactics should do justice to the learners' "points of departure" [1, p. 6]. The Model of Educational Reconstruction, which is epistemologically based on the constructivist position, calls for precisely this consideration [1][2]. The model comprises the triad of *content clarification*, *learners' conceptions*, and *didactic design*; it considers the scientific concepts and the student conceptions as equivalents.

To be able to use this model in Software Engineering (SE) education, we have to take a step back and clarify which misconceptions undergraduates bring to university. Thus, a Systematic Literature Review (SLR) as a secondary data analysis provides information about known SE misconceptions.

Therefore, the paper is structured as follows: It starts with terminological aspects, as a plurality of terms evolved, and related work in other disciplines. The SLR process is explained in Section II, complemented by the results (Section III). Before the paper closes, a short discussion is given (Section IV).

A. Terminological Aspects

Due to many different ways of looking at the research object '*(mis-)conceptions*' as well as the critical examination of the terminology, an abundance of terms has developed. The different understandings have led to a plurality of terms with multiple connotations. The abundance of technical terms has risen so much in the course of research (especially in natural sciences didactics) that it is now almost impossible to survey. The fact that the terms cannot be clearly distinguished from each other often leads to a more or less synonymous use and thus to an undifferentiated mix. As a result of the dissatisfaction with this situation, researchers have again constructed and defined additional terms, which expands the existing term dilemma.

In addition to [3] [4], also others include entire collections of terms. This list (merely referenced by single publications due to restricted page space) gives an impression of the broad spectrum:

- *Preconceptions* [3]–[6]
- *(Students') conceptions* [3][4]
- *Alternative conceptions* [3]
- *Naïve conceptions* [4]
- *Naïve theories* [3][4]
- *Naïve beliefs* [3]
- *Beliefs* [7]
- *Alternative beliefs* [3]
- *Alternative frameworks* [3][4][6]
- *Intuitive theories/science* [6]
- *Prior knowledge* [6]
- *Misconceptions*, the "standard term" as [3, p. 119] state – despite the negative connotation [4] [6].

In spite of the heterogeneity of terms, opposed opinions and discussions on the different types of expression, it can be stated consensually that individuals each develop different conceptions of certain concepts, which should and must be used as a starting point in teaching. These conceptions can, but do not have to be in line with modern scientific theories [4] and therefore may act as learning obstacles [8], often referred to as *misconceptions*.

B. Related Work on Misconceptions in Didactics

The research and publications about misconceptions in natural sciences in the context of school are immense, as a bibliography by Duit [9] proves. When looking at the catalogue, encompassing over 8,300 publications and summarizing them per decade (Figure 1), it is obvious that since the mid-1970s international researchers have been investigating the field.

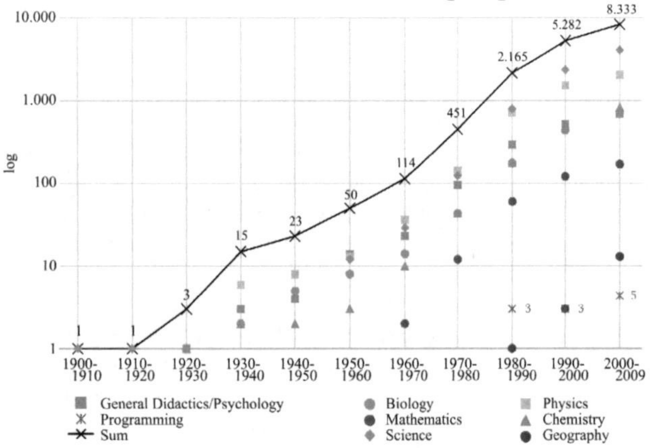

Fig. 1. Diagram of Accumulated Number of Publications per Decade, Sorted by Discipline Listed in [9]; esp. Focused on 'Programming'

Out of these, merely five publications [10]–[14] can be assigned to 'programming' as nearest to SE, but also to science and/or maths; i.e. they are equivocal.

Moreover, in the last few years, several papers on misconception research in computer sciences appeared concerning:

- ... programming [15]–[18] and object-oriented programming in particular [19][20].
- ... artifacts, e.g., computers, smartphones, and so on [21, and others].
- ... the Internet [22].

All publications listed have in common that they do not particularly deal with SE and are contextualised within school education. This results in research needs for SE in university.

II. Method: SLR on Misconceptions in SE

In order to be able to present the state of research on (undergraduate) conceptions in SE, there is a need for a SLR, which summarizes all available information about this phenomenon thoroughly and impartially [23, p. 7]. Conducting a SLR is a quantitative methodology of secondary data collection for the synthesis of research results from primary studies. The guidelines – used here – that Kitchenham and Charters have drawn up for SE are derived from several approaches in medicine and the social sciences [23, p. vi].

The following explanations, which describe the three-phase process of the SLR – carried out as a computer-based, automated search – are divided into the initial planning in Section II-A, the actual practical implementation (Section II-B) and the subsequent presentation and use of the results (Section III), see also [23][24].

A. Phase 1: Initial Planning

The planning of the SLR contains some parameters that require previous definition in order to minimize bias. The SLR is determined as follows:

1) Research Question(s): To what extent does research on misconceptions in SE already exist? Which misconceptions in SE are known/documented?

2) Search Strategy:

a) Language Selection: At this point, the language radius, which is one of the inclusion criteria, should be anticipated. The reason for this is the following definition of the Search Query (SQ). Since research on conceptions is international, publications in German and English are considered.

b) Queries and Synonyms: Regardless of the various connotations (Section I-A), the search should encompass the previous research on misconceptions in SE as broadly as possible. Therefore, the search query is based on the numerous synonymously used English terms shown in Table I. (Indicating wildcards, i.e. placeholders, by an asterisk (*).)

TABLE I. Development of the English Search Query Using Synonyms

Synonyms	Substrings	
	Noun	**Adjective**
preconceptions	preconception*	–
students' conceptions	conception*	–
alternative conceptions		alternative
naïve conceptions		naïve
naïve theories	–	
naïve beliefs	belief*	
beliefs		–
alternative beliefs		alternative
alternative frameworks	–	
intuitive theories	–	intuitive
intuitive science	–	
prior knowledge	–	prior
misconceptions	misconception*	–

In contrast to *preconception*, *conception*, *belief* and *misconception*, the terms *theory*, *framework* and *science* (plus plurals) are only included in combination with the respective adjectives (Table I), since they are often used as technical terms in SE and unspecific for answering the research question. Same applies to the terms *student*, *knowledge* and *science*, because of the usage of pedagogical databases. These are combined with the disciplinary focus on SE, resulting in Search Query 1; including wildcards (*) and search for exact phrases (quotation marks). (The equivalent German SQ is not attached here.)

c) Database: Electronic literature databases are selected based on Kitchenham et al. [25] in combination with [26]. Kitchenham et al. have already dealt intensively with SLRs in the area of SE and set up a list of important English-language journals and conferences, which they themselves use for their literature research (see Table II).

("software engineer*" OR "software development*" OR "software process*")
AND
("preconception*" OR "conception*" OR "belief*" OR "misconception*"
OR
"naïve theor*" OR "alternative framework*" OR
"intuitive theor*" OR "intuitive science" OR "prior knowledge")

Query 1. English Search Query

TABLE II. SELECTION OF ELECTRONIC DATABASES FOR SLR BASED ON [25] [26]

Source	IEEE	ACM	SD	SC	SL	ERIC	WoS	GS	arXiv	dblp
Information and Software Technology			X	X				X		
Journal of Systems and Software			X	X				X		
IEEE Transactions on SE	X							X		
IEEE Software	X							X		
Communications of the ACM		X								
ACM Computer Surveys		X								
ACM Transactions on SE Methodologies		X								
Software Practice and Experience								X		
Empirical SE Journal					X					
IEEE Proc. Software (now: IET Software)	X							X		
Proc. Int. Conference on SE	X	X						X		
Proc. Int. Symp. of Software Metrics	X	X						X		
Proc. Int. Symp. on Empirical SE	X	X						X		

These are used as a basis to identify databases that include these compilations, namely: IEEE-Xplore [28], ACM-Digital Library [29], SpringerLink (SL) [30], Scopus (SC) [31], and Science Direct (SD) [32]. This selection is supplemented by further search engines from the educational context (ERIC [33], Web of Science (WoS) [34]) and the metadata database GoogleScholar (GS) [35]. In addition to the proposed ones, arXiv [36], an open access repository for electronic preprints from numerous areas – including computer science –, and the dblp [37], which is co-founded by the German federal government, are used.

3) Selection Strategy: The selection is controlled on the basis of the following predefined Inclusion (IC) and Exclusion Criteria (EC).

IC.1 The publication is written in English or German language.
IC.2 It is explicitly about the discipline SE.
IC.3 Misconceptions in SE are explicitly mentioned.

EC.1 The contribution is an abstract, workshop, poster, or similar, as these do not provide in-depth information.

4) Quality Assessment: The gathered publications have to be qualified against predefined Quality Criteria (QC):

QC.1 *Traceability*: How do the authors know this misconception? It is scientifically important to be able to track where the information comes from.
QC.2 *Validation*: Has it been confirmed that it is a misconception? How did the authors validate the conception to be "at odds with modern scientific theories" [4, p. 2]? If not done, there is no indication that it is really a *mis*conception.
QC.3 *Occurence in the population*: Does this misconception exist in the population? Did the authors test the misconception in a specific target group? Otherwise, the existence of the misconception is not empirically proven at all or limited to individual subjects (e.g. through interviews).

B. Phase 2: Conducting the SLR

The process of conducting the SLR is shown in Figure 2 as *Phase 2* of the overall process.

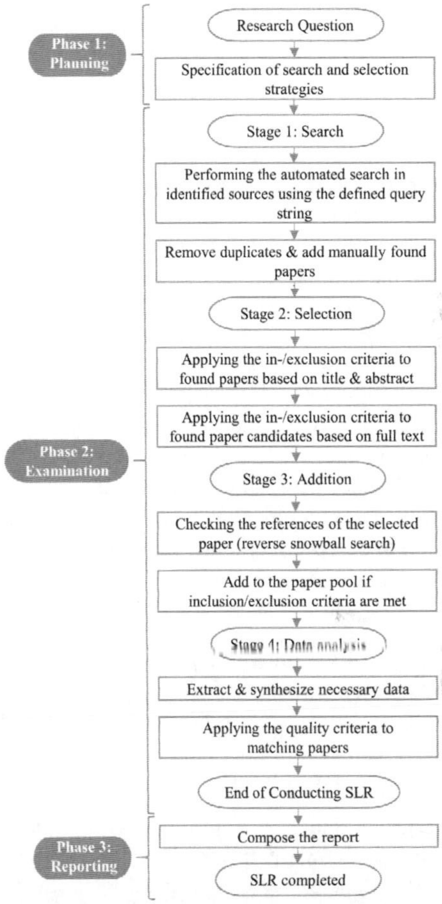

Fig. 2. Flowchart of the SLR process (based on [23][24][27])

1) Stage 1: Conducting the Automated Search: For the search – if possible – use of extended/advanced search functions, wildcards (e.g., "misconception*"), and Boolean operators is made in order to be able to exploit the predefined syntax of the query (see String 1). Nevertheless, the string must be adapted to the options of the search engine. Care is taken to ensure no semantic changes take place.

The SQ is limited to document title and abstract, as recommended by [27, p. 2050] as well as others. (Deviations from this definition, due to the search options of the individual databases, are documented accordingly in the evaluation in Section III). The reason for this is that both metadata are already indicators of the relevance of a publication.

TABLE III. SUMMARY OF SLR RESULTS AFTER APPLYING IN-/EXCLUSION CRITERIA ON TITLE & ABSTRACT

		Search Engines										Sum
		IEEE	ACM	SD	SC	SL	ERIC	WoS	GS	arXiv	dblp	
Results of English SQ		250	410	93	847	0	29	4	87	257	41	2,018
Results of German SQ		16	54	7	46	0	3	0	7	2	5	140
Sum of Search Results		266	464	100	893	0	32	4	94	259	46	**2,158**
No Papers (e.g. Proc.)		2	2	0	53	0	2	0	34	6	0	99
Duplicates		15	85	18	383	0	10	4	16	18	29	578
Balance without Duplicates		249	377	82	457	0	20	0	44	235	17	1,481
IC.1a:	English	249	352	81	442	0	20	0	40	231	10	1,425
IC.1b:	German	0	0	0	5	0	0	0	1	0	0	6
IC.2:	SE Discipline-Specific	223	253	65	381	0	18	0	34	162	7	1,143
IC.3:	Misconceptions	30	60	4	43	0	8	0	6	5	2	158
EC.1:	Contribution Type	0	1	0	0	0	1	0	0	0	0	2
EC:	No Information	0	0	0	1	0	0	0	2	0	0	3
Paper Candidates		**29**	**40**	**4**	**37**	**0**	**6**	**0**	**5**	**5**	**2**	**128**

Note: At this point, IC.3 is not completely applicable, since misconceptions are not specifically mentioned in title & abstract, but it is checked, whether the contribution is explicitly about misconceptions.

2) Stage 2: Applying the In-/Exclusion Criteria: The relevance of a publication is determined in a two-stage process (see Figure 2, *Stage 2*). First of all, the title and abstract are examined and evaluated on the basis of the predefined criteria. These provide enough information to decide whether a publication encompasses insights of interest; in doubt they were included. The papers included are then rechecked regarding the in-/exclusion criteria; this time considering the full text.

3) Stage 3: Backward Snowballing: Once *Stage 2* is completed, "the references of the selected papers [are] reviewed and any missing candidate papers [are] assessed against the inclusion/exclusion criteria" [27, p. 2052] as well; this is referred to as 'backward snowballing'.

4) Stage 4: Data Analysis: To assess the quality of the methods and results in the gathered publications, quality criteria have to be predefined against which to assess the data extracted and synthesized.

III. PHASE 3: RESULTS

The results of the coarse search based on the selection criteria (Section II-A3) applied to titles and abstracts (Section III-A) and the detailed search using full texts (Section III-B) are presented. Additionally, the results of the analysis of the misconceptions found in the selected publications is shown in Section III-C, which is based on the QCs (Section II-A4).

A. Results: Coarse Search

The automated search has been completed between April, 30th and May, 1st 2020. Since the search was not limited to a date range, the review process timewise included every research found, covering papers as of 1970. Table III illustrates the number of matches ($n = 2,158$) initially received through the SQs. Excluding data sets that contained entire proceedings/compilations instead of contributions as well as duplicates, results in $n = 1,481$. Finally, after applying the inclusion and exclusion criteria to title and abstract, $n = 128$ papers/articles can be identified as potentially relevant to our interest. Therefore, only these are considered in the next step, in which the full text of these publications is considered.

Duplicates could be localized both internally – within the results of the same SQ, within the same database, or overlaps between English and German SQs – and externally – between the results of different search engines. The number of duplicates can be seen in Table IV including multiple mentioning, as papers might be found in multiple databases. (Therefore, the sums are not equivalent with the numbers of duplicates in Table III.)

TABLE IV. NUMBER OF DUPLICATES

	IEEE	ACM	SD	SC	SL	ERIC	WoS	GS	arXiv	dblp
IEEE	15	32		222		1	2	15	5	12
ACM		54		111				9	4	7
SD			18	60				4		2
SC				53		7	4	31	10	21
SL					0					
ERIC						3		3		
WoS							0	3		4
GS								17		19
arXiv									8	2
dblp										4

B. Results: Full Text Search

Proceeding further, the predefined inclusion and exclusion criteria are then applied to the paper candidates based on the full text of the contributions. This results in $n = 15$ papers that match the criteria (see Table V, on the next page). Papers are excluded that cover the topic 'misconception', but did not explicitly mention at least one statement the respective authors refer to as misconception concerning the topic SE (cf. IC.3). The subsequent backward snowball search – based on the adequate papers found – reveals some additional publications that have been checked against the inclusion/exclusion criteria listed as well. Summing up, a total of $n = 18$ papers are found (see Table V) that are of interest to the research question of this SLR.

Through the selection process in *Stage 2* and Backward Snowballing in *Stage 3* as a whole, we double-checked the contributions by assessing each paper. As Kitchenham et al. suggest, publications are included if we cannot make a consensual decision [27, p. 2052].

TABLE V. SUMMARY OF SLR RESULTS AFTER APPLYING IN-/EXCLUSION CRITERIA ON FULL TEXTS

	Search Engines										Sum
	IEEE	ACM	SD	SC	SL	ERIC	WoS	GS	arXiv	dblp	
Paper Candidates (see Table III)	29	40	4	37	0	6	0	5	5	2	128
IC.1a: English	29	40	4	37	0	6	0	5	5	2	128
IC.1b: German	0	0	0	0	0	0	0	0	0	0	0
IC.2: SE Discipline	29	40	4	37	0	6	0	4	5	2	127
IC.3: Mention Misconceptions	5	3	1	2	0	0	0	1	3	0	15
Papers Found	**5**	**3**	**1**	**2**	**0**	**0**	**0**	**1**	**3**	**0**	**15**
Backward Snowballing	27	5	0	2	0	0	0	1	4	0	39
Already Included in SLR	2	1	0	1	0	0	0	0	2	0	6
After Applying Selection Criteria	0	0	0	1	0	0	0	0	2	0	3
Result	**5**	**3**	**1**	**3**	**0**	**0**	**0**	**1**	**5**	**0**	**18**

The matching papers found ($n = 18$, shown as the result in Table V) are listed below:

- IEEE: [38]–[42]
- ACM: [43]–[45]
- Science Direct: [46]
- SCOPUS: [47] (cites and covers the myths of the primary source [48] and 7 new statements) [48][49]
- Google Scholar: [50]
- arXiv: [51][52] (is included in [53] and thus not considered further) [53][54] (is the basis for [53]); and thus considered together, covering 21 misconceptions in total) [55]

C. Results: Misconceptions Found

Within the publications named, a total of 167 individual statements (see Table VI; without cross-references) are declared as misconceptions by the respective authors. The misconceptions gathered should be evaluated by assessing the quality of the publications in order to determine the capacity of the findings, using the quality criteria from Section II-A4.

The coding of the subcategories of the quality criteria was not determined in advance, but developed during the analysis based on and close to the available data; i.e. the publications themselves. The following subcategories are considered as high-quality (see grey marking in Table VI):

QC.1 *Traceability*: A primary *study* as well as the *reference* to quotable publication(s), in which the misconception(s) were found is defined as satisfying scientific claims. In contrast, no indication is insufficient.

QC.2 *Validation*: The conception has to be *empirically confirmed* as "at odds with modern scientific theories" [4, p. 2] to be a *mis*conception. Whereas, a rejection, an explanation by the author(s) or reference(s) that the statement given is supposed to be a misconception is no sufficient evidence for validation. This is also due to the fact that misconceptions exist in all ages, from primary level to university and even experts and professors can hold them themselves [56, p. 9, 11].

QC.3 *Occurrence in the population*: Practitioners misconceptions are included, as it is very likely that students have them as well, if they can be encountered in professionally experienced. However, no indication of occurrence in the population can initially only be interpreted as a presumption.

The intersection of the QCs results in $n = 20$ misconceptions (Table VI). Yet, the papers [53] and [54] only deal with the topic 'defect prediction', the authors of [45] look at SE covering the software life cycle more holistically; see thematic structuring in Table VII (on the next page).

Note: [45] would actually not be included in the intersection, as it is not explained where the misconceptions come from (QC.1). But the authors validated them (QC.2) and tested their occurrence concerning students (QC.3). Thus, the misconceptions listed are hypotheses, that have been empirically confirmed; thus, nevertheless, they are included in the intersection.

TABLE VI. SUMMARY OF MISCONCEPTIONS FOUND IN THE FULL TEXTS USING THE QUALITY CRITERIA

		Papers Found																	Sum
		[38]	[39]	[40]	[41]	[42]	[43]	[44]	[45]	[46]	[47]	[48]	[49]	[50]	[51]	[53]	[54]	[55]	17
Misconceptions explicitly named		16	12	12	7	6	4	5	12	4	7	7	10	36	4	10	21	4	167
QC.1:	- Study						4							36		21 (in [54])			51
Traceability	- Reference(s)	15	6			6													37
	- No Indication	1	6	12	7			5	12	4	7	7	10		4			4	79
QC.2:	- Empirically Confirmed								12							8 (in [53])			20
Validation	- Empirically Rejected															2 (in [53])			2
	- Reference(s)	6	6		5														17
	- Only based on Explanation						4			4	7	7	10		4				36
	- No Indication	10	6	12	2	6		5						36		11		4	92
QC.3:	- Practitioners	16				6	4									21 (in [54])			37
Occurrence	- Undergraduates		12	12					12										36
	- No Indication				7			5		4	7	7	10	36	4	10/21 (in [53])		4	94
Intersection (of rows marked)									12							8			20

TABLE VII. LIST OF MISCONCEPTIONS MATCHING THE QUALITY CRITERIA

Topic(s): Project	Process Models	Team Skills	Reuqirements	Implementation	Defects	Documentation	Misconception	Reference(s)
	X						A defined software process is only important when you are working with people who are less skilled.	[45, (1)]
		X					A good software developer will often choose to work alone on a project in order to get it done faster.	[45, (2)]
	X	X					When you have a team of good programmers who work well together, a software process will usually get in the way.	[45, (3)]
				X			My code should take advantage of the implementation details in other code.	[45, (4)]
			X				It is expected that clients will describe their requirements accurately before a team begins programming.	[45, (5)]
				X			As a software developer, most of my time will be spent designing and implementing new algorithms and data structures.	[45, (6)]
X							Most of the time when I start a new programming task in industry, I will be working on a new project.	[45, (7)]
				X			Developers do not need to know the high-level context of the system; this allows them to concentrate on their task.	[45, (8)]
					X		A software project is successful only if it ships with very few known defects.	[45, (9)]
						X	Software engineering is about producing lots of documentation on the requirements and implementation of the project.	[45, (10)]
	X	X	X				Process, requirements, and team-management are important to business majors, not software developers.	[45, (11)]
				X			The majority of the cost of a successful software project will be the initial implementation effort.	[45, (12)]
					X		A file with a complex code change process tends to be buggy.	[53, (B1)], [54, (S2)]
					X		A file that is changed by more developers is more bug-prone.	[53, (B2)], [54, (S14)]
					X		A file with more added lines is more bug-prone.	[53, (B3)], [54, (S4)]
					X		Recently changed files tend to be buggy.	[53, (B4)], [54, (S7)]
					X		Recently bug-fixed files tend to be buggy.	[53, (B6)], [54, (S10)]
					X		A file with more fixed bugs tends to be more bug-prone.	[53, (B7)], [54, (S11)]
					X		A file with more commits is more bug-prone.	[53, (B8)], [54, (S12)]
					X		A file with more removed lines is more bug-prone.	[53, (B9)], [54, (S13)]

IV. DISCUSSION

A. Methodology: Threats to Validity

Several aspects regarding the SLR should be remarked upon.

First, one significant limitation is the broad number of synonyms for 'misconception'; it is almost impossible – despite all efforts – to ensure that all relevant papers are found.

Second, we used the four-eyes principle to proceed and discussed to achieve consensus, but enclosed papers causing persistent disagreement. However, this is not an ideal process, affecting reliability of assessment and evidence of results.

Third, a limitation is that own publications could turn out to be matches in the SLR, which must be handled objectively. This can result in a systematic error. It is therefore noted that authors of this paper also authored the publication [50].

B. Discussion of Results

Regarding the results of the SLR, it is noted that the cut of 2,158 publications to merely 3 [45] [53] [54] of interest identified is immense. As a result, it could be assumed that the search (engines/query) or the selection (in-/exclusion/quality criteria) are inadequate. However, this contradicts that ...

- ... SE didactics are still developing.
- ... the consideration of another database (Section I-B, [9]) also indicates that little research is available to date.
- ... other authors report the same for the adjacent field of computer sciences: "At present, hardly any empirical data concerning the issue of expectations and prior knowledge [...] in informatics [...] are available" [57, p. 143].

V. CONCLUSION

The paper's purpose, to identify and analyse known misconceptions in SE to use these insights in higher education, has been pursued using a systematic literature review. Predefined search queries have been applied to search 10 databases before the publications have been filtered using the selection strategy described. Out of 2,158 publications, 18 could be identified as appropriate for the selection criteria. These contain 167 statements, which the authors of these papers refer to as misconceptions. 20 of them met the quality criteria specified; i.e. only 3 publications cover valuable data.

To conclude, the results show that currently evidence-based research on misconceptions in SE is limited; this secondary study demonstrates, there is not enough research on evidence-based misconceptions in SE to use these insights for higher education. So, in addition a primary study to identify misconception in SE is indispensable before addressing them.

ACKNOWLEDGEMENT

The present work as part of the EVELIN project was funded by the German Federal Ministry of Education and Research (BMBF) under grant numbers 01PL17022B and 01PL17022A. The authors are responsible for the content of this publication.

REFERENCES

[1] R. Duit, "Science education research internationally: Conceptions, research methods, domains of research," *EURASIA Journal of Mathematics, Science & Technology Education*, vol. 3, no. 1, pp. 3–15, 2007.

[2] R. Duit, H. Gropengießer, U. Kattmann, M. Komorek, and I. Parchmann, "The model of educational reconstruction," in *Science Education Research and Practice*, D. Jorde and J. Dillon, Eds. Springer, 2012, pp. 13–37.

[3] J. P. Smith, A. A. diSessa, and J. Roschelle, "Misconceptions reconceived: A constructivist analysis of knowledge in transition," *Journal of the Learning Sciences*, vol. 3, no. 2, pp. 115–163, 1994.

[4] J. R. Read, "Children's misconceptions and conceptual change in science education," 2004, [retrieved: 09, 2020]. [Online]. Available: http://acell.chem.usyd.edu.au/Conceptual-Change.cfm

[5] I. Diethelm and S. Zumbrägel, "An investigation of secondary school students' conceptions on how the internet works," in *Koli Calling International Conference on Computing Education Research*, M.-J. Laakso and R. McCartney, Eds. ACM Press, 2012, pp. 67–73.

[6] S. Todtenhaupt, *To develop an understanding of chemistry in schoolchildren: An investigation into the redox topic at a high school. (Original title: "Zur Entwicklung des Chemieverständnisses bei Schülern: Eine Untersuchung zur Redox-Thematik an einem Gymnasium" [German]).* Frankfurt a.M.: Lang, 1995.

[7] A. Taylor Kujawski, and P. Kowalski, "Naïve psychological science: the prevalence, strength, and source of misconceptions," *The Psychological Record*, vol. 54, pp. 15–25, 2004.

[8] R. Reuter, F. Hauser, C. Gold-Veerkamp, J. Mottok, and J. Abke, "Towards a definition and identification of learning obstacles in higher software engineering education," in *Annual International Conference on Education and New Learning Technologies (EDULEARN)*, IATED, Ed., 2017, pp. 10 259–10 267.

[9] R. Duit, "STCSE: Students' and teachers' conceptions and science education," Bibiography, 2009, [retrieved: 09, 2020]. [Online]. Available: http://archiv.ipn.uni-kiel.de/stcse/download_stcse.html

[10] D. N. Perkins and R. Simmons, "Patterns of misunderstanding: An integrative model of misconceptions in science, math and programming," in *2. Int. Seminar Misconceptions and Educational Strategies in Science and Mathematics: Vol. I*, J. D. Novak, Ed., 1987, pp. 381–395.

[11] ——, "Patterns of misunderstanding: An integrative model for science, math, and programming," *Review of Educational Research*, vol. 58, no. 3, pp. 303–326, 1988.

[12] L. Louca and Z. C. Zacharia, "The use of computer-based programming environments as computer modelling tools in early science education: The cases of textual and graphical program languages," *International Journal of Science Education*, vol. 30, no. 3, pp. 287–324, 2008.

[13] J. Confrey, "Misconceptions across subject matter: science, mathematics, programming," in *2. Int. Seminar Misconceptions and Educational Strategies in Science and Mathematics: Vol. I*, J. D. Novak, Ed., 1987, pp. 81–106.

[14] N. Taylor and G. Corrigan, "New South Wales primary school teachers' perceptions of the role of ICT in the primary science curriculum - A rural and regional perspective," *International Journal of Science and Mathematics Education*, vol. 5, no. 1, pp. 85–109, 2007.

[15] R. D. Pea, "Language-independent conceptual "bugs" in novice programming," *Journal educational computing research*, vol. 2, no. 1, pp. 25–36, 1986.

[16] J. Sorva, "Visual program simulation in introductory programming education." Dissertation, Espoo, Aalto Univ., Finland, 2012.

[17] A. Swidan, F. Hermans, and M. Smit, "Programming misconceptions for school students," in *Conference on International Computing Education Research (ICER)*. ACM, 2018, pp. 151–159.

[18] Ž. Žanko, M. Mladenović, and I. Boljat, "Misconceptions about variables at the K-12 level," *Education and Information Technologies*, vol. 24, no. 2, pp. 1251–1268, 2019.

[19] R. Kelter, M. Kramer, and T. Brinda, "Statistical frequency-analysis of misconceptions in object-oriented-programming: Regularized per models for frequency analysis across oop concepts and related factors," in *Koli Calling International Conference on Computing Education Research*, M. Joy and P. Ihantola, Eds. ACM, 2018, pp. 6:1–6:10.

[20] S. Holland, R. Griffiths, and M. Woodman, "Avoiding object misconceptions," in *SIGCSE technical symposium on Computer science education*, C. M. White, C. Erickson, B. Klein, and J. E. Miller, Eds. ACM, 1997, pp. 131–134.

[21] M. T. Rücker and N. Pinkwart, ""How else should it work?" A grounded theory of pre-college students' understanding of computing devices," *ACM Transactions on Computing Education*, vol. 19, no. 1, pp. 2:1–2:23, 2018.

[22] I. Diethelm, P. Hubwieser, and R. Klaus, "Students, teachers and phenomena: Educational reconstruction for computer science education," in *Koli Calling International Conference on Computing Education Research*, M.-J. Laakso and R. McCartney, Eds. ACM, 2012, pp. 164–173.

[23] B. A. Kitchenham and S. Charters, "Guidelines for performing systematic literature reviews in software engineering: Version 2.3," EBSE Technical Report (EBSE-2007-01), Keele University & University of Durham, 2007.

[24] P. O. Brereton, B. A. Kitchenham, D. Budgen, M. Turner, and M. Khalil, "Lessons from applying the systematic literature review process within the software engineering domain," *Journal of Systems and Software*, vol. 80, no. 4, pp. 571–583, 2007.

[25] B. A. Kitchenham, et al., "Systematic literature reviews in software engineering – a systematic literature review," *Information and Software Technology*, vol. 51, no. 1, pp. 7–15, 2009.

[26] A. Bartel, "Conception and development of a DSM-based gamification authoring system to support university teaching. (Original title: "Konzeption und Entwicklung eines DSM-basierten Gamification Authoring Systems zur Unterstützung hochschulischer Lehre" [German])," Dissertation, Universität Regensburg, 2018.

[27] B. A. Kitchenham and P. O. Brereton, "A systematic review of systematic review process research in software engineering," *Information and Software Technology*, vol. 55, no. 12, pp. 2049–2075, 2013.

[28] IEEE, "IEEE Xplore Digital Library," 2020. [Online]. Available: https://ieeexplore.ieee.org/Xplore/home.jsp

[29] ACM, "ACM Digital Library," 2020. [Online]. Available: http://dl.acm.org/

[30] Springer Nature Switzerland AG, "SpringerLink," 2020. [Online]. Available: https://link.springer.com/

[31] Elsevier B.V., "Scopus," 2020. [Online]. Available: http://www.scopus.com/

[32] ——, "ScienceDirect," 2020. [Online]. Available: https://www.sciencedirect.com/

[33] Institute of Education Sciences of the US Department of Education, "Eric – education resources information center," 2020. [Online]. Available: https://eric.ed.gov/

[34] Clarivate Analytics, "Web of Science," 2020. [Online]. Available: http://www.webofknowledge.com

[35] Google LLC, "Google Scholar," 2020. [Online]. Available: http://scholar.google.de/

[36] Cornell University, "arXiv.org: e-Print archive," 2020. [Online]. Available: https://arxiv.org/

[37] Schloss Dagstuhl and Universität Trier, "dblp: computer science bibliography," 2020. [Online]. Available: https://dblp.uni-trier.de/

[38] P. Devanbu, T. Zimmermann, and C. Bird, "Belief evidence in empirical software engineering," in *International Conference on Software Engineering (ICSE)*, 2016, pp. 108–119.

[39] M. M. Inuwa and A. Varol, "Intensity of misconception in software engineering," in *International Informatics and Software Engineering Conference (UBMYK)*, 2019, pp. 1–6.

[40] J. Ivins, B. R. von Konsky, D. Cooper, and M. Robey, "Software engineers and engineering: A survey of undergraduate preconceptions," in *Frontiers in Education (FIE)*, 2006, pp. MIF–6–11.

[41] B. Özkan and O. Demirors, "On the seven misconceptions about functional size measurement," in *Joint Conference of the International Workshop on Software Measurement and the International Conference on Software Process and Product Measurement (IWSM-MENSURA)*, 2016, pp. 45–52.

[42] J. S. van der Ven and J. Bosch, "Busting software architecture beliefs: A survey on success factors in architecture decision making," in *Euromicro Conference on Software Engineering and Advanced Applications (SEAA)*, 2016, pp. 42–49.

[43] A. Begel and B. Simon, "Struggles of new college graduates in their first software development job," *SIGCSE Bull*, vol. 40, no. 1, pp. 226–230, 2008.

[44] D. DeMarco Brown, "Five agile ux myths," *Journal of Usability Studies*, vol. 8, no. 3, pp. 55–60, 2013.

[45] L. A. Sudol and C. Jaspan, "Analyzing the strength of undergraduate misconceptions about software engineering," in *International Computing Education Research (ICER)*. ACM, 2010, pp. 31–39.

[46] R. H. Wilcox, "Behavioral misconceptions facing the software engineer," in *Computer and Information Sciences*, ser. SEN Report Series Software Engineering, J. T. Tou, Ed. Elsevier, 1971, vol. 2, pp. 285–287.

[47] J. P. Bowen and M. G. Hinchey, "Seven more myths of formal methods: Dispelling industrial prejudices," in *FME'94: Industrial Benefit of Formal Methods*, ser. LNCS 873. Springer, 1994, pp. 105–117.

[48] A. Hall, "Seven myths of formal methods," *IEEE Software*, vol. 7, no. 5, pp. 11–19, 1990.

[49] D. Carlson, "Debunking agile myths," *CrossTalk*, vol. 30, no. 3, pp. 32–36, 2017.

[50] S. Jahn, C. Gold-Veerkamp, R. Reuter, J. Mottok, and J. Abke, "Secure software engineering in academic education: Students' preconceptions of it security," in *International Conference of Education, Research and Innovation (ICERI)*, IATED, Ed., 2019, pp. 6825–6834.

[51] P. Ralph and B. J. Oates, "The dangerous dogmas of software engineering," 2018, [retrieved: 09, 2020]. [Online]. Available: arXiv: 1802.06321v1

[52] Shrikanth N. C. and T. Menzies, "Assessing developer beliefs: A reply to "perceptions, expectations, and challenges in defect prediction"," 2019, [retrieved: 09, 2020]. [Online]. Available: arXiv:1904.05794v1

[53] ——, "Assessing practitioner beliefs about software defect prediction," 2020, accepted at ICSE'20, [retrieved: 09, 2020]. [Online]. Available: arXiv:1912.10093v3

[54] Z. Wan et al., "Perceptions, expectations, and challenges in defect prediction," *IEEE Transactions on Software Engineering*, pp. 1–26, 2018.

[55] D. Rombach and F. Seelisch, "Formalism in software engineerings: Myths versus empirical facts," in *Balancing Agility and Formalism in Software Engineering*, D. Hutchison, et al., Ed. Springer, 2008, pp. 13–25.

[56] R. Duit, "Schülervorstellungen – von Lerndefiziten zu neuen Unterrichtsansätzen [German]," in *Schülervorstellungen in der Physik*, R. Müller, R. Wodzinski, and M. Hopf, Eds. Köln: Aulis, 2011, pp. 8–14.

[57] C. Schulte and J. Magenheim, "Novices' expectations and prior knowledge of software development," in *First international Workshop on Computing education research*, R. Anderson, S. A. Fincher, and M. Guzdial, Eds. ACM Press, 2005, pp. 143–153.

Agile Specification of Code Generators for Model-Driven Engineering

Kevin Lano, Qiaomu Xue
Dept. of Informatics
King's College London, UK
Email: kevin.lano@kcl.ac.uk, qiaomu.xue@kcl.ac.uk

Shekoufeh Kolahdouz-Rahimi
Dept. of Software Engineering
University of Isfahan, Iran
Email: sh.rahimi@eng.ui.ac.ir

***Abstract*—The production of code or other text from software models is an essential task in Model-Driven Engineering (MDE) approaches for software development. Automated code generation is key to the productivity improvements observed in MDE approaches. Nonetheless, there has been a lack of systematic research into optimising the construction of code generators, and in the current state of the art such generators are usually developed manually, which involves detailed programming in 3GLs, or in specialised code generation languages. In either case, high expertise in the source language abstract syntax is necessary. In this paper, we survey different approaches for the construction of code generators, and we define an approach for declarative specification of code generators by text-to-text mappings, in terms of the concrete syntax of both source and target languages. We show that this approach enables the rapid development of code generators, which are also more concise and efficient compared to previous generators.**

Keywords — Code generation; Agile development; UML; Model-Driven Engineering.

I. Introduction

Code generation is the production of programming language code (e.g., Java) or other text (e.g., XML) from a model of a source language, such as a subset of UML, or a Domain-Specific Language (DSL). Code generation is an essential step in the application of Model-Driven Engineering (MDE) [18] to software application development, enabling the automated production of software artifacts from specification or design models, which are usually at a higher abstraction level than the artifacts (i.e., they abstract away from details of a specific implementation platform or programming language). This means that an application can be specified once and different code versions generated automatically from the specification, targeted at several different platforms. For example, a mobile app could be specified in a platform-independent form, and then separate implementations generated from the specification, targetted at the iOS and Android mobile platforms [14]. For a new target platform or language version, a new code generator needs to be produced, but existing application specifications can be reused.

Despite the importance of code generation, there has been relatively little research published on optimising the overall production process of code generators [5][25]. Instead, most published work has focussed on describing particular code generators [1][10][19][26], and issues specific to a particular generator. There are no general guidelines for assuring the quality of code generators, and perhaps as a consequence of this lack, the quality of automatically generated code is sometimes poor in comparison with manually-written code [13][17].

The task of developing a code generator consists of three main activities:

1) Defining a semantically valid representation of the source language in the target language and verifying this representation;
2) Defining a code generation strategy to create the target representation of each source model;
3) Writing and testing code generation rules in a 3GL or code generation language.

If we restrict attention to source languages which are subsets of UML, crucial concepts which need to be represented in a target language are *classes and interfaces*, *features* (attributes, references and operations), *inheritance and polymorphic operation semantics*, *object creation/deletion*, *object communication*, *object state changes*, and *Object Constraint Language (OCL) data types and operators*.

The task of finding a valid representation may be relatively simple if there is small semantic distance between UML and the target (e.g., in the case of OO programming languages, such as Java, C# and C++, which support orthodox class/inheritance concepts). But for other target languages (e.g., for C, Python, JavaScript) there is considerable semantic distance from UML, and no simple encoding of UML concepts.

In this paper we focus on items 2) and 3) above. Section II reviews the state of the art in code generation approaches, and Section III introduces our approach to code generation specification and implementation, using the $\mathcal{CSTL}$ concrete syntax transformation language. Section IV provides a comparative evaluation of the approach, Section V discusses threats to validity, and Section VI gives related and future work.

II. Code generation approaches

A code generator can be defined either in terms of the *abstract syntax* of the languages it relates, or in terms of their *concrete syntax*: abstract syntax refers to the conceptual elements of a language, represented as a Backus-Naur Form (BNF) grammar or metamodel, and the features and inter-relations and constraints of these elements. Concrete syntax refers to the written textual form or graphical form of models/programs or other artifacts in a language.

For example, part of the metamodel of the C language is shown in Figure 1.

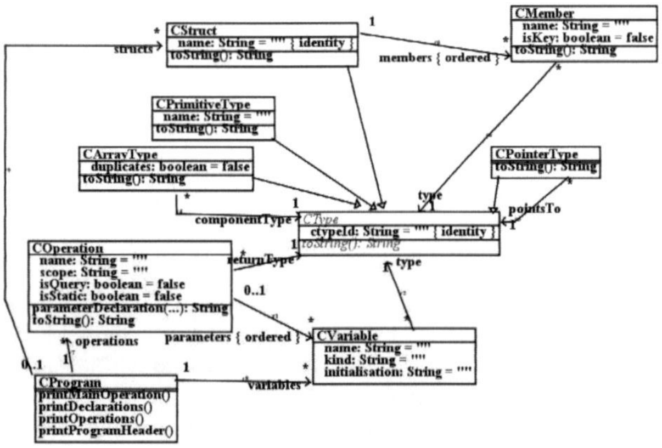

Figure 1. C language metamodel

The *CStruct* class is the abstract syntax representation of C `struct` type definitions, which have the concrete syntax:

```
struct S
{ MT1 cm1;
  ...
  MTn cmn;
};
```

where each of the `MTi cmi;` are the concrete syntax of *CMember* elements that are the members of the *CStruct*.

In these terms there are three general approaches to writing code generators:

1) *Abstract syntax to abstract syntax*: code generation rules are written in a programming language or in a general Model Transformation (MT) language, to map from elements of the abstract syntax of the source language, to elements of the abstract syntax of the target language.
2) *Abstract syntax to concrete syntax*: templates using target concrete syntax are defined, with variable parts or slots within these templates having content depending upon source model elements and expressions written in terms of source language abstract syntax.
3) *Concrete syntax to concrete syntax*: the mapping is defined only in terms of source and target language concrete syntax, with rules specifying how source concrete syntax fragments should be represented in target concrete syntax.

In cases where abstract syntax is used, this involves navigation over the elements of a source or target model using the data structures of a 3GL, or via an expression language, which is usually based on OCL [24].

An example of the first approach is the UML to C code generator of [19], which is written in OCL. The second approach is supported by specialised model-to-text MT languages, such as EGL [8], Acceleo [2], and Xtext/Xtend [9]. The third approach is supported by concrete syntax MT languages, such as the concrete graph transformation language of [12].

A. *Issues in code generation*

The task of code generation may require the resolution of several fundamental problems:

1) *Language abstraction gap*: the distance between the source and target languages is too great to be bridged by a single generation step, and multiple steps or human input is needed. For example, declarative specification in Agile UML [6] is expressed using OCL predicates as invariants or postconditions. This specification is quite distant from executable code, and several translation stages are required to refine the specification into an executable form.
2) *Structural gap*: the source and target languages may have different structures, so that one source element can contribute to the target syntax of multiple target elements (a 1-many relationship), or information from multiple source elements could be combined to form one target element (a many-1 relationship). For example, a UML class attribute is represented by a C struct member, and by possibly multiple setter and getter operations, in separate header and code files [19].
3) *Semantic gap*: where source language concepts cannot be directly represented in the target language because of semantic differences, so that a more complex and indirect encoding is needed. For example, UML inheritance has no direct representation in C [19], and differs in its semantics from Python or JavaScript inheritance. Likewise, the constructs of UML statemachines have no direct correspondence with conventional programming language constructs [1][26].

Each of the three general approaches listed above address these problems in different ways, and there are also various tradeoffs in each approach. Abstract syntax to abstract syntax specifications can address the language abstraction gap by using intermediate languages between the source and target, and chaining transformations in sequence (Figure 2). Structural and semantic gaps can be addressed by complex coding in terms of the abstract syntaxes. However this approach requires deep understanding of the metamodels of both source and target languages, and understanding of OCL-style navigation expressions, in addition to knowledge of target language concrete syntax. Because abstract syntax is typically more verbose and detailed than concrete syntax, such specifications can become very large and complex programs or transformations, which are not easy to understand or maintain.

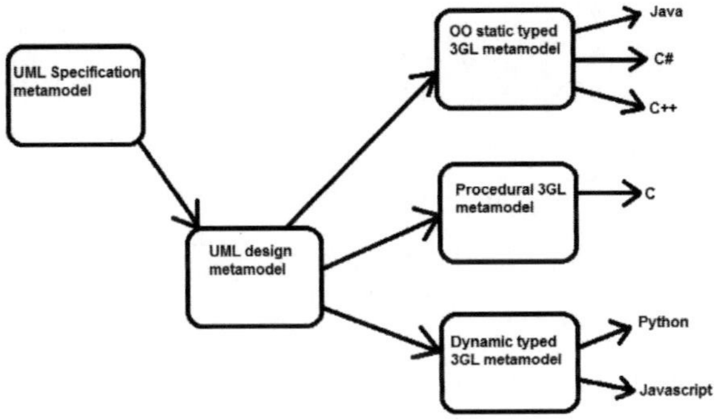

Figure 2. Staged code generation

Abstract to concrete syntax approaches using template languages involve specification with a combination of abstract syntax source language expressions and concrete target text. Thus to use these approaches, knowledge of the source language metamodel and of the target language concrete syntax is needed, but not of the target language metamodel. Again, complex navigation expressions are typically needed to refer to and select source model elements. The structure of a template-based specification is usually closely tied to the structure of the target language program components.

To address language gaps, preliminary model-to-model transformations could be used as in Figure 2, with only the final step being model-to-text [15]. The preliminary transformations could construct a design model suitable for direct translation to any target language in a given language family. For structural and semantic gaps, auxiliary operations and data would need to be used, with possibly multiple passes through the source model, and multiple output templates (e.g., for C production from UML, a C header file template and a C code file template would be needed). This again requires complex specification in the source abstract syntax. The mix of source and target languages in one artifact can be confusing, and such specification can be prone to errors due to misuse of delimiters between the language texts [21].

Concrete syntax to concrete syntax approaches have the advantage that no knowledge of abstract syntax is needed. In addition, any navigation over source and target models is implicit, based on the concrete syntax structures. Thus, the code generation rules can be defined in an intuitively natural manner in terms of the concrete source and target syntax. However, for cases of abstraction, structural or semantic gaps, more complex mapping mechanisms are needed, with auxiliary operations and possibly multiple rules/multiple passes over the source text. In principle, concrete syntax to concrete syntax transformations could be chained as in Figure 2 to use intermediate textual languages to bridge gaps.

III. CONCRETE SYNTAX TO CONCRETE SYNTAX SPECIFICATION USING $\mathcal{CSTL}$

Our experience of building large code generators in Java [20] and in OCL [19] convinced us that a more usable, agile and lightweight approach was needed.

For the simpler specification of code generators, we have developed a textual concrete syntax transformation notation $\mathcal{CSTL}$. This is a DSL for code generation, which enables the direct definition of code-generation transformations by means of concrete syntax to concrete syntax mappings.

A. $\mathcal{CSTL}$ concepts

$\mathcal{CSTL}$ is designed to be a small language, which can be used by general software practitioners, and does not require a high degree of MDE expertise. Its execution semantics can be understand in terms of familiar string matching and replacement concepts. Figure 3 shows the metamodel of $\mathcal{CSTL}$.

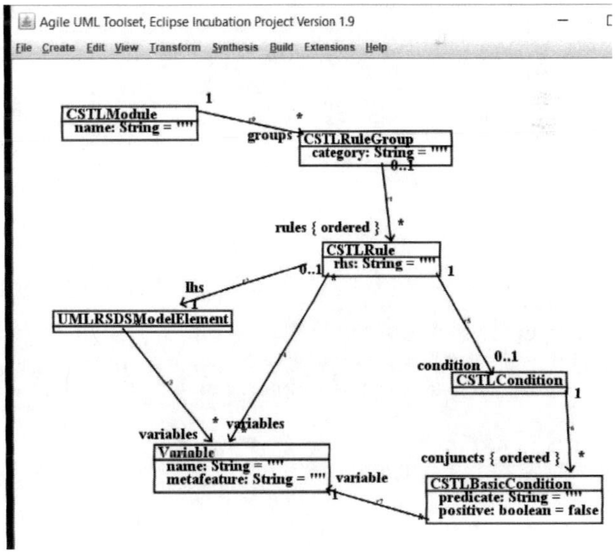

Figure 3. $\mathcal{CSTL}$ metamodel

A $\mathcal{CSTL}$ module consists of a sequence of rules grouped into categories. Individual rules in $\mathcal{CSTL}$ notation have the form:

```
selement |-->telement<when> Condition
```

The <*when*> clause and condition are optional. The left hand side (LHS) of a $\mathcal{CSTL}$ rule is some piece of concrete syntax in the source language, e.g., in Kernel Metamodel (KM3) [16] textual notation for UML class models, and the right hand side (RHS) is the corresponding concrete syntax in the target language (e.g., C, Java, Swift, etc), which the LHS should translate to. Apart from literal text concrete syntax, the LHS may contain variable terms _1, _2, etc, representing arbitrary source concrete syntax fragments (possibly constrained by the optional condition), and the RHS may refer to the translation of these fragments also by _1, _2, etc. This enables $\mathcal{CSTL}$ mappings to be applied recursively. Rules are grouped into source language syntactic categories, such as binary expressions or statements, and apply to elements in these categories. Specialised rules are listed before more general rules.

For example, to map a KM3 text syntax of a UML class to type and data declaration text in a C header file, assuming that the class contains only simple data feature definitions $x : T$, we could write the following rules to translate UML types, attribute declarations and class declarations:

```
Type::
Integer |-->int
Real |-->double
Boolean |-->unsigned char
String |-->char*
Set(_1) |-->_1*
Sequence(_1) |-->_1*
_1 |-->struct _1*<when> _1 Class

Attribute::
_1 : _2; |--> _2 _1;\n
_1 : _2; _3 |--> _2 _1;\n _3

Class::
class _1 { _2 } |-->struct _1\n{_2};
class _1 extends _2 { _3 } |-->
struct _1\n{ struct _2* super;\n_3};
```

These rules translate a class declaration

```
class Customer extends Person
{ name : String;
  age : Real;
}
```

into:

```
struct Customer
{ struct Person* super;
  char* name;
  double age;
};
```

Rule conditions can be combined by conjunction (comma) and negation, for example:

```
_1 = _2 |-->_1 == _2<when>
  _1 not String, _1 not object,
  _1 not collection
```

Negation can often be avoided by using the ordering of rules. The above rule could alternatively be expressed as a default case after specific = rules for strings, objects and collections.

Any stereotype of an LHS model element may also be used as a condition on it, for example:

```
Attribute::
_1 : _2 |-->  let _1 : _2<when>_1 readOnly
```

for a mapping from UML to Swift.

The *metafeature* notation _*i*'*f* enables access to features *f* of the abstract syntax. For example, _1'*elementType* returns the element type of whatever language element is held in variable _1.

Furthermore, a set of rules can be grouped together in a single file, representing one way of mapping source elements to target elements. Separate files can define alternative or additional mappings. For example, separate files *cheader.cstl* and *cbody.cstl* could be used to create the header and body files of a C program derived from a UML model. This addresses the issue of 1-many structural gaps, and enables context-dependent alternative translations of source syntactic elements. If *f.cstl* is a file containing a $\mathcal{CSTL}$ module, then the notation _1'*f.cstl* applies this module to the contents of _1.

B. $\mathcal{CSTL}$ semantics

The execution semantics of $\mathcal{CSTL}$ is based on string pattern matching and rewriting. Given a source text element *elem* of syntactic category *CT*, the first *CT* rule whose LHS matches *elem* and whose conditions are true is applied to *elem*, with metavariables _*i* of the LHS being bound to corresponding source fragments within *elem*. These fragments are then themselves mapped by the rule set and the result of transformation is substituted for _*i* on the RHS of the rule. If no rule applies, an element is mapped to itself.

Formally, a $\mathcal{CSTL}$ specification module *cg* contained in a file *cg.cstl* defines a function τ_{cg} from the texts of source language $\mathcal{L}_1$ to those of target language $\mathcal{L}_2$ as follows.

For each source text $e \in \mathcal{L}_1$, of $\mathcal{L}_1$ category *C*, successive rules *r* of the *C* :: group in *cg* are checked to determine if *r.lhs* can match to *e*.

Each *r* is of the form

```
lhs |-->rhs<when> Conditions
```

An absent condition is interpreted as *true*. r matches e if e equals $r.lhs$ with substitutions of subtexts e_i of e for the variables $\_i$ of $r.lhs$, i.e., e equals $r.lhs[e_i/\_i]$ (ignoring leading or trailing spaces). r is then applicable to e if $Conditions[e_i/\_i]$ also hold. In this case, the result of cg applied to e is

$$\tau_{cg}(e) \;=\; r.rhs[\tau_{cg}(e_i)/\_i]$$

where r is the first C :: rule matching e. If no rule of the C :: group matches e, then e is copied to the output:

$$\tau_{cg}(e) \;=\; e$$

in either case, the specifier must ensure that the result $\tau_{cg}(e)$ is a valid text of $\mathcal{L}_2$.

For example, the UML attribute declaration `s : Sequence(Real);` matches the LHS `_1 : _2;` of the first *Attribute* rule above, with `_1` bound to `s` and `_2` bound to `Sequence(Real)`. The latter type text is then rewritten to `double*` by the *Type* rules for *Sequence* and *Real*, so that the overall result of the attribute rule application is `double* s;\n`.

Metafeatures $\_i`f$ are evaluated as $\tau_{cg}(e_i`f) = \tau_{cg}(\overline{e_i}.f)$, where $\overline{e_i}$ is the abstract syntax element corresponding to e_i.

A module application $\_i`f.cstl$ is evaluated as $\tau_{cg}(e_i`f.cstl) = \tau_f(e_i)$.

C. $\mathcal{CSTL}$ applications

We have applied $\mathcal{CSTL}$ to the translation of UML to Java (UML2Java8), and to Swift (UML2Swift). These are used as part of UML to Android and UML to iOS mobile app generation tools. $\mathcal{CSTL}$ is also provided as part of the Agile UML toolset [6] as a facility to enable users to quickly specify new code generators from UML to different programming languages, hence extending the toolset for their own needs.

The emphasis in the UML2Java8 and UML2Swift code generators is on the generation of fully functional code from OCL expressions. OCL has over 100 operators [24], thus at least these many rules are needed to translate OCL expressions to program code. 152 of the 183 rules (83%) of the UML2Java8 generator are either mapping rules for different kinds of OCL expression (139 rules) or for statements (13 rules). Some examples of expression rules from this generator are:

```
BinaryExpression::
_1 & _2 |-->_1 && _2
_1->count(_2) |-->Collections.frequency(_1,_2)
_1->select(_2 | _3) |-->
  Ocl.selectSet(_1,(_2)->{return _3;})
    <when> _1 Set

_1->includes(_2) |-->_1.contains(_2)
_1->includesAll(_2) |-->_1.containsAll(_2)
```

A Java 8 library of OCL functions, Ocl.java, is also defined to support the implementation of some operators, such as $\rightarrow$*select*. The UML2Swift generator is similarly constructed.

$\mathcal{CSTL}$ can also be used for general DSL to code synthesis, provided that the DSL elements can be expressed as a subset of our UML source language. Stereotypes can be used to label UML elements as representing DSL elements, and rules for DSL code generation expressed in terms of these stereotypes.

IV. Evaluation

We evaluate the approach by comparing UML to 3GL code generators specified using different approaches (Table I). We compare the development effort of the generators, and their sizes, syntactic complexity and efficiency. The size is measured in lines of code (LOC). *MaxES* is the maximum OCL expression size used in navigation expressions (operators + identifiers in the expression). This is the *MEL* measure of [28]. All approaches cover the structural parts of the generated code, but differ in how they synthesise behaviour (constructor and method bodies).

TABLE I. COMPARISON OF CODE GENERATION APPROACHES

Generator	*Implemented*	*Size*	*MaxES*	*Scope*
UML2C++ [20]	Java	18,100	–	Behaviour from OCL
UML2Java [7]	Acceleo/ Java	3,957	27	Outline behaviour
UML2Java [27]	EGL	1,425	35	Statemachine behaviour
UML2Java8 [6]	$\mathcal{CSTL}$	426	11	Behaviour from OCL
UML2Swift [6]	$\mathcal{CSTL}$	398	5	Behaviour from OCL

Table I shows that the $\mathcal{CSTL}$ Java generator is substantially smaller compared with other UML to Java approaches. Unlike the Acceleo and EGL generators, it is focussed on behaviour implementation instead of structural implementation. The declarative nature of the specification should also make it easier to comprehend and to change than imperative or hybrid code generators involving explicit model navigation. The syntactic complexity is indicated by the maximum condition or navigation expression size for the $\mathcal{CSTL}$ solution this is also significantly smaller than for the other solutions.

In Table II we compare the performances of the Acceleo, $\mathcal{CSTL}$ and a Java-coded UML to Java code generator on the Acceleo test model *example.uml*, which consists of 6 classifiers, 8 data features, 6 operations and 5 inheritance relations (Figure 4).

Larger examples were created by duplicating this basic structure. We also added some functionality to the operations of the example. The results in Table II show that the $\mathcal{CSTL}$

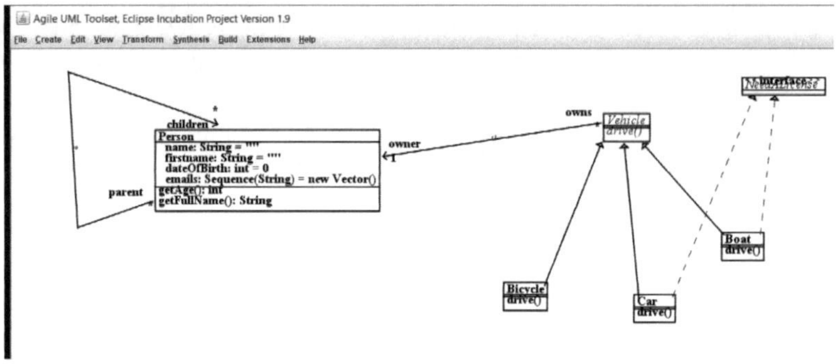

Figure 4. Acceleo example model

generator is approximately 10 times more efficient than the Acceleo generator, despite including OCL expression processing. This improvement is likely to be caused by the purely tree-based processing of $\mathcal{CSTL}$, in contrast to the graph navigations of Acceleo. $\mathcal{CSTL}$ specifications contain no global variables or other 'memory' of which rules have been applied, so that rule applications (e.g., upon separate classes) are independent and could be parallelised. The $\mathcal{CSTL}$ solution is similar in efficiency to the Java-coded UML2Java4 generator of [6].

TABLE II. PERFORMANCE COMPARISON OF UML TO JAVA CODE GENERATION APPROACHES

Model	*Size*	*Acceleo*	$\mathcal{CSTL}$ *(UML2Java8)*	*Java (UML2Java4)*
1	25	480ms	45ms	28ms
2	50	750ms	70ms	47ms
4	100	800ms	36ms	37ms
10	250	1.12s	80ms	79ms
15	375	1.52s	104ms	194ms

TABLE III. COMPARISON OF CODE GENERATOR DEVELOPMENT EFFORT

Approach/Generator	*Effort*
Acceleo/Java: UML2Java [7]	3000+ hours
Java: UML2C++ [20]	2170 hours
OCL: UML2C [19]	1375 hours
$\mathcal{CSTL}$: UML2Java8	36 hours
$\mathcal{CSTL}$: UML2Swift	50 hours

Table III compares the development effort of different generators, in terms of person hours. These show substantial reductions in effort for the $\mathcal{CSTL}$ developments, compared to developments using 3GL programming, templates or OCL. This reduction arises because (i) the code generator file has a modular structure based on the source language syntax categories; (ii) no programming language or OCL code needs to be written; (iii) the overall size of the generator is substantially reduced and is contained in 2 or 3 small files. Not only is the initial effort lower in the $\mathcal{CSTL}$ generators, but also the cost of making changes to the specification.

We can also compare the size of the generated code for the example model of Figure 4: this is 107 LOC for the $\mathcal{CSTL}$ UML2Java8 generator, 380 LOC for the Acceleo UML2Java, and 1628 LOC for the Java coded UML2Java4 translator of [6]. The latter provides many additional functionalities, such as input and export of models from XML and CSV, which the $\mathcal{CSTL}$ and Acceleo generators do not.

V. Threats to Validity

We address *instrumental bias* by performing all measurements in a consistent manner. Regarding *selection bias*, our evaluation example is taken from the Acceleo repository, and hence it is independent of the authors. Regarding generalisation from the single example presented here, we have also used $\mathcal{CSTL}$ to generate app code for several Android and iOS apps of different kinds, and found similar results in terms of high efficiency and low generated code size. Regarding *relevance*, we have only implemented UML to code mappings, DSL to code mappings are the subject of future work.

VI. Related and Future Work

Investigations into the use of machine learning, specifically Long Short Term Memory (LSTM) neural nets, to synthesise model transformations from examples of input and output models have shown that this can be practically useful [4], however it requires large numbers of examples and significant training time. The same approach could potentially be used to derive code generators from examples presented either in abstract or concrete syntax.

Tools have also been created that convert UI sketches into UI code [3][22]. These are based on object recognition approaches, so could be used as a means of processing manually-drawn concrete syntax graphical models (such as class diagrams or activity diagrams) prior to code generation from these models. Other low-code approaches for code production are template-based or data-based app builders, such as Microsoft PowerApps [23] or Google AppSheet [11].

A disadvantage of ML approaches, such as LSTM neural nets, are that they only produce implicit 'black box' specifications of generators. In contrast, $\mathcal{CSTL}$ specifications provide a clear and explicit expression of how source language syntax maps to target language syntax. Compared to app builders, we use a wide range of UML features to define application data and functionality. The $\mathcal{CSTL}$ rules give precise control over which code elements are produced for these specifications.

An important area for future work is ensuring the quality of generated code [13]: code generators should not increase the technical debt burden of a software system, and where possible should ensure that code quality standards are met. There should not be unnecessary code generated, and duplicated and excessively complex code should be avoided, together with other flaws, such as bidirectional module dependencies. Our approach can avoid complex duplicated code by factoring out complex code definitions into the OCL support library. An example is the complex Swift code needed for regular expression matching: the Ocl.swift library defines a function $matches(str : String, pattern : String)$, which encapsulates this code, so that the $\mathcal{CSTL}$ translation rule can be simplified to:

```
_1->matches(_2) |-->
  Ocl.matches(str: _1, pattern: _2)
```

VII. Conclusion

We have considered alternative approaches for the definition of code generators, and proposed a novel declarative approach, which permits simpler and more concise specifications, compared to existing approaches. We showed that the approach can produce smaller and more efficient code generators for UML to Java transformation.

References

[1] A. Aabidi, A. Jakimi, R. Alaoui and E. Hassan El Kinani, "An object-oriented approach to generate Java code from hierarchical-concurrent and history states", Int. Journal of Information and Network Security, vol. 2, 2013, pp. 429–440.

[2] Acceleo project, https://www.eclipse.org/acceleo, accessed 18.8.2020.

[3] T. Beltramelli, "pix2code: Generating code from a GUI screenshot", https://arxiv.org/abs/1705.07962, 2017. Accessed 18.8.2020.

[4] L. Burgueno, J. Cabot, and S. Gerard, "An LSTM-based neural network architecture for model transformations", MODELS '19, 2019, pp. 294–299.

[5] A. Dieumegard, A. Toon, and M. Pantel, "Model-based formal specification of a DSL library for a qualified code generator", OCL 2012, pp. 61–62.

[6] Eclipse Agile UML project, https://projects.eclipse.org/projects/modeling.agileuml, accessed 18.8.2020.

[7] Eclipse UML2Java code generator, https://git.eclipse.org/c/umlgen/, accessed 18.8.2020.

[8] Epsilon project, https://projects.eclipse.org/projects/modeling.epsilon, accessed 18.8.2020.

[9] M. Eysholdt and H. Behrens, "Xtext: implement your language faster than the quick and dirty way", OOPSLA 2010, pp. 307–309.

[10] M. Funk, A. Nysen, and H. Lichter, "From UML to ANSI-C: an Eclipse-based code generation framework", RWTH, 2007.

[11] Google, https://www.appsheet.com, accessed 18.8.2020.

[12] R. Gronmo, B. Moller-Pedersen, and G. Olsen, "Comparison of three model transformation languages", ECMDA-FA, 2009, pp. 2–17.

[13] X. He, P. Avgeriou, P. Liang, and Z. Li, "Technical debt in MDE: A case study on GMF/EMF-based projects", MODELS 2016, pp. 162–172

[14] H. Heitkotter, T. Majchrzak, and H. Kuchen, "Cross-platform MDD of mobile applications with MD^2", SAC 2013, ACM Press, 2013, pp. 526–533.

[15] Z. Hemel, L. Kats, D. Groenewegenn, and E. Visser, "Code generation by model transformation: a case study in transformation modularity", Sosym, 9: 375–402, 2010.

[16] F. Jouault and J. Bezivin, "KM3: a DSL for metamodel specification", ATLAS team, INRIA, 2006.

[17] L. Kapova, T. Goldschmidt, S. Becker, and J. Henss, "Evaluating maintainability with code metrics for model-to-model transformations", QoSA 2010: Research into Practice – Reality and Gaps, Springer, 2010, pp. 151–160.

[18] K. Lano, *Agile model-based development using UML-RSDS*, CRC Press, 2016.

[19] K. Lano, S. Yassipour-Tehrani, H. Alfraihi, and S. Kolahdouz-Rahimi, "Translating from UML RSDS OCL to ANSI C", OCL 2017, STAF 2017, pp. 317–330.

[20] K. Lano, H. Alfraihi, S. Kolahdouz-Rahimi, M. Sharbaf, and H. Haughton, "Comparative case studies in agile MDD", FlexMDE 2018, MODELS 2018, pp. 203–212.

[21] K. Lano, S. Fang, H. Alfraihi, and S. Kolahdouz-Rahimi, "Simplified specification languages for flexible and agile modelling", FlexMDE, MODELS 2019, pp. 460–467.

[22] Microsoft, *sketch2code*, https://www.microsoft.com/en-us/ai/ai-lab-sketch2code, accessed 18.8.2020.

[23] Microsoft, *PowerApps*, https://powerapps.microsoft.com, accessed 18.8.2020.

[24] OMG, *Object Constraint Language Specification v2.4*, 2014.

[25] I. Stuermer, M. Conrad, H. Doerr and P. Pepper, "Systematic testing of model-based code generators", IEEE TSE, 33(9), 2007, pp. 622–634.

[26] E. Sunitha and P. Samuel, "Object-oriented method to implement the hierarchical and concurrent states in UML state chart diagrams", Software engineering research, management and applications, Springer-Verlag, 2016, pp. 133–149.

[27] TU/e, SLCOtoJava1.0 code generator, https://gitlab.tue.nl/SLCO, 2020.

[28] M. Wimmer, S. Martinez, F. Jouault, and J. Cabot, "A Catalogue of Refactorings for model-to-model transformations", Journal of Object Technology, vol. 11, no. 2, 2012, pp. 1–40.

Plagiarism Detection Systems for Programming Assignments: Practical Considerations

Maxim Mozgovoy and Evgeny Pyshkin
University of Aizu

Tsuruga, Ikki-Machi, Aizu-Wakamatsu, Fukushima, 965-8580, Japan
Email: {mozgovoy,pyshe}@u-aizu.ac.jp

***Abstract*—We discuss a project contributing to the quality of software engineering education by producing a state of the art code duplication and plagiarism detection system, aimed at college and university teachers. Though detecting plagiarism (as unauthorized "borrowings" of code fragments) consumes time and energy of the teachers, ignoring this issue makes a negative impact on students' discipline and lowers motivation of course participants. While plagiarism detection in software code is a well-known research task, there are no open source modern plagiarism detection systems that are designed for actual classroom use by implementing state of the art detection techniques, convenient visualizations, integration with course management systems, and supporting common use case scenarios.**

***Keywords*–Education; plagiarism; software; programming; exercises; online learning.**

I. Introduction

Societal lock-down of 2020 caused by Covid-2019 outspread pushed educational institutions to enforce teaching and learning processes based on active using of online and distant education technology. Distant learning tools have many advantages (flexibility in using them at any time from virtually any device, convenient access, possibilities for user collaboration, creating less stressful study process), but also considerable limitations. That's why methodological and organizational solutions for distant learning should be developed so that they would improve the teaching process in a way serving both remote and traditional face-to-face teacher/student communication. Further digitalization of learning process does not mean its transfer to online environments only, developing better computer-assisted tools to support traditional teaching is equally important.

Programming is commonly considered as an activity favoring outsourcing, task distribution and online communication, which make the project work of experienced engineers more efficient and well organized. However, in programming teaching, the lack of direct in-person communication often makes difficult to fairly check the solutions of students and to support them in their practical work. Even within the scope of traditional face-to-face classes, it is hard to manage all the students' projects, especially if you have big groups of students. Thus, instructors need good instruments to support practical exercise assignments and their checks.

Teachers who conduct online classes, as we observe, typically do not seek to use a single universal tool covering all their needs. Instead, they tend to choose the most suitable software for the given task. For example, a teacher might publish video recordings on YouTube, communicate with students via Slack, organize videoconferences using Zoom, and publish learning materials on Moodle. Some activities are, however, easier to organize than others. Videoconferencing and messaging is a relatively straightforward process with today's technology, while conducting exercise sessions and ensuring proper homework evaluation can be more laborious. Since the students may work on their assignments in an unsupervised environment (and organizing a proper proctoring procedure might be complicated and not always desirable), ensuring fair study conditions for everyone and reducing the amount of cheating is essential.

Plagiarism is a type of academic dishonesty that consists in reusing documents composed by other authors without proper acknowledgement of the original source [1]. Plagiarism is a common phenomenon among students, as some of them may tempt to reuse solutions developed by their peers or copied online, thus, eliminating their educational value.

Many authors note that plagiarism can often be prevented by designing better, more personalized assignments, training students to avoid unintentional plagiarism, and administrative measures [2] [3]. It is also often suggested that preventive measures should be combined with computer-assisted plagiarism detection practices. Most detection tools, such as Turnitin [4], are designed for detecting overlapping online sources for a given document (an essay or a research paper), but some recently developed instruments are specifically tailored for detecting duplications in offline collections of software code [5].

II. Plagiarism Detection in Student Projects: Challenges and Practical Goals

Plagiarism detection in student-submitted software source code is an established research topic, stemming from the task of identifying duplicated fragments in large software systems, which has its own importance, since the duplicated code impairs project architecture, conditions worse project maintainability, increases the risk of software bugs, and may seriously affect code efficiency. The problem of detecting software code improper reuse differs from natural language plagiarism detection due to several factors:

- Code collections under testing are typically available offline, since it is nearly impossible to find online a fragment of code that solves a particular teacher-supplied task, unless it is a well-known classical algorithm;
- Students typically receive the same or very similar assignments, so they tend to borrow code from their peers or predecessors;
- Software code is easy to modify, refactor or obfuscate, keeping its functionality intact;
- In principle, code reuse itself is a common engineering practice, which does not always refer to plagiarism.

Thus, though it seems obvious to apply some natural language processing algorithms suitable for general-purpose text processing, we have to mention a number of important issues demonstrating serious particularities of plagiarism detection in software programs.

Contradiction between standard software engineering practices and pedagogical aims. Teachers fight plagiarism, since, first, it itself contradicts major pedagogical aims. However, at the same time (specifically, in engineering disciplines), teachers should introduce existing standard solutions. Software engineering practices naturally favor reusing the successful solutions and standardized models, but the proper reuse should be differentiated from large scale source code copying.

Detecting structural source code similarity. In process of comparing the source code fragments, we are not so interested in finding exact matches, but their structural resemblance and/or functional equivalence. One may expect that recognizing structural similarity of math equations may provide useful insights in detecting structurally similar source code fragments [6] [7], the latter being nothing but the texts in a formal language. However, especially in the cases when students are encouraged to use structural software organization and presentation models (such as software design patterns, specific project architectures, etc.), we could not accuse a student in plagiarism, based on structural similarity only.

Few solutions may be used in classroom environments. Surprisingly, there are very few systems designed specifically for actual classroom use. Most researchers tend to be focused on purely algorithmic aspects of the problem, such as robust file comparison procedure, high speed of detection process or explicit support for specific programming languages. Therefore, the tasks of designing appropriate user interfaces or providing specific functionality relevant for teachers of programming classes is challenging, and often neglected.

Most commercial solutions are for texts in natural languages. The gap between the achievements in developing algorithms for source code processing and their applicability to classroom environments is not filled by commercial companies offering solutions focused primarily on detecting matches for natural-language texts. As a result, teachers still often rely on manual detection, which is a very time-consuming and laborious process, they could not gain all the possible benefits from using the online submission systems (such as Moodle and/or automated code testing / grading instruments).

Thus, the problem of identifying reliable similarity detection methods, suitable for academic environment and applicable to a wide range of programming languages is far from being resolved. That is why, in sum, the practical goal of our project is to automate teachers' daily routine tasks that consume much time and energy. We believe that the existence of a convenient plagiarism detection instrument can be a noticeable contributing factor for better quality of courses offered at educational institutions. The teachers really need to have more time to be concentrated on developing the course content, creating interesting tasks, or organizing problem-based learning teams, while it is in the interests of our society that the students study harder, honestly, more efficiently and have lower chances to pass the course by copying their peers' work. Some researchers observe that even skillful students often feel demotivated when they see others passing courses using "borrowed" solutions (which happens in large courses, where the teachers have no time for appropriate checks of the whole corpus of student submissions) [8], so an automated plagiarism detection system would have a positive effect on all parties involved in course activities.

III. Plagiarism Prevention and Detection Techniques

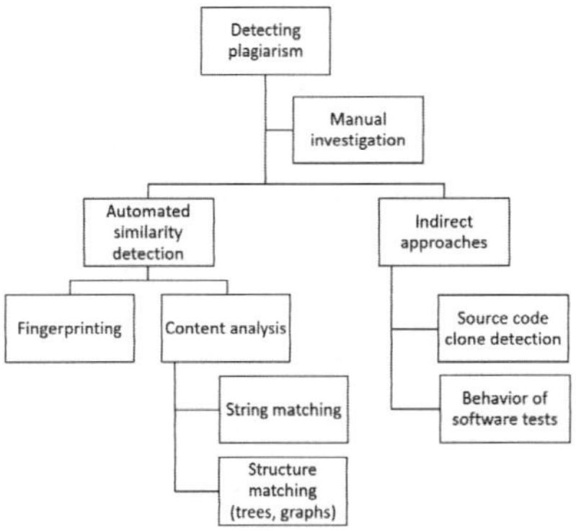

Figure 1. Taxonomy of plagiarism detection methods.

It is often noted in the literature that plagiarism prevention should be the main goal of a teacher, while detection is seen as a "last resort" measure. Various methods of plagiarism prevention were suggested. Generally, they are aimed to make plagiarism technically hard, socially unacceptable, and legally dangerous [3]. The teachers are advised to design personalized assignments and conduct onsite problem solving sessions, when possible. School policymakers are expected to devise "honor codes" and similar mechanisms to make the students aware of high importance of "fair play" principles at a given institution. Furthermore, violators of the code are expected to face severe disciplinary punishment.

Nevertheless, plagiarism detection is still seen as a valuable activity, since the very knowledge of plagiarism checking may deter cheating. As noted above, numerous works are dedicated to the technical side of the problem. Even systems belonging to a relatively narrow group of "hermetic detection systems for source code" [9] can be categorized into several classes according to their basic approach to detection [3] (see Figure 1). By "hermetic" we mean that borrowings are expected to be found in the same collection rather than in an online source [9]

Over the last decades, a number of software similarity and source code clone detection methods were developed [10] [11] [12] [13]. However, the evaluation of their relative detection performance, applicability to particular programming languages, and robustness to refactoring techniques is still a subject of research works [5].

In addition to formal clone detection algorithms, the workflow analysis can be promising: if the system can detect that a learner copied and then pasted a large amount of source code at once, such a behavior may be considered as a possible plagiarism issue [14]. In particular, the chosen method(s) should be able to identify matching fragments of the source code files, which is not always possible for techniques based on normalization by decompilation.

IV. Introducing the Project: Sources and Project Goals

The principal challenge of the project is to create a system that would combine high plagiarism detection efficiency with the simplicity of use and appeal to a broad teacher audience by providing capabilities consistent with pedagogical goals and teaching practice.

At least, the following goals should be achieved in a system, applicable in a programming course context:

- "Hermetic" plagiarism detection in a collection of student-submitted assignments.
- Exclusions of certain fragments marked as "templates" by the teacher. Teachers often provide code templates that are expected to be integrated into a student's solution, and these templates should not be considered unauthorized borrowings.
- Simplified detection and reporting procedure "historical" submissions. When students copy from their peers, it is desirable to identify specific pairs of similar documents and deal with their authors on individual basis. However, if a student copied an assignment submitted in the past, it might be enough to provide a simplified report merely proving the fact of cheating.
- Rich reporting and visualization capabilities, which would enable the teachers to find clusters of matching documents efficiently and perform manual analysis of identified similarities.
- Support for a variety of programming languages, and an option to "tokenize" code (see, for example, [15]), which helps to identify plagiarism even if the source code is refactored (lines rearranged, variables renamed, etc.).
- An efficient approximate matching algorithm, able to find partial matches located in non-contiguous areas of source documents.
- Integration with online course management systems (such as Moodle) and/or online code testing tools (such as Aizu online judge [16]).

Some of these capabilities can be are found in earlier systems [17]. For example, WCopyfind [18] for NLP plagiarism detection provided features for HTML reporting and worked with user-defined document collections. Sherlock [19] supported templates, text tokenization, as well as certain visualization instruments.

V. Conclusion

Since, this paper describes an ongoing project, many issues still need more study and efforts. We need conduct interviews with other programming class teachers to identify all actual classroom practices including the use of online submission systems, current plagiarism prevention and detection measurements, and grading policy. Careful analysis of these practices will help in revealing the practical use cases for plagiarism detection to be used as a basis for our system. In large, achieving the project goals may significantly affect further development of innovative programming teaching practices (such as those described in [20]) within the scope of improving computer education.

Acknowledgement

The work is supported by the University of Aizu Research Funding.

References

[1] T. Kakkonen and M. Mozgovoy, "Students cyber-plagiarism," in Encyclopedia of Cyber Behavior. IGI Global, 2012, pp. 1168–1177.

[2] R. A. Posner et al., The little book of plagiarism. Pantheon, 2007.

[3] M. Mozgovoy, Enhancing computer-aided plagiarism detection. University Of Joensuu Joensuu, 2007.

[4] M. N. Halgamuge, "The use and analysis of anti-plagiarism software: Turnitin tool for formative assessment and feedback," Computer Applications in Engineering Education, vol. 25, no. 6, 2017, pp. 895–909.

[5] C. Ragkhitwetsagul, J. Krinke, and D. Clark, "A comparison of code similarity analysers," Empirical Software Engineering, vol. 23, no. 4, 2018, pp. 2464–2519.

[6] K. Yokoi and A. Aizawa, "An approach to similarity search for mathematical expressions using mathml," Towards a Digital Mathematics Library. Grand Bend, Ontario, Canada, July 8-9th, 2009, 2009, pp. 27–35.

[7] E. Pyshkin and M. Ponomarev, "Mathematical equation structural syntactical similarity patterns: A tree overlapping algorithm and its evaluation," Informatica, vol. 40, no. 4, 2016.

[8] D. Chuda, P. Navrat, B. Kovacova, and P. Humay, "The issue of (software) plagiarism: A student view," IEEE Transactions on Education, vol. 55, no. 1, 2011, pp. 22–28.

[9] T. Kakkonen and M. Mozgovoy, "Hermetic and web plagiarism detection systems for student essaysan evaluation of the state-of-the-art," Journal of Educational Computing Research, vol. 42, no. 2, 2010, pp. 135–159.

[10] M. Novak, "Review of source-code plagiarism detection in academia," in 2016 39th International Convention on Information and Communication Technology, Electronics and Microelectronics (MIPRO). IEEE, 2016, pp. 796–801.

[11] D. Kılınç, F. Bozyiğit, A. Kut, and M. Kaya, "Overview of source code plagiarism in programming courses," International Journal of Soft Computing and Engineering (IJSCE), vol. 5, no. 2, 2015, pp. 79–85.

[12] M. Akhin and V. Itsykson, "Clone detection: Why, what and how?" in 2010 6th Central and Eastern European Software Engineering Conference (CEE-SECR). IEEE, 2010, pp. 36–42.

[13] A. Sheneamer and J. Kalita, "A survey of software clone detection techniques," International Journal of Computer Applications, vol. 137, no. 10, 2016, pp. 1–21.

[14] A. S. Carter and C. D. Hundhausen, "Using programming process data to detect differences in students' patterns of programming," in Proceedings of the 2017 ACM SIGCSE Technical Symposium on Computer Science Education, 2017, pp. 105–110.

[15] M. Ďuračík, E. Kršák, and P. Hrkút, "Current trends in source code analysis, plagiarism detection and issues of analysis big datasets," Procedia engineering, vol. 192, 2017, pp. 136–141.

[16] C. M. Intisar and Y. Watanobe, "Classification of online judge programmers based on rule extraction from self organizing feature map," in 2018 9th International Conference on Awareness Science and Technology (iCAST). IEEE, 2018, pp. 313–318.

[17] M. Mozgovoy, T. Kakkonen, and G. Cosma, "Automatic student plagiarism detection: future perspectives," Journal of Educational Computing Research, vol. 43, no. 4, 2010, pp. 511–531.

[18] L. Bloomfield, "Software to detect plagiarism: Wcopyfind (version 2.6)," 2009.

[19] M. Joy and M. Luck, "Plagiarism in programming assignments," IEEE Transactions on education, vol. 42, no. 2, 1999, pp. 129–133.

[20] E. Pyshkin, "Liberal arts in a digitally transformed world: Revisiting a case of software development education," in Proceedings of the 13th Central & Eastern European Software Engineering Conference in Russia, ser. CEE-SECR '17. New York, NY, USA: ACM, 2017, pp. 23:1–23:7.

Implementing Service Design Methods and Tools into Software Development

A case study: Service Design sprint

Jemina Luodemäki, Jouni Similä, Hannu Salmela
Department of Management and Entrepreneurship
Turku School of Economics, University of Turku
Turku, Finland
Email: jemina.m.luodemaki@utu.fi, jouni.simila@utu.fi, hannu.salmela@utu.fi

Abstract— **Service Design is a comprehensive and collaborative design approach for creating value for all stakeholders. Service Design includes several methods and tools for the improvement of a new or an existing service. The implementation of Service Design into software development has been only partially studied. Likewise, research regarding the benefits and challenges concerning the utilization of Service Design precisely in software development is rather deficient. The aim of this study was to experiment applying Service Design methods and tools into software development through a pilot project carried out in a Finnish software development company. This research presents possible benefits and challenges that implementing Service Design into software development may have. In addition, critical factors to be considered while implementing Service Design are proposed.**

Keywords-service design; agile software development; SaaS; design sprint.

I. INTRODUCTION

Nowadays, all companies are involved in the software business either directly or indirectly. Software affects all industries and can be seen as the main driver for innovation [1]. Software development teams often experience pressure to keep up with the dynamic business environment and continuously changing customer requirements. The success of a product or service is determined by the created customer value and therefore software development teams constantly aim to create and develop innovative features to provide added value for the customer [2]. Customer participation and active involvement throughout the software development process are key factors to ensure focusing on the correct matters and consequently creating customer satisfaction. However, there are often several layers of people and processes between the end-users and the software development team, which complicates the user involvement. Service Design offers methods to bridge the gap between developers and users [3].

Service Design is a comprehensive and collaborative design approach for creating value for all stakeholders. In Service Design the creation of value is not limited to the end-user or customer but includes creating added value throughout the process. Therefore, Service Design can be utilized for Business-to-Business (B2B), as well as for internal services or public services [4]. Service Design includes several methods and tools for the improvement of a new or an existing service. Service Design has been studied widely in the field of creating new products and services [5] [6]. The implementation of Service Design into software development has been only partially studied. Likewise, research regarding the benefits and challenges concerning the utilization of Service Design precisely in software development is rather deficient.

The aim of this research was to experiment applying Service Design methods and tools into software development through a pilot project carried out in a small Finnish software development company, referred to as Company X. The company follows the principles of agile software development and provides Software-as-a-Service (SaaS) for human resource management. This research presents possible benefits and challenges that implementing Service Design into software development may have. In addition, critical factors to be considered while implementing Service Design are proposed. The field of research is relevant, because Service Design has been a ponderable subject during the past years, but it has not yet been studied as widely in software development as in many other fields.

The main research questions are:

RQ1: *How can Service Design methods and tools be implemented into internal processes in B2B software development?*

RQ2: *What are the benefits, challenges and critical factors when implementing Service Design methods and tools into software development?*

The key findings of this research consist of suggested factors to be considered while implementing Service Design into internal processes in B2B software development and an aggregation of the benefits, challenges and critical factors of implementing Service Design into software development.

The paper is initiated with Section 1 including the introduction. This is followed by Section 2, which describes background and related work around the subject. In Section 3 the empirical research design is presented, and this is followed by Section 4 and the introduction to the actual case study: the Service Design sprint. In Section 5 results and discussion are presented. Lastly, Section 6 combines the conclusions of the research.

II. BACKGROUND AND RELATED WORK

A. Service Design

In this research, Service Design means a holistic and collaborative approach to create value for the service user as well as the service provider [7]. The Service Design approach includes multiple tools and methods for different phases of the development process to enable comprehensive understanding of user emotions and motivations for all stakeholders [8]. In the context of this research Service Design has an outside-in aspect on the development of services and the emphasis is especially on applying different design methods and techniques to the design process of services [9]. Service Design combines different methods and approaches that have been utilized before [10].

Service Design highlights the fact that value is co-created between the customer and the service provider. This is not similarly emphasized in other design approaches like participatory design [11] or digital interaction design [12]. Even though, the term "service" is common in both of the above-mentioned, the center of attention does not exceed the customer experience beyond the user experience or use experience outside of the service touchpoints. In a way, Service Design has been able to revive other design approaches [13].

B. Implementing Service Design

In order to successfully implement Service Design methods and tools to the software development processes of a company, it is crucial to recognize all the people involved in the required changes, both internally and externally. The implementation of Service Design may require change management. Junginger & Sangiorgi [14] present a framework for the link between organizational change and Service Design based on their findings in their research. They found four similarities in their case studies regarding the link between organizational change and Service Design.

Firstly, Service Design often begins at the organizational periphery, which means that the marginal location where Service Design work is first started might limit the interference in the daily operations. Secondly, building trust relationships for change between the Service Design team and stakeholders was recognized as a similarity. A collaborative, flexible and transparent approach as well as generating interest were in a key role when building trust relationships. The third similarity was developing transformative insights into the values, norms, assumptions and behaviors of the organization in order to build trust, stimulate interest and co-create a new vision. Lastly, pilot projects as a seed for change were recognized in both case studies. Pilot projects can have an essential role in opening the way for transformative changes as they can help designers make behavioral values, norms and patterns tangible.

As a conclusion from the framework research Junginger and Sangiorgi [14] state that Service Design is still an emergent discipline based mainly on informal and tacit knowledge. Applying this framework into a wide range of contexts is suggested as a future research focus in the paper. This research puts the theoretical framework by Junginger and Sangiorgi [14] into context and further studies how it can be utilized in B2B software development.

C. Service Design and agile software development

This research has a focus on how agile software development affects the implementation of Service Design methods. Therefore, the principles of agile software development will be compared to the principles of Service Design and similarities and differences will be pointed out. Following agile methods in software development means the ability to adapt to change. Environments and requirements change continuously, and agile methods aim to respond to the changes by being iterative, incremental and cooperative [15]. Agile methods are people-centric and strive to recognize the value that proficient people and their relationships bring to software development. Improving customer satisfaction through cooperation and involving customers and other important stakeholders are also in a key role while following agile methods. The organizations ability to emphasize learning, self-organization and teamwork has a notable impact on the created value [16].

Customer involvement is one of the key benefits that adopting agile methods brings. Satisfaction with the product has increased among both customers and developers after following agile software development methods [17]. Building successful software products and services requires understanding customers' requirements and involving them throughout the development process. Customer involvement refers to different ways of active participation by the customer or the end-user in the software development process with different interactive techniques [18].

Customer collaboration is a key principle also in Service Design. The new principles of Service Design by Stickdorn et al. [4] include human-centered and collaborative as key aspects when applying Service Design. Involving customers to the design process can be carried out by organizing workshops with the customers and utilizing different design tasks and tools like prototyping in the workshops. Service Design approaches based on collaborative workshops have enabled applying Service Design as an abbreviated, but efficient design sprint as a pre-development phase in agile software development [3].

Applying Service Design methods into an agile Scrum process as sprints may support the service provider to recognize the correct small tasks for delivering a better Minimum Viable Product (MVP) for the customer [3]. This again enhances the basic principles of agile software development as early and frequent deliveries are emphasized in several definitions of agile software development [19]. Table 1 presents principles of agile software development and Service Design that have the most resemblance.

TABLE I. RESEMBLANCE BETWEEN AGILE AND SERVICE DESIGN PRINCIPLES

Agile principle	Definition	Service Design principle	Definition
Collaboration	Business people should work with developers throughout the project on a daily basis.	Collaborative	Stakeholders from different backgrounds should be involved throughout the service design sprocess.
Motivated individuals, good environment, support & trust	Projects should be built in a supporting environment and around motivated individuals.	Human-centered	Highlights the importance of involving all the people affected by the service.
Customer satisfaction, continuous delivery, value	Satisfying the customer with early and continuous delivery of valuable software.	Holistic	Services should address the needs of all stakeholders across the business.
Sustainability, people	Promoting sustainable development. Sponsors, developers and users should maintain an ongoing pace.	Iterative	An experimental, adaptable and continual approach, iterating towards implemen-tation.
Adaptability, competitiveness	Taking changing requirements into account.	Sequential	Taking interrelated actions into account.

The principles of Agile and Service Design have similarities, which can support applying Service Design methods into the software development process of an organization following agile methods. Both principles highlight the importance of collaboration between different stakeholders, involving all relevant people as well as sustainable and iterative development. These similarities can create synergistic effects when following both agile and Service Design principles. However, Service Design and agility have also slight differences, for example when considering the focus of the approaches in a bigger picture. Even though both approaches are user-centric agile has more focus on early delivery of valuable software to the customer, whereas Service Design highlights understanding the services from the customer perspective, but also the importance of creating value through the entire development process for all stakeholders.

On the other hand, when comparing Service Design to traditional software development models, such as the waterfall model, the benefits of Service Design stand out more clearly. In the waterfall model progress is seen flowing steadily downwards like a waterfall and changes during the design phase should be avoided. It is a linear model, where each step of the process is frozen before moving on to the next one, and changes to the requirements will not be considered in later phases [20]. These are opposite to many Service Design principles such as continuous iteration, adaptiveness and involving stakeholders throughout the design process.

III. EMPIRICAL RESEARCH DESIGN

The research was composed with an action research approach, which included several data collection methods. Action research is a methodology that aims to support organizational learning to develop practical outcomes. In the end of the 1990's the importance and popularity of action research in information systems increased notably. One basic principle in action research is that the best way of studying complex social processes is changing these processes and observing the results and effects of the implemented changes [21].

Frequently, action research uses several different methods for the collection of data. Using multiple methods like analysis of relevant documents, in depth interviews and participative socio-technical design concurrently is encouraged. Similar methods are also utilized in Service Design and therefore the two approaches support each other. Service Design tools and methods are in line with qualitative research methods as both are holistic processes that require participation in a real-life setting. As action research focuses on organizational learning through problem solving together with Service Design tools and methods it can provide a comprehensive way of collecting data [22]. The data was mainly collected through a focus group interview, semi-structured interviews, a questionnaire survey and the actual case study: The Service Design sprint. Due to the global pandemic regarding Covid-19 the Service Design sprint had to be held remotely, contrary to the original plan. The remote implementation brought its own challenges to the planning phase, but also enhanced the efficiency of the workshops held during the sprint.

The trustworthiness of this research will be evaluated through four aspects: credibility, transferability, dependability and conformability [23]. In doing so, it should be taken into account that the researcher is part of the organization where the case study was carried out. The role of the researcher in the Service Design sprint was the role of a project manager. The researcher was responsible of the process in its entirety, including the scope, budget, deadlines and reporting. This may affect the objectiveness of the results to some point, but precautions were taken to ensure the objectiveness. The researcher did not facilitate or lead the sessions and workshops during the actual case study to ensure as objective results as possible and to make sure that the workshops were not even accidentally directed to a desired direction from the researcher point of view.

The credibility of this research is desirable as the empirical material is rather inclusive and based on the empirical results another person could end up with the same findings and conclusions. The transferability of the research is reliable as the research is grounded on similar previous research. The results are examined in comparison to the findings of these previous studies, and similar findings from previous research are presented. Dependability is ensured by following a logical research process and carefully documenting each phase of the process. In addition, the conformability of the research is ensured by presenting logical links between the results and conclusions.

IV. THE SERVICE DESIGN SPRINT

The structure of the Service Design sprint was combined from different approaches and frameworks and further modified to best fit the needs of Company X. The structure of the Service Design sprint was mainly formed based on the idea of the Design Sprint developed at Google Ventures, the Double Diamond model [24] designed by the Design Council and the three-day Service Design session presented by Stickdorn [4]. The final version of the Service Design sprint held in Company X was basically a combination of an internal design sprint and a co-creative workshop with the customers. The sprint was held as a pre-development phase of the agile software development process.

As discovered by Junginger & Sangiorgi [14] pilot projects can have an essential role in successful organizational change. Stickdorn et al. [4] also propose starting with small Service Design projects as these can be used to modify the Service Design process as well as the company's structures and culture. Therefore, a pilot project was carried out in Company X, to demonstrate and explore the benefits, challenges and critical factors that applying Service Design has in software development.

Service Design has not been applied to internal processes in Company X before this case. However, several different design methods such as user stories and prototyping have been utilized in the software development process already previously. Thus, it was also mutually agreed in Company X that the company would benefit more of examining the use of the Service Design methods and tools during the research and ideation phase, than in the prototyping and implementation phase. Hence, the Service Design sprint will focus on the first diamond of the Double Diamond model, which includes the phases discover and define.

The selected Service Design methods and tools for the remote implementation of the Service Design sprint include the following methods and tools: desk research, semi-structured interviews, developing key insights, mapping key findings, 5 x Why's?, voting and prioritization methods, "How might we..?" questions, brainwriting, brainstorming, mindmapping, feature planning, mapping features, idea portfolio, personas, user stories, wireframing, prototyping, warm-ups as check-in methods, feeling canvases as check-out methods and compiling research reports. The methods and tools were utilized during pre-sprint research, the actual three-day Service Design sprint and post-sprint debriefing.

See Figure 1 for the structure of the remote version of the Service Design sprint. The Service Design sprint was experimented as a pre-development phase of the agile software development process of Company X.

V. RESULTS AND DISCUSSION

The results of the action research cycle are compared to previous research on the field. The findings of this research support some of the previous findings, but also differences and additional factors were identified during this research.

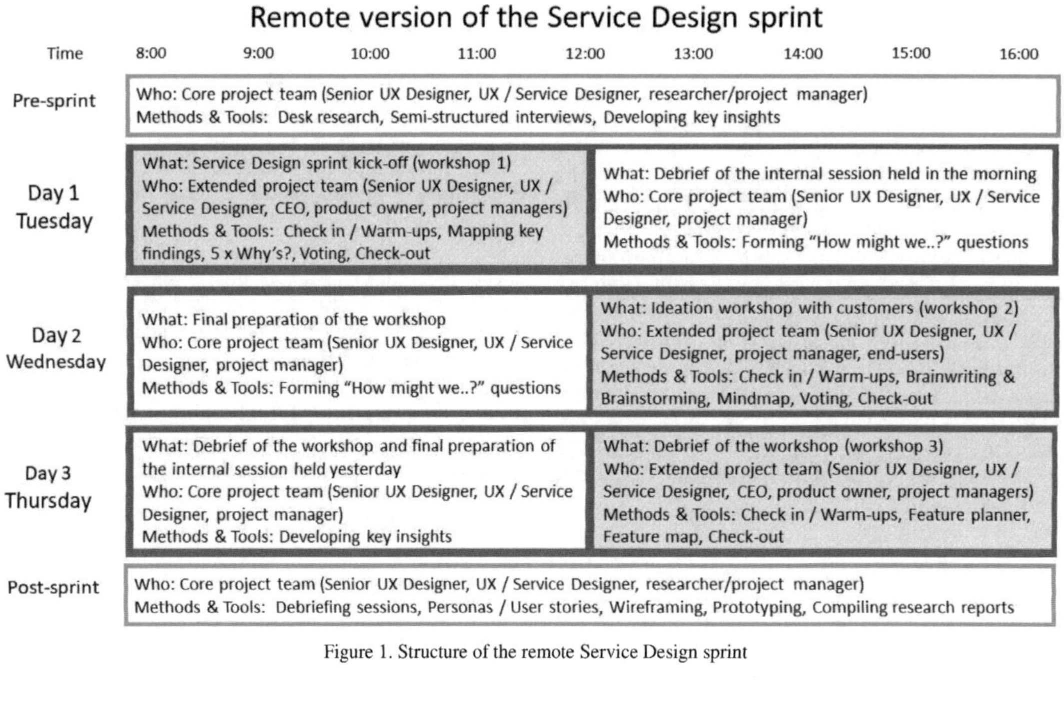

Figure 1. Structure of the remote Service Design sprint

The key findings and the discussion with previous research will be presented under three aspects based on the benefits, challenges and critical factors of implementing Service Design into software development. Each subchapter will be approached with the support of a table to present the key findings regarding the aspect in question.

A. Identified benefits

The benefits of Service Design that have been identified in previous literature regarding software development [2] include improved communication, instant feedback, increased motivation and innovation, mindset change, learning and decision making, identification and prioritization of features or potential market segments and value creation. The research done by Sauvola et al. [3] focused on experimenting the prototyping methods of Service Design whereas this research had the focus on research and ideation methods. However, several similar benefits that Sauvola et al. [3] have identified previously can be recognized based on this research. For example, improved internal motivation, delivering added value to the customer and improving the understanding of the customer and typical use cases of the software were identified based on the empirical research and are reminiscent to the benefits identified by Sauvola et al. [3]. Based on this research, the identified benefits that implementing Service Design can bring for software development are listed outright in Table 2 below.

TABLE II. IDENTIFIED BENEFITS

Key findings – benefits	Provided empirical support	Related findings in previous studies
Improved internal motivation	Focus group interview, Case: Service Design sprint	Sauvola et al. (2018)
Improved understanding of the customer and typical use cases of the software	Focus group interview, Case: Service Design sprint, Questionnaire survey	Sauvola et al. (2018), Furrer et al. (2018)
Identifying the actual needs and challenges of the customer	Focus group interview, Case: Service Design sprint, Questionnaire survey	Sauvola et al. (2018), Stickdorn et al. (2018)
Efficient resource allocation	Focus group interview, Case: Service Design sprint	Stickdorn et al. (2018), García et al. (2013), Sauvola et al. (2018)
Delivering added value to the customer	Case: Service Design sprint, Questionnaire survey	Sauvola et al. (2018), Furrer et al. (2016)
Improved customer satisfaction	Case: Service Design sprint, Participant observation, Questionnaire survey	Stickdorn et al. (2018), Furrer et al. (2018)

B. Identified challenges

The identified challenges of Sauvola et al. [2] differ partly with the ones identified during this research. This may be due to the difference between the utilized Service Design methods. However, one similar challenge was discovered in this research regarding the finding of Sauvola et al. [2] concerning stakeholder availability. In this research, the related identified challenges are commitment, selling Service Design as a concept to the customers and involving the relevant people to the process. Moreover, another discovered challenge of this research is that prototyping methods are difficult to execute in a workshop context remotely. In further iterations, as prototyping methods are also experimented within the workshops, the findings can be more profoundly compared to the previous findings of Sauvola et al. [2]. The possible challenges outright identified during this research, and that can be faced while implementing Service Design to software development, are listed in Table 3.

TABLE III. IDENTIFIED CHALLENGES

Key findings – challenges	Provided empirical support	Related findings in previous studies
Lack of time	Focus group interview, Case: Service Design sprint	Stickdorn et al. (2018)
Commitment	Focus group interview, Case: Service Design sprint	Sauvola et al. (2018), Junginger & Sangiorgi (2009)
Internal assumptions	Focus group interview, Participant observation, Case: Service Design sprint, Questionnaire survey	Junginger & Sangiorgi (2009)
Selling Service Design as a concept to the customers	Focus group interview, Case: Service Design sprint, Questionnaire survey	Sauvola et al. (2018)
Involving the relevant people to the process	Focus group interview, Participant observation, Case: Service Design sprint, Questionnaire survey	Sauvola et al. (2018), Stickdorn et al. (2018)
Prototyping methods in remote workshops	Case: Service Design sprint	
Implementing Service Design as an ongoing activity	Case: Service Design sprint	Junginger & Sangiorgi (2009)

C. Identified critical factors

The most important critical factor when implementing Service Design to an organization can be perceived as carrying out a pilot project. In order to achieve the above-mentioned benefits and avoid recognized challenges, this research suggests taking into account the following critical factors when implementing Service Design into an organization. The critical factors are proposed to be considered when planning and executing a pilot project for implementing Service Design to an organization. The critical factors identified by this research are listed in Table 4.

TABLE IV. IDENTIFIED CRITICAL FACTORS

Key findings – critical factors	Provided empirical support	Related findings in previous studies
Pilot project	Focus group interview, Case: Service Design sprint	Junginger & Sangiorgi (2009), Stickdorn et al. (2018)
Encompassing and detailed preparation	Case: Service Design sprint, Questionnaire survey	Sauvola et al. (2018)
Discovering suitable Service Design methods and tools	Focus group interview, Case: Service Design sprint, Questionnaire survey	Stickdorn et al. (2018)
Scoping the sprint challenge	Case: Service Design sprint, Questionnaire survey	
Focusing on appropriate challenges	Case: Service Design sprint	
Finding a "light-weight" solution	Focus group interview, Case: Service Design sprint,	Stickdorn et al. (2018)
Providing concrete results and findings	Case: Service Design sprint, Questionnaire survey	Stickdorn et al. (2018)
Taking into account the possible impacts of a remote implementation	Case: Service Design sprint	

The findings of the empirical research of this study support the above-mentioned critical factors. Similar factors have been highlighted in previous literature [4][14] regarding Service Design as well. However, this research presents the critical findings in respect of software development and hence supports the corresponding findings of Sauvola et al. [2].

VI. CONCLUSIONS

The first research question "*How can Service Design methods and tools be implemented into internal processes in B2B software development?*" was addressed by mapping out a suitable way of experimenting the implementation of Service Design to the case company. The research question was first approached with the focus group interview in order to acquire understanding of the assumptions and knowledge that the employees of Company X had related to Service Design. The results of the focus group interview disclosed that employees of Company X saw potential benefits regarding Service Design such as improving internal motivation and understanding the customer more profoundly. However, employees were simultaneously concerned of the lack of time and commitment regarding both internal and external stakeholders. The factors that were highlighted in the focus group interview were taken into account while planning the pilot project for implementing Service Design methods and tools in Company X.

The Service Design sprint was created based on the knowledge gained from previous literature as well as utilizing the know-how of the employees of Company X. On the grounds of the research process it was discovered that implementing Service Design methods and tools into internal processes requires Service Design to be considered as an ongoing activity in the organization. This means that in order to embed Service Design to the organization permanently further Service Design iterations are required. The Service Design activities should be continuously improved and modified if needed to achieve even better results.

It can be stated that a carefully planned pilot project is in a key role when implementing Service Design into B2B software development. Regarding the second research question it can be concluded that Service Design can be implemented to B2B software development through a pilot project, for example a Service Design sprint, which involves both internal and external stakeholders. Moreover, it was experimented that a compact Service Design sprint can be used as a pre-development phase in agile software development. In addition, to be able to carry out a successful Service Design pilot project it is crucial to communicate the objectives of the pilot project as well as the results and findings to all stakeholders.

The second research question "*What are the benefits, challenges and critical factors when implementing Service Design methods and tools into software development?*" was first addressed through the focus group interview by initially mapping out the benefits, challenges and critical factors that employees of Company X saw possible regarding the implementation of Service Design. These findings were then taken into account while planning action and creating the pilot project which was based on the three-day Service Design sprint. Lastly, the final results of the pilot project were mirrored and compared to the previous findings of the focus group interview while evaluating and specifying learning.

Regarding the second research question it can be concluded that the possible benefits of Service Design in software development include improved internal motivation, improving understanding of the customer and typical use cases of the software, identifying the actual needs and challenges of the customer, efficient resource allocation, delivering added value to the customer and improved customer satisfaction. Furthermore, achieving all these benefits while utilizing Service Design can simultaneously assist the organization in finding a common language between different teams and stakeholders. On the other hand, the possible challenges that may be faced when implementing Service Design in software development are related with the lack of time and commitment, internal assumptions, selling Service Design as a concept to the customer, involving the relevant people to the process, prototyping methods in remote workshops and implementing Service Design as an ongoing activity.

Related to the identified benefits and challenges it can be further concluded that the motivation or reason behind the above-mentioned factors often depends on the stakeholder in question. For example, the lack of time for Service Design activities from the developers point of view may be related to the pressure of delivering new features promptly, whereas from the customers point of view this may be due to the fact that they might need a permission for participating to a Service Design sprint from their superiors, who might not realize the value of Service Design activities with the service provider. In order to truly understand the motivations behind the identified benefits and challenges, further research about the background of different stakeholders may be required. The findings could then be advisable to consider while planning the pilot project for implementing Service Design.

This research proposes that by taking into account the following critical factors when implementing Service Design into software development the above-mentioned challenges are more likely to be overcome and consequently the above-mentioned benefits are more likely to be achieved. The critical factors when implementing Service Design are composed on the pilot project carried out in Company X. The key critical factor identified by this research is starting the implementation of Service Design through a pilot project. Other critical factors identified are suggested to be considered while planning and executing the Service Design pilot project in question. The critical factors regarding the pilot project consist of detailed and encompassing planning, discovering suitable Service Design methods and tools, scoping the sprint challenge, focusing on appropriate challenges, finding a lightweight solution and providing concrete results and findings.

In addition, this research demonstrated that carrying out a design sprint remotely is possible and profitable. While planning a remote implementation of Service Design the remote aspect should be consciously investigated as working remotely may bring its own challenges to the implementation.

The limitations of this research include that the research was carried out in a single case company, which means that the results may differ in distinct circumstances. Therefore, generalizations based on the results of this research are limited. Albeit, the results provide an approach for implementing Service Design to software development, the sprint was just one way of carrying out a pilot project. Different approaches may be discovered more suitable and functional in other organizations. Therefore, each organization should discover the best practices for embedding Service Design in the organization in question.

For future studies, this research suggests validating the Service Design sprint model. It can be stated that the Service Design sprint model presented in this research requires further iterations before it can be considered practical. For example, experimenting the Service Design sprint as the first phase in agile software development could be further studied. The way Service Design and agile software development may be able to complete one another is worth examination in practice. In addition, evaluation of combining a design sprint and a co-creation workshop would be interesting. An interesting similar approach combining design thinking, lean startup and agile development is provided by Flores et al. [25].

Another topical subject of research would be comparing the results of traditionally held workshops to the remote workshops. The remote working aspect is truly actual considering the current situation globally.

REFERENCES

[1] C. Elbert, "Looking into the future," IEEE Software, Vol. 32(6), pp. 92–97, 2015.

[2] T. Sauvola, M. Kelanti, J. Hyysalo, P. Kuvaja, and K. Liukkunen, "Continuous Improvement and Validation with Customer Touchpoint Model in Software Development," CSEA 2018: The Thirteenth International Conference on Software Engineering Advances, pp. 52–60, 2018.

[3] T. Sauvola, S. Rontti, L. Laivamaa, M. Oivo, and P. Kuvaja, "Integrating Service Design Prototyping into Software Development," ICSEA 2016: The Eleventh International Conference on Software Engineering Advances, pp. 325–332, 2016.

[4] M. Stickdorn, M. E. Hormess, A. Lawrence, and J. Schneider, "This Is Service Design Doing: Applying Service Design Thinking in the Real World". O'Reilly Media, England, 2018.

[5] P. Arslan, "Applications of service design in the software industry," In: Miettinen, S. (edit.) An Introduction to Industrial Service Design, pp. 25-34. Routledge. New York, 2017.

[6] R. Garcia, "Creating and Marketing New Products and Services," CRC Press. Boca Raton, 2014.

[7] Service Design Network. [Online]. Available from: https://www.service-design-network.org/about-service-design, [retrieved: 8, 2020.]

[8] S. Miettinen, S. Rontti, and J. Jeminen, "Co-Prototyping Emotional Value," 19th DMI: Academic Design Management Conference Design Management in an Era of Disruption, pp. 1–19, 2014.

[9] R. Alves and N. J. Nunes, "Towards a taxonomy of service design methods and tools," Lecture Notes in Business Information Processing 2013, Vol.143, pp. 215–229, 2013.

[10] E. Yu and D. Sangiorgi, "Service Design as an Approach to Implement the Value Cocreation Perspective in New Service Development," Journal of Service Research 2018, Vol. 21(1), pp. 40–58, 2018.

[11] F. Kensing, "Methods and Practices in Participatory Design," ITU Press, Copenhagen, Denmark, 2003.

[12] D. Saffer, "Designing for Interaction," New Riders Press. ISBN 0-321-43206-1, 2006.

[13] S. Holmlid, "Participative, co-operative, emancipatory: From participatory design to service design. DeThinking Service

ReThinking Design," First Nordic Conference on Service Design and Service Innovation, pp. 105–118, 2009.

[14] S. Junginger and D. Sangiorgi, "Service design and organisational change: Bridging the gap between rigor and relevance," International Association of Societies of Design Research, pp. 4339–4348, 2009.

[15] J. Chaves and S. de Freitas, "A Systematic Literature Review for Service-Oriented Architecture and Agile Development," ICCSA 2019: Computational Science and Its Applications – ICCSA 2019, pp. 120–135, 2019.

[16] S. Nerur and V. Balijepally, "Theoretical reflections on agile development methodologies," Communications of the ACM—Emergency Response Information Systems: Emerging Trends and Technologies, Vol. 50(3), pp. 79–83, 2007.

[17] T. Dybå and T. Dingsøyr, "Empirical studies of agile software development: A systematic review," Information and Software Technology, Vol. 50, pp. 833–859, 2008.

[18] S.G. Yaman et al. "Customer Involvement in Continuous Deployment: A Systematic Literature Review," In: Daneva M., Pastor O. (eds) Requirements Engineering: Foundation for Software Quality. REFSQ 2016. Lecture Notes in Computer Science, Vol. 9619, pp. 249–265, 2016.

[19] M. Laanti, J. Similä, and P. Abrahamsson, "Definitions of Agile Software Development and Agility," Communications in Computer and Information Science, Vol. 364, pp. 247–258, 2013.

[20] S. Balaji and MS. Murugaiyan, "Waterfall vs. V-Model vs. Agile: A comparative study on SDLC," International Journal of Information Technology and Business Management, Vol. 2 (1), pp. 26–30, 2012.

[21] R. Baskerville, "Investigating Information Systems with Action Research," Communication of the Association for Information Systems, Vol. 2, Article 19, pp. 2-32, 1999.

[22] H. Madden and A.T. Walter, "Using an Action Research Approach to Embed Service Design in a Higher Education Institution," Swedish Design Research Journal, pp. 40-50, 2016.

[23] P. Eriksson and A. Kovalainen, "Qualitative Methods in Business Research. Introducing Qualitative Methods: Qualitative methods in business research." SAGE Publications Ltd. pp. 194–209, 2011.

[24] M. E. Porter "The Competitive Advantage of Nations," New York: Free Press, 1990.

[25] M. Flores et al. "How Can Hackathons Accelerate Corporate Innovation?," In: Moon I., Lee G., Park J., Kiritsis D., von Cieminski G. (eds) Advances in Production Management Systems. Production Management for Data-Driven, Intelligent, Collaborative, and Sustainable Manufacturing. APMS 2018. IFIP Advances in Information and Communication Technology, vol 535. Springer, Cham, 2018.

A Machine Learning Approach Towards Automatic Software Design Pattern Recognition Across Multiple Programming Languages

Roy Oberhauser[0000-0002-7606-8226]
Computer Science Dept.
Aalen University
Aalen, Germany
e-mail: roy.oberhauser@hs-aalen.de

Abstract—**As the amount of software source code increases, manual approaches for documentation or detection of software design patterns in source code become inefficient relative to the value. Furthermore, typical automatic pattern detection tools are limited to a single programming language. To address this, our Design Pattern Detection using Machine Learning (DPDML) offers a generalized and programming language agnostic approach for automated design pattern detection based on Machine Learning (ML). The focus of our evaluation was on ensuring DPDML can reasonably detect one design pattern in the structural, creational, and behavioral category for two popular programming languages (Java and C#). 60 unique Java and C# code projects were used to train the artificial neural network (ANN) and 15 projects were then used to test pattern detection. The results show the feasibility and potential for pursuing an ANN approach for automated design pattern detection.**

Keywords–software design pattern detection; machine learning; artificial neural networks; software engineering.

I. INTRODUCTION

In the area of software engineering, software design patterns have been well-documented and popularized, including the Gang of Four (GoF) [1] and POSA [2]. The application of documented solutions to recurring software design problems has been a boon to improving software design quality and efficiency.

However, as the design patterns are mostly described informally, their implementation can vary widely depending on the programming language, natural language, pattern structure and terminology awareness of the programmer, experience, and interpretation. The actual detection and documentation of these software design solution patterns has hitherto relied on the experience, recollection, and manual analysis of experts. The pattern books referenced above were published over 25 years ago, and while many millions of lines of code have since been programmed, they have not been subjected to any comprehensive analysis. Furthermore, any project documentation of applied patterns, if existent, may be inconsistent with the current source code reality (e.g., prescriptive documentation of intentions, adaptations during development, maintenance changes) and thus not reflected or necessarily trustworthy. Additionally, known pattern variants may occur, the patterns may evolve over time with technology, and in fact new patterns may unknowingly be developed that the experts may be unaware of. The many different programming languages used, the different natural languages of programmers that affect naming, tribal community effects, the programmer's (lack of) knowledge of these patterns and use of (proper) naming and notation or markers, make it difficult to identify pattern usage by experts or tooling. While many code repositories are accessible to the public on the web, many more repositories are hidden within companies or other organizations and are not necessarily accessible for analysis. While determining actual pattern usage is beneficial for identifying which patterns are used where and can help avoid unintended pattern degradation and associated technical debt and quality issues, the investment necessary for manual pattern extraction, recovery, and archeology is not economically viable.

While automated feature extraction of software design patterns from documentation or code repositories is not yet commonly available among popular software development tools, research has attempted to find automated techniques that work. However, most of the published techniques have not applied ML to this problem area. One implicit challenge for most approaches is to demonstrate coverage of all 23 of the GoF patterns, which very few if any achieve.

This paper contributes Design Pattern Detection using Machine Learning (DPDML), a generalized and programming language independent approach for automated design pattern detection based on ML. Our realization of the core of the solution approach shows its feasibility, and an evaluation using 75 unique Java and C# code projects with three common GoF patterns for training and testing provides insights into its potential and limitations.

The structure of this paper is as follows: the following section discusses related work. Section 3 describes our solution approach. In Section 4, our realization is presented. This is followed by our evaluation and then a conclusion.

II. RELATED WORK

Various approaches have been used for software design pattern detection, and they can be categorized based on different analysis styles, such as structural, behavioral, or semantic, with some utilizing a combination of styles. Many approaches include some form of structural analysis for pattern detection. Within this style, ML approaches use classification, decision tree, Artificial Neural Networks (ANNs), or support vector machines (SVMs), mapping the pattern detection problem to a learning problem. Examples include MARPLE-DPD [3], Galli et al. [4], and Ferenc et al. [5]. Wang et al. [6] uses a reason-based approach based on matrices. Examples of rule-based approaches include

Sempatrec [7] and FiG [8], which use an ontology representation. Metric-based approaches include MAPeD [9] and PTIDEJ [10]. Fontana et al. [11] describe a micro-structure-based structural analysis approach. In the behavioral analysis style, graph-based approaches include: DPIDT [12] that analyzes subpatterns in UML, and a UML semantic graph by Mayvan and Rasoolzadegan [13]. An example semantic-analysis style approach is Issaoui et al. [14], which uses an XML representation. DP-Miner [15] is a matrix-based approach using UML that involves structural, behavioral, and semantic analysis. Uchiyama et al. [16] uses a metric-based approach that involves both structural and behavioral analysis.

The styles and approaches used are quite fractured and none has reached a mature and high-quality result with an accessible and executable implementation that we could evaluate. We are not aware of any approach yet that can automatically and reliably detect all 23 GoF design patterns. Most have some limitation or drawback, and the success rate reported among the approaches varies tremendously. We conclude further investigation and research in this area is essential to enhancing the knowledge surrounding this area. Our solution approach is unique in offering: 1) a generalized code-centric approach that combines available data (rather than focusing on only one category of information) without necessarily requiring behavioral analysis, 2) being programming language-independent to support multiple popular programming languages, and 3) leveraging ML.

III. Solution

Our full holistic DPDML solution approach is shown in Figure 1, indicating the realized DPDML-C core subset. It is based on the following principles:

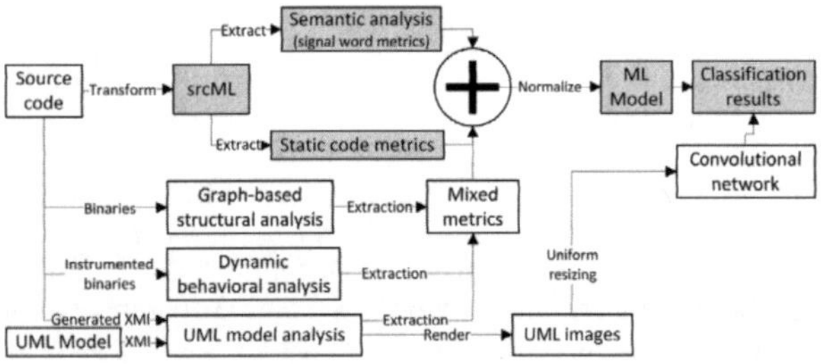

Figure 1. General DPDML comprehensive solution approach with realized core DPDML-C (shown in grey).

ML model: by utilizing ML to analyze sample data, the model learns how to classify new unknown data, in our case to differentiate design patterns. Our realization may apply or combine any ML model that suites the situation. Currently, an ANN is used because we were interested in investigating its performance, and intend in future work to detect a wide pattern scope, pattern variants, and new patterns. From our standpoint, alternative non-ML methods such as creating a rule-based system by hand would require labor and expertise as the number of patterns increases and new undiscovered patterns should be detected. With an appropriate ML model, these should be learned automatically and be more readily detected.

Programming language-independent: the source code is converted into an abstracted common format for further processing. For this, in our realization we currently utilize srcML [17], thus our realization can currently support any programming languages that have a mapping to the srcML XML-based format, including C, C++, Java, and C#. If other abstract syntax formats are standardized and available for analysis, these also can be considered. Our main purpose is to extract various metrics in a common fashion from the source code.

Semantic analysis: common pattern signal words in the source code can be used as an indicator or hint for specific pattern usage. Additional natural languages can be supported to detect usage of pattern names or their constituent components in case they were coded in other languages. Our realization supports German, Russian, and French.

Static code metric extraction: various static code metrics are utilized to detect and differentiate design patterns.

Graph analysis: code repositories are analyzed using graph-based tools like jQAssistant and metrics extracted.

Dynamic analysis: tracing runtime code behavior can detect behavioral similarities in event sequencing, especially for the creational or behavior patterns. From these traces event and related runtime metrics can be extracted.

UML structural analysis: in case a UML model exists, the XMI structures can be analyzed and indicators extracted, such as signal words or other structural metrics. If no UML diagrams or XMI exist, they could be generated by reverse engineering UML tools and structural metrics extracted. Furthermore, a convolutional network could analyze UML images for similarities to support pattern classification.

Metric normalization: the value ranges of metrics are normalized to a scale of 0-1 to improve ANN performance.

The hypothesis driving our DPDML solution and investigation is that by utilizing all available data and more specifically metrics related to the design patterns, and feeding this input into an ANN or other ML models, we can achieve suitable classification accuracy. From a practicality standpoint, this could reduce the overall manual labor involved in identifying potential patterns, classifying them, and can potentially assist developers, maintainers, or experts involved in software archeology.

IV. (Partial) Realization

For our realization to apply ML, a sufficient data set of different and realistic projects was needed to support supervised learning. Not all portions of the full solution approach could yet be realized due various unexpected obstacles and project resource constraints, and we plan to address the complete DPDML realization in future work.

A. Comprehensive DPDML Challenges

UML structural analysis: most of the 60 design pattern code repositories we used did not contain any or sufficient UML for us to use in supervised training or testing. If they contained UML, it would be time-consuming to manually verify the code to determine if they are correspondingly valid UML diagrams. If they were created manually rather than generated, they may contain some additional information or signal words not necessarily available in the code. If, however, round-trip UML tools were used, then the code reflects the information found in the diagrams, and thus the diagrams hold no additional information. While UML can be helpful for human analysis and verification because it distills code structure visually, they are difficult to automatically verify against code and machine-based analysis does not necessarily benefit from or need the simplification. If UML diagrams were generated directly from the code by a UML tool triggered by DPDML, little additional value would currently be gained, since the basis is the code itself, and no structural information not already contained or derivable from the code is created. Given a common UML generator, structural visual image comparison techniques could be applied with a convolutional network to determine if it helps with classification. Lacking a UML training and testing dataset of sufficient size, this portion of our solution concept will be evaluated in future work.

Dynamic analysis: many available code projects have different runtime environments, languages, libraries, concurrent processing, and require specialized tooling to acquire behavior tracing data, which is very computing resource intensive, time consuming to manually setup and acquire, and requires specialized automated analysis tools, since no formats or tool standards exist in this area. In the tracing, one would have to ensure that the patterns are actually substantially executed, which can be issue for larger projects. Furthermore, creating sufficiently large training sets for ML would be challenging. For most users of the approach we are seeking, requiring this level of analysis would perhaps be an academic exercise and could improve our understanding, but it is neither practical nor economically viable for continued usage, and we thus did not realize this portion of our solution concept.

Graph analysis: Analysis of code repositories using graph-based tools such as jQAssistant could be used, but similar to the dynamic analysis issues, tools such as jQAssistant require compiled binaries for analysis. Given this, it could be used to query various aspects and enhance our classification results and can be used to assist with manual verification. However, since our training data did not consist wholly of compiled code, we intend to address the realization of this aspect in future work.

Various analysis tools could potentially improve the results, but these are usually developed with a certain purpose that influences the interaction modes and the output. For instance, plugins for the Eclipse IDE are often focused on Java, are primarily graphical to help a developer analyze the current project, but are not designed for automated analysis of many projects in various languages from the command line. Since we chose to include both Java and C# support, no IDE-specific tooling was utilized. Beyond IDE tools, reverse-engineering tools such as Imagix 4D or code analysis tools like SourceMeter require either commercial licenses or are missing a command-line mode, and are limited in how they can be used for automated analysis situations in our context.

B. Core DPDML-C Implementation

A key aspect of our investigation was to determine if the core of the DPDML solution, metrics-based ML using an ANN, works as intended. Also, since source code should usually be readily available, whereas other information (binaries may not build, instrumentation and UML may not exist), our prototype realization effort focused on the source code analysis, known as the core DPDML-C as shown in grey in Figure 1. Due to resource and time constraints, we initially focused on having the network learn to detect one pattern out of each of three pattern categories: from the structural category, Adapter; from the creational patterns, Factory; and from the behavioral patterns, Observer. This pattern scope could then be expanded in future work if the outcome is positive.

Python was used to implement our prototype due to its versatility and the available libraries to support the implementation of ANNs. TensorFlow was chosen along with Keras as a top-layer API.

Metric-based matching: The ElementTree parser was used to traverse srcML and count the specific XML-tags. The metric values were not separated by roles or classes, but are merged and evaluated as a whole. The metrics used were inspired by Uchiyama et al. [16] and are shown in Table I.

TABLE I. OVERVIEW OF METRICS

Abbreviation	Description
NOC	Number of classes
NOF	Number of fields
NOSF	Number of static fields
NOM	Number of methods
NOSM	Number of static methods
NOI	Number of interfaces
NOAI	Number of abstract interfaces

Semantic-based matching: An obvious approach to pattern detection is naming. If a developer already used common design pattern terminology in the code, then this should be utilized as a pattern detection indicator. For our signal word detection, we translated the signal words to German, French, and Russian to improve results for non-English code.

Semantic variations: To determine if other signal words beyond the design pattern name were used in implementations, we analyzed several examples of implemented design patterns and any UML diagrams, if provided. 12 additional signal words were selected, four for each pattern as shown in Table II.

TABLE II. SIGNAL WORDS FOR DESIGN PATTERNS

Pattern	Signal Words			
Adapter	Adapter	adaptee	target	adapt
Factory	Factory	create	implements	type
Observer	observer	state	update	notify

Internationalization: To test internationalization, the Python library *translate* was used to translate the signal words to German, French, and Russian. Rather than extending the list of metrics passed to the ANN, a match with a translated word is counted in the same input parameter as the original English words. Applying Natural Language Processing (NLP) to reduce words by stemming or creating lemmas to compare to a defined word list would also be possible, and may improve or deteriorate the results, if for instance the input array contained further zeros when no signal words were found.

C. *Artificial Neural Network (ANN)*

Based on our realization scope, since the input array is not multidimensional, deep neural networks (DNNs) with additional layers would not necessarily yield improved results. We thus chose to realize one input layer, two hidden layers, and one output layer as shown in Figure 2. We created the network with the Keras API with the TensorFlow Python library.

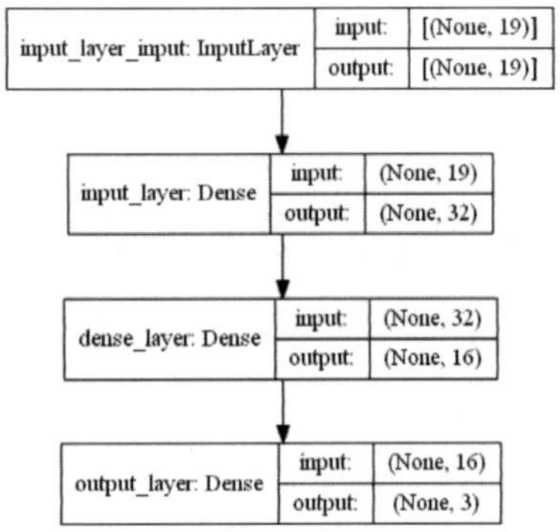

Figure 2. ANN model overview created with Keras.

The input layer size matches the data points, and as there are 7 metrics and 12 semantic match values, this makes 19 input values total. The input model structure is a numpy array as follows:

```
[NOC, NOF, NOSF, NOM, NOSM, NOI, NOAI, ASW1,
  ASW2, ASW3, ASW4, FSW1, FSW2, FSW3, FSW4,
         OSW1, OSW2, OSW3, OSW4]
```

The first 7 values correspond to Table I while the rest indicate the number of signal word matches from Table II. SW=Signal Word, A=Adapter, F=Façade, and O=Observer, 1-4 implies the corresponding table column. Only 7 metric values are utilized when no signal words exist.

The first hidden layer is a dense layer (with each neuron fully connected to the neurons in the prior layer) consisting of 32 neurons. The activation function was a rectified linear unit (ReLU). The second layer is a dense layer with 16 neurons. This conforms with the general guideline to gradually decrease the neurons as one approaches the output layer. The output layer consists of three neurons to match the three design patterns that should be detected. The "Softmax" activation method is used, which is often used in classification problems and supports identifying the confidence of the network in its decision. The "Adam" algorithm is a universal optimizer that is recommended in a wide assortment of papers and guides. As no specialized optimizer was needed, "Adam" with its default values was chosen as defined in [18]. No regularization was applied in each layer. Adam automatically adjusts and optimizes the learning rate. Sparse categorical crossentropy was applied as the loss function for this multi-class classification task.

The size of the ANN should fit the size of the problem. Small adjustments to the ANN structure showed no significant performance impact, whereas significantly increasing the neuron count or layer count negatively impacted results. With two hidden layers and 48 neurons, the first layer contains 640 parameters, the second layer 528, and the output layer 51, resulting in 1219 parameters that are adjusted during training.

The network is trained in epochs, wherein the complete training set is sent through the network with weights adjusted. As the weights and metrics change per epoch, an early-stopping callback stops the training if the accuracy of the network decreases over more than 10 epochs, saving the network that had the best accuracy. A validation dataset is typically used during training to monitor results on unlearned data after each epoch, but as our training set was limited, we used a prepared testing dataset with known labels.

D. *Training Datasets*

As to possible design pattern training sets, the Pattern-like Micro-Architecture Repository (P-MARt) includes a collection of microstructures found in different repositories such as JHotdraw and JUnit. However, because these patterns are intertwined with each other, they do not provide isolated example specimens for training the ANN. The Perceptrons Reuse Repositories could theoretically provide many instances of design patterns for a training dataset, but no results were provided on the website during the timeframe of our realization, and while the source code analyzer is free, the servers could not be reached.

We did manage to find training data as detailed in the next section. Since our initial intent for DPDML was a much broader scope for data pattern mining, and because we expected a large supply of sample data, we focused on an ANN realization. We were also interested in determining if we could train an ANN to detect these patterns with relatively few samples. However, due to unexpected additional resource and time constraints involved in finding pattern samples manually, we had to reduce the number of design patterns involved, and could not compare the ANN with alternative classification schemes such as Naïve Bayes, Decision Tree, Logistic Regression, and SVMs, but this will be considered in future work.

V. EVALUATION

The evaluation corresponds to the three patterns that were the focus of the realization: from the structural category, Adapter; from the creational patterns, Factory; and from the behavioral patterns, Observer. The reason for choosing these three is that each represents a different pattern category and these are popular patterns. Furthermore, the number of While such simple design patterns might well be better detected with other ML models, our overall DPDML is much more ambitious, and we thus wanted to validate that an ANN would still work suitably (perhaps not optimally) in a more constrained low-data case.

A. *Dataset*

As shown in Figure 3, the dataset consisted of 75 small single-pattern code projects from public repositories, 49 in Java and 26 in C# (mostly from github and the rest from pattern book sites, MSDN, etc.), evenly distributed into 25 unique code projects per pattern. They were specifically labeled as examples of these patterns, and manually verified. These popular languages are supported by srcML, and the mix permits us to demonstrate the programming language independent principle. The inequality between language examples is likely due to the language popularity and age.

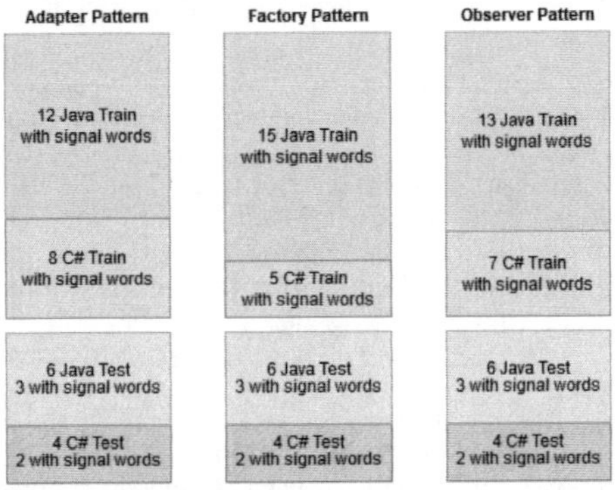

Figure 3. Pattern-specific datasets in columns with programming language specific training sets on the top rows and test sets on the bottom.

Training data: Of the 75 projects, 20 per pattern category (60 total) were selected for training the ANN, with between 60-75% of the code projects being in Java (green) and the remainder in C# (blue) as shown in the upper section of Figure 3.

Test data: The remaining 15 projects of the 75 (five per pattern category with 3 in Java and 2 in C#) were used for the test dataset. In order to test whether signal word pattern matching significantly impacts the ANN results, these projects were duplicated and their signal words removed or renamed, resulting in 6 Java (orange) and 4 C# (purple) projects per pattern/category as shown in the lower section of Figure 3. This resulted in 10 test projects per pattern.

B. *Supervised Training*

As shown in Figure 4, during training the accuracy improves from 47% to 95% in the first seven epochs, thereafter fluctuating between 85-95% with a peak of 96.7% in the 27th epoch. The network loss metrics are shown in Figure 4. The loss value drops from an initial 1.0841 to 0.2816 in epoch 17 before small fluctuations begin, with the trend continuing downward. The loss value of 0.1995 in epoch 27 is an adequate prerequisite for detecting patterns in unknown code projects, and we saw little value in increasing the training epochs. The early stopping callback was not triggered since the overall accuracy of the network is still increasing despite the fluctuations, indicating a positive learning behavior and implying that with the given data points, it is finding structures and values that allow it to differentiate the three design patterns from each other. We thus chose to stop the training at 30 epochs, which took 2-45 seconds depending on the underlying hardware environment (any Graphical Processing Unit (GPU) with CUDA support will improve processing times).

Considering that the worst case of random guessing would result in an accuracy of 33%, the accuracy result of 97% is significantly better and shows the potential of the approach.

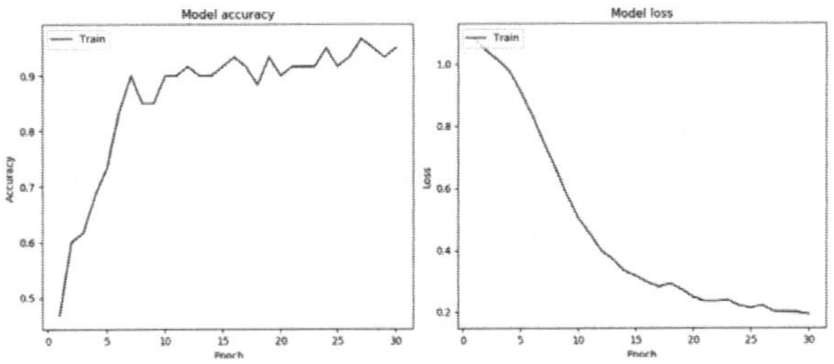

Figure 4. Network accuracy and loss over 30 epochs of training.

The training results show that not only is the ANN learning to differentiate the patterns, its confidence for these determinations increases during the training. By epoch 27 with an accuracy of 96.7% and a loss of 0.1995, only two out of the 60 total code projects spread evenly across the three design patterns are incorrectly classified.

C. *Testing*

Recall from Section V.A. that for the test dataset, 15 unique code projects were taken (five unique projects per pattern), and these were then duplicated and their signal words removed, resulting in 30 code projects. By removing the signal words, we can determine the degree of dependence of the network on these signal words.

During testing, the reported accuracy dropped to 83.3%, meaning 25 of the 30 patterns were correctly identified. Furthermore, the loss went to 0.4060, meaning a loss in confidence of its determination. A deterioration in these values is to be expected when working with unfamiliar data.

The results show that the network was able to use its learned knowledge in training to correctly classify a majority of unknown projects (25 out of 30).

TABLE III. CONFUSION MATRIX BASED ON 30 CODE PROJECTS

Predicted Labels	True Labels			Accuracy	Precision	F_1 Score
	Factory	*Adapter*	*Observer*			
Factory	7	0	0	90%	100%	0.82
Adapter	1	9	1	90%	81%	0.86
Observer	2	1	9	86.7%	75%	0.82
Recall	70%	90%	90%			

The confusion matrix is shown in Table III. The precision column indicates how many of the predicted labels are correct, while the recall row indicates how many true labels were predicted correctly. Fewer false positives improve the precision, while fewer false negatives improve the recall value. All the code projects predicted to be Factory were correct (a precision of 100%), while the remaining 30% of the Factory pattern projects were incorrectly classified as another pattern (these false negatives result in a recall of 70%). This indicates that the Factory is more easily confused with the other patterns, a possible explanation being that the metrics we used may better differentiate more involved (more complex) patterns. The other patterns had less precision (81% or 75%), but a better recall of 90%. The overall F_1 score is 0.83.

As to the influence of signal words, our hypothesis that signal words would improve the results proved hitherto unfounded. The classification precision was not affected by signal words, with 12 projects with signal words and 13 without being correctly classified. Additional test runs showed similar results (+/- one project). However, in future work we will investigate this further as we increase the statistical basis.

The results show suitable accuracy of the DPDML-C, and we believe a generalization of the DPDML approach across the GoF and further patterns to be promising.

VI. Conclusion

This paper presented our DPDML solution approach, a generalized and source code-based but programming language-independent approach for automated design pattern detection based on ML. Our realization of the core DPDML-C shows its feasibility for source code-based analysis. An evaluation using 60 unique Java and C# code projects for training and then 15 code projects for testing. With an accuracy of 83% and loss of 0.4060 during testing, the results show the feasibility and potential for pursuing an ANN approach for automated design pattern detection as well as some of the limitations. Furthermore, no cost-intensive behavioral analysis was involved to achieve this result. Our results for the three patterns did not show that signal words substantially improve results, indicating that other pattern characteristics can potentially suffice as indicators. While our initial focus on three fundamental patterns is obviously not of practical use yet, it shows promise for extending it to others.

Future work will investigate the inclusion of additional pattern properties and key differentiators to improve the results even further. This includes analyzing the network classification errors in more detail to further optimize the network accuracy, adding support for the remaining GoF patterns, utilizing semantic analysis with NLP capabilities on the code for additional natural languages, supporting additional programming languages such as C++, and extending our prototype realization to include additional code metrics, UML structural analysis (if UML is available), graph-based analysis, and dynamic behavioral analysis if traces are provided. Also, we intend to evaluate pattern detection when they are intertwined with other patterns and evaluate accuracy, performance, and practicality on large code bases. We will also investigate the detection of new design patterns and variants to the traditional patterns. Furthermore, we intend to apply cross-validation and consider alternative classification schemes such as Naïve Bayes, Decision Tree, Logistic Regression, and SVMs. Thereafter, we intend to do an empirical industrial case study.

Acknowledgment

The author thanks Florian Michel for his assistance with the design, implementation, evaluation, and diagrams.

References

[1] E. Gamma, Design patterns: elements of reusable object-oriented software. Pearson Education India, 1995.

[2] F. Buschmann, R. Meunier, H. Rohnert, P. Sommerlad, and M. Stal, Pattern-oriented software architecture: a system of patterns, Vol. 1. John Wiley & Sons, 2008.

[3] M. Zanoni, F. A. Fontana, and F. Stella, "On applying machine learning techniques for design pattern detection," J. of Systems & Software, 2015, vol. 103, no. C, pp. 102-117.

[4] L. Galli, P. Lanzi, and D. Loiacono, "Applying data mining to extract design patterns from Unreal Tournament levels," Computational Intelligence and Games. IEEE, 2014, pp. 1-8.

[5] R. Ferenc, A. Beszedes, L. Fulop, and J. Lele, "Design pattern mining enhanced by machine learning," 21st IEEE Int'l Conf. on Softw. Maintenance (ICSM'05), IEEE, 2005, pp. 295-304.

[6] Y. Wang, H. Guo, H. Liu, and A. Abraham, "A fuzzy matching approach for design pattern mining," J. Intelligent & Fuzzy Systems, vol. 23, nos. 2-3, pp. 53-60, 2012.

[7] A. Alnusair, T. Zhao, and G. Yan, "Rule-based detection of design patterns in program code," Int'l J. on Software Tools for Technology Transfer, vol. 16, no. 3, pp. 315-334, 2014.

[8] M. Lebon and V. Tzerpos, "Fine-grained design pattern detection," IEEE 36th Annual Computer Software and Applications Conference, IEEE, pp. 267-272, 2012.

[9] I. Issaoui, N. Bouassida, and H. Ben-Abdallah, "Using metric-based filtering to improve design pattern detection approaches," Innovations in Systems and Software Engineering, vol. 11, no. 1, pp. 39-53, 2015.

[10] Y. G. Guéhéneuc, J. Y. Guyomarc'h, and H. Sahraoui, "Improving design-pattern identification: a new approach and an exploratory study," Software Quality Journal, vol. 18, no. 1, pp. 145-174, 2010.

[11] F. A. Fontana, S. Maggioni, and C. Raibulet, "Understanding the relevance of micro-structures for design patterns detection," Journal of Systems and Software, vol. 84, no. 12, pp. 2334-2347, 2011.

[12] D. Yu, Y. Zhang, and Z. Chen, "A comprehensive approach to the recovery of design pattern instances based on sub-patterns and method signatures," Journal of Systems and Software, vol. 103, pp. 1-16, 2015.

[13] B. B. Mayvan and A. Rasoolzadegan, "Design pattern detection based on the graph theory," Knowledge-Based Systems, vol. 120, pp. 211-225, 2017.

[14] I. Issaoui, N. Bouassida, and H. Ben-Abdallah, "Using metric-based filtering to improve design pattern detection approaches. Innovations in Systems and Software Engineering," vol. 11, no. 1, pp. 39-53, 2015.

[15] J. Dong, Y. Zhao, and Y. Sun, "A matrix-based approach to recovering design patterns," IEEE Transactions on Systems, Man, and Cybernetics-Part A: Systems and Humans, vol. 39, no. 6, pp. 1271-1282, 2009.

[16] S. Uchiyama, H. Washizaki, Y. Fukazawa, and A. Kubo, "Design pattern detection using software metrics and machine learning," First International Workshop on Model-Driven Software Migration (MDSM 2011), p. 38-47, 2011.

[17] M. Collard, M. Decker, and J. Maletic, "Lightweight transformation and fact extraction with the srcML toolkit," IEEE 11th international working conference on source code analysis and manipulation, IEEE, 2011, pp. 173-184.

[18] D. Kingma and J. Ba, "Adam: A method for stochastic optimization," arXiv preprint arXiv:1412.6980, 2014.

Systematic Review on the Use of Metrics for Estimating the Effort and Cost of Software Applicable to the Brazilian Public Sector

Washington Henrique Carvalho Almeida[1], Felipe Furtado[1], Luciano de Aguiar Monteiro[1], Fernando Escobar[2] and Sahra Karolina Gomes e Silva[3]
[1]Center for Studies and Advanced Systems of Recife – CESAR School
Recife, Brazil
[2]PMI-DF
Brasília, Brazil
[3]UNINASSAU
Teresina, Brazil
E-mail: {whca, fsfs, lam}@cesar.school
E-mail: {fernando.escobar.br, sahrask}@gmail.com

***Abstract*— This article presents a systematic literature review concerning the use of metrics for estimating effort, cost, and timescale in the scope of software development services for the federal public administration sector, which seeks to obtain subsidies to reply to what metrics are used around the world and can be adopted within the Brazilian normative framework and applied to the sourcing of Information Technologies services. The systematic review is strongly related to the knowledge of associated literature, which can help us to understand the question. The research was conducted in some databases (AMC Digital Library, IEEE Xplore, Science Direct – Elsevier, Springer, Annals SBES and Annals SBQS) to which many filters were applied to obtain a set of articles that with thematic synthesis can highlight the adoption of expert-based estimation technique and metrics that address complexity. Finally, it was possible to find that there is truly little material related to the Brazilian case, which can highlight the importance of both systematic review and research.**

Keywords-systematic review; metrics; cost; effort.

I. INTRODUCTION

The evolution of Information Technology (IT) in the information era, boosted by the digital transformation of corporations, brings up several questions concerning the improvement of software quality. This is due to the amount of investment made by these corporations, whether they belong to the public or the private sector.

In Brazilian Federal Public Administration (FPA), software development is submitted to a very restrictive normative scope when it comes to setting delivery dates at the moment of hiring specialized services for these specific ends. With the advent of Normative Instruction IN 04/2008 and its constant alterations culminating in the current version, the IN 01/2019 from the Digital Government Department in the Ministry of Economy (DGD/ME) has equivalent legislation related to the other powers (Legislative and Judiciary). The IN 01/2019 regulates the requirements for hiring Information Technology services in the sphere of the Federal Executive Power. This period of time (2008-2019) and the adoption of metrics like the Function Point (FP) technique for compensating the hired effort have brought a several discrepancies that, in many cases, do not comprehend the real cost attributed to a commission.

Brazilian law requires payment for results but there is a discrepancy between the effort undertaken and the pricing process carried out by the contracting public institution [1].

Thus, as a way to fill this normative gap, this article aims to identify metrics for effort estimation used in software development projects with agile methods that seek to identify metrics or estimation processes that can be used to meet current Brazilian normative restrictions.

The remainder of this article is structured as follows: Section 2 approaches some concepts, which are essential for understanding the terminology that composes the scenario. Section 3 presents the review protocol, research conduction, and extraction results regarding this systematic review. In Section 4, we present the research results. Section 5 presents discussions, Section 6 the research limitations, and finally in Section 7, we present conclusions and future works.

II. CONCEPTS

Since the early days of Software Engineering, one of its fundamental problems is the estimation of effort, deadlines, and cost involved in software development. A lot has evolved in this area, but this key question is still the theme of some studies [2].

Earlier studies stated that large scale software development estimations and associated costs had a history of being more often wrong than right [3]. In this setting, several processes and metrics were established seeking to improve cost control [4], which is the basis of any area of Engineering.

Software measuring is concerned with the quantification of certain attributes in a software system, such as its complexity or its reliability. By comparing measured values among themselves and then to standards applied to an organization, it is possible to draw conclusions about the quality of the software or evaluate the efficiency of software processes, tools, and methods [5].

Software metrics aims to control and efficiently identify essential parameters that affect software development, as well as characteristics that cannot always be objectively measured. The term "software metrics" includes many activities that involve a certain level of software measurement and has a relationship with a series of concepts that base the adoption of metrics [2]. Some of these activities are listed as follows:

- models and measurements for estimating the cost and effort;
- data collection;
- models and quality measurements;
- models of reliability;
- security metrics;
- structural and complexity metrics;
- evaluation of the maturity of capacity;
- metrics management;
- evaluation of methods and tools;
- development by different teams of people.

In addition to that, the project and the analysis of software metrics are important in the life cycle of software development. Software metrics play a vital role in cost, quality, programming, reliability, and maintenance. There are many methods to decide what metrics must be used and for what ends [6]. The attributes of metrics can be either independent or they might depend on each other. In software engineering, there is not a consensus on what to measure and how to evaluate the result from these measurements [5].

Boehm [7], in his studies, assigned six (6) categories to the techniques to estimate the cost of a software system. This classification will be the basis for the thematic synthesis of metrics found in our selected studies.

The classification is defined as follows.

- **Based on the Opinion of Specialists**: this estimation is also known as an analogy-based estimate. It is the most used and it is generally accurate. The problem is that it is very subjective and can be biased. Techniques like Work Breakdown Structure (WBS) and techniques of group consensus like Delphi are used to eliminate the bias. Another deficiency is that the number of requirement alterations over time can render this method ineffective.
- **Based on Models**: there are many parametrical models but the most used one is COCOMO II. It is based on the assessment of various factors for estimates and it often needs dimension metrics such as Line of Code (LOC) – or its derivations, such as kLOC – or FP. The problem with these models is that they were designed having in mind a factory-like software development process based on a waterfall model.
- **Based on Regression**: linear regression is a statistical model where an equation estimates the expected value of a variable y given the values of some variables x. However, it has many deficiencies and needs a wide array of data. Another problem occurs in extreme cases, which are common in software engineering: usually, data used for building data clusters that will be tested in the equation are not collected properly due to limitations in time and budget.
- **Combined with Bayesian Statistics**: another alternative that attracts the methods of pure regression is a Bayesian approach, which combines the strengths of experience and methods based on regression. The Bayesian approach provides a formal process through which prior judgment by specialists can be combined with sampling (data) for producing a robust subsequent product. The Bayesian analysis is a method of inductive thinking that has been used in many scientific subjects.
- **Learning-Oriented**: a learning-oriented method is reasoning based on cases, in which it is possible to learn more adaptatively what cases in a sample of projects are better adjusted to the dominion application. It is currently based on machine learning and comes with Neural Networks methods, Genetic Algorithms, among others.
- **Based on Dynamic Systems**: techniques based on dynamics explicitly recognize that the effort applied to a software project or other factors of cost change throughout development; that is, they are dynamic rather than static. However, factors like deadlines, personnel level, project requirements, training needs, budget, etc. fluctuate over the course of development and it can cause fluctuations in the personal productivity of the project. This, in turn, has consequences on the probability of a project to be concluded within the planned deadline and budget – generally negative. System dynamics is a methodology of continuous modeling simulation in which the results and the behavior of the model are shown as information charts that change over time. The models are represented with modified networks with positive or negative feedback.

With the classification proposed, we will present COCOMO II, due to its wide adoption worldwide, and FP functional metrics, due to its wide application in service contraction for software development in Brazil [1].

A. COCOMO II

COCOMO II is a technique and tool for algorithmic modeling of costs. This empirical model was derived from the collection of data from various software projects of different sizes. These data were analyzed to discover formulas that would fit the observation in the best way. These formulas approached the system size and factors from the product, the project, the team, and the effort to develop a system [5].

COCOMO II was developed based on the first COCOMO cost estimation models (Constructive Cost Modelling), which were mostly based on the development of the original code [7]. This technique is usually linked to metrics and has four (4) basic models (application composition model; early design model; reuse model; and, post-architecture model), depending on the metrics used, as seen in the FP and LOC studies.

B. Function Point Metrics

In 1979, Allan Albrecht, from International Business Machines (IBM), published a paper that brought to light a new metrics that, according to his experiences, proved itself effective for measuring software and posed as an alternative to metrics based on LOC. The above metrics started being used by many software companies as of the 1980s [8].

FP metrics were created from a principle stating that projects must be completed at a pre-established deadline, respecting the budget, and satisfying the client. From the beginning, it must have specific functional objectives and the desired value for money objectives. If the project can reach these objectives respecting the timetable and the budget, the client will be satisfied. Thus, it is necessary to measure productivity to identify and select the development systems and technologies that offer the most functionalities for application with the least effort and the lowest cost [1].

In Brazil, this technique has had accentuated growth, especially in the federal government sphere, with actions from Brazil's Federal Court of Accounts (TCU) and the publication of IN 02/2008 and IN 04/2008, both from the actual Ministry of Economy. It was determined that the services hiring should use the unit that would allow the measurement of results despite the existence of models other than the one standardized by International Function Point Users Group (IFPUG), and the fact that all of them are standardized by International Organization for Standardization (ISO). The IFPUG model is the most commonly used one in Brazil [1].

III. Methods

A. Systematic Review of Planning

To understand the process adopted for conducting the systematic review, the following activities were defined, as shown in Figure 1:

- Formulate the research question: refers to define a question to support the research conduction;
- Define Research Protocol: regards to elaborate a protocol to research rules control.
- Search research bases: in this activity, a string is used to find studies in selected databases.
- Identify studies through title and abstract: refers to studies selection from reading titles and abstracts.
- Retrieve articles from databases: get the chosen studies from databases for more detailed analysis.
- Select studies according to the criteria: this activity includes selecting studies according to previously established criteria.
- Extract data: regards to gettting relevant information related to the research question.
- Evaluate quality: refers to quality assessment of the studies cited.

This way, in the first stage and step 1, the research question was formulated

1) What metrics adequately reward the effort applied in the construction of software functionality?

Complementarily, as secondary questions, which are inherently aligned with the answer to the main question, we have listed:

2) What metrics, according to the normative Brazilian framework, can be used to reward a supplier in cases where software development is outsourced by an FPA entity?
3) What metrics techniques are used in prompt methods and measure effort, deadline, cost, and size involved in software development?
4) Is FP Metrics used for calculating the payment of services in contracts outside of Brazil?

In the research protocol, we did define the Search Strings, databases to be consulted, and the criteria of quality for selecting the articles. Then, we move on to the Execution stage.

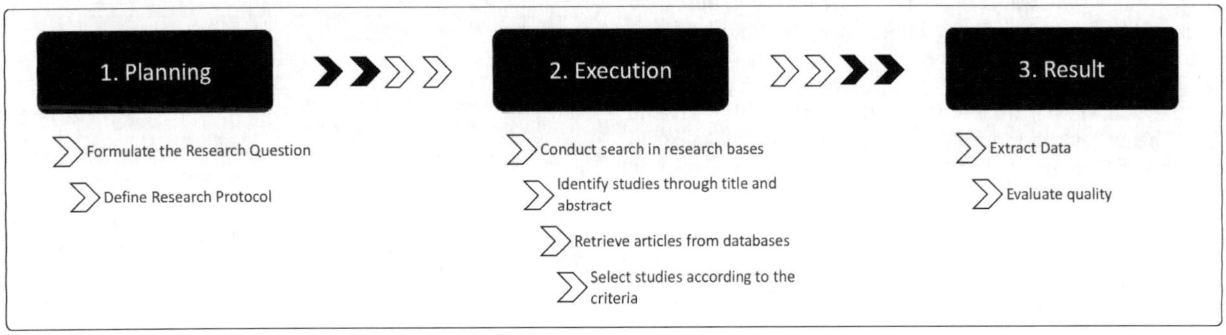

Figure 1. Diagram of the methodology of the systematic review.

B. Research Bases

The gathering of the articles was conducted on four bases with the automatic search strategy and two bases with the manual search strategy, as shown in Table I. Besides that, they were used due to the relevance of each base in this theme, by Kitchenham [4].

The literature repositories in the area seem to be promising. As one of the questions concerns a problem identified in Brazil, the study adopted the search from the Annals of Software Engineering Symposiums (SBES) and Software Quality (SBQS) held by the Brazilian Computer Society (SBC), which are reference events in the area and the theme of metrics is strongly based on Software Engineering and the studies of Software Quality.

TABLE I. SELECTED BASES.

Base	Address	Search
ACM Digital Library	https://dl.acm.org/	Automatic
IEEE Xplore	https://ieeexplore.ieee.org	Automatic
ScienceDirect – Elsevier	https://www.sciencedirect.com/	Automatic
Springer	https://link.springer.com/	Automatic
Annals SBES	The address is changed every year according to the organization of the event.	Manual
Annals SBQS	The address is changed every year according to the organization of the event.	Manual

In the manual searches in both events, there was a peculiarity. After a certain period, the books start being indexed to the ACM base, hence the manual research comprehended the years 2010 – 2019.

C. Research Strings

Considering such bases for research, some combinations of terms were fundamental for obtaining articles that would help systematic review and to obtain its state of the art.

We proceeded to cross the main keywords related to the themes we investigated, which were: "Smart Contract", "Metric", "Agile", "Effort", and "Cost", in addition to other occasionally necessary ones for enriching our research sources, aiming to comprise a bigger amount of productions, avoiding the exclusion of a very important study or one that would stand out. Thus, some Search Strings were set up and all the selected papers referred to the 2010 – 2019 period. The Search Strings for each database are shown in Table II. In the initial stage, the number of articles found is shown in Table III.

TABLE II. SEARCH STRINGS.

Id	Database	Query applied
1	ACM Digital Library	[[All: "smart contract"] OR [All: metric]] AND [[All: "agile development"] OR [All: "agile"]] AND [[Abstract: "effort"] OR [Abstract: "cost"]] AND [[All: "smart contract"] OR [All: "metric"]] AND [Publication Date: (01/01/2010 TO 12/31/2019)]
2	IEEE Explore	(((("All Metadata":smart contract OR Metric) AND "All Metadata":"agile development" OR agile) AND "All Metadata":effort) AND "All Metadata":cost)
3	ScienceDirect – Elsevier	("smart contract" OR metric) AND ("agile development" OR agile) AND (effort OR cost) Abstract Effort OR cost
4	Springer	'("smart contract" OR metric) AND ("agile development" OR agile) AND (effort OR cost) AND "effort estimation"'

TABLE III. ARTICLES IN EACH BASE.

Database	Total
ACM Digital Library	185
IEEE Explore	61
Science Direct - Elsevier	813
Springer	161
Annals SBES	0
Annals SBQS	1
Total	**1221**

D. Criteria for Selection

Many criteria were selected so a certain article could be included to or excluded from the analysis for this research, such criteria are defined in Table IV and Table V. Inclusion criteria 5 was provided because the first FP contracts in Brazil were drawn in 2010. Exclusion criteria 3 refers to studies that are not entirely online accessible or fully inaccessible. The definition of exclusion criterion 7 is important to exclude studies that did not explain any metric for payment for services, such as FP, UCP, etc.

TABLE IV. CRITERIA FOR INCLUDING ARTICLES.

CI	Criteria for the inclusion of articles
1	Studies that show empirical or theoretical data or reports of experiences about metrics applied to payment based on the effort involved in the development of a software system;
2	Studies of quantitative and qualitative research;
3	Primary and secondary studies;
4	Studies wrote in English and Portuguese;
5	Studies published since 2010 [9].

TABLE V. CRITERIA FOR THE EXCLUSION OF ARTICLES.

CE	Criteria for the exclusion of articles
1	Repeated articles;
2	Similar articles;
3	Inaccessibility;
4	The article is not written in Portuguese or English;
5	Published as short paper or only as a poster;
6	Article without an abstract;
7	Studies did not focus on metrics for the payment of services;
8	Studies based solely on the opinion of specialists, not pointing to a specific experience;
9	Editorials, prefaces, forewords, article abstracts, interviews, news articles, analysis, tutorials, correspondence, discussions, commentaries, letters to readers, tutorial summaries, workshops, and panels.

E. Result Studies

After applying the criteria for inclusion and exclusion, we selected a set of studies that would be likely to answer the research question. At this stage, the articles were analyzed by using the web application Rayyan, for cataloging the studies and sorting which ones were excluded and which were selected. The procedure described in the subsections above resulted in the number of articles per year and per database, as shown in Table VI.

In Table VII, we have a division by type, being 85 of the primary studies, 2 systematic mappings, 6 literature reviews, and 13 systematic reviews. Literature reviews are papers concerned with various metrics, but in their methodology, they do not show the thoroughness of a systematic review.

TABLE VI. ARTICLES PER BASE.

Database	2010	2011	2012	2013	2014	2015	2016	2017	2018	2019	TOTAL
ACM Digital Library	1	2	1	0	1	1	2	5	4	3	20
IEEE Explore	2	2	2	4	7	1	6	2	2	0	28
Science Direct - Elsevier	2	0	1	2	1	4	2	1	4	3	20
Springer	3	2	4	2	7	1	0	2	8	8	37
SBQS (Manual Research)	0	0	0	0	0	0	0	0	0	1	1
SBES (Manual Research)	0	0	0	0	0	0	0	0	0	0	0
Total											**106**

TABLE VII. TYPE OF STUDY.

Technique for Estimation	Quantity
Primary Study	85
Systematic Mapping	2
Literature Review	6
Systematic Review	13
Total	**106**

In terms of how these studies were published, we observed that 46 of these articles (43.4%) were presented in conferences, 35 (33.02%) were published in journals, 24 (22.64%) were chapters from books and 1 (0.94%) is a book, as seen in Figure 2.

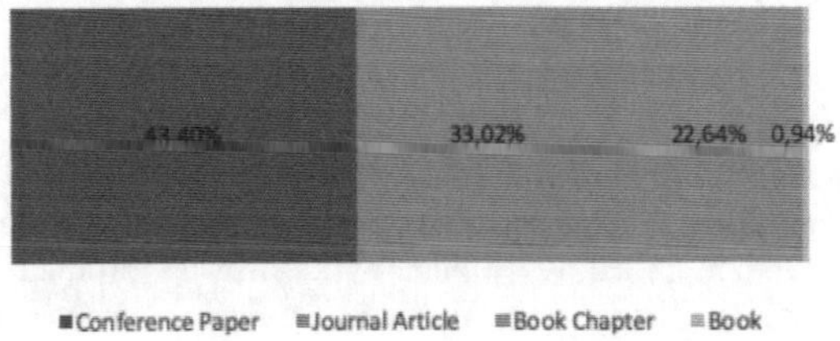

Figure 2. How the papers were published.

Among the 36 articles published in conferences, Figure 3 shows them, sorted according to their countries of origin.

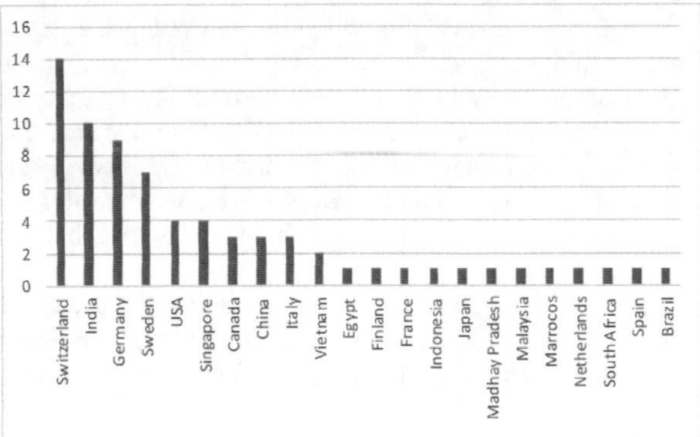

Figure 3. Countries where the conferences were held.

Moreover, the most relevant journals are listed ahead. 7 papers were published in the Journal of Systems and Software, 6 in Empirical Software Engineering, 5 in Information and Software Technology, 3 in Innovations in Systems and Software Engineering, 3 in Procedia Computer Science, 2 in the Journal of King Saud University – Computer and Information Sciences and Others with 1 article each, as shown in Table VIII.

TABLE VIII. ARTICLES SELECTED ACCORDING TO BASE.

Journal	Publisher	Quantity
Journal of Systems and Software	Elsevier	7
Empirical Software Engineering	Springer	6
Information and Software Technology	Elsevier	5
Innovations in Systems and Software Engineering	Springer	3
Procedia Computer Science	Elsevier	3
Journal of King Saud University - Computer and Information Sciences	Elsevier	2
Others (with 1 study)	ACM, Springer, and Elsevier	9
Total		**35**

After analyzing the articles and submitting them to a systematic synthesis with the classification of the estimation techniques, we found 6 articles that relate to the review of several techniques and 69 articles with primary studies that use various metrics, as shown in Table IX.

TABLE IX. CLASSIFICATION OF ARTICLES AND THE ESTIMATION TECHNIQUE THEY ADOPTED.

Estimation Technique	Quantity
Regression-Based	2
Model-Based	7
Learn-Based	20
Expert-Based	38
Dynamic-Based	2
Total	**69**

Amid this classification, we found the following metrics, though it is possible to observe that in some cases there is a combination of studies and several forms of metrics [10], and the combination of techniques like

COCOMO II and the metrics it naturally uses, as it is part of this model.

In addition to that, several studies related to metrics in agile methods, but they are complemented with some calibration done by using multiple factors or even machine learning, Bayesian statistics, neural networks, genetic algorithms, or other algorithms proposed in case studies. In the topic of discussions, we will present a review with the studies and techniques, methods, and approached metrics. The list of articles can be found in Appendix A, with the grade resulted from the classification as shown in Table X to the thematic synthesis also with techniques and metrics used.

TABLE X. TECHNIQUES AND METRICS FOUND.

Metrics	Kind of Measurement	Quantity
FP	Functional	10
COSMIC	Functional	4
UCP (Use Case Point)	Functional	5
SP (Stories Points)	Complexity	21
Velocity	Complexity	4
LOC or kLOC	Size	4

In this topic, we are bound to assess a narrative synthesis among 69 papers with classified metrics. This method builds a history based on the evidence found in the studies that were included [11].

According to Rodgers et al. [12], the recommended steps for conducting this synthesis are (i) development of theory; (ii) development of a preliminary synthesis; (iii) exploration of relationships inside and among studies; and (iv) assessment of the robustness of the product of synthesis. The robustness is presented in item 3.7 of the criteria and quality assessment.

F. Criteria of quality

Criteria of quality were adopted for classifying the results. The main goal when using quality criteria is to assess methodological aspects in the studies. When trying to assess the quality of the primary studies through quality criteria, the researcher seeks to increase reliability and generalization in the results [13].

Another way to measure quality in primary studies is through the application of a checklist, that is, a form that contains items that will be used to assess the quality of each study independently [11]. Therefore, a list was created for verifying the following criteria, as exposed in Table XI.

TABLE XI. QUALITY CRITERIA.

ID	Check List Item
1	Do the metrics adequately reward the effort applied to the construction of new software functionality?
2	Can the metrics be used following with the Brazilian normative framework for rewarding the supplier of software development is outsourced by an entity of the federal public administration?
3	Are the metrics used in agile methods that measure the effort, the deadline, the cost, and size involved in the construction of a software system?
4	Are the metrics used for rewarding services in contracts outside of Brazil?
5	Does the research show evidence or is it only a literature review?
6	Was there a detailed description of the review process?
7	Is the object of the research clearly defined?
8	Is there enough evidence to support a conclusion?
9	Does it show any charts, figures, or tables making a synthesis of the system?

Thus, a score of 0 or 1 was assigned in case the studies meet each of the 9 requirements, allowing the creation of a ranking. Out of the 106 studies initially selected, 69 were classified as likely to answer the questions – they are listed in Appendix A. Another 37 did not have a direct answer to the questions or showed inconclusive results.

G. Tools

To support the process, some tools had to be defined. Initially, the study used the Mendeley software for cataloging the list of articles yielded by the selected databases. For storing the articles (PDF) we used Zotero after the stages of selection of bases and list of articles have been repeated.

When the bases had been defined after the initial validation, the Rayyan software was used, which allowed the analysis of articles for the reading stage. The assessment of their quality was done employing an electronic form with questions and criteria for assessing each one of the selected articles.

IV. RESEARCH RESULTS

This research sought first to raise the metrics used in the industry for the adequate remuneration of the costs involved in the development of a software product, as presented, criteria were defined seeking to answer the research questions.

The research identified the most common metrics and various usage scenarios using the most varied systematics as a result, they were cataloged in the tables presented in the previous sections.

In Brazil, rework, which is common practice in agile methodologies, ends up not being properly remunerated because in the contractor's view it would be like paying for a job that does not deliver results. it is quite true that the rules and manuals of mandatory use due to the legislation seek to include rework when payment is by FP, but in practice, the problem lies in the imbalance that this type of practice ends up generating.

Also, the research helped to identify that the use of PF is not recommended for the support of systems, something that had already been identified in applied research in Brazil [14].

V. DISCUSSION

After the narrative and thematic syntheses, the following evidence was obtained to answer the research question:

Q1: Does the metrics adequately reward the effort applied to the construction of software functionality?

Yes, we found several metrics techniques that can assess the effort applied in the construction of software functionality, from parametric models like COCOMO [15]–[18] to its evolution COCOMO II [19][20] and this model requires a wide historical basis that is often based on functional measurement metrics like FP [21] and COSMIC [22]–[24] in addition to some studies that used LOC [25].

Q2: Can the metrics be used in following the Brazilian normative framework for rewarding the supplier of software development is outsourced by an entity of the federal public administration?

Yes, for functional measurement metrics, FP and COSMIC, but several metrics in more extensive studies using metrics applied to agile methods as Velocity [26], Sprint Points [27], Story Points [28], and Delivery Stories [29]. In some cases, it was combined with multiple factors techniques [30] to improve the precision and algorithms with verification list, even so, machine learning use [31].

Q3: Is the metric used in agile methods and measure effort, deadline, cost, and size involved in software development?

Yes, the same works presented in Q2 are about agile methods and measure these 3 aspects focused on software maintenance activities [32] and bugs fix [33].

Twenty studies focus on the use of machine learning techniques with the most diverse techniques since genetic algorithms [34], Bayesian statistics [35], fuzzy logic [36], [37], neural networks [38][39], and machine learning with multiple approaches [35][37][40][41].

Therefore, the most used are techniques based on expertise with an analogy (Expert-Based). It is presented in the studies several uses of the metrics in agile methods, mixing functional measure as FP already cited, or COSMIC [22]–[24][42] and classic agile metrics combined with multiple factors to precision calibration [26][27][43]–[45].

Q4: Is FP Metric used for calculating the payment of services in contracts outside of Brazil?

FP metric was found in 10 studies. The study of Russo et al. [46] is about FP used by the Italian public sector for critical service outsourcing. However, the metric is used to evaluate the functional size, deriving from this, productivity with effort and cost. Besides, the work explains Scrum Points that would be a fixed value of Hours inside a Sprint, for example, 40 hours, and the deliveries are made within an open scope system.

Another one [47], is about FP within a Dynamic-Model technique, a combination of Dynamic-Bases activity and Model-Based applied on agile development. But an old study from 2010 and another one uses COCOMO as a technique with Unadjusted Function Points (UFP) that would not be the FP use based on the IFPUG manual. The other studies [10][17][21][48]–[51] use analogy estimation mixing teams experience estimation with analogy and some agile metrics besides FP.

VI. RESEARCH LIMITATIONS

The Research looked for metrics used to pay for the effort and that can be adopted in Brazil following the Brazilian normative framework. The research found specific studies that dealt with the adoption of metrics in public organizations outside of Brazil.

Performing the automatic search in the databases, many of the studies did not meet the inclusion and exclusion criteria; therefore, after careful analysis, only 9% of the articles were selected. One of the bases returned 813 studies but most did not meet the criteria.

But one of the limitations is that the search for metrics in scientific works may not cover the practices developed by public organizations, so in an update of this systematic review, multi-vocal research should be adopted.

VII. CONCLUSION AND FUTURE WORKS

The most found metric in the studies was Story Points (which is based on a combination of the amount of effort involved in the development of a feature, with the complexity of that development, and the risk contained in it), very much in line with the development in agile methods, and which together with Velocity complements the metrics that address complexity.

Functional metrics, with a large advantage of Function Points (in the Brazilian case, in response to the regulations and guidelines of the control agencies), are second in the ranking. LOC, code size metric, performs last in studies, as it is a measure that we can consider linked to paradigms and technologies that are no longer in use.

Regarding the techniques, the predominance of Expert Based shows the importance of specialized opinion, with consideration and ponderation by Learn Based techniques, based on machine learning – very aligned with the data sciences. The grades attributed to the works, based on Quality Criteria, confirm this predominance.

The low number of works presented in Brazil contrasts with the importance of the theme for government hiring of these types of services, which constitutes an avenue of opportunities for future works.

Moreover, we can draw some conclusions concerning the research questions. The metrics related to complexity (Story points and Velocity) demonstrated to be more adequate to reward the effort applied in the construction of software functionality.

Also, we can infer some observations from Appendix A. Commonly, based on the defined technique (with a large predominance of Expert-based), the experiences adopt a combination of metrics. Together, they manage to better respond to the challenge of adequately reward the effort applied in the construction of software functionality.

ACKNOWLEDGMENT

The authors would like to thank CESAR School for financial support and especially teachers Alberto César Cavalcanti França and Ana Paula Cavalcanti Furtado who conducted the discipline of Systematic Review at the doctoral program.

REFERENCES

[1] W. H. C. Almeida and F. Furtado, "Análise sobre Métricas em Contratos de Fábricas de Software no âmbito da Administação Pública" (Analysis of metrics in software factory contracts within the public administration). 1ª ed, vol. 1. Rio de Janeiro, Albatroz, 2019.

[2] N. Fenton and J. Bieman, "Software Metrics: A Rigorous and Practical Approach", 3th Edition, CRC Press, 2014.

[3] R. E. Merwin, "Estimating software development schedules and costs", in Proceedings of the 9th Design Automation Workshop, New York, NY, USA, Jun. 1972, p. 1–4.

[4] B. Kitchenham, "What's up with software metrics? – A preliminary mapping study", Journal of Systems and Software, vol. 83, nº 1, p. 37–51, Jan. 2010.

[5] I. Sommerville, "Software engineering", 10th edition, Global edition, Pearson, 2016.

[6] N. Fenton and J. Bieman, "Software Metrics", vol. 1. Chapman and Hall/CRC, 2014.

[7] B. Boehm and K. Sullivan, "Software economics: Status and prospects", in Information & Software Technology, Nov 15, 1999, p. 937–946.

[8] R. Pressman and B. Maxim, "Engenharia de Software" (Software Engineering) - 8ª Edição. McGraw Hill Brasil.

[9] D. Kovags, F. L. Falchi, and A. R. Rivas, "Analysis of the Utilization of Scrum Framework Effort Estimation Metrics in Federal Public Administration", in Proceedings of the XVIII Brazilian Symposium on Software Quality - SBQS'19, Fortaleza, Brazil, 2019, p. 30–38.

[10] R. Popli and N. Chauhan, "Estimation in agile environment using resistance factors", in 2014 International Conference on Information Systems and Computer Networks (ISCON), Mathura, India, Mar. 2014, p. 60–65.

[11] E. Y. Nakagawa, K. R. F. Scannavino, S. C. P. F. Fabbri, and F. C. Ferrari, "Revisão Sistemática da Literatura em Engenharia de Software: Teoria e Prática" (Systematic Review of Software Engineering Literature: Theory and Practice), 2017.

[12] M. Rodgers et al., "Testing Methodological Guidance on the Conduct of Narrative Synthesis in Systematic Reviews: Effectiveness of Interventions to Promote Smoke Alarm Ownership and Function", Evaluation, vol. 15, nº 1, p. 49–73.

[13] B. Kitchenham and S. Charters, "Guidelines for performing Systematic Literature Reviews in Software Engineering", EBSE Technical report, Ver. 2.3., 2007.

[14] A. Trendowicz and R. Jeffery, "Software Project Effort Estimation", Software Project Effort Estimation, 2014.

[15] V. Nguyen, L. Huang, and B. Boehm, "An analysis of trends in productivity and cost drivers over years", in Proceedings of the 7th International Conference on Predictive Models in Software Engineering - Promise '11, Banff, Alberta, Canada, 2011, p. 1–10.

[16] S. Basri, N. Kama, F. Haneem, and S. A. Ismail, "Predicting effort for requirement changes during software development", in Proceedings of the 7th Symposium on Information and Communication Technology - SoICT '16, 2016, p. 380–387, Accessed: May 20, 2020. [Online].

[17] M. Farah-Stapleton, M. Auguston, and K. Giammarco, "Executable Behavioral Modeling of System and Software Architecture Specifications to Inform Resourcing Decisions", Procedia Computer Science, vol. 95, p. 48–57, 2016.

[18] J. A. Pow-Sang and R. Imbert, "Effort Estimation in Incremental Software Development Projects Using Function Points", vol. 340, T. Kim, C. Ramos, H. Kim, A. Kiumi, S. Mohammed, e D. Ślęzak, Orgs.

[19] R. Litoriya, N. Sharma, and A. Kothari, "Incorporating Cost driver substitution to improve the effort using Agile COCOMO II", in 2012 CSI 6th International Conference on Software Engineering (CONSEG), Indore, Madhay Pradesh, India, set. 2012, p. 1–7.

[20] S. Sunkle and V. Kulkarni, "Cost Estimation for Model-Driven Engineering", in Model Driven Engineering Languages and Systems, vol. 7590, R. B. France, J. Kazmeier, R. Breu, and C. Atkinson, Orgs. Berlin, Heidelberg: Springer Berlin Heidelberg, 2012, p. 659–675.

[21] J. Shah, N. Kama, and N. A. A. Bakar, "Estimating Change Effort Using a Combination of Change Impact Analysis Technique with Function Point Analysis", in Proceedings of the 2019 8th International Conference on Software and Information Engineering - ICSIE '19, Cairo, Egypt, 2019, p. 9–14, doi: 10.1145/3328833.3328836.

[22] I. Hussain, L. Kosseim, and O. Ormandjieva, "Towards Approximating COSMIC Functional Size from User Requirements in Agile Development Processes Using Text Mining", in Natural Language Processing and Information Systems, vol. 6177, C. J. Hopfe, Y. Rezgui, E. Métais, A. Preece, and H. Li, Orgs. 2010, p. 80–91.

[23] M. Salmanoglu, T. Hacaloglu, and O. Demirors, "Effort estimation for agile software development: comparative case studies using COSMIC functional size measurement and story points", in Proceedings of the 27th International Workshop on Software Measurement and 12th International Conference on Software Process and Product Measurement on - IWSM Mensura '17, 2017, p. 41–49.

[24] A. Kaur and K. Kaur, "A COSMIC function points based test effort estimation model for mobile applications", Journal of King Saud University - Computer and Information Sciences, p. S131915781831317X, Mar. 2019.

[25] H. K. Sharma, R. Tomar, A. Dumka, and M. S. Aswal, "OpenECOCOMO: The algorithms and implementation of Extended Cost Constructive Model (E-COCOMO)", in 2015 1st International Conference on Next Generation Computing Technologies (NGCT), Dehradun, Sep. 2015, pp. 773-778.

[26] A. A. Mohallel and J. M. Bass, "Agile Software Development Practices in Egypt SMEs: A Grounded Theory Investigation", in Information and Communication Technologies for Development. Strengthening Southern-Driven Cooperation as a Catalyst for ICT4D, vol. 551, P. Nielsen and H. C. Kimaro, Orgs. Cham, 2019, p. 355–365.

[27] R. Popli and N. Chauhan, "A sprint-point based estimation technique in Scrum", in 2013 International Conference on

Information Systems and Computer Networks, Mathura, Mar. 2013, p. 98–103.
[28] J. Choudhari and U. Suman, "Story Points Based Effort Estimation Model for Software Maintenance", Procedia Technology, vol. 4, p. 761–765, 2012.
[29] M. Daneva et al., "Agile requirements prioritization in large-scale outsourced system projects: An empirical study", Journal of Systems and Software, vol. 86, n° 5, Art. n° 5, May 2013.
[30] M. Usman, R. Britto, L.-O. Damm, and J. Börstler, "Effort estimation in large-scale software development: An industrial case study", Information and Software Technology, vol. 99, p. 21–40, Jul. 2018.
[31] V. Khatibi Bardsiri, D. N. A. Jawawi, S. Z. M. Hashim, and E. Khatibi, "A flexible method to estimate the software development effort based on the classification of projects and localization of comparisons", Empir Software Eng, vol. 19, n° 4, p. 857–884, Aug. 2014.
[32] A. Espinoza and J. Garbajosa, "A study to support agile methods more effectively through traceability", Innovations in Systems and Software Engineering, vol. 7, n° 1, p. 53–69, Mar. 2011.
[33] S. Porru, A. Murgia, S. Demeyer, M. Marchesi, and R. Tonelli, "Estimating Story Points from Issue Reports", in Proceedings of the 12th International Conference on Predictive Models and Data Analytics in Software Engineering - PROMISE 2016, Ciudad Real, Spain, 2016, p. 1–10.
[34] S. Bilgaiyan, P. K. Panigrahi, and S. Mishra, "Chaos-Based Modified Morphological Genetic Algorithm for Effort Estimation in Agile Software Development", in A Journey Towards Bio-inspired Techniques in Software Engineering, vol. 185, J. Singh, S. Bilgaiyan, B. S. P. Mishra, and S. Dehuri, Orgs. 2020, p. 89–102.
[35] J. Khan, Z. A. Shaikh, and A. B. Nauman, "Development of Intelligent Effort Estimation Model Based on Fuzzy Logic Using Bayesian Networks", in Software Engineering, Business Continuity, and Education, vol. 257, T. Kim, H. Adeli, H. Kim, H. Kang, K. J. Kim, A. Kiumi, and B.-H. Kang, Orgs.
[36] A. Saini, L. Ahuja, and S. K. Khatri, "Effort Estimation of Agile Development using Fuzzy Logic", in 2018 7th International Conference on Reliability, Infocom Technologies and Optimization (Trends and Future Directions) (ICRITO), Noida, India, Aug. 2018.
[37] K. E. Rao and G. A. Rao, "Ensemble learning with recursive feature elimination integrated software effort estimation: a novel approach", Evol. Intel., Feb. 2020.
[38] Ch. Prasada Rao, P. Siva Kumar, S. Rama Sree, and J. Devi, "An Agile Effort Estimation Based on Story Points Using Machine Learning Techniques", in Proceedings of the 2nd International Conference on Computational Intelligence and Informatics, vol. 712, V. Bhateja, J. M. R. S. Tavares, B. P. Rani, V. K. Prasad, and K. S. Raju, Orgs. Singapore, 2018, p. 209–219.
[39] A. Panda, S. M. Satapathy, and S. K. Rath, "Empirical Validation of Neural Network Models for Agile Software Effort Estimation based on Story Points", Procedia Computer Science, vol. 57, 2015, p. 772–781.
[40] M. R. Tayyab, M. Usman, and W. Ahmad, "A Machine Learning Based Model for Software Cost Estimation", in Proceedings of SAI Intelligent Systems Conference (IntelliSys) 2016, vol. 16, Y. Bi, S. Kapoor, and R. Bhatia, Orgs.
[41] S. M. Satapathy and S. K. Rath, "Empirical assessment of machine learning models for agile software development effort estimation using story points", Innovations in Systems and Software Engineering, vol. 13, n° 2–3, p. 191–200, Sep. 2017.
[42] J.-F. Dumas-Monette and S. Trudel, "Requirements Engineering Quality Revealed through Functional Size Measurement: An Empirical Study in an Agile Context", in 2014 Joint Conference of the International Workshop on Software Measurement and the International Conference on Software Process and Product Measurement, Rotterdam, Netherlands, Oct. 2014, p. 222–232.
[43] S. Bilgaiyan, S. Mishra, and M. Das, "Effort estimation in agile software development using experimental validation of neural network models", International Journal of Information Technology, vol. 11, n° 3, p. 569–573, Sep. 2019.
[44] Mohd. Owais and R. Ramakishore, "Effort, duration and cost estimation in agile software development", in 2016 9th International Conference on Contemporary Computing (IC3), Noida, India, Aug. 2016, p. 1–5.
[45] W. Rosa, R. Madachy, B. Clark, and B. Boehm, "Early Phase Cost Models for Agile Software Processes in the US DoD", in 2017 ACM/IEEE International Symposium on Empirical Software Engineering and Measurement (ESEM), Toronto, Canada, Nov 2017, pp. 30-37
[46] D. Russo, G. Taccogna, P. Ciancarini, A. Messina, and G. Succi, "Contracting agile developments for mission critical systems in the public sector", in the 40th International Conference, Gothenburg, Sweden, 2018.
[47] S. Kang, O. Choi, and J. Baik, "Model-Based Dynamic Cost Estimation and Tracking Method for Agile Software Development", in 2010 IEEE/ACIS 9th International Conference on Computer and Information Science, Aug. 2010, p. 743–748.
[48] H. Huijgens, A. van Deursen, L. L. Minku, and C. Lokan, "Effort and Cost in Software Engineering: A Comparison of Two Industrial Data Sets", in Proceedings of the 21st International Conference on Evaluation and Assessment in Software Engineering - EASE'17, 2017, p. 51–60.
[49] E. G. Wanderley, A. Vasconcelos, and B. T. Avila, "Using Function Points in Agile Projects: A Comparative Analysis Between Existing Approaches", in Agile Methods, vol. 802, V. A. dos Santos, G. H. L. Pinto, and A. G. Serra Seca Neto, Orgs.
[50] W. Rosa, T. Packard, A. Krupanand, J. W. Bilbro, and M. M. Hodal, "COTS integration and estimation for ERP", Journal of Systems and Software, vol. 86, n° 2, Art. n° 2, Feb. 2013.
[51] M. Usman and R. Britto, "Effort Estimation in Co-located and Globally Distributed Agile Software Development: A Comparative Study", in 2016 Joint Conference of the International Workshop on Software Measurement and the International Conference on Software Process and Product Measurement (IWSM-MENSURA), Berlin, Oct. 2016, p. 219–224.
[52] A. Kaushik, D. Kr. Tayal, and K. Yadav, "A Comparative Analysis on Effort Estimation for Agile and Non-agile Software Projects Using DBN-ALO", Arabian Journal for Science and Engineering, vol. 45, n° 4, Art. n° 4, Apr. 2020.

[53] L. L. Minku, "A novel online supervised hyperparameter tuning procedure applied to cross-company software effort estimation", Empir Software Eng, vol. 24, n° 5, Art. n° 5, Oct. 2019.

[54] V. Khatibi Bardsiri, D. N. A. Jawawi, S. Z. M. Hashim, and E. Khatibi, "A PSO-based model to increase the accuracy of software development effort estimation", Software Quality Journal, vol. 21, n° 3, Art. n° 3.

[55] S. Baker and E. Mendes, "Aggregating Expert-Driven Causal Maps for Web Effort Estimation", in Advances in Software Engineering, vol. 117, T. Kim, H.-K. Kim, M. K. Khan, A. Kiumi, W. Fang, and D. Ślęzak, Orgs. Springer Berlin Heidelberg, 2010, p. 264–282.

[56] R. Popli and N. Chauhan, "Agile estimation using people and project related factors", in 2014 International Conference on Computing for Sustainable Global Development (INDIACom), New Delhi, India, Mar. 2014, p. 564–569.

[57] S. Dragicevic, S. Celar, and M. Turic, "Bayesian network model for task effort estimation in agile software development", Journal of Systems and Software, vol. 127, p. 109–119.

[58] R. Popli and N. Chauhan, "Cost and effort estimation in agile software development", in 2014 International Conference on Reliability Optimization and Information Technology (ICROIT), Faridabad, Haryana, India, Feb. 2014, p. 57–61.

[59] M. Usman, K. Petersen, J. Börstler, and P. Santos Neto, "Developing and using checklists to improve software effort estimation: A multi-case study", Journal of Systems and Software, vol. 146, p. 286–309, Dec. 2018.

[60] A. W. Md. M. Parvez, "Efficiency factor and risk factor-based user case point test effort estimation model compatible with agile software development", in 2013 International Conference on Information Technology and Electrical Engineering (ICITEE), Yogyakarta, Indonesia, 2013.

[61] V. Lenarduzzi, I. Lunesu, M. Matta, and D. Taibi, "Functional Size Measures and Effort Estimation in Agile Development: A Replicated Study", in Agile Processes in Software Engineering and Extreme Programming, vol. 212, C. Lassenius, T. Dingsøyr, and M. Paasivaara, Orgs.

[62] A. Zakrani, A. Najm, and A. Marzak, "Support Vector Regression Based on Grid-Search Method for Agile Software Effort Prediction", in 2018 IEEE 5th International Congress on Information Science and Technology (CiSt), Marrakech, 2018.

[63] O. Malgonde and K. Chari, "An ensemble-based model for predicting agile software development effort", Empirical Software Engineering, vol. 24, n° 2, Art. n° 2, Apr. 2019.

[64] D. Taibi, V. Lenarduzzi, M. O. Ahmad, and K. Liukkunen, "Comparing Communication Effort within the Scrum, Scrum with Kanban, XP, and Banana Development Processes", in Proceedings of the 21st International Conference on Evaluation and Assessment in Software Engineering - EASE'17, Karlskrona, Sweden, 2017, p. 258–263.

[65] A. Magazinius and R. Feldt, "Confirming Distortional Behaviors in Software Cost Estimation Practice", in 2011 37th EUROMICRO Conference on Software Engineering and Advanced Applications (SEAA), Oulu, Finland, Aug. 2011.

[66] K. Moharreri, A. V. Sapre, J. Ramanathan, and R. Ramnath, "Cost-Effective Supervised Learning Models for Software Effort Estimation in Agile Environments", in 2016 IEEE 40th Annual Computer Software and Applications Conference (COMPSAC), Jun. 2016, p. 135–140.

[67] D. K. Goswami, S. Chakrabarti, and S. Bilgaiyan, "Effort Estimation of Web Based Applications Using ERD, Use Case Point Method and Machine Learning", in Automated Software Engineering: A Deep Learning-Based Approach, vol. 8, 2020.

[68] E. Mendes, "Improving Software Effort Estimation Using an Expert-Centred Approach", in Human-Centered Software Engineering, vol. 7623, M. Winckler, P. Forbrig, and R. Bernhaupt, Orgs.

[69] P. Ram, P. Rodriguez, and M. Oivo, "Software Process Measurement and Related Challenges in Agile Software Development: A Multiple Case Study", in Product-Focused Software Process Improvement, vol. 11271, M. Kuhrmann, K. Schneider, D. Pfahl, S. Amasaki, M. Ciolkowski, R. Hebig, P. Tell, J. Klünder, and S. Küpper, Orgs. Cham, 2018, p. 272–287.

[70] E. Scott and D. Pfahl, "Using developers' features to estimate story points", in Proceedings of the 2018 International Conference on Software and System Process - ICSSP '18, Gothenburg, Sweden, 2018, p. 106–110.

[71] S. R. Sree and C. P. Rao, "A Study on Application of Soft Computing Techniques for Software Effort Estimation", in A Journey Towards Bio-inspired Techniques in Software Engineering, vol. 185, J. Singh, S. Bilgaiyan, B. S. P. Mishra, and S. Dehuri, Orgs.

[72] A. Effendi, R. Setiawan, and Z. E. Rasjid, "Adjustment Factor for Use Case Point Software Effort Estimation (Study Case: Student Desk Portal)", Procedia Computer Science, vol. 157, p. 691–698, 2019.

[73] N. Ramasubbu and R. K. Balan, "Overcoming the challenges in cost estimation for distributed software projects", in 2012 34th International Conference on Software Engineering (ICSE 2012), Zurich, 2012, pp. 91-101.

[74] T. Schulz, Ł. Radliński, T. Gorges, and W. Rosenstiel, "Predicting the Flow of Defect Correction Effort using a Bayesian Network Model", Empirical Software Engineering, vol. 18, n° 3.

[75] P. Jodpimai, P. Sophatsathit, and C. Lursinsap, "Re-estimating software effort using prior phase efforts and data mining techniques", Innovations in Systems and Software Engineering, vol. 14, n° 3, Art. n° 3, Sep. 2018.

[76] P. Pospieszny, "Software estimation: towards prescriptive analytics", in The 27th International Workshop on Software Measurement and 12th International Conference on Software Process and Product Measurement, Gothenburg, Sweden, 2017, [Online]. Available: http://dl.acm.org/citation.cfm?doid=3143434.3143459.

[77] B. Tanveer, L. Guzmán, and U. M. Engel, "Understanding and improving effort estimation in Agile software development: an industrial case study", in Proceedings of the International Workshop on Software and Systems Process - ICSSP '16, Austin, Texas, 2016, p. 41–50.

[78] L. Kompella, "Advancement of Decision-Making in Agile Projects by Applying Logistic Regression on Estimates", in 2013 IEEE 8th International Conference on Global

Software Engineering Workshops, Bari, Italy, Aug. 2013, p. 11–17.

[79] S. Thakur and H. Singh, "FDRD: Feature Driven Reuse Development Process Model", in 2014 IEEE International Conference on Advanced Communications, Control and Computing Technologies, Ramanathapuram, 2014, pp. 1593-1598.

[80] F. Fellir, K. Nafil, R. Touahni, and L. Chung, "Improving Case Based Software Effort Estimation Using a Multi-criteria Decision Technique", in Software Engineering and Algorithms in Intelligent Systems, vol. 763, R. Silhavy, Springer International Publishing, 2019.

[81] S. Puhl and R. Fahney, "How to assign cost to avoidable requirements creep: A step towards the waterfall's agilization", in 2011 IEEE 19th International Requirements Engineering Conference, 2011, p. 307–312.

[82] M. Lusky, C. Powilat, and S. Böhm, "Software Cost Estimation for User-Centered Mobile App Development in Large Enterprises", in Advances in Human Factors, Software, and Systems Engineering, AHFE 2017. Advances in Intelligent Systems and Computing, vol 598. Springer, Chamvol, T. Ahram and W. Karwowski, Orgs. Cham, 2018.

APPENDIX A. ARTICLES, QUALITY CRITERIA, TECHNIQUES, AND METRICS

Ref.	Grade	Technique	Metric
[46]	7	Expert-Based	FP or SCRUM POINTS
[45]	7	Expert-Based	SP, UCP, FP, LOC, and OBJECT POINTS
[9]	7	Expert-Based	SP and UCP
[52]	6	Learn-Based	Data Set, DBN (Deep Belief Network) and ALO (Ant Lion Optimization)
[24]	6	Dynamic-Model	Data et, FP, SP and Algorithm
[30]	6	Expert-Based	Story Points to Maintenance
[40]	6	Learn-Based	ML (Machine Learning)
[47]	6	Expert-Based	COSMIC for Test
[28]	6	Learn-Based	Data Set and PSO
[53]	5	Model-Based	COCOMO and UFP (Unadjusted FP)
[54]	5	Learn-Based	SP and HH, ML
[27]	5	Learn-Based	Data Set, SP, and Multifactor
[55]	5	Expert-Based	EXPERT
[56]	5	Model-Based	Data Set and Statistical
[57]	5	Learn-Based	Data Set, Agile and COCOMO-II and ML and Data mining
[58]	5	Regression Based	Data Set, SP, and Velocity.
[20]	5	Model-Based	COCOMO II and Multifactor
[50]	5	Learn-Based	Data Set and ML
[59]	5	Dynamic-Model	Causal Structure Aggregation Model
[35]	5	Expert-Based	Multifactor and SP, Velocity
[60]	5	Expert-Based	Expert and Multifactor
[18]	5	Learn-Based	ML and Bayesian
[44]	5	Expert-Based	COSMIC
[41]	5	Expert-Based	Scrum adopted
[39]	5	Learn-Based	ML, NN, Fuzzy, Data Set
[37]	5	Expert-Based	FP, LOC, EOP (Enhanced Object Points for ERP)
[10]	5	Expert-Based	Sprint Points and Multifactor
[61]	5	Model-Based	PSO, Data Set, Algorithm
[19]	5	Expert-Based	UCP for Test
[62]	5	Learn-Based	Bayesian
[22]	5	Learn-Based	Data Set, and Algorithm
[29]	4	Expert-Based	FP
[26]	4	Expert-Based	EXPERT
[38]	4	Model-Based	SP, HH, EXPERT, Algorithm ensemble-based model
[63]	4	Learn-Based	SP, HH, EXPERT
[34]	4	Expert-Based	Data Set, Size (FP), Effort, Cost, and Duration
[64]	4	Expert-Based	COSMIC
[65]	4	Expert-Based	Data Set, User Stories, Story Points and Sprint Time
[66]	4	Model-Based	COCOMO and KLOC with Tool
[48]	4	Expert-Based	Interview and Multifactor
[23]	4	Expert-Based	COSMIC and SP, User Stories
[43]	4	Expert-Based	Velocity, Testing Performance, Issues' Estimation Accuracy, and Code Quality
[30]	4	Expert-Based	FP with Agile
[36]	4	Learn-Based	EXPERT
[67]	4	Expert-Based	EXPERT
[21]	4	Expert-Based	Velocity, SP
[68]	4	Learn-Based	ML and SP, Rede Neural.
[25]	4	Expert-Based	Scrum and FP, SP
[42]	4	Learn-Based	User Stories, Expertise, and Complexity using Fuzzy Logic to Predict
[69]	4	Expert-Based	Effort in Communication in Agile Environment
[70]	4	Expert-Based	UCP, size, and productivity
[49]	4	Learn-Based	Genetic Algorithm
[71]	3	Model-Based	COCOMO and KLOC
[72]	3	Expert-Based	UCP
[15]	3	Expert-Based	COCOMO and FP
[33]	3	Learn-Based	Data Set, Bayesian, and aspects for Maturity (CMMI)
[17]	3	Expert-Based	Maturity to Best Estimations
[73]	3	Learn-Based	NN, Fuzzy, and another ML
[74]	3	Expert-Based	Expert, Changes Requirements
[75]	3	Learn-Based	ML
[76]	3	Expert-Based	Data Set, Data Mining
[77]	3	Expert-Based	SP for Issues
[78]	2	Expert-Based	Multifactor (RF, RNF, and DP-Domain Properties)
[79]	2	Learn-Based	COCOMO and Change Request
[80]	2	Regression Based	Logistic Regression Model
[16]	2	Expert-Based	FDD and Reuse
[81]	1	Expert-Based	Delphi
[82]	1	Expert-Based	Data Set and Quality of Requirements

Defining Leadership and its Challenges while Transitioning to DevOps

Krikor Maroukian
Microsoft
Modern Service Management
Athens, Greece
e-mail: krmaro@microsoft.com

Stephen R. Gulliver
Henley Business School
University of Reading
Reading, United Kingdom
e-mail: s.r.gulliver@henley.ac.uk

Abstract— **DevOps practices and principles adoption is no longer restricted to technology-specific skills. Many studies indicate that successful DevOps adoption is part of continuous corporate transformation at all levels, and that includes cultural and behavioural patterns, process-driven perspective and toolchain readiness for usage. Our research method involves the analysis and evaluation of 30 interviews with participants from the private and public sectors in the EMEA region. Analysis and evaluation of a survey completed by 250 participants (73% from Europe) and 76% who have held previous leadership positions is also included. A mixed methods approach was used. Thirty (30) participants from consultancy firms and service provider organisations generated coded themes to expand our understanding of relevant factors. From the 250 survey participants, 81% had 10+ years of professional experience and two-thirds were currently practicing DevOps. The aim of our research was to unveil leadership-specific observations on characteristics and factors that would indicate certain reasoning behind challenges faced by organisations while transitioning to DevOps. Our results show that top leadership factors identified are: communication and collaboration, customer-centric mindset, having a technical background, and being an active listener. The least important factors identified were: gaining a relevant certification, design thinking, previous experience on transformation projects, and talent seeking.**

Keywords-DevOps adoption; resistance factors; leadership characteristics; metrics.

I. Introduction

The 1990s saw the birth of pre-agile approaches, such as the Rapid Unified Process [1] and XP [2] [3], which eventually led to Agile Software Development, which is characterised mainly by lightweight, flexible, adaptive processes linked to rapidly changing corporate business environments aiming to eliminate waste [44]. The traditional 'waterfall' approach to release and deployment management requires a release cycle of 6-18 months, which shifts focus to maintenance-only. This practically means that operations teams in Information Technology (IT) organisations are focused on purely reactive maintenance activities including bug fixes. There is, however, a lack of development of new feature development, i.e., change of features or functions that would fundamentally change the program architecture [13].

Software has become pervasive in day-to-day human activities, and the world economy is now dependent on software use. This in turn has increased the importance of having software-intensive products and services that are useful, secure and reliable at all times during operational use.

A retrospective view of the last twenty years of software product development practices and principles shows that a decline of Extreme Programming (XP) publications has been succeeded by the gradual increase, i.e., since about 2009, in the popularity of agile and lean practices, such as SCRUM [42] and Kanban [43]. Moreover, two other areas that seem to be gaining popularity are technical debt and code smells, which address software product development and code maintenance suboptimisation - in terms of agile team velocity to deliver sprint artefacts for the minimum-viable product. Furthermore, certain agile practices, e.g., pair-programming since 2003, user stories since 2003, test-driven development since 2007, and code refactoring since 2009, are relatively stable. In addition, DevOps, Continuous Integration, Continuous Deployment, Continuous Delivery are characterised as 'hot research topics', with considerable increases in popularity since 2014 [14].

Leading DevOps practice and principle adoption has become a fundamental element to the success of DevOps teams [4] [39]. A high-performing organisation is characterised by adoption of DevOps practices by multiple teams and departments, high responsiveness to mean-time-to-recover from product system failure, i.e., end-user experience degradation, mean-time-to-market, change failure rate, and embedding security deep into the source code [15]. However, there is still limited research outlining the leadership style, traits, competencies and skillset accompanied with high-performing DevOps-oriented organisations. Speed in the development and delivery of new software features provides the opportunity to respond quickly to customer needs, business opportunities, and get quick feedback about the new software features [16]. Feedback loops facilitate information that is useful to make informed decisions regarding software development efforts; conducted by different stakeholders of the software product development value stream.

The purposes of our study are (RQ1) to provide a better understanding of the leadership characteristics required to enable DevOps practice and principle adoption, (RQ2) to gain insights into the DevOps adoption inhibitors or resistance factors slowing down change, and (RQ3) to examine the associated metrics to these set of competencies and leadership style.

This paper is divided into four further sections. Section II lays out the thoroughly researched account of literature behind DevOps adoption and pertinent leadership research, the challenges faced in the transitional period towards

DevOps practice and principle adoption and which type of technology-agnostic i.e., team-driven, process driven, metrics can be associated to DevOps. Section III describes the research method, design and collection process. Section IV outlines the analysis and evaluation of the interview and survey results, including an examination of research validity. Lastly, Section V concludes the paper including future research considerations.

II. BACKGROUND AND RELATED WORK

A. DevOps Adoption and Leadership

The adoption of DevOps practices and principles requires several factors to be taken into account. The most popular model among DevOps adoption is known as Culture-Automation-Lean-Monitoring-Sharing (CALMS) [17], which requires a change of people's mindset, skill and toolsets. This orientation requires gradual and minor changes in an organisation's daily operations. For companies to move from structured to agile structures in software development, there needs to be first an adoption stage of agile practices and a shift to smaller cross-functional teams, and later, when a certain level of maturity is attained, DevOps practices can be adopted, such as automated system integration and continuous integration [18]. When continuous integration is in place, customers express an interest in receiving enhancements and bug fixes more frequently. Therefore, adoption of continuous delivery practices is required. The final step occurs when the organisation not only releases software continuously, but also develops mechanisms to conduct rapid experimentation in order to drive innovation.

The DevOps Institute's Collective Body of Knowledge (CBOK) focuses on three pillars: DevOps, Lean and Leadership [19]. In addition, successful adoption of DevOps requires agile software development [29]. For practitioners in the industry, there is a decline of interest in XP, and a steady increase in SCRUM over time. Between 2006 and 2015, there was an increase in interest concerning continuous integration, however, there was a sharp increase in DevOps adoption in the last few years [20]. This sharp increase has most likely been triggered by DevOps leaders who have acquired the transformational acumen required to contribute to the design, influence, and motivate cultural transformation, which is proven to be a critical success factor in DevOps adoption: making it a multidisciplinary topic that requires application of a mix of skills, practices, and principles [21].

The State of DevOps Report published by Puppet discovered a correlation between transformational leadership and organisational performance [23]. Transformational leadership comprises of four dimensions: idealised influence, inspirational motivation, intellectual stimulation, and individualised consideration and the leader aims to inspire and transform followers by appealing to their ideas and emotions [41]. In addition, the State of DevOps Report conveys that DevOps leaders with a servant leadership mentality inspired better team performance [23]. In essence, the leader is serving rather than being served and, therefore, creates an environment of trust, collaboration and reciprocal service, which ultimately leads higher performance [40]. Servant leadership was developed as a theory of ethical leadership, which is comprised of values, such as integrity, altruism, humility, empathy and healing, personal growth, fairness, justice and empowerment [41]. Our study attempts to identify the characteristics presented by a mixed methods research design approach and how obtained results and outcomes relate to transformational and servant leadership.

B. DevOps Adoption Challenges

Following a decade of DevOps, there is no firm consensus amongst software practitioners and scholars as to what the DevOps definition actually includes [4] [30]-[34]. Moreover, DevOps is unclear but also evolving [13]. Literature defines DevOps in numerous ways, although, the majority of descriptions specifies 'DevOps' as a term that is used to emphasise the collaboration between software development and operations. There is, however, a research and industrial need to develop a better understanding of the DevOps scope [20], since DevOps has been described as: a new role within a software organisation [35]; a movement for change in software industry [30]; a set of software development practices [4]; a leagile approach [22] – i.e., the combination of the lean and agile paradigms; and High Velocity IT [5], which ITIL4® defines as involving techniques for valuable investments, fast development, resilient operations, co-created value and assured conformance.

Cultural enablers, used to promote the adoption of DevOps practices, are required, such as focus on decision making, customer focus, engineering practices, learning and development, leadership, team recognition, innovation, guilds and performance feedback [21] [36] [37]. Moreover, to achieve performance gains, while adopting DevOps, the following are shown to be essential [38]:

- Tightened feedback loops between Dev and Ops teams;
- Established practices of automated performance monitoring;
- Measurement of key performance metrics in Continuous Integration, Test and Ops teams;
- Shared tools and performance metrics across teams.

According to the State of DevOps Report [23], published by Puppet and the DevOps Research and Assessment (DORA), there is an increasing inclusion of IT team members into DevOps teams such that:

- Sixteen percent (16%) of the respondents identified themselves as working in DevOps teams in 2014;
- Nineteen percent (19%) of the respondents identified themselves as working in DevOps teams in 2015;
- Twenty-two percent (22%) of the respondents identified themselves as working in DevOps teams in 2016;
- Twenty-seven percent (27%) of the respondents identified themselves as working in DevOps teams in 2017.

Furthermore, there are considerable challenges in DevOps practice adoption in the IT industry. DevOps adoption challenges include, but are not limited to, the insufficient communication, deep-seated company culture, industry constraints and feasibility, heterogeneous environments. Moreover, a Delphi study of 42 Norwegian experts indicated a comprehensive list of problems influencing poor cooperation between software development and operations [24], however, the most serious problems in poor software development – operations cooperation - included the following aspects:

- Operations not being involved in the requirements specifications;
- Poor communication and information flow;
- Unsatisfactory test environment;
- Lack of knowledge transfer;
- Systems being put into production before they are complete;
- Operational routines not being established prior to deployment.

Additionally, the hierarchical approach of organisational structures that welcome static team structures can also become a bottleneck to information flow. Moreover, obstacles to flow can also be characterised as anything that acts as an impediment to cognitive load of a DevOps team topology [45]. Cognitive load refers to the amount of working memory being used at any one moment within a team structure. Flow challenges can be due to disengaged teams, software too big for team structure, confusing organisational design options, team getting pulled into too many directions, painful reorganisation every few years, flow is blocked by certain factors and too many reactive-natured surprises for the team to handle [45].

For modern software companies, speed facilitates fast and repeatable software development and delivery processes [25]. Complexity of performance engineering approaches is a barrier for wide-spread adoption by practitioners. Accordingly, performance engineering approaches must be lightweight and must smoothly integrate with existing tools in the DevOps pipeline [37]. This is evident by the emergence and the growing interest of a continuous deployment paradigm in the software industry. Continuous deployment entails the capability of an organisation to deliver new software features at multiple times and in the shortest time possible. DevOps is an approach that has been reported to enable the continuous deployment paradigm as it embodies a set of useful principles crucial to the development and deployment of software [26]. Practices that have posed as barriers to continuous deployment include time pressure, increased technical debt, customer unwillingness to update and conflicting goals between rapid released and achieving high reliability and test coverage. In addition, the adoption challenges that have also been identified in large scale organisations are cultural barriers, risk of disintermediation of roles, lack of DevOps education and awareness, resistance to change, silo mentality and lack of strategic direction from senior management [36].

In general, organisations and IT professionals place DevOps in high regard, but DevOps practices adoption is associated with challenges. These challenges can arise mainly from a combination of necessity in maintaining a legacy system, lack of senior management buy-in, managerial structure, and resistance [21]. Other points which pose as barriers are blame-culture, communication difficulties, and delays in producing software releases [4] [30]-[34].

C. *Measuring DevOps*

Metrics in traditional highly structured corporate environments produce development cycles that focus a lot on defect density of the software product: yet, this is not the most effective way to measure quality in the context of software product development [6] [7]. The effect that traditional approaches have had to software development is that 'surrogation' can lead to enterprise strategy being replaced with metrics [27], with employees consciously aiming to contribute to local optima rather than global corporate optima to increase flow in the value stream [8].

Software development teams commonly express significant differences in behavioural patterns of developers and testers when senior management first establishes a key performance metric of 'least defects in deployable code' into a production environment and announce the downsizing of the quality assurance team [6]. Software development should be attempting to get closer to the metrics most frequently utilised to evaluate the speed with which releases can move to production environments before performance inefficiencies start to appear [6]. Additionally, software development pipeline health is essential to maintaining high quality software. Measurement approaches in DevOps teams include, but are not limited to, source code version control, optimum branching strategy, static analysis, >80% code coverage, vulnerability scan, open source scan, artifact version control, auto provisioning, immutable servers, integration testing, performance testing, build deploy testing automated for every commit, automated rollback, automated change order, zero downtime release, feature toggle [12].

In addition to the aforementioned, there is increased research interest in understanding how DevOps teams measure cognitive load using relative domain complexity without measuring lines of code produced, number of modules, classes, or methods [7]. This can be further complemented by flow metrics – i.e., flow distribution, flow velocity, flow time, flow load, flow efficiency [10], which represent the proportion of each flow work item being active in a given sprint. In particular, flow velocity measures features, defects, risks and technical debt in the product development flow whereas flow time resembles lead time and process time as defined in value stream maps [27]. Moreover, flow load represents active or waiting work in the value stream, and flow efficiency is the result of measuring flow load, i.e., duration of work inactivity in the value stream.

Workflow can be further categorised according to the Deployment Pipeline stages [11]. At the requirements planning level, new and unique work, including repetitive work, is considered for optimisation purposes. Moreover, optimizing it requires fast feedback and a focus on end-to-end cycle time for an all-round customer feedback.

Another dimension to DevOps can be Microsoft's perception on the triage of people, process and technology while providing a strong focus on the following seven DevOps habits [28]:

1. Flow of customer value.
2. Team autonomy and enterprise alignment.
3. Backlog groomed with learning.
4. Evidence gathered in production.
5. Managing technical debt.
6. Production-first mindset.
7. Infrastructure is a flexible resource.

In regard to the seven habits, firstly, flow of customer value entails automated testing, Continuous Integration (CI), Continuous Deployment (CD) and release engineering and management. Moreover, scaling that in terms of agile to self-managing teams and feature crews regards team autonomy and enterprise alignment. Thirdly, within Microsoft feature crews, another habit is to refine and reprioritise backlog items through usage monitoring, telemetry, Testing In Production (TIP) and stakeholder feedback. In fact, evidence collected from production environments include all aforementioned steps for backlog refinement plus the use of feature flags and continuous experimentation, regarded as one of key DevOps practices. In addition, managing technical debt concerns peer code reviews, automated testing, continuous measurement and agile documentation. In terms of production first mindset application performance management and Infrastructure-as-Code (IaC) play big role in achieving it, coupled with configuration management and automated recovery. Finally, IaC, automated scaling, sandboxing for development and test environments as well as the usage of microservices and containers make Infrastructure a flexible resource to work with while adopting DevOps practices and principles.

The aforementioned literature on DevOps metrics at the team structure-process-toolset level should be taken into account in a cross-functional manner and be communicated transparently to both leadership and engineering teams to establish progress and quality in a consistent format [9].

III. Research Method

Having defined the agile, lean, and DevOps adoption benefits and challenges described in literature, it is crucial to determine whether these views align with industry domain practitioners.

A. Research Design

This paper presents contextually relevant data generated from thirty (30) semi-structured interviews, see Figure 1, that were conducted between September 2018 and January 2019 with practitioners in companies working within a wide range of countries (Czech Republic, Estonia, Italy, Georgia, Greece, The Netherlands, Saudi Arabia, South Africa, United Arab Emirates (UAE), United Kingdom). Additionally, a survey was conducted during the period August 2019 and December 2019 whereby the responses of 250 participants were recorded.

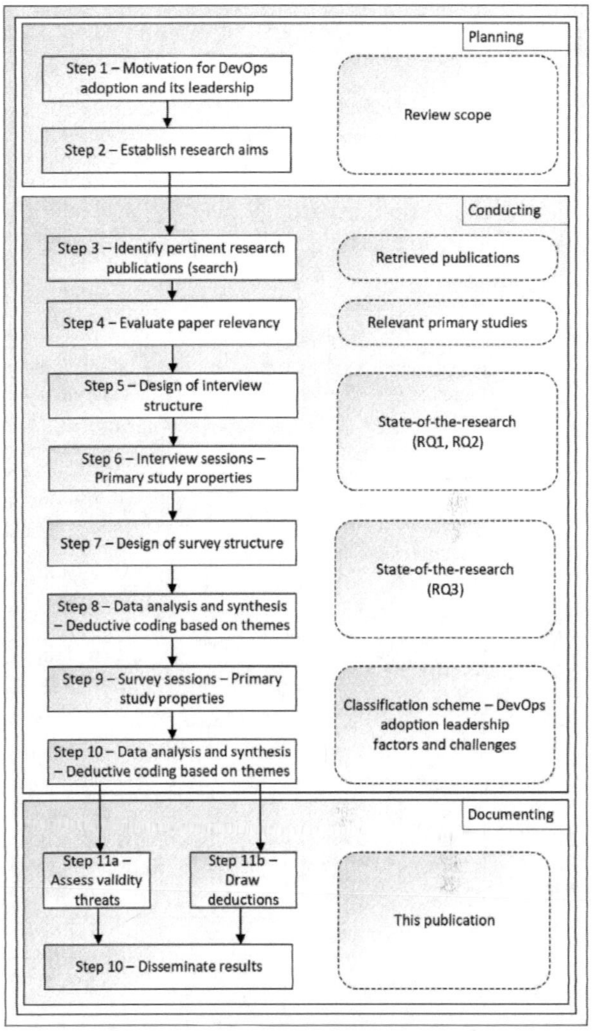

Figure 1. Research study process.

B. Data Collection for Interviews

The interview participants were identified with their roles, organisation size and country within which they work. Participants selected for the interview process had previous experience of agile, lean and DevOps practices and principles. We invited participants through IT events in Europe and through professional social media networks, see Table I.

TABLE I. LIST OF INTERVIEW PARTICIPANTS

	Industry Practitioner Profile		
	Job Title	***Country of Work***	***Domain***
P1	PMO Director	Saudi Arabia	Aviation
P2	Principal Consultant,	Italy	IT

	Industry Practitioner Profile		
	Job Title	***Country of Work***	***Domain***
	IT Service Management		Consulting Services
P3	CIO	Greece	Insurance
P4	Principal Consultant, IT Service Management	UK	IT Consulting Services
P5	Managing Director, IT Service Management	UK	IT Consulting Services
P6	Smart Systems Manager	Greece	IT Consulting Services
P7	Senior Digital Transformation Technologist & Solution Practice Lead	United Arab Emirates	IT Consulting Services
P8	Principal Consultant, IT Service Management	United Kingdom	IT Consulting Services
P9	Founding Consultant, IT Service Management	United Kingdom	IT Consulting Services
P10	Managing Director	United Kingdom	IT Consulting Services
P11	Head of Remote Transactions	Greece	Banking
P12	Consultant	Netherlands	IT Consulting Services
P13	Deputy Chief Information Officer	Greece	Construction Management
P14	Head of Applications	Greece	Lottery
P15	Principal Consultant, IT Service Management	South Africa	IT Consulting Services
P16	Founding Consultant, IT Service Management	United Kingdom	IT Consulting Services
P17	Managing Director, IT Service Management	United Kingdom	IT Consulting Services
P18	Managing Director and Lead Consultant	United Kingdom	IT Consulting Services
P19	IT Operations Manager	Greece	Lottery
P20	IT Operations Manager	United Kingdom	Government
P21	Founding Consultant, IT Service Management	United Kingdom	IT Consulting Services
P22	Assistant General Manager, IT Operations	Greece	Banking
P23	Chief Digital Office	Estonia	Government

	Industry Practitioner Profile		
	Job Title	***Country of Work***	***Domain***
P24	Chief Information Officer	Greece	Insurance
P25	Chief Information Officer	Greece	Aviation
P26	Development Team Lead	Greece	Lottery
P27	IT Operations Lead	Georgia	Government
P28	Business Development Director	Greece	IT Consulting Services
P29	Operations and Innovation Lead, IT Services	Czech Republic	Courier Services
P30	CIO	Greece	Automotive

To achieve a heterogeneous perspective, and to increase the wealth of information, practitioners from a variety of organisations were invited and consulted. The information provided to interview participants prior to the interview commencing stated that names or organisation titles would not be disclosed as part of this research.

Data collection and analysis was mapped to answer the research questions posed at the end of Introduction section, see Table II. The entire set of interview questions is accessible at [46].

TABLE II. RESEARCH QUESTIONS MAPPED TO INTERVIEW QUESTIONS

Research Question	**Interview Question (No.)**
Data collection for segmentation purposes e.g., participant age, professional experience, job role, country of work, industry of work.	1, 2, 3, 21
RQ1) Leadership characteristics required to enable DevOps practice and principle adoption	17, 18, 19, 20, 21
RQ2) What are the DevOps adoption inhibitors (resistance factors)?	4, 5, 6, 7, 8, 9, 10, 11, 12, 13, 14, 21
RQ3) How should DevOps leadership be measured?	4, 20, 21

There were twenty (20) questions - consisting of two types of questions – participant demographics questions and questions mapped to the three research questions in this paper.

The interview series consisted of thirty (30) participants from nine countries Greece (11), UK, (10), Saudi Arabia (2), Czech Republic (1), Estonia (1), Georgia (1), Italy (1), Netherlands (1), South Africa (1), United Arab Emirates (1). Fifteen (15) were IT consultants and another fifteen (15) were from service provider organisations. The service consumers of IT consultants can be service providers or other IT consultants. The service consumers for the service provider organisation can also be either internal or external. All Greek participants were service providers. UK participants consisted of nine (9) consultants and one (1) service provider. There was a distinct diversity of participant roles, e.g., Principal Consultant (10), Managing Director (4), Chief Information Officer / Chief Digital Officer (6), IT Operations Manager (3), PMO Director (1), Head of Remote Transactions (1), Smart Systems Manager (1), Head of Applications (1), Development Team Lead (1), Business Development Director (1), Operations and Innovation Lead (1). Furthermore, the industries of participants were Consulting Services (14), Aviation (3), Government (3), Lottery (2), Insurance (2), Finance (2), Manufacturing (1), Logistics (1), ISV (1), Automotive (1).

The interview participants were aware of, and had considerable previously experience applying a range of frameworks, international standards, methodologies, practices, and principles; such as ITIL (26), SCRUM (22), DevOps (19), Lean IT (15), ISO20000 (8), PMBOK (10), PRINCE2 (8), XP (4), SAFe (3).

C. *Data Collection for Survey*

The survey was divided into four sections: 1) questions about the participant's professional information; 2) questions about DevOps practices adopted, 3) questions about leadership related to DevOps, and 4) questions on DevOps metrics. The target audience of the survey is defined mainly as Consultant, Product/Software Developer, C-Suite, Operations engineer, IT Architect. The entire set of survey questions is accessible at [47].

TABLE III. RESEARCH QUESTIONS MAPPED TO SURVEY QUESTIONS

Research Question	Survey Question (No.)
Data collection for segmentation purposes e.g., participant age, professional experience, job role, country of work, industry of work.	1, 2, 3, 4, 5, 20
RQ1) Leadership characteristics required to enable DevOps practice and principle adoption	7, 8, 13, 14, 17, 18, 19, 20
RQ2) What are the DevOps adoption inhibitors (resistance factors)?	1, 12, 13, 14, 20
RQ3) How should DevOps leadership be measured?	8, 11, 15, 16, 20

The 250 participants of the survey answered six demographics questions. The participant role segmentation is shown in Figure 2.

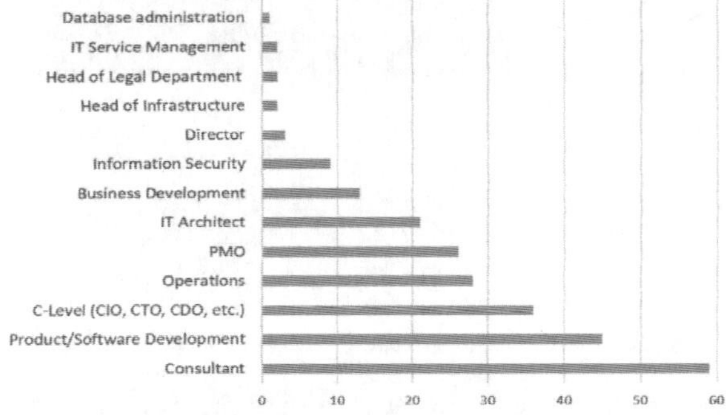

Figure 2. Survey participant job role.

Moreover, the industries in which the survey participants worked in are IT Services/Consulting (33%), Government (22%), Financial Services (13%), Technology/Telecommunications (8%), Manufacturing (4%), Financial Services/Consulting (3%), Aviation (3%), Construction (3%), Retail/Consumer Services (2%), Healthcare (2%), Education (2%), Recycling (1%), Insurance (1%), Energy/Utilities (1%), Leisure & Hospitality (1%).

IV. RESULTS

A. *DevOps Adoption and its Challenges*

In terms of DevOps adoption inhibitors and resistance factors, P15 (Principal Consultant, South Africa) mentioned that "Extremely hierarchical organisational structures are communication barriers to DevOps adoption". Another failure point for DevOps adoption can be that "DevOps practice adoption has to be at a wider enterprise scale for it to be labelled successful". In addition, P27 (IT Operations Manager, Georgia) stated that "Top management is not interested in agile and DevOps practice adoption. They do care about customer satisfaction levels, which can mean a reactive attitude towards the number of complaints received". Notably, P3 (CIO, Greece) mentioned that "We identified the bottlenecks that we adopted while adopting these structured approaches". However, P8 (Principal Consultant, UK) argues that "senior management and team members should not blame the person who introduced the new practice" since "continuous experimentation is crucial to the success of DevOps adoption and any new practice adoption". It is vital to establish the right organisational culture when it comes to the shift of mindset that DevOps adoption requires. To that extent P10 (Managing Director, UK) stated that "the team leading the adoption of the new way of working has to have the right skills and cultural drivers to succeed".

In the survey of 250 participants, there were certain close-ended questions which aimed to unravel more around DevOps practice and principle adoption and Figure 3 indicates the results.

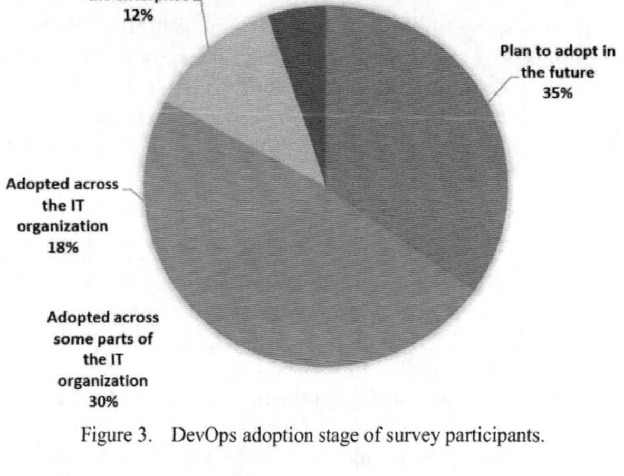

Figure 3. DevOps adoption stage of survey participants.

In addition, the roles responsible for the decision making process in DevOps adoption initiatives are shown in Table IV.

TABLE IV. DECISION MAKING ROLE IN DEVOPS ADOPTION PROCESS

Role responsible for decision making in DevOps adoption process	Participant Preference (%)
C-Level (Chief Information Officer, Chief Digital Officer, etc.)	33.6
Development Lead	20.8
Product Owner	16
Architect	10.4
Operations Lead	6
Business Domain	3.6
DevOps Engineer	3.2
Developer	3.2
System/Network/Database Administrator	1.2
Executive Committee	0.8
Team Leader	0.4
Analyst	0.4
Not Sure	0.4

It is worrisome that Information Security and DevOps Engineer are given low importance. In addition, there seems to be low involvement of the business domain in DevOps adoption initiative. On the other hand, the high concentration of responses to C-level executive (Chief Information Officer, Chief Digital Officer, etc.) and development team lead could suggest that the development teams themselves have to shift from a highly hierarchical organisational structure to more autonomous self-organising team behaviours, which characterise DevOps teams.

Lack of commitment by customer is recognised as the top inhibitor and resistance factor of DevOps adoption followed by lack of organisational practice adoption capability. A 4-point Likert scale was chosen for this question to record opinions. These results are similar to the overall expressed opinion during the interviews and indicate that there is overwhelming agreement on these types of inhibitors to DevOps adoption. Having identified the set of most frequently adopted DevOps practice and principles, the next section attempts to provide clarity on DevOps adoption leadership.

B. *DevOps Leadership*

It is worth looking into the level of acceptance of a leadership role being an individual or team role and the influential effect it can have on team performance in the context of software product development and coding pipeline health. Nine (9) service providers and (6) consultants agreed that the leadership role should be an individual role whereas five (5) service providers and five (5) consultants agreed that the leadership role should be a team role. Lastly, one (1) service provider and three (3) consultants stated that both approaches are required interchangeably throughout the course of a transitioning initiative towards DevOps practice and principle adoption.

Throughout the series of interviews, there was focus on DevOps adoption and the leadership role. In fact, P5 (Managing Director, UK) and P19 (IT Operations Manager, Greece) stated that "Leadership skillset is the most important thing to adoption barrier breakdown". P7 (Consultant, United Arab Emirates) stated that "In the beginning of an adoption initiative there is a constant link to fear of people for loss of power, loss of position, etc.". Moreover, P12 (Principal Consultant, Netherlands) mentioned that there is "Lack of Leadership (walk-the-talk, lead by example, confront 'undesirable behaviours, reward new behaviours)". In addition, P23 (CDO, Estonia, P28 (Business Development Director, Greece) and P30 (CIO, Greece) added that "end-to-end ownership of the leadership role is required in terms of cross-functional team leadership".

Moreover, the survey showed that 76% of participants have held or hold a leadership position and 91% claimed that DevOps leadership role is required and that it should be an individual role (67%). These results are similar to the results produced from the thirty (30) interview participants.

C. *DevOps Metrics*

The interview series revealed that version control and issue tracking have been vastly adopted by the respondents i.e., 95%. Additionally, performance monitoring, test automation and automated deployment seem to have important penetration in the software product development practices. On the contrary, Infrastructure-as-Code, code coverage, static code analysis, trunk-based development, automated provisioning of IT resources, and containerised environments didn't score as high as the aforementioned, three areas.

The main aim of this survey section was to uncover more around the metrics related to DevOps adoption and its leadership role. DevOps adoption practices and principles adoption levels can be measured with the ways indicated in Figure 4.

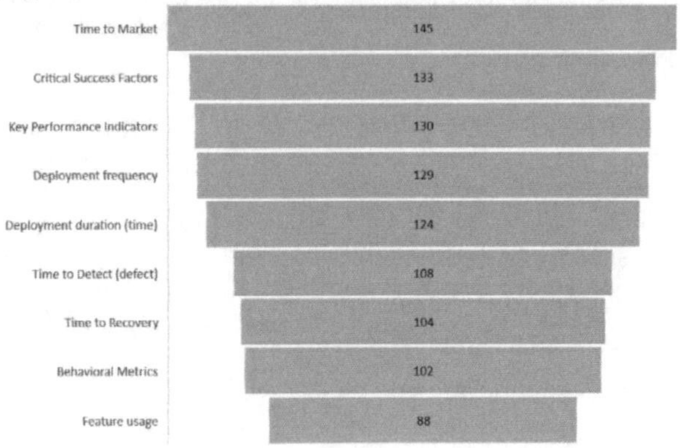

Figure 4. DevOps adoption metrics indicated by survey participants.

The traditional approach to measuring adoption in software development surfaced in the results shown in

Figure 4, in terms of time to market, Key Performance Indicators (KPI) and Critical Success Factors (CSF). The most prominent DevOps oriented metrics were deployment frequency, deployment duration, time to detect a defect, time to recovery and behavioural metrics. Feature usage seems to be an emerging practice for DevOps adoption. Moreover, 88% of respondents agreed that the leadership role should be associated and have ownership of the aforementioned metrics in order to facilitate the DevOps teams efforts in the adoption of practices and principles. Lastly, regarding the software development-oriented metrics described in section Background and Related Work – Measuring DevOps, there was negligible mention in the interviews and the survey.

D. Research Validity

Initially, we considered the internal validity. The main validity threat relates to possible bias in the participant selection process. The communication channels, utilised to invite interview and survey participants, were conferences of DevOps, Lean IT and IT service management. In addition, the majority of interview participants related their work to closed-sourced software products. Future study could focus on DevOps adoption leadership by considering Open-Source Software (OSS) products. Next, we considered the construct validity. A threat to construct validity is that half of the questions of the online survey consisted of closed-ended questions. The authors evaluated the survey structure and deduced that the advantages of closed-ended questions outweighed the disadvantages. Furthermore, concerning external validity, although the viewpoint of the interviewed and surveyed practitioners is considered with different backgrounds, working in varying industry domains and geographical regions, the authors do not claim that research results from this contribution are valid to other scenarios. However, saturation was achieved after the 20th interview.

V. CONCLUSIONS

This paper indicates that DevOps practice and principle adoption maintained strong linkage to agile and lean practice and principle adoption for thirty (30) interview participants from private and public sectors in the EMEA region. In addition, the evaluation of a survey completed by 250 participants, of which 76% have held previous leadership positions further enhanced the linkage of DevOps, agile and lean practices and principles. Moreover, a mixed methods approach was used. The 30 interviews generated coded themes to expand our understanding of relevant factors from most to least recurring in interview transcripts; (1) DevOps leadership, (2) practice and principle adoption, (3) employee culture, (4) product development and (5) skills. The data collected from a series of interviews and a survey indicate a clear list of specific agile, lean and DevOps practices and principles including leadership characteristics which form a crucial part to DevOps adoption theory.

A. Discussion

The most important findings of this review, which are organised according to the study's research questions, are summarised below.

RQ1) What are the leadership characteristics required to enable DevOps practice and principle adoption?

From the 250 survey participants, with 81% possessing over 10+ years of professional experience, results indicated that a new practice and principle adoption leadership role should exist for transformation initiatives; i.e., that the C-Suite should be the direct report of the DevOps leader. The most prominent identified DevOps leadership characteristics associated to leadership skills were: communication and collaboration, customer-centric mindset, having a technical background, and being an active listener.

The results obtained from the survey participants shed more light on the already established beliefs extracted from the interview participants. For instance, there was strong indication by interview participants that a shift of skillset towards acquiring, developing and applying more soft skills is necessary to achieve new practice and principle adoption, in this case agile, lean and DevOps. In fact, communication and collaboration as well as customer-centric or even customer-obsessed mindset is an extension to that viewpoint. Another example spurs from the technical and/or business backgrounds that could play a role in DevOps adoption leadership. Ever since the term "DevOps" was coined back in 2009, the worldwide IT and business community have come to an assumingly obvious realisation; "DevOps" is associated to the IT organisation and that is where it stays. This belief seems to reflect in the survey findings where possessing a technical background is more important than a business background by as much as 15% in the "Strongly Agree" category. However, the survey findings also suggest that possessing a business background is beneficial to a certain extent with interview participants state that a balanced background is preferable to technical-only or business-only.

The least important DevOps leadership characteristics were: gaining a relevant certification, design thinking, previous experience on transformation projects and talent seeking. Furthermore, the Information Security Officer is mostly seen as a collaborator to the DevOps adoption leader.

Survey results indicate that certification was, by a considerable degree, the least preferred characteristic for the DevOps leader. Although there is availability of DevOps leader certifications e.g., DevOps Leader (DOL) certification, by the DevOps Institute, it seems that the desire to become certified in DevOps leadership is not regarded to be an important characteristic or requirement. In addition, design thinking which entails observation, insights generation, ideation, prototype and testing for product development purposes was clearly not considered a crucial characteristic or requirement. Furthermore, previous experience of transformation projects did not yield any connection to DevOps leadership. The authors' intent was to investigate a finding from the interview series, where there was an indication that constant coaching by an external entity e.g., consultant is required, although not always, to sustain transformation initiatives. However, most of the time, the IT organisation cannot sustain newly adopted practices in their structure and default to the "old habits of working", which could suggest that an individual with previous experience on transformation projects would know how to avoid a similar situation in the transition process to DevOps practice and principle adoption.

RQ2) What are the DevOps adoption inhibitors?

The analysis and evaluation of interviews showed that several DevOps adoption inhibitors were recognised (1) communication barriers, (2) lack of cross-functional collaboration, (3) lack of senior management buy-in, (4) lack of leadership, (5) lack of cross-functional leadership, (6) lack of enterprise-wide DevOps adoption, (7) plethora of IT systems coupled with numerous IT support roles and (8) lack of cross-functional collaboration. In addition, the survey added the (9) lack of commitment by customer and (10) lack of organisational practice adoption capability.

The interview participants established that the cultural behaviour of making organisational group distinctions of defining responsibility, especially in terms of "us" and "them", is immensely detrimental to the cross-functional team collaboration mode and the cross-functional leadership DevOps aims to achieve. In essence, this inhibitor leads to DevOps enterprise-wide adoption facing failure from the off start of such an initiative, implying that it is important to first let the cultural character within the IT organisation take form and shape and then aim for adoption at a wider scale, outside the IT organisation. To that extent, the interviews showed that Human Resources departments can be a first step outside the IT organisation where DevOps adoption can contribute in terms of shift of culture-skillset-toolset. Simply put, as one interviewee stated, "Leadership skillset is the most important thing to adoption barrier breakdown". In addition, the set of inhibitors identified could have a direct cause of exacerbation from the perspective of the Human Resources department, whereby utilising a rudimentary selection approach that qualifies new hires based on the right toolset experience without considering mindset and skillset-specific aspects falls short of DevOps-oriented team structure expectations. Thus, this selection process could insinuate that IT teams that fail or partially fail to adopt DevOps practices and principles are because the transition to the right mindset e.g., embrace continuous experimentation, cross-collaboration between development, operations, quality assurance and information security teams, etc. and skillset is simply, under-developed. There are findings in the survey to indicate that talent seeking is not considered an important characteristic of the DevOps leader since that is a responsibility area normally covered by Human Resources. Therefore, the perception that DevOps teams and their leaders should not engage or engage minimally with talent seeking opportunities could affect the future staffing of those teams.

RQ3) How should DevOps leadership be measured?

During the survey, participants indicated that DevOps adoption leadership practices should still be governed by traditional approaches, such as CSF, KPI and time-to-market. However, agile and lean metrics formed a significant part of the wider picture with the top five most popular being (1) deployment frequency, (2) deployment duration, (3) time to detect defect, (4) time to recovery , and (5) behavioural metrics. The DevOps-oriented metrics from the aforementioned, i.e., (1) to (4), indicate software product development measurements that can apply to a DevOps team structure as well as to the DevOps leadership role. From the cultural perspective, (5) can refer to behaviour that aims to increase knowledge sharing in cross-functional fashion, the frequency that a leader performs one-to-ones with DevOps teams and their members to understand what is on top of mind, similar to Gemba walks in the physical or virtual format, the number of absentees during DevOps adoption sessions, etc.

Moreover, feature usage is an emerging practice for DevOps adoption and it regards monitoring usage of a released product feature in a production system environment and whether performance is as expected. Lastly, the vast majority of respondents agreed that the leadership role should be associated and have ownership of the aforementioned metrics.

Presently, we conclude that DevOps adoption leadership is very much a multidisciplinary topic requiring a specific identified skillset coupled with a set of DevOps practices and principles. The leadership approach of the organisational structure is vital to the level of resistance exhibited by IT professionals during the transitioning period from a highly structured software product development approach to DevOps. We also deduce that the transitional phase of DevOps adoption requires an individual to lead DevOps teams which leads to the belief that DevOps has a substantial leadership component at its transitional level.

B. Future Research Directions

DevOps adoption leadership and its relationship to software product development teams is becoming a vastly popular research topic. The authors' intent is to maintain focus on the analysis and evaluation of presently collected research data and to provide further insights relative to current findings in order to witness which leadership styles can become part of the transitional journey of organisations towards DevOps practice and principle adoption. The organisational change required to achieve a successful state of a DevOps-oriented environment in today's global market raises a number of challenges and resistance factors in terms of the triage of mindset-skillset-toolset. The effects of the change need to be continuously monitored to identify the link to the shift of the triage experienced. In that aspect, one of the future research aims could be to invite and/or select IT practitioners with prior and/or current Open Source Software (OSS) experience. Additionally, it is the authors' belief that DevOps adoption velocity and its continuous applicability whether in an IT organisation-wide or enterprise-wide context, regards the levels of cognitive load under which DevOps team structures learn to perform. Therefore, future research could focus in gaining more insights on the extent of influence posed on DevOps teams and their leadership role due to cognitive load. Lastly, the current pandemic crisis, which has shifted the working experience to its virtual format, colocation; one of DevOps practices, for software product development, operations, quality assurance and information security teams is no longer the case. As long as the "work-from-home" paradigm is enforced in the global software product development community teams, that could potentially be affecting the interplay of DevOps adoption leadership characteristics and can be part of future research considerations.

REFERENCES

[1] P. Kruchten, "The rational unified process: an introduction," Addison-Wesley Longman Publishing Co., Inc., USA, 1999.

[2] K. Beck, "Extreme programming explained: embrace change," Addison-Wesley, Don Mills, Ontario, Canada, 2000.

[3] M. Fowler, "Refactoring: improving the design of existing code," Addison-Wesley, Don Mills, Ontario, Canada, 1999.

[4] L. Bass, I. Weber and L. Zhu, "DevOps: A Software Architect's Perspective," Addison Wesley, 2015.

[5] AXELOS, "ITIL4® Managing Professional High Velocity IT," The Stationery Office, London, UK, 2020, ISBN: 9780113316403.

[6] M. Herring, "DevOps for the Modern Enterprise," IT Revolution, Portland, Oregon, 2018.

[7] M. Kersten, "From Project to Product," IT Revolution, Portland, Oregon, 2018.

[8] E. Goldratt, "Theory of Constraints and How it Should be Implemented," North River Press, 1994.

[9] M. Herring, D. DeGrandis, N. Forsgren and S. Guckenheimer, "Measure efficiency, effectiveness and culture to optimize devops," IT Revolution, Portland, Oregon, 2015.

[10] G. Gruver, "Start and Scaling DevOps in the Enterprise," Bookbaby, 2016.

[11] K. Martin and M. Osterling, "Value stream mapping: how to visualize work and align leadership for organizational transformation," McGraw-Hill Education, UK, 2014.

[12] M. Nygard, T. Pal, S. Magill, S. Guckenheimer and J. Willis, "DevOps Governance Architecture," IT Revolution, Portland, Oregon, 2019.

[13] H. Alahyari, T. Gorschek and R. B. Svensson, "An exploratory study of waste in software development organizations using agile or lean approaches: A multiple case study at 14 organizations," Information and Software Technology, vol. 105, pp. 78-94, Jan. 2019, doi.org/10.1016/j.infsof.2018.08.006.

[14] P. Rodríguez et al., "Chapter Four - Advances in Using Agile and Lean Processes for Software Development," Advances in Computers, Elsevier, vol. 113, pp. 135-224, 2019, doi.org/10.1016/bs.adcom.2018.03.014.

[15] W. J. W. Geurts, "Faster is Better and Cheaper," Wiley Online, vol. 26, pp. 1002-1015, Jul. 2016, doi.org/10.1002/j.2334-5837.2016.00207.x.

[16] T. Schlossnagle, "Monitoring in a DevOps world," ACM Queue, 2017, dl.acm.org/doi/pdf/10.1145/3178368.3178371.

[17] J. Willis. *What DevOps means to me*. [Online]. Available from: https://blog.chef.io/what-devops-means-to-me/, 2020.10.16

[18] P. Rodríguez et al., "Continuous deployment of software intensive products and services: A systematic mapping study," Journal of Systems and Software, vol. 123, pp. 263-291, 2017, doi.org/10.1016/j.jss.2015.12.015.

[19] DevOps Institute. *DevOps Collective Body of Knowledge* [Online]. Available from: devopsinstitute.com/resources/, 2020.10.16

[20] T. Dingsøyr and C. Lassenius, "Emerging themes in agile software development: Introduction to the special section on continuous value delivery," Information and Software Technology, pp. 56-60, 2016

[21] S. Jones, J. Noppen and F. Lettice, "Management challenges for DevOps adoption within UK SMEs." ACM, 2016, 978-1-4503-4411-1/16/17.

[22] W. Xiaofeng, K. Conboy and O. Cawley, ""Leagile" software development: An experience report analysis of the application of lean approaches in agile software development," J. Syst. Softw. Vol. 85, 2012.

[23] Puppet, DORA. *State of DevOps Report 2019* [Online]. Available from: puppet.com/resources/report/state-of-devops-report/, 2020.10.16

[24] J. Iden, B. Tessem and T. Päivärinta, "Problems in the interplay of development and IT operations in system development projects: A Delphi study of Norwegian IT experts," Information and Software Technology, vol. 53(4), pp. 394-406, 2011, DOI: 10.1016/j.infsof.2010.12.002.

[25] D. Feitelson, E. Frachtenberg and K. Beck, "Development and Deployment at Facebook," IEEE 1089-7801/13, 2013.

[26] J. Humble and J. Molesky, "Why enterprises must adopt devops to enable continuous delivery," Cutter IT Journal, vol. 24(8), pp. 6-12, 2011.

[27] Harvard Business Review, M. Harris, B. Tayler. *Don't Let Metrics Undermine Your Business* [Online]. Available from: hbr.org/2019/09/dont-let-metrics-undermine-your-business/, 2020.10.16

[28] Azure DevOps Microsoft Documentation. *DevOps at Microsoft* [Online]. Available from: docs.microsoft.com/en-us/azure/devops/learn/devops-at-microsoft/, 2020.10.16

[29] L. E. Lwakatare, P. Kuvaja and M. Oivo, "Relationship of DevOps to Agile, Lean and Continuous Deployment," 17th International Conference on Product-Focused Software Process Improvement (PROFES), Nov. 2016, pp. 399-415, doi:10.1007/978-3-319-49094-6.

[30] B. B. N. de França, H. Jeronimo and G. H. Travassos, "Characterizing DevOps by hearing multiple voices," Proceedings of the 30th Brazilian Symposium on Software Engineering (SBES), Association for Computing Machinery, New York, pp. 53–62, 2016.

[31] A. Dyck, R. Penners and H. Lichter. 2015. Towards Definitions for Release Engineering and DevOps, 3rd International Workshop on Release Engineering (RELENG), doi: 10.1109/RELENG.2015.10

[32] L. E. Lwakatare, P. Kuvaja and M. Oivo, "An exploratory study of DevOps: extending the dimensions of DevOps with practices," 11th International Conference on Software Engineering Advances, pp. 91–99, IARIA, Rome, 2016.

[33] J. Smeds, K. Nybom and I. Porres, "DevOps: A definition and perceived adoption impediments," Agile Processes in Software Engineering and Extreme Programming (XP2015), Lecture Notes in Business Information Processing, vol. 212, Springer, Cham, 2015.

[34] R. Jabbari, N. bin Ali, K. Petersen and B. Tanveer, "What is DevOps? A Systematic Mapping Study on Definitions and Practices," Proceedings of the Scientific Workshop Proceedings (XP2016). Association for Computing Machinery, New York, NY, USA, Article 12, pp. 1–11, doi.org/10.1145/2962695.2962707.

[35] N. Kerzazi and B. Adams, "Who needs release and devops engineers, and why?," Proceedings of the International Workshop on Continuous Software Evolution and Delivery (CSED2016). Association for Computing Machinery, New York, NY, USA, pp. 77–83, 2016, doi.org/10.1145/2896941.2896957.

[36] M. B. Kamuto and J. J. Langerman, "Factors inhibiting the adoption of DevOps in large organisations: South African context," 2nd IEEE International Conference on Recent Trends in Electronics, Information & Communication Technology (RTEICT), 2017, DOI: 10.1109/RTEICT.2017.8256556.

[37] C. P. Bezemer et al., "How is Performance Addressed in DevOps?" Proceedings of ACM/SPEC International Conference on Performance Engineering (ICPE 2019), Association for Computing Machinery, New York, NY, USA, pp. 45–50, 2019, doi.org/10.1145/3297663.3309672.

[38] W. Gottesheim, "Challenges, benefits and best practices of performance focused DevOps," Proceedings of the 4th International Workshop on Large-Scale Testing (LT2015), 2015.

[39] K. Maroukian and S. R. Gulliver, "Leading DevOps practice and principle adoption," Proceedings of the 9th International Conference on Information Technology Convergence and Services (ITCSE2020), AIRCC, Computer Science and Information Technology, pp. 41-56, 2020, ISBN13: 978-1-925953-19-0.

[40] R. K. Greenleaf, "Servant leadership: A journey into the nature of legitimate power and greatness", Paulist Press, 2002, ISBN: 978-0809105540

[41] G. A. Yukl and W. L. Gardner, III, "Leadership in organizations", Pearson Education, Essex, 2020, ISBN13:978-1-292-31440-2.

[42] J. Sutherland and K. Schwaber, "The Definitive Guide to Scrum: The Rules of the Game", 2017, USA.

[43] J. Anderson, "Kanban: Successful Evolutionary Change for Your Technology Business", 2010, Blue Hole Press, USA.

[44] M. Poppendieck and T. Poppendieck, "Lean Software Development: An Agile Toolkit", Addison-Wesley Professional, 2003, Boston, USA.

[45] M. Skelton, M. Pais, "Team Topologies", IT Revolution, 2019, Portland, USA.

[46] Research Interview Structure. *Interview Introduction and Settings* [Online]. Available from: https://tinyurl.com/ybxrcujq, 2020.10.16

[47] Research Survey Structure. *Survey* [Online]. Available from: https://tinyurl.com/yapl9u3u, 2020.10.16

Software Quality Evaluation via Static Analysis and Static Measurement: an Industrial Experience

Luigi Lavazza

Dipartimento di Scienze Teoriche e Applicate
Università degli Studi dell'Insubria
Varese, Italy
Email: luigi.lavazza@uninsubria.it

Abstract—**Business organizations that outsource software development need to evaluate the quality of the code delivered by suppliers. In this paper, we illustrate an experience in setting up and using a toolset for evaluating code quality for a company that outsources software development. The selected tools perform static code analysis and static measurement, and provide evidence of possible quality issues. To verify whether the issues reported by tools are associated to real problems, code inspections were carried out. The combination of automated analysis and inspections proved effective, in that several types of defects were identified. Based on our findings, the business company was able to learn what are the most frequent and dangerous types of defects that affect the acquired code: currently, this knowledge is being used to perform focused verification activities.**

Keywords–Software quality; Static analysis; Software measurement; Code clones; Code measures.

I. INTRODUCTION

Today, software is necessary for running practically any kind of business. However, poor quality software is generally expensive, because poor quality code can cause expensive failures, increased maintenance cost and security breaches. Hence, organizations that rely on software for running their business need to keep the quality of their software under control.

Many companies do not have the possibility or the will of developing the software they need. Hence, they outsource software development. In this case, an organization has no direct visibility and control of the development process; instead, they can only check the quality of the delivered product.

In this paper, we report about an experience in setting up the toolset needed for evaluating the quality of the code provided by a supplier to an organization. The software involved in the reported activities is used by the organization to run two Business-to-Consumer (B2C) portals.

The organization needed to evaluate the quality of the supplied code; specifically, they wanted to check that the code was correctly structured, cleanly organized, well programmed, and free from defects that could cause failures or could be exploited by attackers. The organization had already in place a testing environment to evaluate the quality of the code from the point of view of behavioral correctness. They wanted to complement test-based verification with checks on the internal qualities that could affect maintainability, fault-proneness and vulnerability.

To accomplish this goal, we selected a set of tools that provide useful indications based on static analysis and measurement of code. The toolset was intended to be used to evaluate two releases of the portal, and then to be set up at the company's premises, and used to evaluate the following releases.

The contributions of the paper are twofold. We provide methodological guidance on the selection and usage of a small set of tools that can provide quite useful insights on code quality. We also provide some results, which can give the reader a measure of the results that can be achieved via the proposed approach.

Because of confidentiality constraints, in this paper we shall not give the names of the involved parties, and we shall omit some non-essential details.

The paper is structured as follows. In Section II, we provide some details concerning the evaluated software and the tools used for the static analysis and measurement. Section III illustrates the methodological approach. In Section IV, the results of the evaluation are described. Section V provides some suggestions about the organization of a software development process that takes advantage of a static analysis and measurement toolset. Section VI illustrates the related work, while Section VII draws some conclusions and outlines future work.

II. THE CONTEXT

In this section, we describe the problem and the tools that were available to be employed in the problem context.

A. The Software to be Evaluated and the Aim of the Study

The evaluation addressed two B2C portals, coded almost entirely in Java. The analyses concentrated exclusively on the Java code. Table I provides a few descriptive statistics concerning the two portals (LLOC is the number of logical lines of code, i.e., the lines that contain executable code).

TABLE I. CHARACTERISTICS OF THE ANALYZED PORTALS.

	Portal 1	Portal 2
Number of files	1507	280
LLOC	100375	37467
LOC	202249	55934
Number of Classes	1158	247
Number of Methods	13351	5370

The aim of the study consisted in evaluating the quality of the products, highlighting weaknesses and improvement opportunities. In this sense, it was important to spot the types of the most frequently recurring issues, rather than finding *all* the actual defects and issues.

It was also required that the toolset could be transferred to the company's premises. To this end, open-source (or free to use) software was to be preferred.

Accordingly, we looked for tools that can

- Detect bad programming practices, based on the identification of specific code patterns.
- Detect bad programming practices, based on code measures (e.g., methods too long, classes excessively coupled, etc.).
- Detect duplicated code.
- Identify vulnerabilities.

After some search and evaluation, we selected the tools mentioned in Table II. These tools are described in some detail in the following sections.

TABLE II. TOOLS USED AND THEIR PURPOSE.

Purpose	Tool	Main features
Identify defects	SpotBugs	Static analysis is used to identify code patterns that are likely associated to defects.
Collect static measures	SourceMeter	Static measurement is applied at different granularity levels (class, method, etc.) to provide a variety of measures.
Detect code clones	SourceMeter	Structurally similar code blocks are identified.
Identify security issues	FindSecBugs	A plug-in for FindBugs, specifically oriented to identifying vulnerable code.

B. Tools Used

1) Static Analysis for Identifying Defects: SpotBugs (formerly known as FindBugs) is a program which uses static analysis to look for bugs in Java code [1][2]. SpotBugs looks for code patterns that are most likely associated to defects. For instance, SpotBugs is able to identify the usage of a reference that is possibly null.

SpotBugs was chosen because it is open-source and one among the best known tools of its kind. Besides, SpotBugs proved to be quite efficient: on a reasonably powerful laptop, it took less than a minute to analyze Portal 1.

SpotBugs provides "confidence" and "rank" for each of the issued warnings. Confidence indicates how much SpotBugs is confident that the issued warning is associated to a real problem; confidence is expressed in a three-level ordinal scale (high, medium, low). The rank indicates how serious the problem is believed to be. The rank ranges from 1 (highest) to 20 (lowest); SpotBugs also indicates levels: "scariest"($1 \leq$rank≤ 4), "scary" ($5 \leq$rank≤ 9), "worrying" ($10 \leq$rank≤ 14), "of concern" ($15 \leq$rank≤ 20).

2) Static Analysis for Identifying Vulnerabilities: Having selected SpotBugs as a static analyzer, it was fairly natural to equip it with FindSecBugs [3], a plug-in for SpotBugs that addresses security problems.

FindSecBugs works like FindBugs and SpotBugs, looking for code patterns that can be associated to security issues, with reference to problems reported by the Open Web Application Security Project (OWASP) [4] an the weaknesses listed in the Common Weaknesses Enumeration (CWE) [5].

3) Static Measures of Code: Several tools are available to measure the most relevant characteristics of code, including size, complexity, coupling, cohesion, etc.

SourceMeter [6] was chosen because it is free to use, efficient and provides many measures, including all the most popular and relevant.

4) Code Clone Detection: Noticeably, SourceMeter is also able to detect code clones. Specifically, SourceMeter is capable of identifying the so-called Type-2 clones, i.e. code fragments that are structurally identical, but may differ in variable names, literals, identifiers, etc.

III. THE METHOD

Since the most interesting properties of code are undecidable, tools that perform static analysis often issue warnings concerning problems that are likely—but not certain—to occur. In practice, the issues reported by static analysis tools can be false positives. Therefore, we always inspected manually the code that had been flagged as possibly incorrect by the tools.

Similar considerations apply to static measures. For instance, consider a method that has unusually high McCabe complexity: only via manual inspection we can check whether the program was badly structured or the coded algorithm is intrinsically complex.

Problem detection was performed as described in Figure 1. The real problems identified via the process described in Figure 1 were classified according to their type, so that the company that asked for the code quality analysis could focus improvement efforts on the most frequent and serious problems.

IV. RESULTS

Here, we describe the code quality problems that were identified.

A. Warnings issued by SpotBugs

Tables III and IV illustrate the number of warnings that SpotBugs issued for the analyzed code, respectively by confidence level and by rank. In Table III, the density indicates the number of warnings per line of code.

TABLE III. SPOTBUGS WARNINGS BY CONFIDENCE.

	Portal 1		Portal 2	
Metric	Warnings	Density	Warnings	Density
High Confidence	68	0.07%	50	0.13%
Medium Confidence	774	0.77%	502	1.34%
Low Confidence	824	0.82%	420	1.12%
Total	1666	1.66%	972	2.59%

SpotBugs also classifies warning by type (for additional information on warning types, see [7]). Table V illustrates the warnings we obtained, by type. It can be noticed that most warnings concerned security (types "Security" and "Malicious code vulnerability").

1) Results deriving from the inspection of SpotBugs warnings: The effort allocated to the project did not allow analyzing all the warnings issued by SpotBugs. Therefore, we inspected the code where SpotBugs had identified issues ranked "scary" and "scariest." Specifically, we analyzed the warnings described in Table VI.

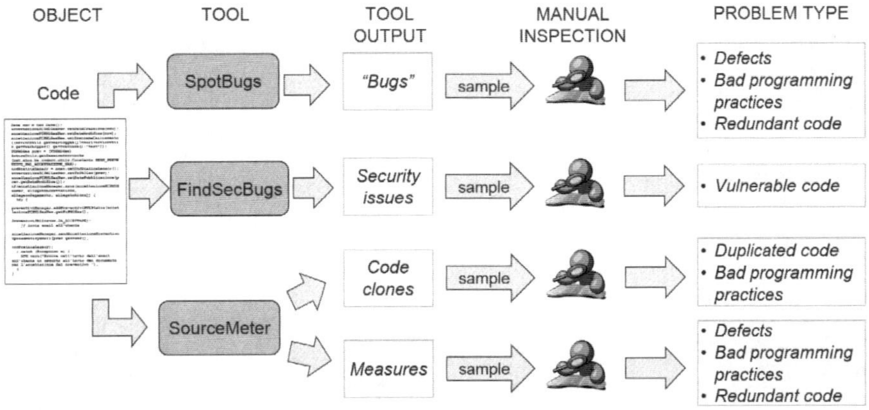

Figure 1. The evaluation process: problem detection phase.

TABLE IV. SPOTBUGS WARNINGS BY RANK

Rank	1	6	7	8	9	10	11	12	14	15	16	17	18	19	20
Portal 1	24	9	1	42		12	39	21	2	604	17	129	562	82	122
Portal 2	10			6	1	7	8	27	18	191	10	59	401	66	168

TABLE V. SPOTBUGS WARNINGS BY TYPE.

	Portal 1		Portal 2	
Warning Type	Number	Percentage	Number	Percentage
Bad practice	73	4.38%	81	8.33%
Correctness	91	5.46%	30	3.09%
Experimental	0	0.00%	1	0.10%
Internationalization	16	0.96%	39	4.01%
Malicious code vulnerability	496	29.77%	316	32.51%
Multithreaded correctness	28	1.68%	1	0.10%
Performance	74	4.44%	143	14.71%
Security	631	37.88%	215	22.12%
Dodgy code	257	15.43%	146	15.02%
Total	1666	100%	972	100%

TABLE VI. SPOTBUGS WARNINGS THAT WERE VERIFIED MANUALLY.

		Occurrences	
Rank	Type	Portal 1	Portal 2
1	Suspicious reference comparison	10	9
1	Call to `equals()` comparing different types	14	1
6	Possible null pointer dereference	8	–
8	Possible null pointer dereference	–	2
8	Method ignores return value	–	4
9	Comparison of `String` objects using == or !=	–	1

Our inspections revealed several code quality problems:

- The existence of problems matching the types of warning issued by SpotBugs was confirmed.
- Some language constructs were not used properly. For instance, class `Boolean` was incorrectly used instead of `boolean`; objects of type `String` were used instead of `boolean` values; etc.
- We found redundant code, i.e., some pieces of code were unnecessarily repeated, even where avoiding code duplication—e.g., via inheritance or even simply by creating methods that could be used in different places—would have been easy and definitely convenient.
- We found some pieces of code that were conceptually incorrect. The types of defect were not of any type that a static analyzer could find, but were quite apparent when inspecting the code.

Concerning the correctness of warnings issued by SpotBugs, we found just one false positive: the "comparison of `String` objects using == or !=" was not an error, in the examined case. We also found that the four instances of "Method ignores return value" were of little practical consequences. In summary, the great majority of warnings indicated real problems, which could cause possibly serious consequences. The remaining warning indicated situations where a better coding discipline could make the code less error prone, if applied systematically.

2) Results deriving from the inspection of FindSecBugs warnings: The great majority of the security warnings (types "Security" and "Malicious code vulnerability") were ranked by FindSecBugs as not very worrying. Specifically, no "scariest") warning was issued, and only one "scary" warning was issued. Therefore, we inspected the only "scary" warning (rank 7, see Table VII), and all the warnings at the highest rank of the level "troubling" (rank 10, see Table VII).

We found that all the warnings pointed to code that had security problems. In many cases, SpotBugs documentation provided quite straightforward ways for correcting the code.

TABLE VII. FINDSECBUGS WARNINGS THAT WERE VERIFIED MANUALLY.

		Occurrences	
Rank	Type	Portal 1	Portal 2
7	HTTP response splitting vulnerability	1	–
10	Cipher with no data integrity	4	2
10	ECB mode is insecure	4	2
10	URL Connection Server-Side Request	1	–
	Forgery and File Disclosure	–	–
10	Unvalidated Redirect	2	–
10	Request Dispatcher File Disclosure	–	1

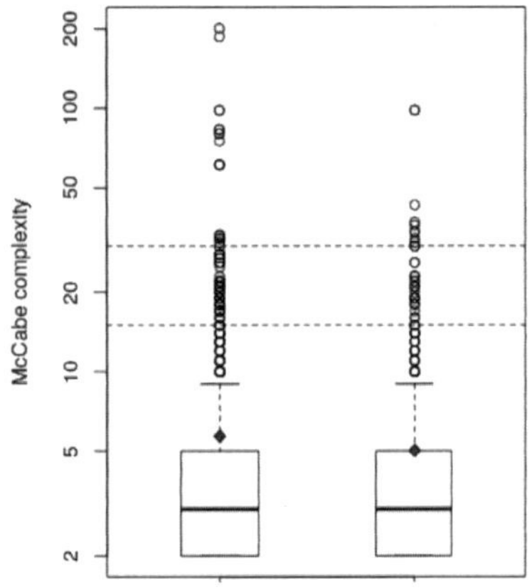

Figure 2. Boxplots illustrating the distributions of McCabe complexity in the two portals (blue diamonds indicate mean values). The scale is logarithmic.

B. Inspection of code elements having measures beyond threshold

Static measures concerning size, complexity, cohesion, coupling, among others, are expected to provide indications on the quality of code. In fact, one expects that code characterized by large size, high complexity, low cohesion, strong coupling and similar "bad" characteristics is error-prone. Accordingly, we inspected code elements having measures definitely out or the usually considered safe ranges. Specifically, we considered McCabe complexity [8], Logical Lines of Code and Response for Class (RFC) [9] as possibly correlated with problems. In fact, we also looked at Coupling Between Objects, Lack of Cohesion in Methods and Weighted Method Count, but these measures turned out to provide no additional information with respect to the aforementioned three measures, i.e., they pointed to the same classes or methods identified as possibly problematic by the aforementioned measures.

We found that several methods featured McCabe complexity well over the threshold that is generally considered safe. Figure 2 shows the distributions of McCabe complexity of methods (excluding setters and getters) together with two thresholds representing values that should and must not be exceeded, according to common knowledge [8][10][11][12]. Specifically, we found methods with McCabe complexity close to 200.

When considering size, we found several classes featuring over 1000 LLOC; the largest class contained slightly less then 6000 LLOC. When considering RFC, we found 12 classes having RFC greater than 200. Interestingly, the class with the highest RFC (709) was also the one containing the method with the greatest McCabe complexity. The biggest class contained the second most complex method. These results were not surprising, since it is known that several measures are correlated to size.

Inspections revealed that the classes and methods featuring excessively high values of LLOC, RFC and McCabe complexity were all affected by the same problem. The considered code had to deal with several types of services, which where very similar under several respects, although each one had its own specificity. The analyzed code ignored the similarities among the services to be managed, so that the code dealing with similar service aspects was duplicated in multiple methods. The code could have been organized differently using basic object-oriented features: a generic class could collect the features that are common to similar services, and a specialized class for every service type could take care of the specificity of different service types.

In conclusion, by inspecting code featuring unusual static measures, we found design problems, namely inheritance and late binding were not used where it was possible and convenient.

C. Inspection of duplicated code

SourceMeter was also used to find duplicated code. Specifically, structurally similar blocks of 10 or more lines of code where looked for. Many duplicated blocks were found. For instance, in Portal 1, 434 duplicated blocks were found. In many cases, blocks included more than one hundred lines. The largest duplicated blocks contained 205 lines. A small minority of detections concerned false positives.

We found three types of duplications:

a) Duplicates within the same file. That is, the same code was found in different parts of the same file (or the same class, often).
b) Duplicates in different files. That is, the same code fragment was found in different files (of the same portal).
c) Duplicates in different portals. That is, the same code fragment was found in files belonging to different portal.

Duplicates of type c) highlighted the existence of versioning problems: different versions of the same class were used in the two portals.

Duplicates of types a) and b) pointed to the same type of problem already identified, i.e., not using inheritance to factor code that can be shared among classes dealing with similar services. Concerning this issue, it is worth noting that static measures revealed a general problem with the design of code, but were not able to indicate precisely which parts of the code could be factorized. On the contrary, duplicated code detection was quite effective in identifying all the cases where code could be factorized, with little need of inspecting the code. In this sense, code clone detection added some value to inspections aiming at understanding the reasons for 'out of range' measures.

V. Suggestions for Improving the Development Process

Given the results described in Section IV, it seems convenient that the capabilities of static analysis and measurement tools are exploited on a regular basis. To this end, we can observe that two not exclusive approaches are possible.

1) Evaluation of code: The toolset can be used to evaluate the released code as described in Section III. However, it would be advisable that developers verify their own code via SpotBugs and SourceMeter even before releasing it: in such a way, a not negligible number of bugs would be removed even before testing and other Verification&Validation activities, thus saving time and effort. With respect to the evaluation described in Section III, where just a sample of the issues reported by the tools were inspected, in the actual development process all issues should be inspected.

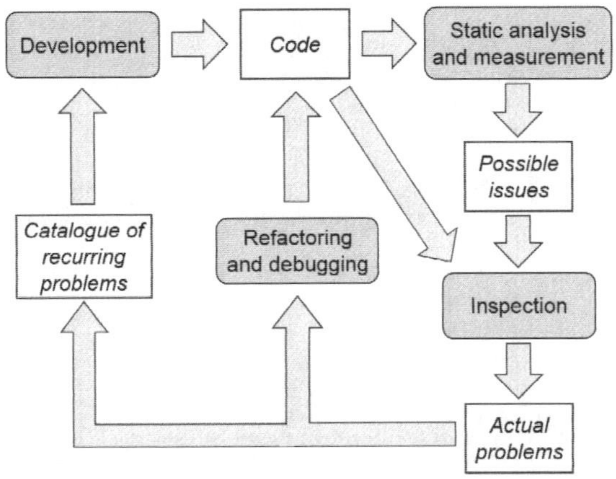

Figure 3. Suggested Development Process.

2) Prevention: The practice of issue identification and verification leads to identifying the most frequently recurring types of problems. It is therefore possible to compile a catalogue of the most frequent and dangerous problems. Accordingly, programmers could be instructed to carefully avoid such issues. This could imply teaching programmers specific techniques and good programming practices.

As a result of the considerations illustrated above, software development activities could be organized as described in Figure 3. If development is outsourced, as in the cases described in this paper, the catalogue of recurrent problems could be used as part of the contract annex that specifies the required code quality level.

Finally, it is worth noting that the proposed approach can be applied in practically any type of lifecycle. For instance, in an agile development environment, the proposed evaluation practices could be applied at the end of every sprint.

VI. Related Work

The effectiveness of using automated static analysis tools for detecting and removing bugs was documented by Zheng et al. [13]. Among other facts, they found that the cost per detected fault is of the same order of magnitude for static analysis tools and inspections, and the defect removal yield of static analysis tools is not significantly different from that of inspections.

Thung et al. performed an empirical study to evaluate to what extent could field defects be detected by FindBugs and similar tools [14]. To this end, FindBugs was applied to three open-source programs (Lucene, Rhino and AspectJ). The study by Thung et al. takes into consideration only known bugs, and is performed on open-source programs. On the contrary, we analyzed programs developed in an industrial context, and relied on manual inspection to identify actual bugs.

Habib and Pradel performed a study to determine how many of all real-world bugs do static bug detectors find [15]. They used three static bug detectors, including SpotBugs, to analyze a version of the Defects4J dataset that consisted of 15 Java projects with 594 known bugs. They found that static bug detectors find a small but non-negligible amount of all bugs.

Vetrò et al. [16] evaluated the accuracy of FindBugs. The code base used for the evaluation consisted of Java projects developed by students in the context of an object-oriented programming course. The code is equipped with acceptance tests written by teachers of the course in such a way that all functionalities are checked. To determine true positives, they used temporal and spatial coincidence: an issue was considered related to a bug when an issues disappeared at the same time as a bug get fixed (according to tests). In a later paper [17] Vetrò et al. repeated the analysis, with a larger code set and performing inspections concerning four types of issues found by FindBugs, namely the types of findings that are considered more reliable.

Tomassi [18] considered 320 Java bugs from the BugSwarm dataset, and determine which of these bugs can potentially be found by SpotBugs and another analyzer—namely, ErrorProne (https://github.com/google/error-prone)—and how many are indeed detected. He found that 40.3% of the bugs were of types that SpotBugs should detect, but only one of such bugs was actually detected by SpotBugs.

In general, the papers mentioned above have goals and use methods that are somewhat similar to ours, but are nonetheless different in important respects. A work that shares context, goals and methods with ours was reported by Steidl et al. [19]. They observed that companies often use static analyses tools, but they do not learn from results, so that they fail to improve code quality. Steidl et al. propose a continuous quality control process that combines measures, manual action, and a close cooperation between quality engineers, developers, and managers. Although there are evident differences between the work by Steidl et al. and the work reported in this paper (for instance, the situation addressed by Steidl et al. does not involve outsourcing), the suggestions for improving the development process given in Section V are conceptually coherent with the proposal by Steidl et al.

Similarly, Wagner et al. [20] performed an evaluation of the effectiveness of static analysis tools in combination with other techniques (including testing and reviews). They observed that a combination of the usage of bug finding tools together with reviews and tests is advisable if the number of false positives is low, as in fact is in the cases we analyzed (many false positives would imply that a relevant effort is wasted).

An alternative to static analyzers like SpotBugs is given by tools that detect the presence of "code smells" [21] in code. A comparison of these types of tools was performed by applying SpotBugs and JDeodorant [22][23] to a set of set of open-source applications [24]. The study showed that the considered tools can help software practitioners detect and remove defects in an effective way, to limit the amount of resources that would otherwise be spent in more cost-intensive activities, such as software inspections. Specifically, SpotBugs appeared to detect defects with good Precision, hence manual inspection of the code flagged defective by SpotBugs becomes cost-effective.

Another empirical study evaluated the persistence of SpotBugs issues in open-source software evolution [25]. This study showed that around half the issues discovered by SpotBugs are actually removed from code. This fact is interpreted as a confirmation that SpotBugs identifies situations that are considered worth correcting by developers.

VII. Conclusions

Evaluating the quality of software is important in general, and especially for business organization that outsource development, and do not have visibility and control of the development process. Software testing can provide some kind of quality evaluations, but to a limited extent. In fact, some aspects of code quality (e.g., whether the code is organized in a way that favors maintainability) cannot be assessed via testing.

This paper describes an approach to software quality evaluation that consists of two phases: in the first phase, tools are used to identify possible issues in the code; in the second phase, code is manually inspected to verify whether the reported issues are associated to real problems. The tools used are of two kinds: the first performs static analysis of code looking for patterns that are likely associated to problematic code; the second type yields measures of static code properties (like size, complexity, cohesion, coupling etc.), thus helping identifying software elements having excessive, hence probably problematic, characteristics.

The mentioned approach was applied to the code of the web portals used by a European company to let its customers use a set of services. The experience was successful, as tool-driven inspections uncovered several types of defects. In the process, the tools (namely SpotBugs and SourceMeter) identified problems of inherently different nature, hence it is advisable to use both types of tools.

Based on our findings, the business company was able to learn what are the most frequent and dangerous types of defects that affect the acquired code: this knowledge is being used to perform focused verification activities.

The proposed approach and toolset (possibly composed of equivalent tools) can be useful in several contexts where code quality evaluation is needed. Noticeably, the proposed approach can be used in different types of development process, including agile processes.

Among the future possible evolutions of this work, the most intriguing one concerns studying the possibility of replacing inspection via some sort of AI-based models that can discriminate false positives and true problems.

Acknowledgment

This work has been partially supported by the "Fondo di ricerca d'Ateneo" of the Università degli Studi dell'Insubria.

References

[1] D. Hovemeyer and W. Pugh, "Finding bugs is easy," ACM Sigplan notices, vol. 39, no. 12, 2004, pp. 92–106.

[2] https://spotbugs.github.io/ [retrieved: August 2020].

[3] https://find-sec-bugs.github.io/ [retrieved: August 2020].

[4] "Open Web Application Security Project (OWASP)," https://www.owasp.org [retrieved: August 2020].

[5] "Common Weaknesses Enumeration," https://cwe.mitre.org [retrieved: August 2020].

[6] R. Ferenc, L. Lang, I. Siket, T. Gyimthy, and T. Bakota, "Source meter sonar qube plug-in," in 2014 IEEE 14th International Working Conference on Source Code Analysis and Manipulation, 2014, pp. 77–82.

[7] https://spotbugs.readthedocs.io/en/stable/bugDescriptions.html/ [retrieved: August 2020].

[8] T. J. McCabe, "A complexity measure," IEEE Transactions on software Engineering, no. 4, 1976, pp. 308–320.

[9] S. R. Chidamber and C. F. Kemerer, "A metrics suite for object oriented design," IEEE Transactions on software engineering, vol. 20, no. 6, 1994, pp. 476–493.

[10] A. H. Watson, D. R. Wallace, and T. J. McCabe, Structured testing: A testing methodology using the cyclomatic complexity metric. US Department of Commerce, Technology Administration, National Institute of , 1996, vol. 500, no. 235.

[11] M. Bray, K. Brune, D. A. Fisher, J. Foreman, and M. Gerken, "C4 software technology reference guide-a prototype." Carnegie-Mellon Univ., Pittsburgh PA, Software Engineering Inst, Tech. Rep., 1997.

[12] JPL, "JPL Institutional Coding Standard for the C Programming Language," Jet Propulsion Laboratory, Tech. Rep., 2009.

[13] J. Zheng, L. Williams, N. Nagappan, W. Snipes, J. P. Hudepohl, and M. A. Vouk, "On the value of static analysis for fault detection in software," IEEE transactions on software engineering, vol. 32, no. 4, 2006, pp. 240–253.

[14] F. Thung, L. Lucia, D. Lo, L. Jiang, P. Devanbu, and F. Rahman, "To what extent could we detect field defects? an extended empirical study of false negatives in static bug-finding tools," Automated Software Engineering, vol. 22, no. 4, 2015, pp. 561–602.

[15] A. Habib and M. Pradel, "How many of all bugs do we find? a study of static bug detectors," in Proceedings of the 33rd ACM/IEEE International Conference on Automated Software Engineering, 2018, pp. 317–328.

[16] A. Vetrò, M. Torchiano, and M. Morisio, "Assessing the precision of FindBugs by mining java projects developed at a university," in 2010 7th IEEE Working Conference on Mining Software Repositories (MSR 2010). IEEE, 2010, pp. 110–113.

[17] A. Vetrò, M. Morisio, and M. Torchiano, "An empirical validation of findbugs issues related to defects," in 15th Annual Conference on Evaluation and Assessment in Software Engineering (EASE 2011). IET, 2011, pp. 144–153.

[18] D. A. Tomassi, "Bugs in the wild: examining the effectiveness of static analyzers at finding real-world bugs," in Proceedings of the 2018 26th ACM Joint Meeting on European Software Engineering Conference and Symposium on the Foundations of Software Engineering, 2018, pp. 980–982.

[19] D. Steidl, F. Deissenboeck, M. Poehlmann, R. Heinke, and B. Uhink-Mergenthaler, "Continuous software quality control in practice," in 2014 IEEE International Conference on Software Maintenance and Evolution. IEEE, 2014, pp. 561–564.

[20] S. Wagner, J. Jürjens, C. Koller, and P. Trischberger, "Comparing bug finding tools with reviews and tests," in IFIP International Conference on Testing of Communicating Systems. Springer, 2005, pp. 40–55.

[21] M. Fowler, Refactoring: improving the design of existing code. Addison-Wesley Professional, 2018.

[22] M. Fokaefs, N. Tsantalis, and A. Chatzigeorgiou, "Jdeodorant: Identification and removal of feature envy bad smells," in 2007 IEEE International Conference on Software Maintenance. IEEE, 2007, pp. 519–520.

[23] "JDeodorant website," 2020. [Online]. Available: https://github.com/tsantalis/JDeodorant

[24] L. Lavazza, S. Morasca, and D. Tosi, "Comparing static analysis and code smells as defect predictors: an empirical study," in Empirical Software Engineering and Measurement – ESEM 2020, 2020.

[25] L. Lavazza, D. Tosi, and S. Morasca, "An empirical study on the persistence of spotbugs issues in open-source software evolution," in 13th International Conference on the Quality of Information and Communications Technology – QUATIC, 2020.

Capacity Planning of Cloud Computing Workloads

A Systematic Review

Carlos Diego Cavalcanti Pereira
CESAR – Recife Center for Advanced Studies and Systems
Recife, Brazil
Email: cdcp@cesar.org.br

Felipe Silva Ferraz
CESAR – Recife Center for Advanced Studies and Systems
Recife, Brazil
Email: fsf@cesar.org.br

***Abstract*—Cloud Computing is a prominent field of research with several areas of knowledge to be explored. The current state of the art of cloud computing regarding capacity planning is a more specific field to address in research and further studies. This work has the objective of identifying, evaluating and interpreting published research that examines sizing and capacity planning for cloud computing workloads. To achieve that, a systematic literature review was conducted. This review resulted in the finding of 504 works, of which 52 were identified as primary studies. The studies were then classified according to research focus and aspect of cloud capacity planning. The work investigates what is known about capacity planning models for cloud computing workloads. The results show statistical data about cloud capacity planning, gaps in current research and models for sizing cloud computing workloads with no historical use and workloads based on functional characteristics or architecture.**

Keywords - cloud capacity planning; capacity planning; cloud computing.

I. INTRODUCTION

Cloud Computing is a way of referring to the use of shared computing resources [1]. Cloud Computing groups gather a large number of servers and other computing resources and generally offer combined capacity based on payment on demand and by cycle [2]. Conceptually, Cloud Computing deals equally with partial or complete abstraction of computational capacity, delivering infrastructure components in the form of service to the end customer [3].

Cloud Computing brought us a new paradigm after the evolution of the use of mainframes for x86 servers [4]. In this model, users no longer have control over the physical technology infrastructure [5]. Cloud computing describes a new approach for how computing services and components are available to users.

One of the key aspects to define and implement a cloud computing workload is to understand the appropriate amount of resources needed to meet demand. Mainly, this activity is conducted by applying empirical approaches [6]. On the other hand, "empirical methods" generally imply that the workloads use some sort of historical data to address the sizing – which is not always possible, especially in innovative systems. Another aspect is that to define the amount of resources needed by a specific workload, it is important to understand its architecture, since, even though historical data may be available, it is not effective to assume that this workload has appropriate enhancements in terms of the amount of resources needed to meet the demand.

To understand how those gaps are usually managed, a Systematic Literature Review (SLR) was conducted to map out how to address those issues and processes with regards to capacity planning of cloud computing workloads.

This work is structured as follows: Section I presents the introduction of Capacity Planning of Cloud Computing Workloads; in Section II, related works are presented; in Section III, a brief introduction to cloud capacity planning is addressed; in Section IV, the applied protocol of this systematic review is presented; in Section V, all results are presented; in Section VI, all findings are addressed and discussed; finally, in Section VII, conclusions are presented.

II. RELATED WORK

Considering that Cloud Computing is a relatively new research field, especially in the case of Capacity Planning, there was no related work found regarding Systematic Literature Reviews on this subject. Even so, the different aspects addressed in this research can be found individually in the primary studies found as a result of this Systematic Literature Review (SLR).

In regards of capacity planning models for cloud computing workloads, most of current approaches somehow apply historical use data as key source of information to establish workload resource needs [6]. Although this assertion can be confirmed as presented on the results of this research, there was no research found in the systematic review addressing cloud capacity planning. When evaluating the results of this study, when relating systematic reviews and cloud computing, the only topic addressed in the research found was Cloud Migration [1]. So, is possible to assume that capacity planning of cloud computing workloads is a subject that has unanswered questions that are relevant to be studied.

III. CLOUD CAPACITY PLANNING

Restrictions regarding software development projects, especially considering shortened schedule horizons and contracted time-to-market deadlines, manifest in traditional approaches to capacity planning, where often a gap is seen and is a major risk compromising their production plans [6]. A formal Capacity Planning approach facilitates forecasting of sizing requirements based on the opportunistic use of whatever performance data and tools are available [1][6][54]-[56]. One of the key aspects when analyzing the relevance of capacity planning in cloud computing projects is the amount of resources needed to meet demand. Depending on the stage at which a project based on cloud computing is, it may be economically unfeasible. This is because architectural decisions can directly impact the need for resources and consequently make the project unviable [4]. Thus in scenarios where there are resource limitations, it is essential to establish a formal capacity planning model [7].

IV. Applied Protocol

For the development of this study, general approaches for performing systematic reviews in software engineering [8] and also for its analysis [9] were applied. Our review process has six steps: (1) establish research protocol, (2) inclusion and exclusion criteria definition, (3) perform search (4) content assessment, (5) data extraction, and (6) synthesis.

The objective of this review is to identify current approaches in scientific literature on sizing and capacity planning for cloud computing workloads. The following questions help identify primary studies:

- What are the capacity planning models for cloud computing workloads available in scientific literature?
- Do capacity planning models consider workloads with no historical use?
- Are there capacity planning models for cloud computing workloads based on functional characteristics or its architecture?

A. *Inclusion and Exclusion Criteria*

For this systematic review, we considered studies that focus in analyzing cloud capacity planning models. The studies could refer to cloud capacity planning specifically or have a broader scope, taking in consideration both cloud computing and capacity planning individually. Considering that this field of research is recent but also in constant development, this review examined studies published from the year 2017.

We also excluded:

- Studies not published in the English language;
- Studies that were unavailable online.

B. *Search Strategies*

The databases considered in the study are in the list below:

- ACM Digital Library;
- IEEE Xplore;
- ScienceDirect – Elsevier.

To ensure that relevant studies would not be excluded when querying different scientific databases, the search strings were tested on each one of databases to guarantee that it would work for all of them. As a result, a general search string was defined:

1. "cloud capacity planning" OR;
2. "capacity planning" AND "cloud computing" OR;
3. "capacity planning" AND "cloud".

As mentioned before, the due process of database search and search strings were tested individually on each database until a final statement was defined. The searches were performed between March 2020 and April 2020. The results of each search were summarized and later examined in order to identify duplicity among them. Table 1 presents the number of studies found on each database.

TABLE I. NUMBER OF STUDIES FOUND IN EACH DATABASE

Database	**Number of Studies**
ACM Digital Library	139
IEEE Xplorer	155
Science Direct	219
Amount of Studies	**513**

C. *Studies Selection Process*

The papers that were collected in the search process were gathered and added to the Mendeley [61] tool. It was found that there were 9 duplicated works among all databases, resulting in a total of 504 non-duplicated papers. Then, they all had their titles analyzed to determine their relevance and adherence to this study. At this stage, the works that did not have a relationship to capacity planning of cloud computing workloads were eliminated. Papers where the titles were unclear about their relation with the subject of this study were put aside to be analyzed in the next step. At the end of this stage, 365 works were excluded and remaining were 137 items for further analysis of abstracts.

At this stage, all works found previously had their abstracts analyzed. Many were also eliminated due to not conforming to the scope of capacity planning of cloud computing workloads. Papers where it was difficult to determine if they conform to the scope of this study due to the aforementioned reasons were included to be filtered out at a further step. As result of this phase of analysis, 75 papers were excluded, thus remaining were 62 to be analyzed more closely. Table 2 presents the number of studies filtered in each step of selection process.

TABLE II. NUMBER OF STUDIES IN SELECTION PHASE

Phase of Selection Process	**Number of Studies**
1. Databases Search	504
2. Title Analysis	137
3. Abstract Analysis	62

D. *Quality Assessment*

After analyzing the search results that did not conform to the scope of this review, we moved on to the quality assessment stage. In this stage, all 62 studies were analyzed, and not only titles or abstracts. In the quality assessment, relevance criteria were established to analyze several aspects regarding each paper selected on prior stages.

To assess the quality of publications, eight questions were defined, based on [9], to support in quality assessment process. Questions supported the analysis, ensuring that relevance and credibility of all papers were being considered. Of the eight questions raised, the first and last one were used to establish whether the paper was relevant for this review. In this case, both questions were used as final exclusion criteria. The other six questions were useful to determine the quality of papers regarding research methods and other related aspects. In this case, those grades supported a formal quality analysis of publications. The questions were:

1. Does the study examine capacity planning models for cloud computing workloads?
2. Is the study based on formal research methods - not just empirical applications?
3. Are the objectives of the study clearly defined?
4. Is the study context adequately described?
5. Were the methods for data collection used and described correctly?
6. Was the research project adequate to achieve the research objectives?
7. Have the research results been properly validated?
8. Does the study directly contribute to this research?

Of the 62 select studies in prior stages, 52 passed to the stage of synthesis and were thus considered primary studies. In the results section, quality assessment process will be described in detail along with the assessment of the 52 remaining studies.

V. Results

As presented previously, 52 studies were identified [9] – [60] as primary studies. In general, all of them address aspects of this systematic review, whether in terms of scope or research questions.

A. *Quantitative Analysis*

The research process conducted resulted in 52 primary studies. They were written by 185 authors affiliated to institutions from 19 different countries and were published between 2017 and 2020. A total of 82 different keywords were identified in all papers.

Regarding country of origin, most of the publications were from United States and India (both with eight publications, each, comprising 15% of all primary studies), followed by Brazil (six publications, comprising 12% of all primary studies). United Kingdom had four publications, Australia, China, Finland, Iran and Italy, had three publications, followed by Spain with two publications. Germany, Chile, France, Macedonia, Malaysia, Qatar, Sweden, Taiwan, and Ukraine each had one publication. Considering the various different origins, it can be concluded that capacity planning of cloud computing workloads is a globally widespread topic.

The most common keywords used in selected works, with their respective frequency were: cloud computing (13), capacity planning (8), performance model (5), resource management (5), prediction (4), application (3), performance (3), simulation (3), workload (3), auto-scaling (2), big data (2), quality of service (2), resource provisioning (2), web application (2), workload characterization (2). The first two keywords - cloud computing and capacity planning - reflect exactly the subject of this research.

B. *Quality Analysis*

As presented before, all primary studies were assessed considering eight quality aspects to ensure their credibility and relevance to this review. The purpose of this analysis was to establish an objective evaluation that all papers selected could actually contribute to the conclusions of this review. To do that, each quality criteria was classified as positive (1) or negative (0).

Table 3 presents the results of this quality assessment of each one of all 52 selected papers. Columns "Q1" to "Q8" represent all of the criteria defined by questions to evaluate the following aspects of publications: Focus, Research, Objectives, Context, Data Collection, Research Project, Validation and Added Value. As mentioned before, all of the selected papers were marked "1" in both "Focus" and "Added Value" criteria. All studies with negatives answers (0) in one of those two criteria were removed during the selection stage.

TABLE III. QUALITY ANALYSIS OF PRIMARY STUDIES

Study	Q1	Q2	Q3	Q4	Q5	Q6	Q7	Q8	Total
[9]	1	1	1	1	1	0	1	1	88%
[10]	1	1	1	0	1	1	1	1	88%
[11]	1	1	0	1	1	1	1	1	88%
[12]	1	1	1	1	1	1	1	1	100%
[13]	1	1	1	0	1	1	1	1	88%
[14]	1	1	1	0	1	1	1	1	88%
[15]	1	1	0	1	0	1	1	1	75%
[16]	1	1	1	1	0	0	1	1	75%
[17]	1	1	1	1	0	1	1	1	88%
[18]	1	1	0	1	1	1	1	1	88%
[19]	1	1	0	0	1	1	1	1	75%
[20]	1	1	0	1	0	1	0	1	63%
[21]	1	1	0	1	0	1	0	1	63%
[22]	1	1	1	0	0	1	0	1	63%
[23]	1	1	1	0	0	1	1	1	75%
[24]	1	1	0	0	1	1	1	1	75%
[25]	1	1	1	1	0	1	1	1	88%
[26]	1	1	0	1	1	0	1	1	75%
[27]	1	1	0	1	0	1	0	1	63%
[28]	1	1	1	1	1	1	0	1	88%
[29]	1	1	1	1	1	1	1	1	100%
[30]	1	1	0	1	1	0	1	1	75%
[31]	1	1	1	1	1	1	1	1	100%
[32]	1	1	1	1	0	1	1	1	88%
[33]	1	1	1	1	0	1	1	1	88%

Study	Q1	Q2	Q3	Q4	Q5	Q6	Q7	Q8	Total
[34]	1	1	0	1	0	1	0	1	63%
[35]	1	1	0	1	0	1	0	1	63%
[36]	1	1	0	1	1	1	0	1	75%
[37]	1	1	0	1	1	1	0	1	75%
[38]	1	1	1	0	1	1	1	1	88%
[39]	1	1	1	0	1	1	1	1	88%
[40]	1	1	1	0	0	0	1	1	63%
[41]	1	1	1	1	0	0	1	1	75%
[42]	1	1	1	1	1	0	1	1	88%
[43]	1	1	1	1	1	0	1	1	88%
[44]	1	1	1	1	0	1	1	1	88%
[45]	1	1	1	1	1	1	0	1	88%
[46]	1	1	1	1	1	0	1	1	88%
[47]	1	1	1	1	1	0	1	1	88%
[48]	1	1	1	1	1	0	1	1	88%
[49]	1	1	1	1	0	0	1	1	75%
[50]	1	1	1	1	1	1	1	1	100%
[51]	1	1	1	1	1	1	1	1	100,00%
[52]	1	1	1	1	1	1	1	1	100%
[53]	1	1	1	1	1	1	1	1	100%
[54]	1	1	1	1	1	0	1	1	88%
[55]	1	1	1	0	1	1	0	1	75%
[56]	1	1	1	0	1	1	0	1	75%
[57]	1	1	1	1	1	1	1	1	100%
[58]	1	1	1	1	1	1	1	1	100%
[59]	1	1	1	1	1	1	1	1	100%
[60]	1	1	1	1	1	1	1	1	100%

All of the papers that were analyzed in this review provided information on the research method, adding an important value regarding its relationship with the scientific method. Considering that all studies applied some sort of formal research method, all criteria scored above 70%, except one where data collection scored 67%. Even so, this lack of clarity as to the methods of data collection in some of the works does not generally compromise the quality of the selected papers.

VI. Discussion

After performing the search, data extraction and synthesis of primary studies, the authors were able to identify some patterns regarding capacity planning of cloud computing workloads. At first, it was possible to conclude that cloud computing - and the process of capacity planning for workloads running on cloud - is a very recent field of research and also subject to a lot of entropy, given the characteristic of being fast evolving within computer science.

It is also possible to conclude that there is a lack of standardization of capacity planning methods for cloud computing workloads and methods that are not intensive on historical use data. This was identified after the classification of primary studies in a parallel to research questions - that covers both aspects mentioned previously. The majority of studies applied historical use data to predict future resource demands for a specific type of workload - such as IoT (Internet of Things) solutions, database and so forth - using machine learning and artificial intelligence techniques.

A. Cloud Capacity Planning models

Capacity planning is a process that is not applied only in the field of computer science. Most engineering sciences - or any field that works with limited resources - need to address how to manage and properly apply resources to meet changing and constant evolving demands.

As such, in cloud computing environments, in which resources are offered as services, they are considered as practically infinite - as long as the customer pays for it. Capacity planning models are being applied to manage how to use resources efficiently and in a well architected way.

This research has found that although scientific literature covers formal methods to perform capacity planning for cloud computing workloads, there is no standardization regarding inputs and outputs, processes and generalization, to cover broader scenarios and types of workloads.

B. Cloud Capacity Planning models for cloud computing workloads with no historical use

An important finding of this review was that most of capacity planning methods for cloud computing workloads consider historical data use for understanding demands needs and for planning. This empirical approach shows some efficiency – especially when using historical data as an input for prediction models – but it often fails to deliver a higher percentage of assertiveness on new workloads. Another gap on this type of approach is that when performing capacity planning for an unprecedented type of workload – such as innovative or disruptive software – whereby there is no historical data for that workload; this leads current methods to apply a benchmark as input for those prediction models, decreasing percentage of assertiveness on capacity planning metrics for new or unprecedented workloads.

C. Cloud Capacity Planning models based on type of workloads and architectural characteristic

Scientific literature analyzed in this review showed that there are methods to perform capacity planning for specific types of workloads – such as IoT, database, fog computing and so forth. However, those models vary widely in their method, calculations, and, especially, assertiveness.

In this sense, this systematic review has not found generalist models which could cover capacity planning broadly and which could also consider specific characteristics of different types of workloads. The authors believe that standardization and generalization in the method would enhance scientific evolution for capacity planning of cloud computing workloads.

D. *Towards Cloud Capacity Planning*

As presented previously, one of the main challenges of working with cloud computing environments is how to properly plan and calculate the amount of resources needed for a specific set of workload. Besides the use of historical data as major input to predict resource demands and the absence of generalist models for capacity planning, our study found another set of challenges:

- Standardization: The lack of standards in gathering and provisioning capacity planning models makes reuse difficult;
- Assertiveness: Although current models deliver some capacity planning metrics, those calculations often fail to deliver a high percentage of assertiveness to define resource needs;
- Generalization: Most of current models address specific types of workloads, and do not cover a more generalist workload based on its architecture, for instance.

VII. CONCLUSION

This systematic review focuses on mapping and identifying studies that aim to establish a formal process for capacity planning of cloud computing workloads. In the search phase, 504 papers were found, of which 52 were classified as primary studies, following applied selection and quality criteria.

All papers were classified considering their focus on answering the research questions. After this stage, a quality analysis was performed to access how the papers addressed eight different quality criteria, as this method was applied to ensure that each study covered formal scientific methods and covered relevant aspects of this systematic review.

In regards to the aspects of capacity planning, the majority of studies covered some type of formal method to perform capacity planning of cloud computing workloads. Most of them focused on historical data use to somehow predict future resource demands. To do that, machine learning and artificial intelligence techniques were generally applied. Another important aspect in parallel to research questions is that no general method or framework was found to cover different type of workloads - although there are methods to perform cloud capacity planning for specific workloads, as mentioned before, each method however establishes a different approach and is focused in analyzing a specific type of workload.

In order to expand the results found and to improve the conclusions of this systematic review, some considerations about the limitations of this study need to be highlighted:

- Perhaps considering a wider period of publications - more than 3 years of publishing - even the great entropy of the subject;
- Apply search strings that include more keywords with terms related to the object of this research, such as "Resource Management";
- Look for capacity planning challenges in other science and engineering references, given that resource-limited scenarios is a characteristic not only present in computer science.

For future work and further research, it would be important to analyze specifically capacity planning methods that do not apply historical data use - considering that not all software projects have a precedent of use, such as for innovative and disruptive software - and also to cover different types of workloads - since current methods aim to analyze specific types of cloud computing workloads.

REFERENCES

[1] P. Jamshidi, A. Ahmad, and C. Pahl, "Cloud Migration Research: A Systematic Review," IEEE Trans. Cloud Comput., vol. 1, no. 2, pp. 142–157, 2013, [Online]. Available: https://ulir.ul.ie/bitstream/handle/10344/3656/Jamshid_cloud.pdf?sequence=2.

[2] S. Bhardwaj, L. Jain, and S. Jain, "Cloud Computing : a Study of Infrastructure As a Service (Iaas)," Int. J. Eng., vol. 2, no. 1, pp. 60–63, 2010, [Online]. Available: http://ijeit.org/index_files/vol2no1/CLOUD COMPUTING A STUDY OF.pdf.

[3] L. Wang et al., "Cloud computing: A perspective study," New Gener. Comput., vol. 28, no. 2, pp. 137–146, 2010, doi: 10.1007/s00354-008-0081-5.

[4] W. Hasselbring and S. Frey, "Model-Based Migration of Legacy Software Systems to Scalable and Resource-Efficient Cloud-Based Applications: The CloudMIG Approach," First Int. Conf. Cloud Comput. GRIDs, Virtualization Model., no. c, pp. 155–158, 2010.

[5] S. Sheshadhri and R, Nithiya, "Mapping multi-tier architecture into cloud environment using slicing and virtualization," 40th IRF Int. Conf., pp. 6–10, 2016.

[6] N. Gunther, Guerrilla capacity planning: A tactical approach to planning for highly scalable applications and services. Springer, 2007.

[7] Barbara A. and Kitchenham. Systematic review in software engineering: where we are and where we should be going. In Proceedings of the 2nd international workshop on Evidential assessment of software technologies. Association for Computing Machinery, New York, NY, USA, September, 2012, 1–2. DOI:https://doi.org/10.1145/2372233.2372235

[8] T. Dybå and T. Dingsøyr, "Empirical studies of agile software development: A systematic review," Inf. Softw. Technol., vol. 50, no. 9, pp. 833–859, 2008, doi: https://doi.org/10.1016/j.infsof.2008.01.006.

[9] W. Iqbal, A. Erradi, and A. Mahmood, "Dynamic workload patterns prediction for proactive auto-scaling of web applications," J. Netw. Comput. Appl., vol. 124, pp. 94–107, 2018, doi: https://doi.org/10.1016/j.jnca.2018.09.023.

[10] M. Amiri and L. Mohammad-Khanli, "Survey on prediction models of applications for resources provisioning in cloud," J. Netw. Comput. Appl., vol. 82, pp. 93–113,

2017, doi: https://doi.org/10.1016/j.jnca.2017.01.016.
[11] M. Amiri, L. Mohammad-Khanli, and R. Mirandola, "A sequential pattern mining model for application workload prediction in cloud environment," J. Netw. Comput. Appl., vol. 105, pp. 21–62, 2018, doi: https://doi.org/10.1016/j.jnca.2017.12.015.
[12] V. de N. Personé and A. Di Lonardo, "Approximating finite resources: An approach based on MVA," Perform. Eval., vol. 131, pp. 1–21, 2019, doi: https://doi.org/10.1016/j.peva.2018.11.005.
[13] J. O. de Carvalho, F. Trinta, D. Vieira, and O. A. C. Cortes, "Evolutionary solutions for resources management in multiple clouds: State-of-the-art and future directions," Futur. Gener. Comput. Syst., vol. 88, pp. 284–296, 2018, doi: https://doi.org/10.1016/j.future.2018.05.087.
[14] R. Tolosana-Calasanz, J. Á. Bañares, and J.-M. Colom, "Model-driven development of data intensive applications over cloud resources," Futur. Gener. Comput. Syst., vol. 87, pp. 888–909, 2018, doi: https://doi.org/10.1016/j.future.2017.12.046.
[15] K.-J. Wang and P. H. Nguyen, "Capacity planning with technology replacement by stochastic dynamic programming," Eur. J. Oper. Res., vol. 260, no. 2, pp. 739–750, 2017, doi: https://doi.org/10.1016/j.ejor.2016.12.046.
[16] M. Zakarya and L. Gillam, "Modelling resource heterogeneities in cloud simulations and quantifying their accuracy," Simul. Model. Pract. Theory, vol. 94, pp. 43–65, 2019, doi: https://doi.org/10.1016/j.simpat.2019.02.003.
[17] M. Amiri, L. Mohammad-Khanli, and R. Mirandola, "An online learning model based on episode mining for workload prediction in cloud," Futur. Gener. Comput. Syst., vol. 87, pp. 83–101, 2018, doi: https://doi.org/10.1016/j.future.2018.04.044.
[18] V. Medel, R. Tolosana-Calasanz, J. Á. Bañares, U. Arronategui, and O. F. Rana, "Characterising resource management performance in Kubernetes," Comput. Electr. Eng., vol. 68, pp. 286–297, 2018, doi: https://doi.org/10.1016/j.compeleceng.2018.03.041.
[19] M. S. Aslanpour, M. Ghobaei-Arani, and A. Nadjaran Toosi, "Auto-scaling web applications in clouds: A cost-aware approach," J. Netw. Comput. Appl., vol. 95, pp. 26–41, 2017, doi: https://doi.org/10.1016/j.jnca.2017.07.012.
[20] B. Treynor, M. Dahlin, V. Rau, and B. Beyer, "The calculus of service availability," Commun. ACM, vol. 60, no. 9, pp. 42–47, Aug. 2017, doi: 10.1145/3080202.
[21] A. Kiani, N. Ansari, and A. Khreishah, "Hierarchical Capacity Provisioning for Fog Computing," IEEE/ACM Trans. Netw., vol. 27, no. 3, pp. 962–971, 2019, doi: 10.1109/TNET.2019.2906638.
[22] S. R. Shishira, A. Kandasamy, and K. Chandrasekaran, "Workload Characterization: Survey of Current Approaches and Research Challenges," in Proceedings of the 7th International Conference on Computer and Communication Technology, 2017, pp. 151–156, doi: 10.1145/3154979.3155003.
[23] M. Ciavotta, E. Gianniti, and D. Ardagna, "Capacity Allocation for Big Data Applications in the Cloud," in Proceedings of the 8th ACM/SPEC on International Conference on Performance Engineering Companion, 2017, pp. 175–176, doi: 10.1145/3053600.3053630.
[24] J. C. Mogul, R. Isaacs, and B. Welch, "Thinking about Availability in Large Service Infrastructures," in Proceedings of the 16th Workshop on Hot Topics in Operating Systems, 2017, pp. 12–17, doi: 10.1145/3102980.3102983.
[25] J. Ericson, M. Mohammadian, and F. Santana, "Analysis of Performance Variability in Public Cloud Computing," in 2017 IEEE International Conference on Information Reuse and Integration (IRI), 2017, pp. 308–314.
[26] I. Stypsanelli, O. Brun, S. Medjiah, and B. J. Prabhu, "Capacity Planning of Fog Computing Infrastructures under Probabilistic Delay Guarantees," in 2019 IEEE International Conference on Fog Computing (ICFC), 2019, pp. 185–194.
[27] M. Torquato, L. Torquato, P. Maciel, and M. Vieira, "IaaS Cloud Availability Planning using Models and Genetic Algorithms," in 2019 9th Latin-American Symposium on Dependable Computing (LADC), 2019, pp. 1–10.
[28] O. Biran et al., "Heterogeneous Resource Reservation," in 2018 IEEE International Conference on Cloud Engineering (IC2E), 2018, pp. 141–147.
[29] L. Tang and H. Chen, "Joint Pricing and Capacity Planning in the IaaS Cloud Market," IEEE Trans. Cloud Comput., vol. 5, no. 1, pp. 57–70, 2017.
[30] R. Vaze, "Online Knapsack Problem Under Expected Capacity Constraint," in IEEE INFOCOM 2018 - IEEE Conference on Computer Communications, 2018, pp. 2159–2167.
[31] B. Xia, T. Li, Q. Zhou, Q. Li, and H. Zhang, "An Effective Classification-based Framework for Predicting Cloud Capacity Demand in Cloud Services," IEEE Trans. Serv. Comput., p. 1, 2018.
[32] C. Melo, R. Matos, J. Dantas, and P. Maciel, "Capacity-Oriented Availability Model for Resources Estimation on Private Cloud Infrastructure," in 2017 IEEE 22nd Pacific Rim International Symposium on Dependable Computing (PRDC), 2017, pp. 255–260.
[33] M. Noreikis, Y. Xiao, and A. Ylä-Jaäiski, "QoS-oriented capacity planning for edge computing," in 2017 IEEE International Conference on Communications (ICC), 2017, pp. 1–6.
[34] K. N. Kumar and R. Mitra, "Resource Allocation for Heterogeneous Cloud Computing Using Weighted Fair-Share Queues," in 2018 IEEE International Conference on Cloud Computing in Emerging Markets (CCEM), 2018, pp. 31–38.
[35] T. P. Roseline, C. J. M. Tauro, and M. Miranda, "An approach for efficient capacity management in a cloud," in 2017 IEEE International Conference on Current Trends in Advanced Computing (ICCTAC), 2017, pp. 1–6.
[36] K. M. Maiyama, D. Kouvatsos, B. Mohammed, M.

Kiran, and M. A. Kamala, "Performance Modelling and Analysis of an OpenStack IaaS Cloud Computing Platform," in 2017 IEEE 5th International Conference on Future Internet of Things and Cloud (FiCloud), 2017, pp. 198–205.

[37] H. A. Kholidy, "An Intelligent Swarm Based Prediction Approach For Predicting Cloud Computing User Resource Needs," Comput. Commun., vol. 151, pp. 133–144, 2020, doi: https://doi.org/10.1016/j.comcom.2019.12.028.

[38] M. Liaqat et al., "Federated cloud resource management: Review and discussion," J. Netw. Comput. Appl., vol. 77, pp. 87–105, 2017, doi: https://doi.org/10.1016/j.jnca.2016.10.008.

[39] V. K. Prasad, M. Shah, N. Patel, and M. Bhavsar, "Inspection of Trust Based Cloud Using Security and Capacity Management at an IaaS Level," Procedia Comput. Sci., vol. 132, pp. 1280–1289, 2018, doi: https://doi.org/10.1016/j.procs.2018.05.044.

[40] N. Sadashiv, S. M. Dilip Kumar, and R. S. Goudar, "Cloud capacity planning and HSI based optimal resource provisioning," in 2017 Second International Conference on Electrical, Computer and Communication Technologies (ICECCT), 2017, pp. 1–6.

[41] M. Noreikis, Y. Xiao, and Y. Jiang, "Edge Capacity Planning for Real Time Compute-Intensive Applications," in 2019 IEEE International Conference on Fog Computing (ICFC), 2019, pp. 175–184.

[42] S. Gupta and D. A. Dinesh, "Online adaptation models for resource usage prediction in cloud network," in 2017 Twenty-third National Conference on Communications (NCC), 2017, pp. 1–6.

[43] C. Verbowski, E. Thayer, P. Costa, H. Leather, and B. Franke, "Right-Sizing Server Capacity Headroom for Global Online Services," in 2018 IEEE 38th International Conference on Distributed Computing Systems (ICDCS), 2018, pp. 645–659.

[44] C. H. G. Ferreira et al., "A Low Cost Workload Generation Approach through the Cloud for Capacity Planning in Service-Oriented Systems," 2017, doi: 10.1145/3018896.3018900.

[45] D. Ardagna et al., "Performance Prediction of Cloud-Based Big Data Applications," in Proceedings of the 2018 ACM/SPEC International Conference on Performance Engineering, 2018, pp. 192–199, doi: 10.1145/3184407.3184420.

[46] J. C. Christopher, "Analytics Environments on Demand: Providing Interactive and Scalable Research Computing with Windows," 2017, doi: 10.1145/3093338.3093369.

[47] M. Marin, V. Gil-Costa, A. Inostrosa-Psijas, and C. Bonacic, "Hybrid capacity planning methodology for web search engines," Simul. Model. Pract. Theory, vol. 93, pp. 148–163, 2019, doi: https://doi.org/10.1016/j.simpat.2018.09.016.

[48] A. Brunnert and H. Krcmar, "Continuous performance evaluation and capacity planning using resource profiles for enterprise applications," J. Syst. Softw., vol. 123, pp. 239–262, 2017, doi: https://doi.org/10.1016/j.jss.2015.08.030.

[49] T. Le Duc, R. G. Leiva, P. Casari, and P.-O. Östberg, "Machine Learning Methods for Reliable Resource Provisioning in Edge-Cloud Computing: A Survey," ACM Comput. Surv., vol. 52, no. 5, 2019, doi: 10.1145/3341145.

[50] S. K. Moghaddam, R. Buyya, and K. Ramamohanarao, "Performance-Aware Management of Cloud Resources: A Taxonomy and Future Directions," ACM Comput. Surv., vol. 52, no. 4, 2019, doi: 10.1145/3337956.

[51] D. Irwin and B. Urgaonkar, "Research Challenges at the Intersection of Cloud Computing and Economics," National Science Foundation, USA, 2018.

[52] P. Mitrevski, F. Mitrevski, and M. Gusev, "A Decade Time-Lapse of Cloud Performance and Dependability Modeling: Performability Evaluation Framework," 2019, doi: 10.1145/3320326.3320400.

[53] R. Han et al., "Workload-Adaptive Configuration Tuning for Hierarchical Cloud Schedulers," IEEE Trans. Parallel Distrib. Syst., vol. 30, no. 12, pp. 2879–2895, 2019.

[54] P. Östberg et al., "Reliable capacity provisioning for distributed cloud/edge/fog computing applications," in 2017 European Conference on Networks and Communications (EuCNC), 2017, pp. 1–6.

[55] M. Carvalho, D. A. Menascé, and F. Brasileiro, "Capacity planning for IaaS cloud providers offering multiple service classes," Futur. Gener. Comput. Syst., vol. 77, pp. 97–111, 2017, doi: https://doi.org/10.1016/j.future.2017.07.019.

[56] K. C. Anupama, R. Nagaraja, and M. Jaiganesh, "A Perspective view of Resource-based Capacity planning in Cloud computing," in 2019 1st International Conference on Advances in Information Technology (ICAIT), 2019, pp. 358–363.

[57] M. Carvalho et al., "Multi-Dimensional Admission Control and Capacity Planning for IaaS Clouds with Multiple Service Classes," in Proceedings of the 17th IEEE/ACM International Symposium on Cluster, Cloud and Grid Computing, 2017, pp. 160–169, doi: 10.1109/CCGRID.2017.14.

[58] E. Zharikov, O. Rolik, and S. Telenyk, "An integrated approach to cloud data center resource management," in 2017 4th International Scientific-Practical Conference Problems of Infocommunications. Science and Technology (PIC S T), 2017, pp. 211–218.

[59] R. I. Cartwright and B. Gilmer, "The Infinite Capacity Media Machine," SMPTE Motion Imaging J., vol. 128, no. 9, pp. 1–7, 2019.

[60] B. T. Sloss, S. Nukala, and V. Rau, "Metrics That Matter," Queue, vol. 62, no. 4, p. 88, 2018, doi: 10.1145/3305263.3309571.

[61] Elsevier Mendeley Tool. Available at https://www.mendeley.com/

An Architectural Smell Evaluation in an Industrial Context

Francesca Arcelli Fontana
University of Milano-Bicocca
Milano, Italy
email: arcelli@disco.unimib.it

Federico Locatelli
Anoki
Milano, Italy
email: f.locatelli@anoki.it

Ilaria Pigazzini
University of Milano-Bicocca
Milano, Italy
email: i.pigazzini@campus.unimib.it

Paolo Mereghetti
Anoki
Milano, Italy
email: p.mereghetti@anoki.it

***Abstract*—A known symptom of architectural erosion is the presence of architectural smells in software systems. They are the result of design decisions which negatively impact on software quality, and may lead to what is called Architectural Technical Debt. When such problems arise, developers feel difficulties in maintaining and evolving their architectures. Some tools have been developed to automatically identify architectural smells and in this study we propose the evaluation of architecture erosion in an industrial context through Arcan, an analysis tool able to identify eight architectural smells. In particular, we report the results of an industrial case study born from the collaboration between a Laboratory of the University of Milano-Bicocca and an italian company active in the software consulting field. The study has been structured as a survey on the architectural smells detected by the tool, from which we collected the feedback and opinions of the three projects' developers. Developers learned about architectural smells and became aware of the fact that their project had additional problems with respect to what they knew. We propose this work as a pilot for future works on the perception of AS in industrial context.**

Keywords–Architectural Smells; Architectural Debt; Industrial study; Refactoring; Criticality.

I. INTRODUCTION

Architectural Smells (AS) are design decision which negatively impact on software quality. They represent the main source of investigation in order to evaluate and manage architectural debt [1][2]. While code smells [3], in particular some of them (such as Large Class, Long Methods, Duplicate Code) are all well known from the developer/practitioner perspective, architectural smells are not so well known. Developers are often unaware of these smells, and they focus their attention on short term tasks, such as bug fixing and other code level issues. They are not aware of the possible accumulating debt due to the presence of architectural smells in their projects.

In order to better investigate how architectural smells are perceived by the developers, we describe in this work an evaluation we performed in an industrial context on the detection and perception of architectural smells by the developers/practitioners. With this purpose, we started a collaboration between the Evolution of Software Systems and Reverse Engineering Laboratory (ESSeRE Lab) of the University of Milano Bicocca [4] and the Anoki company in Milano [5]. The architectural smells considered in this evaluation are those currently recognized by the Arcan tool [6] developed by the ESSeRE Lab. The developers of the company received material and explanations on the considered architectural smells. Then we proposed a survey with different questions that they had to answer related to each instance of the inspected smells.

Through this study we aim to answer the following Research Questions:

RQ1: How are architectural smells perceived in an industrial context? With the answer to this question we aim to investigate whether the concept of AS is known and whether developers perceive them as problems with some kind of impact on software quality attributes. We are also interested in exploring other possible smells/problems present in the analyzed project considered harmful by developers, in order to improve the Arcan tool with new detectors.

RQ2: What practitioners suggest according to the refactoring of the smells? The effort required to fix AS, such as Cyclic Dependency, is higher than fixing a code smell [3], because it implies to move/modify both methods and classes of a system [7]. For this reason, we aim to investigate the opinion of the developers about the possible actions to be taken regarding the refactoring of the AS.

RQ3: Which are the most critical smells according to the practitioners perception? We aim to identify the smells perceived as most critical according to the evaluation of the interviewees. This information could be useful during software development by trying to avoid them and remove them first, since the most critical smells could lead to a progressive architecture degradation.

Moreover, with our study we aimed to reach further goals related to the validation of the Arcan tool, namely: *The evaluation of 8 different types of architectural smells* detected by Arcan through the feedback of the developers of the company, which could provide also useful hints to enhance the AS detection strategies and the possible definitions of new metrics (severities) able to discriminate the different smells by their criticality and *Additional feedback* on the possible usefulness of architectural smell detection, as the one outlined by the practitioners, related to the migration towards a microservice architecture.

The paper is organized through the following sections: in Section 2 we describe some related work, in Section 3 we introduce the AS considered during this evaluation, in Section 4 we describe the study design and the different questions used in the survey, in Section 5 we outline the main results, in Section 6 the lessons learned and in Section 7 the threats to validity. Finally, in Section 8 we report the answers to our RQ, the conclusions and future developments.

II. RELATED WORK

Several works have been done on the evaluation of code smells or other kind of code violations in collaboration with practitioners, such as for example a survey on code smells performed by Yamashita et al. [8] which outlines that a large proportion of developers did not know about code smells. A study of Soh et al. [9] where professionals were hired to perform maintenance tasks in order to assess whether code smells affect maintenance activities. Palomba et al. [10] conducted a study on developer's perception of the nature and severity of code smells. Tahir et al. [11] investigated how developers discuss code smells and anti-patterns across three technical Stack Exchange sites.

Few works focused on the evaluation of AS, in particular in an industrial context through the feedback of the developers/practitioners. Arcelli et al. [6] evaluate the precision of the detection results provided by the Arcan tool on the detection of three smells in two industrial projects. Wu et al. [12] present their experience in using a software architecture measurement standard through a collaboration with a company to evaluate, measure, and improve the architectures of their software products. Mo et al. [13] report their experiences of applying three complementary automated software architecture analysis techniques, in some industrial projects. Pigazzini et al. [14] describe an approach based on AS detection and topic detection for the migration towards a microservice architecture in an industrial case study, where the developer provided also several feedbacks on the usefulness of the AS detection during the migration steps.

In a previous study [2], we conducted an in-depth investigation on the identification and prioritization of architectural debt in an industrial context through a survey, interviews and inspection of the code with the practitioners of an industry in Sweden. With respect to this work, in this study we consider a larger number of smells, eight smells instead of three, the developers evaluated a higher number of instances of smells, the previous detection rules of the three smells have been improved and the survey has been changed through the introduction of new questions.

III. ARCHITECTURAL SMELLS

We consider eight AS, which correspond to the currently detected smells by the Arcan tool [6] on Java *components* i.e. classes and/or packages:

Cyclic Dependency (CD): refers to a component that is involved in a chain of relations that break the desirable acyclic nature of a component dependency structure. Arcan detects this smell on classes (CD-C) and packages (CD-P) and according to different shapes as those described by Al-Mutawa et al. [15].

Hub-Like Dependency (HL): occurs when a component has (outgoing and ingoing) dependencies with a large number of other components [7]. This smell is detected on both classes (HL-C) and packages (HL-P).

Unstable Dependency (UD): describes a component that depends on other components that are less stable than itself, with a possible ripple effect of changes in the system [16]. This smell is detected on packages.

God Component (GC): occurs when a component is excessively large either in terms of Lines Of Code (LOC) or number of classes [17]. This smell is detected on packages.

Dense Structure (DS): arises when components in a project have excessive and dense dependencies without any particular structure i.e. without following a specific architectural design [18]. This smell is detected on the entire project under analysis and occurs when the density (the ratio of dependencies over the components) of the project is high. Hence, only one instance can be detected per single project.

Feature Concentration (FC): occurs when an architectural component implements different functionalities in a single design construct [19]. This smell is detected on packages.

Insufficient Package Cohesion (IPC): occurs when an architectural component has low internal cohesion [18]. This smell is detected on packages.

Scattered Functionality (SF): describes a system where multiple components are responsible for realizing the same high-level concern and, additionally, some of those components are responsible for orthogonal concerns [20]. For *concern*, we mean a software system's role, responsibility, concept, or purpose [21]. This smell is detected on packages.

We considered the above AS because they violate different design principles, so that we can ask for developer feedback on different kinds of architectural problems. In particular, CD, HL, UD and DS are based on dependency issues: dependencies are of great importance in software architecture and components that are highly coupled and with a high number of dependencies are considered more critical, since they have higher maintenance costs. GC and IPC smell violate the modularity principle; finally FC and SF violate the separation of concerns principle [21].

Arcan bases all its computations on the **dependency graph** which is the representation of the project under analysis in form of a directed graph. The basic nodes represent the system entities, such as Java classes, packages and methods. Edges represent the relationships among the various entities. We exploit the graph to detect all the smells which affect the dependencies, e.g., Cyclic Dependency smell, which is caused by the presence of circular dependencies in the graph. However, some smells need other kinds of information in order to be detected, for instance the Feature Concentration and Scattered Functionality smells regard how system features are organized inside a project. Hence, Arcan is also able to generate the **feature graph**, whose aim is to represent the *features* (as synonym of concerns) that can be associated to the different parts of the system architecture. The feature graph associates a name in natural language to a set of project files, enabling developers to *read* how features are disposed across the project. Both Arcan graphs can be stored in the Neo4j [22] graph database, which we exploit also to visualize them.

IV. CASE STUDY DESIGN

In this study, a survey with different questions was given to the practitioners in order to obtain meaningful data on the AS listed in Section III. The practitioners were three and they were all developers belonging to the team that was working on the analyzed project at the time the survey was proposed. The first one was a junior developer with 4 years of experience working on the project analysed in this study. The second one was a middle developer with 9 and a half years of experience of which 1 year and a half spent working on the project. The third one, the team leader, was a senior developer with almost 15 years of experience working on the project for 2 years. We now describe the steps followed in the case study:

1) During a meeting at the company, one of the author introduced the practitioners to the notion of AS by explaining them what they are and why it is important to identify and refactor them. In the same meeting, Arcan and its principal functionalities have been introduced.

2) We then sent them a document containing the detailed descriptions of all the AS detected by Arcan, including a description on how Arcan detects them, the metric thresholds and formulas used for the detection. We gave them a week to read (during their normal work at the company) the document and study the AS meaning and relevance.

3) After that time, we instructed them on how to properly answer the questions of the survey, by briefly explaining the different categories and meaning of the questions.

4) We exploited the Google Form tool to create the survey. We provided the URLs to access it and we assigned 15 days to answer all the questions.

The survey contains 12 questions that the three practitioners had to answer individually for each AS instance. In particular, 19 AS instances were presented. For each instance, we provided the description of the smell type it refers to and we contextualized it by reporting all classes/packages affected by the smell. We also attached a visual representation of the smell with the dependency graph thanks to the Neo4j graph visualizer used by Arcan[23]. We presented 19 instances because we selected for each type of AS the ones that, in our opinion, were the most interesting, trying also to include instances with different granularity (for CD and HL) and different characteristics (for IPC, FC and GC). We call *smell characteristics* the smell properties that can be measured by a metric. For IPC we measure the Lack of Component Cohesion (LCC) [24], which is a metric ranging in $(0, 1]$, where 1 corresponds to packages with a complete lack of cohesion. For SF and FC we consider the number of features inside packages. For GC we compute the number of classes in a package and the LCC metric.

We assume that according to the different characteristics, AS can have different *criticalities* intended as the severity and effort needed to remove them: in this paper we also study if the perceived AS severity has a relation with such characteristics. Table III in Section V contains all the instances considered for each AS. We decided to analyse a greater number of instances for the new smells that we did not evaluate in previous works [6][25].

A. Analyzed Project

The analyzed project is a Business Management System written in Java with a monolithic architecture, but the developers are interested in a migration towards a microservices one. Table I reports the project's metrics and the number of AS instances detected by Arcan on it. The analyzed project

TABLE I. ANALYZED PROJECTS METRICS AND ARCHITECTURAL SMELLS

metrics		**architectural smells**									
NOC	NOP	#CD (classes)	#CD (package)	#HL (classes)	#HL (package)	#UD	#GC	#DS	#IPC	#FC	#SF
1343	112	135	5	3	3	19	10	1	107	4	81

is 10 years old and can be considered a medium-large project with 1343 classes and 112 packages. Arcan detected a total of 367 smell instances of which mostly are Cyclic Dependency between classes (135), Insufficient Package Cohesion (107) and Scattered Functionality (81), while smells like Hub-Like (3) and Feature Concentration (4) are much less present.

B. Data Collection through the Survey

The questions asked to the developers in the survey are reported in Table II. Each question aims to gather the developer's evaluation on specific aspects of the analyzed AS, that is particularly valuable considering their deep knowledge on the project. The proposed questions can be grouped by category:

AS detection and awareness $[Q1 - Q3, Q12]$: this set of questions aim to evaluate the precision of the Arcan detection strategies and investigate the awareness of the developers on the presence of the smells.

AS impact$[Q5-Q6]$: these questions aim to collect information about the perceived impact of AS on different software quality attributes.

AS refactoring$[Q7 - Q9]$: such questions gather information about whether refactoring activities, in the opinion of the developers, should be conducted and the type of refactoring needed to remove the smell.

AS severity, refactoring effort and priority$[Q4, Q10 - Q11]$: these questions aim to evaluate the effort/time needed to apply the refactoring and understand whether the smells can be ranked depending on their criticality (severity), i.e. if it is possible to quantify the smell impact thanks to the evaluation of specific smell characteristics, e.g., smell size (the number of affected classes/packages). To evaluate the answers of these questions, we define and compute three metrics (see section 5 for more details on the metrics computation), namely *Average Severity* of the smells, i.e., the average criticality that developers' associate to the smells, the *Average Effort* needed to refactor the smells and the *Average Priority of refactoring* that can be associated to the smells, i.e., the ordering of the smells depending on which should be refactored first. We chose to compute these values in order to summarize the collected data and be able to compare them.

The proposed questions are of three types: binary questions, where the possible answers are Yes or No; closed-ended questions, with multiple possible answers and open-ended questions, which were optional because we did not want to force the practitioners to spend too much time on them and, in some cases, no answer was needed, e.g., Q3 if the smell instance is considered as a problem by the practitioner. In this way we were able to collect both quantitative and qualitative answers, in particular the latter allowed us to gain insights about the concrete opinions of the practitioners.

V. RESULTS

After an accurate analysis of the answers submitted by the practitioners, significant results were extracted and reported in Table III and Table IV. The collected data reported in this section will be exploited to answer the RQs.

A. AS detection and awareness

One of the information we aimed to obtain from this case study was the classification of each AS instance in true positive or false positive. A smell instance discovered by Arcan was classified as true positive if most of the developers asserted that it is an actual issue/problem in the system, otherwise, it

TABLE II. PROPOSED QUESTIONS

ID	Question	Possible Choices
Q1	Does the reported smell represent a problem in the system?	Yes or No
Q2	Were you aware of the presence of this smell in the system?	Yes or No
Q3	If it's not a problem, do you think that this could be a case of false positive AS? Or an AS not critical? For which reasons?	N/A (open-response)
Q4	How significant are the negative impacts caused by the smell in your opinion?	**0** - Not a problem **1** - Low severity **2** - Mid-Low severity **3** - Mid-High severity **4** - High severity
Q5	If it has negative impacts, which of the following software internal qualities has this type of smell an impact on?	• Reliability (R) • Efficiency (E) • Security (S) • Maintainability (M) • Other
Q6	If not removed, the impact of this type of smell get worse as time passes	**0** - Disagree **1** - Somewhat Disagree **2** - Somewhat Agree **3** - Agree
Q7	What refactoring would you suggest to conduct? (e.g. move class, extract class, extract components, extract layers, etc.. Take in consideration your best option only)	N/A (open-response)
Q8	Do you think that conducting the refactoring would create negative side-effects? If yes which ones?	N/A (open-response)
Q9	If no refactoring should be conducted, which is the reasons?	• Not a real AS (false positive) • The smell does not represent a problem because there is not a better solution • The removal of this smell is too expensive • Other
Q10	How much effort/time can be required to refactor the smell?	**0** - No refactoring needed **1** - Low (< 8 h) **2** - Mid-Low (8-50 h) **3** - Mid-High (50-100 h) **4** - High (>100 h)
Q11	What do you think is the overall priority of refactoring this smell?	**0** - No refactoring needed **1** - Low priority **2** - Mid-Low priority **3** - Mid-High priority **4** - High priority
Q12	There is any architectural issue that you know is present in the system, but was not treated in this survey? If there is, describe it briefly	N/A (open-response)

was classified as false positive. The related questions are Q1 and Q3, but in some cases the answers given by a developer to these questions were incoherent, so we considered as more relevant answer the one provided for Q3 because it is an open answer question. **Among all the 19 AS instances presented in this survey, only 6 were classified as false positives, for an overall precision equals to** 70%. The AS with the higher rate of false positives are the HL on Package with 1/1 and SF with 2/3, while only 2/4 of GC and 1/4 of IPC are false positives. All the other AS instances have been indicated as true positives.

The developers explained also why some instances were false positives, i.e., real smells present in the code which do not represent a problem, in their opinion. For example, some false positives are special cases: the Hub-Like Dependency on Packages instance was detected on a package that contains utility classes which "are supposed to be used by classes of any kind", as stated by the developers; one of the God Component was detected on a package that contains many classes hierarchically organized in that package to avoid *boilerplate code* (sections of code that have to be included in many places with little or no alteration [26]) as declared by the practitioners. Regarding Scattered Functionality, only one of them was considered a true positive: this kind of smell is meant to point out defects in a package-by-feature [27] organization which is desirable in some cases, but not when the actual design is layered, as the project analyzed in this study. Developers got aware of that and signaled it to us, except for the case they considered true. Consequently, they also indicated this type of smell as the less critical, meaning that on their architecture the detected instances do not cause harm.

Another information we acknowledged from the answers to question Q2 was the **awareness of the developers regarding the considered AS**. One developer declared that he/she was already aware of the presence of 15 out of 19 (78%) smell instances, while the others 8 out of 19 (42%) and 5 out of 19 (26%). This information points out that the analysis with Arcan allowed them to discover some smells they were not aware of. Finally, we asked them to list smells or other problems that they knew were present in the system, but not included in the list of smells detected by Arcan in order to identify other possible problems/smells to consider for future extension of the tool detection strategies (Q12). However, no problem has been outlined by the developers in answering this question, so we could not extract useful information in this regard.

B. AS impact

Questions Q5 and Q6 had the purpose of gathering data about which software attributes each smell instance affects and if this negative effect of the smell will get worse as time passes. In question Q5, each developer could select more than one software attribute between Maintainability, Efficiency, Security and Reliability and suggest others ones that were not present among the possible choices. On the other hand, by answering question Q6, they could specify how much they agree with the statement "If not removed, the impact of this type of smell get worse as time passes". This information is summed up in Table III: for each AS instance (first column), the number of practitioners that selected each quality attribute is reported next to the letter indicating the attribute (second column), the Agreement on Q6 answer (third column) was computed by assigning a value (from 0 to 3, see Table II) to each possible choice of question Q6 and summing these values based on the answers of the developers. The higher this sum, the higher the agreement.

One relevant observation is that all the smells were considered affecting maintainability by at least one developer. For one smell instance, *God Component A*, a developer suggested an additional aspect, that "they affect the domain structure" i.e. how the domain model is organized across the different packages. **For what concerns smells that get worse as time passes, we discovered that the developers found Hub-Like on Classes and Feature Concentration the most problematic in these terms.** Even if we sum up the agreement for each type of smell and normalize respect to the number of

TABLE III. RESULTS FOR EACH ARCHITECTURAL SMELL INSTANCE

Architectural Smell Instance	Affected Software Aspects	Agreement on Q6
Cyclic Dependency on Classes	M(3), E(2)	6
Cyclic Dependency on Packages	M(3), E(1), R(1)	6
Hub-Like Dependency on Classes	M(3), E(2), R(1)	**8**
Hub-Like Dependency on Packages	false positive	–
Unstable Dependency	M(3), E(1), R(1), S(1)	5
God Component A	M(1), E(1), Domain structure/feature concentration(1)	4
God Component B	M(3), E(1), S(1)	7
God Component C	false positive	–
God Component D	false positive	–
Insufficient Package Cohesion A	false positive	–
Insufficient Package Cohesion B	M(2), E(1), R(1)	3
Insufficient Package Cohesion C	M(3), E(1), R(1)	3
Insufficient Package Cohesion D	M(3), E(1), R(1)	6
Feature Concentration A	M(2), E(1), R(1)	3
Feature Concentration B	M(3), E(1), R(1), S(1)	**8**
Scattered Functionality A	M(1), R(1)	3
Scattered Functionality B	false positive	–
Scattered Functionality C	false positive	–
Dense Structure	M(1), E(1), R(1), S(1)	5

Key: M: Maintainability, E: Efficiency, R: Reliability, S: Security

instances, the smell which get worse the most is still Hub Like Dependency on classes.

C. AS refactoring

We also asked various questions (Q7, Q8, Q9) regarding the possible refactoring of each smell. Answering two of these questions (Q7,Q8) was optional since they are open-ended questions, thus we collected a limited number of answers. However, the few data helped us in confirming a specific aspect: **smells like Scattered Functionality, Insufficient Package Cohesion and Feature Concentration are meant to point out defects in a package-by-feature [27] organization which is desirable in some cases, but not when the actual design is layered.** These smells are detected by Arcan to provide also a microservice migration support, where a package-by-feature organization is preferable and more useful [14]. Hence, the refactoring of these smells is effective with the aim of reorganizing the project as package-by-feature i.e. transforming the layers into microservices.

Instead, with the answer to Q9, developers provided the reason why they would not refactor the smells instances which they indicated as true positive. In particular, there was a similar response for all CD-P, HL-C, UD and FC asserting that they should not be refactored because "their refactoring would be too expensive". For the FC instance, there was also another answer declaring that "it should not be refactored because there is not a better solution". The same answer was given for one GC instance, all the SF and all the IPC. In brief, developers reported that no refactoring should be conducted on the detected smells because the refactoring activity is too expensive and because sometimes the smell presence is unavoidable. We suggested to the developers that a possible solution to avoid the too expensive smells is to periodically run Arcan on the system and remove smells as soon as they appear. Moreover, their new knowledge about AS can help them in avoiding their introduction in the first place.

D. AS severity, refactoring effort and priority

Other useful data collected for each AS are the perceived severity (Q4), refactoring effort (Q10) and refactoring priority (Q11), which we summarize through the metrics introduced in Section IV-B: the *Average Severity*, the *Average Effort* needed to refactor the smell and its *Average Priority of refactoring*. They are computed by assigning a score to each possible choice the developers could pick to answer questions Q4, Q10 and Q11, then calculating, for each smell instance, the sum of the scores indicated by the developers and eventually computing the average sum for each AS. The maximum reachable value is 12, which happens if all developers agree on answering "High". We found out that the metrics values for all the AS are very close to each other, meaning that developers perceive these three metrics as linearly dependent. The only smells for which one of the three metrics mentioned above has a value that is much higher than the other two metrics are *1)* the Cyclic Dependency smells, which have an Average Priority of refactoring of 8, while the other metrics are equal to 5 and *2)* Dense Structure, which has an Average Effort of 8 and an Average Severity of 5. If we consider the percentages computed on all the smells of the answers regarding Severity, Effort and Priority, we find out that the majority of the smells have been classified as having *Medium-Low* Severity (35%), Effort (33%) and Priority (25%).

Furthermore, we ranked the true positive AS depending on the metrics' values. We reported the most notable ones in Table IV. As we previously mentioned the developers assigned values very close to each other for every AS, so the logical consequence is that the **AS with the highest severity has the highest priority of refactoring and requires the highest effort to be removed too** and vice-versa. In this scenario, Hub-Like Dependency on Classes is the smell with the highest values for all the metrics and Insufficient Package Cohesion is the one with the lowest.

Moreover, we analyzed the possible correspondence between the severity of the AS as perceived by the developers and the metrics used to detect the AS by Arcan, with the aim of identifying a specific smell characteristic (see Section IV) that may become a severity criterion. We checked the *1)* Insufficient Package Cohesion smell according to the Lack of Component Cohesion (LCC)[24], *2)* Feature Concentration according to the number of features inside packages and *3)* God Component according to the number of classes in a package and the LCC metric. We did not check smells with only one true positive.

TABLE IV. RELEVANT SMELLS

AS	Severity		Effort		Priority	
	Most critical	Least critical	Most hard-to-remove	Least hard-to-remove	Most urgent-to-remove	Least urgent-to-remove
HL-C	X		X		X	
IPC		X		X		X

We observed that all the Insufficient Package Cohesion instances have a severity of 3 except for one instance that has a severity of 4: this is also the only one with a LCC equals to 1, which indicates a complete lack of cohesion among the classes belonging to the affected package. The two instances of Feature Concentration have respectively a severity of 4 and 7 and a number of features inside the package of 14 and 28, so we think that this characteristic may be linked to the severity of the smells. Finally, **God Component's instances did not show a link between the severity and the number of classes contained in the package even considering only true positives instances, but we identified a relationship between the developers' severity perception and the Lack Of Component Cohesion of the affected package.** The packages corresponding to the most severe instances (severity=5) have also the highest values of LCC (0.57 and 0.78), while the instance with a severity of 4 affects a package with a LCC of 0.45 and the package affected by the least severe instance (severity=2) has a LCC inferior to 0.2: the higher the LCC of the package, the higher the severity of the AS instance. In brief, we identified a link between: *1)* the severity of the IPC instances and the LCC metric; *2)* the severity of the GC instances and the LCC metric; *3)* the severity of the FC instances and the number of features inside the affected packages.

VI. LESSONS LEARNED

We briefly describe below the principal lessons learned and feedback we obtained from the survey that we exploit to answer the RQs in the next section.

Lesson learned for the Arcan tool developers First of all, we received a feedback from project experts on the precision of the results of the Arcan tool and their usefulness, in particular we obtained feedback on how many detected AS were not actual issues and, taking a closer look to these smells, we can improve the tool in order to reduce the number of false positives results. Secondly, we gathered useful data on how critical each AS instance is, which software attributes it affects and which AS's characteristics may be linked to its criticality: we can use this information to add new functionalities to the tool, like assigning a severity value to each AS instance in order to establish a priority ranking that can reduce the developers' overall refactoring effort. One remarkable example is the severity of GC, which we hypothesised linked to the progressive higher number of classes inside the package. Actually, we found out that developers considered more critical GC instances which have higher LCC: hence a large package with a very low internal cohesion represents the worst possible case that a developer can face.

Lesson learned for the developers/practitioners of the company The developers got useful feedback while examining the smells we showed them through the survey. When we asked them about what the survey taught them, they outlined that *1)* an analysis made through the support of a tool, like Arcan, can bring up issues that the developers did not notice before: they discovered new AS that they never considered as problems and they will keep them in mind from now on to avoid falling into the same mistakes. *2)* They also learned that AS can become relevant issues when working with a large system, because coding can easily lead to the creation of several little smells instances that become progressively greater as the project grows. This aspect, in their opinion, can make the system hard to maintain and understand, specially when trying to identify and separate the system functionalities, such as for a possible migration to a microservices architecture which requires to identify, isolate and put in the same microservice all the classes that work on the same functionality. *3)* Finally, they also got aware of the fact that the developer's experience is important in a perspective of knowledge of the project he/she's working on: the junior developer, thus the least experienced among the three, was also the least aware of the reported smells even though he/she has been working on the project for a longer period (4 years vs 1.5/2 years) compared to the others.

VII. THREATS TO VALIDITY

As for **construct validity**, there is a possibility that the practitioners misinterpreted what the AS represent or what we asked in the questionnaire. However, we mitigated this threat by explaining each type of smell and also each smell instance with a detailed description and the support of a graph visualization. As for **internal validity**, it is unlikely that the opinions on the negative impact of the smells on the project quality reported by the practitioners would be affected by factors that are not related to the AS, since we explained and contextualized each smell in the survey in detail and practitioners were careful to inquire the main causes of the perceived negative impact inside the code. The threat to **external validity** is due to the fact that the case-study has been conducted in a single company and on a single project, hence the results may not apply to other application domains. The reason of such limited scope is due to the difficulties of finding available industrial projects to analyze: in the future, we aim to extend our work with more of them. Moreover, the number of studied AS was limited and for some types, such as Hub-Like Dependency on package, only one instance was analyzed. However, we mitigate this aspect by interviewing three developers with different skills and seniority and by measuring their accordance. As for **reliability**, we identified cases where the practitioners contradicted themselves, however we mitigated this problem by proposing also open-ended questions and collecting their concrete opinions. Even if the study is replicable, the results are based on practitioners' experience and perception, hence the real impact and severity of the AS might differ from the one reported here. However, we subjected the survey to the developers who are actively working on the project and are directly interested by the possible presence and impact of the AS, so their opinion is the most valuable for validating the AS and Arcan.

VIII. CONCLUSION

In this paper, we described the evaluation of 8 AS through the feedback of 3 developers on one industrial project. In particular, we ran the AS detection tool Arcan on the project and presented the results to the developers. Then, for each analyzed instance of AS, we collected information about AS impact, severity and its refactoring through a survey composed of 12 questions. Every developer individually answered the questions of the survey and on such data we build our study. We now report the answers to our research questions, which summarise the results of our study:

RQ1: How are architectural smells perceived in an industrial context? Developers did not know about the concept of

AS, however they reported that they were aware of some of them. They also confirmed that AS have a negative impact on software internal qualities, in particular on maintainability. They recognized the risk linked to the presence of AS in their architecture and acknowledged the usefulness of automatic tools, like Arcan, which can detect this kind of anomaly.

RQ2: What practitioners suggest according to the refactoring of the smells? We were not able to extract from the survey answers, valuable suggestions concerning the refactoring of the smells. However, the few data pointed out that developers would not refactor some of the detected instances because the refactoring activities could be too expensive and for some cases, the smell could represent the only possible solution. A specific comment was made on the refactoring of Feature Concentration, Scattered Functionality and Insufficient Package Cohesion: the refactoring of such ASs is useful, when the system architecture is layered, to prepare the migration towards microservices, by structuring the packages by feature and thus easing the identification of the candidate services. This comment confirmed a result investigated in our previous work, where we exploited Arcan to detect the candidate microservices of an industrial project and collected the developers feedback on the proposed solution [14].

RQ3: Which are the most critical smells according to the practitioners perception? The most critical smell, in the context of this study and the developers' opinion, is HL on classes, which is also one of the smell which gets worse the most, as time passes. Developers should pay attention to this kind of AS and remove it as soon as it appears. On the contrary, IPC is the least critical AS.

In the future, we aim to carry out more studies like the one presented in this paper, on different projects of different applications domain and companies in order to better understand how AS are perceived in an industrial context and improve the AS detection support. We also aim to study how to prevent the introduction of AS by leveraging on machine learning techniques [28]: in this way practitioners could avoid the extra costs due to the refactoring of the AS.

REFERENCES

[1] R. Verdecchia, "Architectural technical debt identification: Moving forward," in 2018 IEEE International Conference on Software Architecture Companion, ICSA Companion 2018, Seattle, WA, USA, April 30 - May 4, 2018, pp. 43–44.

[2] A. Martini, F. Arcelli Fontana, A. Biaggi, and R. Roveda, "Identifying and prioritizing architectural debt through architectural smells: a case study in a large software company," in Proc. of the European Conf. on Software Architecture (ECSA). Madrid, Spain: Springer, Sep. 2018.

[3] M. Fowler, Refactoring: Improving the Design of Existing Code. Boston, USA: Addison-Wesley, 1999.

[4] E. Lab, Evolution of Software Systems and Reverse Engineering Laboratory Official Website, 2020 (accessed August 2020). [Online]. Available: https://essere.disco.unimib.it/

[5] Anoki, Anoki s.r.l., 2020 (accessed August 2020). [Online]. Available: https://www.anoki.it/

[6] F. Arcelli Fontana, I. Pigazzini, R. Roveda, D. A. Tamburri, M. Zanoni, and E. D. Nitto, "Arcan: A tool for architectural smells detection," in Int'l Conf. Software Architecture (ICSA) Workshops, Gothenburg, Apr. 2017, pp. 282–285.

[7] G. Suryanarayana, G. Samarthyam, and T. Sharma, Refactoring for Software Design Smells: Managing Technical Debt, 1st ed. San Francisco, CA, USA: Morgan Kaufmann Publishers Inc., 2014.

[8] A. F. Yamashita and L. Moonen, "Surveying developer knowledge and interest in code smells through online freelance marketplaces," in USER 2013, San Francisco, CA, USA, May 26, 2013, pp. 5–8.

[9] Z. Soh, A. Yamashita, F. Khomh, and Y. Guéhéneuc, "Do code smells impact the effort of different maintenance programming activities?" in SANER 2016, Suita, Osaka, Japan, March 14-18, 2016 - vol. 1, pp. 393–402.

[10] F. Palomba, G. Bavota, M. D. Penta, R. Oliveto, and A. D. Lucia, "Do they really smell bad? A study on developers' perception of bad code smells," in 30th IEEE ICSME, Victoria, BC, Canada, September 29 - October 3, 2014, pp. 101–110.

[11] A. Tahir, J. Dietrich, S. Counsell, S. Licorish, and A. Yamashita, "A large scale study on how developers discuss code smells and anti-pattern in stack exchange sites," Information and Software Technology, vol. 125, 2020, p. 106333.

[12] W. Wu, Y. Cai, R. Kazman, R. Mo, Z. Liu, R. Chen, Y. Ge, W. Liu, and J. Zhang, "Software architecture measurement - experiences from a multinational company," in ECSA 2018, Madrid, Spain, September 24-28, 2018, Proc., pp. 303–319.

[13] R. Mo, W. Snipes, Y. Cai, S. Ramaswamy, R. Kazman, and M. Naedele, "Experiences applying automated architecture analysis tool suites," in Proc. of the 33rd ACM/IEEE, ASE 2018, Montpellier, France, September 3-7, 2018, pp. 779–789.

[14] I. Pigazzini, F. A. Fontana, and A. Maggioni, "Tool support for the migration to microservice architecture: An industrial case study," in Software Architecture - 13th European Conference, ECSA 2019, Paris, France, September 9-13, 2019, Proceedings, pp. 247–263.

[15] H. A. Al-Mutawa, J. Dietrich, S. Marsland, and C. McCartin, "On the shape of circular dependencies in java programs," in ASWEC 2014, Milsons Point, Sydney, NSW, Australia, April 7-10, 2014. IEEE Computer Society, 2014, pp. 48–57.

[16] R. Marinescu, "Assessing technical debt by identifying design flaws in software systems," IBM Journal of Research and Development, vol. 56, no. 5, 2012, pp. 9:1–9:13.

[17] M. Lippert and S. Roock, Refactoring in Large Software Projects: Performing Complex Restructurings Successfully. Wiley, Apr. 2006.

[18] T. Sharma, M. Fragkoulis, and D. Spinellis, "Does your configuration code smell?" in Proceedings of the 13th International Conference on Mining Software Repositories, ser. MSR '16. New York, NY, USA: Association for Computing Machinery, 2016, p. 189–200.

[19] H. S. de Andrade, E. S. de Almeida, and I. Crnkovic, "Architectural bad smells in software product lines: an exploratory study," in Proc. of the WICSA 2014 Companion Volume, Sydney, NSW, Australia, April 7-11, 2014. ACM, 2014, pp. 12:1–12:6.

[20] J. Garcia, D. Popescu, G. Edwards, and N. Medvidovic, "Identifying architectural bad smells," in 2009 13th CSMR, Kaiserslautern, Germany, 2009, pp. 255–258.

[21] E. W. Dijkstra, "On the role of scientific thought," 01 1974.

[22] N. Inc., Neo4j, 2020 (accessed August 2020). [Online]. Available: https://neo4j.com/

[23] ——, Neo4j graph visualization, 2020 (accessed August 2020). [Online]. Available: https://neo4j.com/developer/graph-visualization/

[24] T. Sharma, P. Mishra, and R. Tiwari, "Designite: A software design quality assessment tool," in Proc. of the 1st Intern. Workshop on Bringing Architectural Design Thinking into Developers' Daily Activities, ser. BRIDGE '16. NY, USA: ACM, 2016, p. 1–4.

[25] F. Arcelli Fontana, I. Pigazzini, R. Roveda, and M. Zanoni, "Automatic detection of instability architectural smells," in Proc. of the 32nd Intern. Conf. on Software Maintenance and Evolution (ICSME 2016). Raleigh, North Carolina, USA: IEEE.

[26] N. Mitchell and C. Runciman, "Uniform boilerplate and list processing," in Proc. of the ACM SIGPLAN Workshop on Haskell Workshop, ser. Haskell '07. NY, USA: ACM, 2007, p. 49–60.

[27] K. Lee, K. C. Kang, W. Chae, and B. W. Choi, "Feature-based approach to object-oriented engineering of applications for reuse," Software: Practice and Experience, vol. 30, no. 9, 2000, pp. 1025–1046.

[28] F. A. Fontana, P. Avgeriou, I. Pigazzini, and R. Roveda, "A study on architectural smells prediction," in 45th Euromicro Conference on Software Engineering and Advanced Applications, SEAA 2019, Kallithea-Chalkidiki, Greece, August 28-30, 2019, pp. 333–337.

Offensive and Defensive Perspectives in Additive Manufacturing Security

Rohith Yanambaka Venkata, Nathaniel Brown, Daniel Ting and Krishna Kavi

Center for Agile & Adaptive Additive Manufacturing (CAAAM)
and Dept. of Computer Science and Engineering
University of North Texas
Denton, Texas
USA
Email: {ry0080, nathanielbrown, danielting}@my.unt.edu and krishna.kavi@unt.edu

***Abstract*—Additive Manufacturing (AM) is transforming the manufacturing industry by reducing prototyping time and easing the production of complex parts. Notably, use of AM has gained traction in the medical and aerospace fields, and is rapidly increasing in usage in traditional industry. However, AM's cyber-physical nature opens systems up to vulnerabilities that can result in both cyber and physical damage. In this paper, we document and categorize the state of the art in Additive Manufacturing security research in three ways - by using Microsoft's Spoofing, Tampering, Repudiation, Information Disclosure, Denial of Service and Elevation of Privilege (STRIDE) threat model, by the intent of the attacker, and by the overall purpose of the published works. We also provide a list of security recommendations for AM that could aid in the design of secure AM systems. We hope our approach will enable an understanding of AM security from both the attacker's and defender's perspective, and serve as a survey of relevant research in the field, and stimulate more research into securing AM systems.**

Keywords*–*additive manufacturing; cybersecurity; threat modeling.

I. INTRODUCTION

Advanced manufacturing is a key component in what is called Industry 4.0 - manufacturing relying on sophisticated technologies including networked sensors and actuators, cyber technologies and machine learning to make processes flexible, agile and cost-effective. However, the reliance on these interconnected yet emerging technologies make these processes prone to cybersecurity attacks. In this paper, we will provide a high-level, concise but comprehensive survey of the currently known vulnerabilities with manufacturing, focusing on AM in particular, and suggested best practices for mitigating cyber attacks. First, we will briefly describe AM processes.

AM can produce a component in a layer-wise fashion rather than starting with a block of material and removing material using milling, cutting, or lathing processes (referred here as Subtractive Manufacturing, or SM). In this way, additive processes are not constrained in the same way as subtractive processes, meaning that the manufacturing envelope is opened very wide to produce technically or financially infeasible components due to such challenges as shape complexities, cost, new material combinations, etc. Relevant examples of AM include surgical joint replacement components (such as titanium hip or knee replacements), components whose traditional manufacturing methods would be cost or time prohibitive [1], or components for which the original tooling (such as the dies for forging) no longer exists (such as various components replaced on aging aircraft systems expected to continue serving for many years into the future [2]). Using this manufacturing method allows mass customization while simultaneously decentralizing the manufacturing and distribution process. Underlining mass customization, three-dimensional (3-D) printing is being developed to fabricate highly dose-specific medication. In 2015, the U.S. Food and Drug Administration (FDA) approved the first 3-D printed drug available in the United States — Levetiracetam (Spirtam - Aprecia), which is used to treat partial onset, myoclonic, and primary generalized tonic-clonic seizures in patients with epilepsy [3]. There have even been efforts to design and print medical equipment from simple face masks to complex ventilators [4] following the shortage during the COVID-19 pandemic.

Presently, there are many types of AM that vary based on cost, material system, manufacturing method, user capabilities, and characteristics of the desired final component. The most common forms of AM/3-D printing are - Vat Photopolymerization, Material Extrusion, Material Jetting and Powder Bed Fusion [1].

The AM process is a complex interaction of automated and manual workflows with numerous dependencies - both informational and physical. Additionally, AM my be provided as a service which would include several actors, software applications, sensors, actuation mechanisms and logistical activities. Not all of these entities may reside within a service provider's controlled environment. This cyber-physical nature of Additive Manufacturing processes leaves systems vulnerable to a certain array of unique attacks, including:

- Side-channel attacks that steal valuable intellectual property by listening to an AM system's sounds during product synthesis and running the data through a machine-learning model [5].
- Attacks that target the design stage to create fatal deficiencies (like voids) in key parts of synthesized products [6].
- Attacks that alter printing orientation to decrease end products' tensile strength [7].
- Attacks that target insecure methods of transferring stereolithographic (STL) files, such as via USB sticks [8].
- Attacks that exploit vulnerabilities in the code and programming languages that control AM systems; [9].
- Attacks that target AM quality-assurance techniques to ensure low product quality [10].

Our goal in this paper is to provide a high-level, concise but comprehensive survey of the current state of the art in security for AM; first from the attacker's point of view, then from the defender's, using Microsoft's STRIDE security model to reason about security.

The structure of the remainder of the article is as follows. Section II describes related work and how we sourced the material for our research. Section III describes Microsoft's STRIDE threat model and its unique advantages when analyzing AM security. Section IV describes the intents of attackers seeking to exploit vulnerabilities in AM systems. Section V lists security recommendations for AM systems taken from recommendations for similar systems by the National Institute of Standards and Technology (NIST). Finally, Section VI provides conclusions about this work and future extensions.

II. Related Work

There have been a number of practical attacks specific to 3D printing executed in a lab setting. Works that we will touch upon include Sturm et al. [11], Zeltmann et al. [7], and Moore et al. [12]. These papers demonstrate one specific or narrow range of attacks.

Other papers introduce frameworks to reason about threats in this newly emerging domain of cybersecurity. Zhang & Padmanabhan [13] proposed five categories of risk and applied them to six separate stages in the manufacturing pipeline. Yampolskiy et al. [14] discussed multiple taxonomies over the different elements that can be attacked, how they can be attacked, and consequences of an attack. Glavach et al. [8] describe protocols and security recommendations for proper AM system operation.

Table I groups papers into three categories - papers that present or analyze a specific attack, those that propose a security design framework and those that propose/perform risk assessment on cyber attack(s).

In this paper, we organize vulnerabilities that affect Additive Manufacturing systems using the STRIDE threat model, consolidate and catalog research articles to provide an insight into the perspective of an adversary, and identify potential mitigation techniques.

These articles come from a mix of independent research, conferences, and journals focusing on AM or general manufacturing security, and were sourced from searching online databases for research on AM security, as well as from references from other papers. Since AM security is a relatively new field, most of the research we have compiled is recent.

To reiterate, we aim not to propose a new offensive or defensive strategy, but to unify these works under a common theme, the STRIDE model.

III. STRIDE Model

Most software systems today face a variety of cyber threats. The threat landscape is constantly evolving with the advances in technology. Malware that exploits software vulnerabilities grew 151% in the second quarter of 2018 [15]. Threats can originate from within or outside an organization and lead to devastating consequences. To prevent threats from wreaking havoc, system administrators/designers use threat modeling to profile the security posture of a system.

Threat modeling must be performed early in the development cycle to successfully identify and remedy vulnerabilities. Incorporating threat modeling into the design process of a system will lead to proactive architectural decisions that reduce threats from the start. Cyber physical systems in general, and Additive Manufacturing systems in particular, conflate software technology with physical infrastructure, which introduces a unique challenge of multiple stakeholders being involved in the system design process. Performing threat modeling on a cyber physical system from the perspective of multiple stakeholders is essential in identifying and eliminating threats across a wide spectrum of threat types.

Some of the popular threat models are:

- **PASTA :** The Process for Attack Simulation and Threat Analysis (PASTA) is a risk-centric threat model developed in 2012 [16]. PASTA brings business objectives and technical requirements together. It utilizes several design and elicitation tools at various stages of design and approaches threat-modeling from a strategic level by involving key decision makers and requiring input from operations, governance, architecture and development. PASTA employs an attacker-centric perspective to produce an asset-centric output in the form of threat enumeration and scoring [16].
- **LINDDUN :** The Linkability, Identifiability, Non-repudiation, Detectability, Disclosure of information, Unawareness, Non-compliance (LINDDUN) framework focuses primarily on privacy concerns and is used for data security [16]. The frameworks involves constantly iterating over data elements and analyzing them from the perspective of threat categories. The design involves identifying a threat's applicability to the system and building threat trees [16].
- **Attack Trees :** Using trees to model attacks on a system is an old and widely used technique. The trees are diagrams where the root represents the goal of an adversary and the leaves represent ways to achieve that goal. Each goal is represented by a separate tree. For complex systems, the number of attack trees may be too large to provide valuable and actionable insights into the security posture of the system.

The STRIDE threat model was invented in 1999 and adopted by Microsoft in 2002 [16]. This model identifies six main types of threats:

- **Spoofing :** Claiming a false identify in order to gain unauthorized access to resources. This type of threat violates the authenticity requirement of a system. Examples of this threat include spoofing the identity of a user by brute-forcing user credentials and phishing.
- **Tampering :** Malicious modification of data or processes. This modification may occur on data in transit, data at rest or on processes. This type of threat violates the integrity requirement of a system. Examples include SQL injection attacks and code-injection attacks.
- **Repudiation :** Falsely denying the occurrence of an action or event. Typical repudiation attacks involve a user denying performing a destructive action such as deleting records from a database and attackers truncating log files to remove all traces of a system breach.
- **Information disclosure :** Refers to data leaks or breaches. Perhaps, the most common type of threat today, information disclosure violates the confidentiality

requirement of a system. Eavesdropping, data sniffing, unauthorized access to a database are all examples of information disclosure attacks.

- **Denial of Service :** Disruption of a service or network resource. This prevents legitimate users from accessing the desired network service. This type of attack violates the availability requirement of a system. Typical examples include inundating a network service with multiple requests, using up available space on a shared hard drive, etc.
- **Elevation of Privilege :** Unauthorized access to system resources by violating the authorization requirement of a system. A typical example would be a user gaining root privileges on a system using buffer overflow.

We chose STRIDE model for this article because it is the most mature threat model [16]. It provides a balance between risk-assessment, security and privacy, which is vital when modeling complex cyber physical systems. While the other threat models discussed above have useful characteristics in cyber-only systems, we feel that STRIDE is the most well understood and widely used for cyber physical systems. Table II classifies research articles into the constituent attack types of the STRIDE model based on the type and nature of threats described in the articles.

IV. Intent of the Attacker

There are a number of articles focusing on the intent of a possible attacker. Graves et al. [21] propose a framework for the analysis of attacks on or with AM systems. The authors describe the attack targets as the intersection of the effects the attacks would have with the adversarial goals and objectives. The three major threat categories they identified are technical data theft, AM sabotage, and illegal part manufacturing. Table III summarizes research articles into three categories based on the intent or objective of an attacker.

A. Technical Data Theft

Technical data theft is the unauthorized use of Intellectual Property (IP). To an attacker, IP can be the most lucrative target because it forms the basis of an organization's competitive advantage. Stealing IP from an AM system is not so different from other manufacturing systems. However, security in AM systems may be less developed than that in traditional manufacturing, giving an attacker the edge.

AM is very new compared to traditional manufacturing methods that have been extensively tested in the field. An attacker can exploit zero-day flaws in AM systems that would likely have been patched long ago in a SM system. Do, Martini, and Choo [23] demonstrated several severe security oversights in MakerBot consumer 3D printers: print jobs are transmitted and stored unencrypted, allowing anyone on the same network to steal the model. Even worse, although the printer authenticates a computer over Hypertext Transfer Protocol Secure (HTTPS), it does not properly check the legitimacy of the certificate used, allowing them to do an Address Resolution Protocol (ARP) poisoning attack and perform privileged actions on the printer.

Furthermore, AM exhibits unique properties that enable all kinds of attacks. One such property that an attacker could choose to exploit is the fact that 3D printers use a small set of primitive operations that make consistent acoustic and magnetic emissions. Song et al. [24] were able to conduct a side-channel attack using an ordinary smartphone's sensors. By training a support vector machine to convert sensor data into G-code, they could accurately reconstruct the shape of a design being printed by the widely-used Ultimaker 2 Go.

B. AM Sabotage

AM sabotage most commonly exhibits itself in the manipulation of an AM system to degrade the quality of the manufactured part, though it may also refer to damage done to the AM system itself or its surroundings. The bulk of research done about security challenges in AM fall under this category, as the unique properties of AM open up even more possibilities. One attack unique to AM is the insertion of voids in the middle of a product. Sturm et al. [11] discuss such an attack and show that doing so causes a noticeable degradation in strength while slipping undetected by human operators.

Belikovetsky et al. [6] applied this attack to a real-life scenario from start to finish. Exploiting a patched WinRAR vulnerability on an out-of-date test machine, they inserted gaps inside drone propellers that broke apart in flight. The test machine was intentionally left unpatched, but the main takeaway is that once an attacker gains access to an AM system, they have a wider range of opportunities to sabotage manufactured parts. For example, the previous attack required infiltrating the STL file. But if the attacker gains access to the printer's controls, they can choose to alter the orientation that the part is printed in, which also somewhat unintuitively turns out to impact strength as well, as Zeltmann et al. [7] demonstrate.

C. Illegal Part Manufacturing

Illegal part manufacturing is the creation of products prohibited by law. Unlike the other two intentions mentioned above, which consider an attack by an external actor on the end user, illegal part manufacturing is not an attack in the traditional sense. However, it is still an important consideration, more for the printer manufacturer than the end user. As with all technologies with potential for danger, the thin balance between liberty and safety ought to be explored. There are currently little published works that describe scenarios where such attacks were conducted.

V. Security Recommendations

Although currently there are no specific recommendations for AM systems, guidance is available from NIST for industrial control systems (ICS) and general manufacturing processes. We believe ICS recommendations found in [27] contain many valuable recommendations due to the shared security concerns of AM and ICS systems. Additionally, [28], which is primarily distributed for Federal Information Systems, contains many recommendations relevant to the security of Additive Manufacturing systems due to information systems' reliance on a consistent flow information and the relevance of many of the paper's recommendations to general manufacturing security. Where applicable, recommendation names and descriptions have been paraphrased to contain specific terms that fit the context of AM.

This section is a compilation from three major papers and technical articles from the National Institute of Standards and

TABLE I. CATEGORIZATION OF PAPERS BY PURPOSE

Analyzing a specific attack: Papers with the primary purpose of presenting and analyzing a specific AM attack.	Belikovetsky et al. [6] demonstrate an attack in which a largely undetectable void is added to an AM drone part, causing a disastrous loss of structural integrity. Moore et al. [12] demonstrate an attack on AM quality via malicious printer firmware. Sturm et al. [11] examine potential attack vectors along the AM process chain, and present security recommendations for preventing and detecting attacks. Al Faruque et al. [5] demonstrate an attack that derives the intellectual property of an AM-constructed object by listening on the sounds produced by the construction process and running them through a machine-learning model.
Proposing a security framework: Papers with the primary purpose of presenting a new or modified security framework for the benefit of AM cybersecurity.	Hutchins et al. [17] establish a framework that identifies specific vulnerabilities within a manufacturing supply chain. Padmanabhan and Zhang [13] review cybersecurity risk and mitigation strategies in AM, and propose a framework to "detect threats and assess vulnerabilities in the AM process." They also suggest a new encryption technique to help secure the AM process. Yampolskiy et al. [18] propose a new model for outsourcing Additive Layer Manufacturing (ALM) based manufacturing. Vincent et al. [19] propose an approach to detect attacks in cyber-physical manufacturing systems through the use of structural health monitoring techniques.
Risk Assessment/Analyzing Multiple Attacks: Papers that analyze a variety of attacks on AM or the potential attack vectors of Additive Manufacturing systems.	Prinsloo et al. [20] explore cybersecurity risks associated with the transition to Industry 4.0 and address relevant countermeasures. Yampolskiy et al. [14] analyze attacks that can cause AM machines to exhibit weaponized effects. Zeltmann et al. [7] provide a brief overview of AM security risks and evaluate risks posed by two classes of modifications to the AM process that "are representative of the challenges that are unique to AM." Glavach et al. [8] "address cybersecurity threats to the Direct Digital Manufacturing (DDM) community." Graves et al. [21] assess AM from three security awareness perspectives: "exposure to an attack, evaluation of the system, and potential liability for a successful attack." Slaughter et al. [10] identify techniques used to ensure bad quality in metal AM through malicious manipulating an infrared thermography quality assurance device. Straub [22] discusses attacks on the 3D printing process that involve changes in printing orientation, and proposes an imaging-based solution to combat the problem.

TABLE II. A STRIDE ASSESSMENT OF ADDITIVE MANUFACTURING

Threat type	Papers
Spoofing	An attacker may spoof a printer or computer's identity to intercept 3D models [23] or as part of a larger attack to take control of and sabotage an AM system [6].
Tampering	Assuming access was gained through another attack, an adversary may choose a number of ways to sabotage the system, including, but not limited to, inserting invisible voids [11], altering print settings [7], and/or installing malicious firmware [12].
Repudiation	Repudiation is a generally overlooked threat in AM security articles. Considering secure logging is not a built-in standard in 3D printers, an attacker would simply need to target the tracing capabilities of the surrounding infrastructure.
Information Disclosure	Traditional malware could be deployed to steal the 3D model, which can exist in many forms and place [11]. There also exists side-channel attacks that listen to the predictable acoustic and magnetic emissions of a printer to reconstruct IP with a machine learning model [5] [24].
Denial of Service	One who has gained control of a poorly designed 3D printer may hypothetically manipulate its operating parameters e.g. the electron/laser beam or source material to inflict irreversible damage upon itself.
Elevation of Privilege	Privilege escalation is used as a stepping stone to launch further attacks [6]. However, it is not even needed for some AM systems that perform incorrect authentication or none at all [23].

TABLE III. CATEGORIZATION OF ATTACKS BY INTENT

Adversary's intent	Papers
Technical data theft	Al Faruque et al. [5] describe a novel side-channel attack in which a machine learning model is used to derive an object's geometry by analyzing the noise created by a Fused Deposition Modeling (FDM) 3D printer. Yampolskiy et al. [18] emphasize how there are many places along the AM supply chain in which IP can be stolen, and offer a unique outsourcing model to help secure the process. Campbell and Ivanova [25] describe the potential for AM to increase the ease of violating patents and producing patented products.
AM sabotage	Sturm et al. [11] describe the ease of creating voids in products fabricated by AM to sabotage their mechanical strength. Zeltmann et al. [7] describe how embedded defects and altered printing orientation can negatively affect a printed object's integrity as well. Belikovetsky et al. [6] and Vincent et al. [19] demonstrate the consequences of these attacks by testing sabotaged parts on real-life equipment. Moore et al. [12] takes another route and sabotages the printer firmware, replacing it with a malicious version that can corrupt the print jobs as they are received.
Illegal part manufacturing	Kietzmann et al. [26] describe the potential for AM to catalyze the creation of fake medical products and drugs. Campbell and Ivanova [25] describe the potential of bad actors to manufacture illegal gun parts through AM.

Technology (NIST) regarding security practices to counteract malicious attacks in the cyber and cyber-physical domains. The recommendations come from NIST's Guide to Industrial Control Systems (ICS) Security [27], Security and Privacy Controls for Federal Information Systems and Organizations [28], and Framework for Improving Critical Infrastructure Cybersecurity [29]. We organized these recommendations along STRIDE threat model, describing how to mitigate the different threat types.

A. *Spoofing and Repudiation*

- **Identity Management, Authentication and Access Control:** Access to physical and logical assets and associated facilities is limited to authorized users, processes, and devices, and is managed consistent with the assessed risk of unauthorized access to authorized activities and transactions.
- **Security Monitoring:** The system and assets are monitored to identify cybersecurity events and verify the effectiveness of protective measures. This includes monitoring for unauthorized personnel, connections, devices and software.
- **Access Enforcement:** The system enforces approved authorizations for logical access to information and system resources in accordance with applicable access control policies.
- **Remote Access:** The organization establishes usage restrictions, configuration/connection requirements, and implementation guidance for each type of remote access allowed, and authorizes remote access to the system prior to allowing such connections.
- **Least Functionality:** The organization configures the system to provide only essential capabilities; and

prohibits or restricts the use of prohibited or restricted functions, ports, protocols, and/or services.

- **Device Authentication:** The system uniquely identifies and authenticates devices before establishing a connection.
- **Adaptive Identification and Authentication** The organization requires that individuals accessing the system employ supplemental authentication techniques or mechanisms under circumstances or situations determined to need the extra security.
- **Physical Access Authorizations:** The organization develops, approves, and maintains a list of individuals with authorized access to the location of the system and issues authorization credentials for such access.
- **Developer Security Architecture and Design:** The organization requires the developer of the system, system component, or system service to produce a design specification and security architecture that:
  - Is consistent with and supportive of the organization's security architecture which is established within and is an integrated part of the organization's enterprise architecture;
  - Accurately and completely describes the required security functionality, and the allocation of security controls among physical and logical components; and
  - Expresses how individual security functions, mechanisms, and services work together to provide required security capabilities and a unified approach to protection.
- **Boundary Protection:** The system connects to external networks or other systems only through managed interfaces consisting of boundary protection devices arranged in accordance with an organizational security architecture.
- **Network Disconnect:** The system terminates the network connection associated with a communications session at the end of the session or after an organization-determined time period of inactivity.
- **Session Authenticity:** The system protects the authenticity of the communications sessions.
- **Information System Monitoring:** The organization
  - Monitors the system to detect:
    - Attacks and indicators of potential attacks in accordance with organization-defined monitoring objectives; and
    - Unauthorized local, network, and remote connections.
  - Identifies unauthorized use of the system through relevant techniques and methods;
  - Deploys monitoring devices:
    - Strategically within the system to collect essential information; and
    - At ad hoc locations within the system to track specific types of transactions of interest to the organization; and
  - Protects information obtained from intrusion-monitoring tools from unauthorized access, modification, and deletion.
- **Firewalls:** The organization deploys appropriate firewall policies at pertinent locations to avoid unauthorized access to systems and resources.
- **Repudiation:** The information system protects against an individual (or process acting on behalf of an individual) falsely denying having performed organization-defined actions to be covered by non-repudiation, which may include creating information, sending and receiving messages, or approving information.

B. Tampering, Denial of Service and Elevation of Privilege

- **Risk Assessment:** The organization understands the cybersecurity risk to organizational operations (including mission, functions, image, or reputation), organizational assets, and individuals.
- **Anomalies and Events:** Anomalous activity is detected and the potential impact of events is understood.
  - Detected events are analyzed to understand attack targets and methods;
  - Event data are collected and correlated from multiple sources and sensors; and
  - The impact of events is determined.
- **Security Continuous Monitoring:** The system and its assets are monitored to identify cybersecurity events and verify the effectiveness of protective measures.
  - The network is monitored to detect potential cybersecurity events;
  - The physical environment is monitored to detect potential cybersecurity events;
  - Personnel activity is monitored to detect potential cybersecurity events;
  - Malicious code is detected;
  - Unauthorized mobile code is detected;
  - External service provider activity is monitored to detect cybersecurity events; and
  - Vulnerability scans are performed.
- **Detection Processes:** Detection processes and procedures are maintained and tested to ensure awareness of anomalous events.
- **Continuous Monitoring:** The organization develops a continuous monitoring strategy and implements a continuous monitoring program that includes:
  - Establishment of metrics to be monitored.
  - Ongoing security status monitoring of organization-defined metrics in accordance with the organizational continuous monitoring strategy.
- **Software Usage Restrictions:** The organization uses software and associated documentation in accordance with contract agreements and copyright laws, and tracks the use of software and associated documentation protected by quantity licenses to control copying and distribution.
- **User-Installed Software:** The organization establishes policies governing the installation of software by users and enforces software installation policies through organization-defined methods.

- **Incident Monitoring:** The organization tracks and documents security incidents impacting the system.
- **Risk Assessment:** The organization conducts an assessment of risk, including the likelihood and magnitude of harm, from the unauthorized access, use, disclosure, disruption, modification, or destruction of the system and the information it processes, stores, or transmits.
- **Vulnerability Scanning:** The organization:
  - Scans for vulnerabilities in the system and hosted applications and when new vulnerabilities potentially affecting the system/applications are identified and reported;
  - Employs vulnerability scanning tools and techniques that facilitate interoperability among tools and automate parts of the vulnerability management process by using standards for:
    - Enumerating platforms, software flaws, and improper configurations;
    - Formatting checklists and test procedures; and
    - Measuring vulnerability impact.
  - Analyzes vulnerability scan reports and results from security control assessments; and
  - Remediates legitimate vulnerabilities in accordance with an organizational assessment of risk.
- **Supply Chain Protection:** The organization protects against supply chain threats to the system, system component, or system service by employing organization-defined security safeguards as part of a comprehensive, defense-in-breadth information security strategy.
- **Criticality Analysis:** The organization identifies critical system components and functions by performing a criticality analysis.
- **Tamper Resistance and Detection:** The organization implements a tamper protection program for the system, system component, or system service.
- **Customized Development of Critical Components:** The organization re-implements or custom develops system components deemed critical enough by the organization to take such measures.
- **Application Partitioning:** The system separates user functionality (including user interface services) from system management functionality.
- **Security Function Isolation:** The system isolates security functions from nonsecurity functions.
- **Trusted Path:** The system establishes a trusted communications path between the user and organization-defined security functions to include at a minimum, system authentication and re-authentication.
- **Protection of Information at Rest:** The system protects the confidentiality and/or integrity of organization-defined information at rest.
- **Malicious Code Protection:** The organization:
  - Employs malicious code protection mechanisms at system entry and exit points to detect and eradicate malicious code;
  - Updates malicious code protection mechanisms whenever new releases are available in accordance with organizational configuration management policy and procedures;
  - Configures malicious code protection mechanisms to:
    - Perform periodic scans of the system at a defined frequency and real-time scans of files from external sources at specified endpoints and/or entry and exit points as the files are downloaded, opened, or executed in accordance with organizational security policy; and
  - Addresses the receipt of false positives during malicious code detection and eradication and the resulting potential impact on the availability of the system.
- **Software, Firmware, and Information Integrity:** The organization employs integrity verification tools to detect unauthorized changes to organization-defined software, firmware, and information.
- **Information Input Validation:** The system checks the validity of organization-defined information inputs.
- **Error Handling:** The system
  - Generates error messages that provide information necessary for corrective actions without revealing information that could be exploited by adversaries; and
  - Reveals error messages only to trusted personnel or roles.
- **Memory Protection:** The system implements organization-defined security safeguards to protect its memory from unauthorized code execution.
- **Denial of Service Protection:** The system protects against or limits the effects of denial of service attacks by employing aforementioned organization-defined security safeguards.

C. *Information Disclosure*

- **Governance:** The policies, procedures, and processes to manage and monitor the organization's regulatory, legal, risk, environmental, and operational requirements are understood and inform the management of cybersecurity risk.
- **Data Security:** Information and records (data) are managed consistent with the organization's risk strategy to protect the confidentiality, integrity, and availability of information.
- **Information Protection Processes and Procedures:** Security policies (that address purpose, scope, roles, responsibilities, management commitment, and coordination among organizational entities), processes, and procedures are maintained and used to manage protection of systems and assets.
- **Component Authenticity:** The organization develops and implements anti-counterfeit policy and procedures that include the means to detect and prevents counterfeit components from entering the system.

- **Information in Shared Resources:** The system prevents unauthorized and unintended information transfer via shared system resources.
- **Transmission Confidentiality and Integrity:** The system protects the confidentiality and/or integrity of transmitted information.
- **Wireless Link Protection:** The system protects external and internal wireless links from designated types of signal parameter attacks or references to sources for such attacks.
- **Boundary Protection:** Boundary protection devices are implemented to control the flow of information between interconnected security domains to protect the system against malicious cyber adversaries and non-malicious errors and incidents...Boundary protection devices determine whether data transfer is permitted, often by examining the data or associated metadata.

VI. Conclusion and Future Work

Additive Manufacturing is a technology with enormous potential. However, this makes it easy to rush things to market without taking due consideration of security implications. And because AM is still a developing area of research, it is a challenge to properly secure systems against the expanded variety of things that could go wrong. In this paper, we considered the mind of the opposition by analyzing the intent of the attacker and discussing many possible ways for an attacker to achieve their goal. Furthermore, we categorized these attacks into the STRIDE model and compiled a number of steps that one could take to secure each category. Since AM is a developing area of research, there are still a number of questions that should be further explored:

A. Exactly how much work have manufacturers of consumer and industrial AM devices put into securing their systems?

Do, Martini, and Choo [23] have shown an instance where a 3D printer manufacturer neglected fundamental security practices. However, this is just a single case in a consumer printer. Although we believe this may be an expected symptom of the emerging nature of AM, we do not have enough data to conclude if this is an isolated incident or a widespread concern, and how much worse, if at all, it is than in traditional manufacturing.

B. Are there any additional properties unique to AM that an attacker could exploit?

A key benefit of AM is that it gives manufacturers more flexibility, but at the same time gives malicious actors more opportunities to attack. We covered several such attacks that are only possible or simplified on AM, such as those given by [11] and [7]. We anticipate that a motivated adversary will find even more ways to cleverly exploit AM's advantages. More work can be done to explore other attacks and raise awareness among AM users.

C. What steps, if any, should be taken to prevent the use of 3D printers for potential harm, such as illegal part manufacturing?

We have so far exclusively focused on securing 3D printers so that the user is protected from any malicious actions by outside actors. Graves et al. [21] make the case for considering securing 3D printers so that the outside community environment is protected from destructive uses of this technology.

Regardless, we hope this paper provides a useful, understandable overview of AM security from all sides and concrete ideas for what next steps can be taken.

Acknowledgment

The authors would like to acknowledge the infrastructure and support of Center for Agile & Adaptive and Additive Manufacturing funded through State of Texas Appropriation (#190405-105-805008-220).

References

[1] D. Thomas, "Costs, benefits, and adoption of additive manufacturing: a supply chain perspective," The International Journal of Advanced Manufacturing Technology, vol. 85, no. 5, 2016, pp. 1857–1876. [Online]. Available: https://doi.org/10.1007/s00170-015-7973-6

[2] P. O, "3-d printing is changing the way air force fixes its aging planes," URL: https://www.military.com/defensetech/2017/05/02/3-d-printing-is-changing-way-air-force-fixes-its-aging-planes [accessed : 2020-05-21].

[3] J. Kite-Powell, "Fda approved 3d printed drug available in the us," URL: https://www.forbes.com/sites/jenniferhicks/2016/03/22/fda-approved-3d-printed-drug-available-in-the-us [accessed: 2020-06-02].

[4] R. Tino, R. Moore, S. Antoline, P. Ravi, N. Wake, C. Ionita, J. Morris, S. Decker, A. Sheikh, F. Rybicki, and L. Chepelev, "Covid-19 and the role of 3d printing in medicine," 3D Printing in Medicine, vol. 6, 12 2020.

[5] M. A. Al Faruque, S. R. Chhetri, A. Canedo, and J. Wan, "Acoustic side-channel attacks on additive manufacturing systems," in 2016 ACM/IEEE 7th International Conference on Cyber-Physical Systems (ICCPS). IEEE, Apr 2016. [Online]. Available: http://dx.doi.org/10.1109/ICCPS.2016.7479068

[6] S. Belikovetsky, M. Yampolskiy, J. Toh, and Y. Elovici, "dr0wned - cyber-physical attack with additive manufacturing," CoRR, vol. abs/1609.00133, 2016. [Online]. Available: http://arxiv.org/abs/1609.00133

[7] S. Zeltmann, N. Gupta, N. G. Tsoutsos, M. Maniatakos, J. Rajendran, and R. Karri, "Manufacturing and security challenges in 3d printing," JOM, vol. 68, 2016, pp. 1872–1881.

[8] D. Glavach, J. LaSalle-DeSantis, and S. Zimmerman, Applying and Assessing Cybersecurity Controls for Direct Digital Manufacturing (DDM) Systems. Springer International Publishing, 2017, p. 173–194. [Online]. Available: http://dx.doi.org/10.1007/978-3-319-50660-9_7

[9] S. Moore, P. Armstrong, T. McDonald, and M. Yampolskiy, "Vulnerability analysis of desktop 3d printer software," in 2016 Resilience Week (RWS). IEEE, Aug 2016. [Online]. Available: http://dx.doi.org/10.1109/RWEEK.2016.7573305

[10] A. Slaughter, M. Yampolskiy, M. Matthews, W. E. King, G. Guss, and Y. Elovici, "How to ensure bad quality in metal additive manufacturing," in Proceedings of the 12th International Conference on Availability, Reliability and Security - ARES '17. ACM Press, 2017. [Online]. Available: http://dx.doi.org/10.1145/3098954.3107011

[11] L. Sturm, C. Williams, J. Camelio, J. White, and R. Parker, "Cyber-physical vulnerabilities in additive manufacturing systems: A case study attack on the .stl file with human subjects," Journal of Manufacturing Systems, vol. 44, Jul 2017, p. 154–164. [Online]. Available: https://www.sciencedirect.com/science/article/pii/S0278612517300961

[12] S. Moore, W. Glisson, and M. Yampolskiy, "Implications of malicious 3d printer firmware." Proceedings of the 50th Hawaii International Conference on System Sciences, 01 2017, pp. 6089–6098.

[13] A. Padmanabhan and J. Zhang, "Cybersecurity risks and mitigation strategies in additive manufacturing," Progress in Additive Manufacturing, vol. 3, no. 1-2, 2018, pp. 87–93.

[14] M. Yampolskiy, A. Skjellum, M. Kretzschmar, R. A. Overfelt, K. R. Sloan, and A. Yasinsac, "Using 3d printers as weapons," International Journal of Critical Infrastructure Protection, vol. 14, 2016, pp. 58 – 71. [Online]. Available: http://www.sciencedirect.com/science/article/pii/S1874548215300330

[15] W. Ashford, "WannaCry and NotPetya inspiring new attacks," URL: https://www.computerweekly.com/news/252449265/WannaCry-and-NotPetya-inspiring-new-attacks [accessed: 2020-05-21].

[16] N. Shevchenko, "Threat Modeling: 12 Available Methods," URL: https://insights.sei.cmu.edu/sei_blog/2018/12/threat-modeling-12-available-methods.html [accessed: 2020-05-24].

[17] M. J. Hutchins, R. Bhinge, M. K. Micali, S. L. Robinson, J. W. Sutherland, and D. Dornfeld, "Framework for identifying cybersecurity risks in manufacturing," Procedia Manufacturing, vol. 1, 2015, pp. 47 – 63, 43rd North American Manufacturing Research Conference, NAMRC 43, 8-12 June 2015, UNC Charlotte, North Carolina, United States. [Online]. Available: http://www.sciencedirect.com/science/article/pii/S2351978915010604

[18] M. Yampolskiy, T. R. Andel, J. T. McDonald, W. B. Glisson, and A. Yasinsac, "Intellectual property protection in additive layer manufacturing: Requirements for secure outsourcing," in Proceedings of the 4th Program Protection and Reverse Engineering Workshop, ser. PPREW-4. New York, NY, USA: Association for Computing Machinery, 2014. [Online]. Available: https://doi.org/10.1145/2689702.2689709

[19] H. Vincent, L. Wells, P. Tarazaga, and J. Camelio, "Trojan detection and side-channel analyses for cyber-security in cyber-physical manufacturing systems," Procedia Manufacturing, vol. 1, 2015, p. 77–85. [Online]. Available: http://dx.doi.org/10.1016/j.promfg.2015.09.065

[20] J. Prinsloo, S. Sinha, and B. von Solms, "A review of industry 4.0 manufacturing process security risks," Applied Sciences, vol. 9, no. 23, Nov 2019, p. 5105. [Online]. Available: http://dx.doi.org/10.3390/app9235105

[21] L. M. G. Graves, J. Lubell, W. King, and M. Yampolskiy, "Characteristic aspects of additive manufacturing security from security awareness perspectives," IEEE Access, vol. 7, 2019, pp. 103 833–103 853.

[22] J. Straub, "Identifying positioning-based attacks against 3D printed objects and the 3D printing process," in Pattern Recognition and Tracking XXVIII, M. S. Alam, Ed., vol. 10203, International Society for Optics and Photonics. SPIE, 2017, pp. 22 – 34. [Online]. Available: https://doi.org/10.1117/12.2264671

[23] Q. Do, B. Martini, and K.-K. R. Choo, "A data exfiltration and remote exploitation attack on consumer 3d printers," IEEE Transactions on Information Forensics and Security, vol. 11, no. 10, 2016, pp. 2174–2186.

[24] C. Song, F. Lin, Z. Ba, K. Ren, C. Zhou, and W. Xu, "My smartphone knows what you print: Exploring smartphone-based side-channel attacks against 3d printers," in Proceedings of the 2016 ACM SIGSAC Conference on Computer and Communications Security, 2016, pp. 895–907.

[25] T. A. Campbell and O. S. Ivanova, "Additive manufacturing as a disruptive technology: Implications of three-dimensional printing," Technology & Innovation, vol. 15, no. 1, Jan. 2013, pp. 67–79. [Online]. Available: https://doi.org/10.3727/194982413x13608676060655

[26] J. Kietzmann, L. Pitt, and P. Berthon, "Disruptions, decisions, and destinations: Enter the age of 3-d printing and additive manufacturing," Business Horizons, vol. 58, no. 2, 2015, pp. 209 – 215, eMERGING ISSUES IN CRISIS MANAGEMENT. [Online]. Available: http://www.sciencedirect.com/science/article/pii/S0007681314001608

[27] K. Stouffer, V. Pillitteri, S. Lightman, M. Abrams, and A. Hahn, "Guide to industrial control systems (ICS) security," Tech. Rep., Jun. 2015. [Online]. Available: https://doi.org/10.6028/nist.sp.800-82r2

[28] J. T. Force and T. Initiative, "Security and privacy controls for federal information systems and organizations," Tech. Rep. 53, Apr. 2013. [Online]. Available: https://doi.org/10.6028/nist.sp.800-53r4

[29] Critical Infrastructure Cybersecurity, "Framework for improving critical infrastructure cybersecurity," URL: https://nvlpubs.nist.gov/nistpubs/CSWP/NIST.CSWP.04162018.pdf [accessed: 2020-06-18].

Experience of Video Classes Related to Mobile Development Produced by Multidisciplinary Students Who Used the Challenge Based Learning Methodology

Andrew Diniz da Costa, Carlos José Pereira de Lucena, Hendi Lemos Coelho,
Ricardo Almeida Venieris, Gustavo Robichez Carvalho
Informatics' Department
Pontifical Catholic University of Rio de Janeiro (PUC-Rio)
Rio de Janeiro, Brazil
e-mails: {acosta, lucena, guga, rvenieris}@inf.puc-rio.br,
hendi@les.inf.puc-rio.br

Abstract— **In Brazil, many people cannot speak English and at the same time there is increasing interest in learning mobile development. Depending on the subject, it is easy to find good video classes online in English in the form of tutorials and even more traditional lectures from top universities. However, the same is not true for videos in Portuguese, which are scarce and often times poorer in quality. From that scenario, there is a great opportunity to create video classes in Portuguese with high quality that can impact the community interested to learn mobile development. Aiming to help the community, this paper presents the experience of an activity, which requested the creation of video classes covering topics related to mobile development from two multidisciplinary groups of students coming from different courses at a university in South America. These videos aimed to be short and offer direct explanations using practical examples. That group of students learned to develop mobile applications using the Challenge Based Learning (CBL) methodology, which provides an efficient and effective framework for learning while solving real-world challenges. This experience shows how different approaches used to present CBL impacted the creation of videos, and how the offered activity contributed positively to the learning of the students and the mobile community in Brazil.**

Keywords-challenge based learning; video classes; multidisciplinary groups; mobile development.

I. INTRODUCTION

The Learning Pyramid [1][2] approach of study, also known as "cone of learning", developed by the National Training Laboratory, suggests that most students only remember 5% from traditional lectures and 10% from what they read from textbooks. On the other hand, students retain nearly 90% of what they learn through teaching others. According to [1], active activities (e.g., to practice doing and teaching other people) help to better retain contents than passive activities (e.g., lecture and reading). Following that idea, there are several new learning methodologies [3]-[5] that look for a more fulfilling learning journey for students. One of these methodologies is Challenge Based Learning (CBL) [3] created by Apple in 2008. CBL fosters learning while solving real-world challenges. In order to create learning opportunities, CBL offers a framework that motivates collaborative work among learners to identify big ideas, ask thoughtful questions, and identify, investigate and solve challenges. According to [3], this approach helps students gain deep subject area knowledge and develop the necessary skills to thrive in an ever-changing world.

This paper describes learning experiences with two multidisciplinary groups of students, who came from different courses (e.g., computer science, engineering, law, design, communication etc.) from an activity which requested the creation of video classes related to themes about mobile development. Both groups were participating in an educational program that taught how to develop iOS apps [8] using CBL.

As many students did not have any previous programming knowledge, an additional motivation was to leave them to choose the theme for the video. However, the requirement of being a subject related to mobile development in some way had to be respected – examples ranged from creation of sounds to apps to publishing an app in the App Store. According to CBL [6], students have to be engaged to learn something. Thus, that freedom to choose a theme was a strategy to engage them.

Another motivation to offer such activity was to produce content in Portuguese that could contribute to the community interested to learn more about mobile development. According to [7], only around 5% of Brazilians state they have some knowledge of English. Considering that scenario, the second requirement for the activity was that all video classes should be in Portuguese. Beyond describing how that activity was offered, the paper explains how it contributed to the learning of the students, how CBL influenced the video classes created, and which additional impacts happened from these new contents.

This paper is organized as follows. Section II presents an overview of the CBL methodology. Section III describes the profile of each students group that participated in the activity, beyond explaining how that activity was offered. Section IV presents results collected from the activity and discusses this data. Lastly, Section V presents the final considerations about the work performed.

II. The Challenge Based Learning (CBL) Methodology

According to [6], CBL provides an efficient and effective framework for learning while solving real-world challenges. The framework is collaborative and hands-on, asking all participants (students, teachers, families, and community members) to identify big ideas, ask good questions, identify and solve challenges, gain deep subject area knowledge, develop 21st century skills, and share their experience with the world.

CBL is based on the foundation of experiential learning and is divided into three main phases [6], Engage, Investigate, and Act, which are explained below.

- **Engage.** Learners move from an abstract big idea to a concrete and actionable challenge using the Essential Questioning process. This process allows the generation of a variety of essential questions that help learners to think about personal interests and needs of the community. At the end, one essential question should be chosen. From this question a Challenge turns it into a call to action to learn in detail about the subject.
- **Investigate.** The learners plan and participate in a journey that builds the foundation for solutions and addresses academic requirements. This phase begins generating Guiding Questions (GQs) related to the Challenge. GQs are questions that need to be answered to allow the development of a solution. The necessary action that allows answering some GQs is called guiding activity (e.g., interviewing an expert in a specific area, reading some book etc.). At the end, learners analyze the data and consolidate the knowledge acquired from the research.
- **Act.** In the Act phase, learners already have a solid foundation to begin developing solution concepts. After the approval of this solution concept, learners develop prototypes, experiment and test. These actions can contribute to raise new guiding questions that need to be answered in the next steps to be performed. Thus, learners can return to the investigate phase to complete the research. After developing their solutions, learners implement them, measure outcomes, and reflect about the work. The refinement of the solution can go on until learners are satisfied.

Throughout the challenge, learners document the experience using audio, video, and photography. This ongoing collection of content provides the resources for reflection, informative assessment and evidence of learning.

III. Creation of Video Classes

In this section, we describe how the activity to create video classes was offered for two groups of students. Thus, this section is organized as follows. Subsection A presents the profile of the participants. Subsection B describes when and how the activity was executed with the first group, while subsection C describes the application to the second group.

A. *Participants*

Both groups engaged in the activity of creating video classes while they were part of an educational program, which taught how to develop iOS apps. Each group participated during two years of the program and they were required to be dedicated 20 hours per week. Hence, that activity was offered during two years of program.

The first group, which received the activity, had 37 students coming from different courses, as shown in Table I. That group began their learning journey in February, 2016 and ended in December, 2017. Every week students were mentored by four teachers (3 related to computing and 1 designer), who guided them and provided additional support throughout their learning process.

TABLE I. Group 1 with 37 Participants

Courses	Amount
Business	1
Chemistry Bachelor	1
Computing	16
Communication	1
Design	10
Civil Engineering	1
Electric Engineering	2
Mechanic Engineering	1
Law	1
Production Engineering	3

The second group of students had 38 people. Like the first group, these students also came from different courses and were mentored by the same teachers. Their participation began in February, 2018 and ended in December, 2019. Table II presents which courses these students came from.

TABLE II. Group 2 with 38 Participants

Courses	Amount
Architecture	1
Business	1
Computing	16
Communication	1
Design	10
Chemistry Engineering	2
Control and Automation Engineering	1
Mechanical Engineering	1
Production Engineering	5

B. *Approach Applied to Group 1*

Aiming to explain when and how the activity of creating video classes was offered to the first group, this subsection is structured in three parts: (i) first, it is contextualized how the students were using the CBL methodology, before receiving the activity; (ii) second, it is explained when and how the activity was offered; and (iii) third, it is described how and which data related to that experience were collected.

1) CBL application: When students began the program, they were presented CBL in a lecture, which explained each phase and the vocabulary of the methodology (e.g., big idea, essential question, challenge, guiding questions etc.).

Before receiving the activity, students participated in several challenges ranging from 2 weeks to 3 months. Each challenge had different group formations, such as, free, respecting a maximum number of members per team (3 or 4 people per group), teams with people who never worked together before, groups pre-defined by teachers considering the profile of the students (e.g., course and knowledge of programming) etc. Hence, the main goals of the challenges were: providing different learning and practical experiences, engaging students to exchange knowledge between them, learning technical and soft skills to be a world class iOS developer, and enjoying their learning journey. Considering that context, the term challenge was used to refer to the activity of creating video classes.

In order to put students' autonomy, proactivity, and flexibility solving issues to test during challenges, teachers avoided giving immediate answers to questions asked by them. The approach adopted was to recommend resources and ask questions that could motivate them to research and start questioning themselves about how to find the desired answers. These issues mapped were used by teachers to make new lectures, which could help students by providing additional context after having an actual experience with that topic during the challenge.

2) Video class activity: The activity was offered to students twice. The first time was in July, 2016 and the second in July, 2017. The requirements of the activity defined by teachers and presented to them were the following.

- Choosing any theme related to mobile development;
- Validating the theme chosen with at least one teacher;
- Creating at least one video class;
- Respecting the maximum of 10 minutes per video;
- Creating videos in Portuguese, with practical examples, and avoiding explanations with slides with a lot of text;
- Choosing to work alone or with some colleague;
- Creating and delivering a document that described their CBL process was not necessary. During all previous challenges, such document was requested to students. Thus, that was an important difference.

Considering that one of the main goals was to contribute to the community interested to learn more about mobile development, a YouTube channel, called DEV PUC-Rio [9], was created to share these videos.

In order to guarantee technical correctness and good quality in the videos, a set of steps was followed by students and teachers during the activity. Below, the order of these steps is presented.

1. Teachers offered a set of resources, which students could use to create good video classes. Examples of resources were: links that explained how to use video edition tools, examples of videos classes etc.
2. Students brought themes to create videos. Teachers validated these themes 3 days after the activity was announced. In general, the themes were accepted, but a few cases (5 in total) of students with difficulty in defining some theme were identified. In these situations, teachers talked with them individually. Aiming to help them, teachers tried to identify passions that each student had. Next, some options were considered together to support their final decision.
3. Students created the first version of the video classes in 10 days. Teachers recommended students in the first two days to bring a script, which described the narrative of the video(s).
4. Teachers validated the videos delivered. Each teacher was responsible for a set of videos considering their expertise. Thus, feedback was written for each video content and shared with its creator after 7 days the first version was delivered. The main improvements identified by teachers were: (i) adjusting the sound or image presented, (ii) improving or correcting some explanation made, such as including some resource that could support it, and (iii) breaking videos in two parts, because, in some cases, they exceeded the maximum time of 10 minutes.
5. All students produced a new version of the videos. Teachers validated and offered feedback for each new version created. That process was repeated until achieving a final version for all video classes. The time it took was more than 20 days.
6. Teachers published the validated videos on the YouTube channel created. Thus, the community could access them easily.

3) Gathering data: After finishing the second activity, students received a survey with a set of questions. These questions looked mainly to understand how the experience with participating in both activities was, how they felt about the learning acquired from the activity, and if the CBL impacted the video classes created. To make students more comfortable answering the survey, it was anonymous. Below, there is a more detailed list with the points collected from the survey.

1. Time spent to create each video class;
2. How the experience to create the video classes was;
3. Learning improvement related to the theme chosen;

4. Additional learning in topics related to video creation skills (e.g., video edition, audio edition etc.);
5. CBL influence on the final result achieved;
6. Opinion of the students regarding the usefulness of the activity to their learning.

C. *Approach Applied to Group 2*

Following the structure presented previously, in the current subsection we explain when and how the activity of creating video classes was offered to the second group. Here, the main differences are highlighted, such as how the second group had the first contact with CBL, how the activity was offered to them, and the approach used to gather data related to that learning experience of students.

1) CBL application: In the beginning of the program, students had a first contact with CBL in a challenge offered without having any previous lecture mentioning its terms and definitions. The main goal was to understand the methodology from the practical experience, making the process of understanding CBL more natural. Aiming to engage students and relate the challenge to their lives, the big idea (i.e., theme, area) offered was the city where they lived: Rio de Janeiro. That challenge lasted 2 weeks, and students had to propose something that could improve the city. However, to propose some solution, students must first motivate themselves for the challenge (Engage phase), perform research (Investigate phase), and propose a solution during a presentation (Act phase). At the end, the teachers informed the students that the methodology applied was CBL, and next a lecture presenting the original English terms of the methodology was made.

Similarly to the first group (see subsection III.B), the second one also had several challenges ranging from 2 weeks to 3 months of duration, different group formation strategies, mentoring with the same four teachers of the group 1, and they had the same approach to learning that involved motivating them to be more autonomous, proactive, and flexible while solving issues.

Lastly, the term challenge was not used to describe the activity to be offered. The main reason was that some students did not perform the CBL steps that would contribute with their learning. Thus, it was called as activity.

2) Video class activity: It was offered for the students once in September, 2018. The requirements of the activity and the steps adopted during its execution were the same as the ones offered for group 1. Like the first group, all students of group 2 also had to produce at least a second version of each video. The necessary changes were the same identified in group 1. At the end of the activity, the video classes were also published in the YouTube channel created.

3) Gathering data: After the delivery of all video classes, the same survey applied to group 1 was offered to the second group. Thus, the survey was answered anonymously, making students more comfortable to fill it.

TABLE III. THEMES OF VIDEOS PUBLISHED

Themes	Group 1 Activity 1	Group 1 Activity 2	Group 2 Activity 1
Publishing app at AppStore	1	-	-
Monetization	-	2	-
Disclosure of apps	-	1	-
Persistence	4	4	7
Front-end development and/or UIKit	7	10	10
Software Test or control version	1	3	-
Creative commons license	-	1	-
Autolayout and/or constraint	1	1	3
Camera and/or Photos	-	1	1
Architecture and /or code organization	1	2	3
Control version	1	-	-
Game development	7	1	2
Approaches to login	2	-	-
Concepts/paradigms of programming	2	3	1
Dependency manager	2	-	-
Accelerometer and gyroscope	2	-	-
watchOS	1	-	-
TvOS	1	-	3
Vision or Augmented Reality	-	5	2
MachineLearning and/or IA	-	1	6
Sound from Garageband	-	-	2
Learning Approach to create an app	-	-	1
Other Apple Kits	2	5	5
Total:	**35**	**40**	**46**

IV. Data Collected and Discussion

In this section, data gathered from the survey applied to the students' groups are presented and analyzed. As group 1 had taken part in two activities related to creation of video classes, teachers requested from them answers based on both experiences. If some difference was identified, this fact would be mentioned in the survey, which offered an additional area for comments. On the other hand, group 2 considered only the single experience performing the activity offered to them.

Initially, Table III categorizes themes chosen by students and the number of videos created per category. Notice that by activity applied, i.e., two activities for group 1 and one for group 2, "front-end development and/or UIKit" was the theme with the highest number of videos created. According to [11], UIKit is a framework that provides the required infrastructure for iOS or tvOS [14] apps. It provides the window and view architecture for implementing interfaces, the event handling infrastructure for delivering Multi-Touch and other types of input to apps, and the main run loop needed to manage interactions among the user, the system, and the app.

According to teachers, having a good number of students producing videos related to front-end was not a big surprise, because many of them presented high interest about the topic since the beginning of their participation in the program. Besides, considering that some technologies had increased visibility over time, such as Vision [12], Augmented Reality [13], Machine Learning and IA, such themes also aroused great interest from the students.

Another piece of information gathered from the survey was the time spent to create each video. Table IV shows that more than 50% of the students per group spent more than 5 hours creating each video. Analyzing the information in more detail, many of them mentioned that the process of defining the script, creating materials that could support the videos, learning how to edit videos, were examples of tasks which influenced the time.

TABLE IV. Time spent to create each video.

Options	Group 1	Group 2
Less than 1 hour	0	0
1 to 2 hours	1	3
2 to 5 hours	15	7
More than 5 hours	21	28

The survey also aimed at understanding how students felt about the experience of creating video classes for other people. Table V shows that students from group 2 considered the activity more enjoyable than students from group 1. Analyzing comments made by students from the first group, it was possible to identify that some of them were not as enthusiastic about creating content as when the first activity was introduced. That feedback was important and influenced the decision made by teachers to run the activity with the second group only once.

TABLE V. How the experience to create the video(s) was.

Scales	Group 1	Group 2
1 (not enjoyable)	1	2
2	1	2
3	10	4
4	7	1
5	9	13
6	7	10
7 (very enjoyable)	2	6

Another important piece of information analyzed was a self-assessment by the students considering their knowledge level before and after the activity was performed. From Table VI, it is possible to realize that both groups felt learning improvements in relation to the themes chosen. For instance, group 1 had 34 students answering 5 or higher, and the same happened with group 2, also with 34 students.

TABLE VI. Knowledge level per topic.

Scales	Before Activity Group 1	After Activity Group 1	Before Activity Group 2	After Activity Group 2
1 (none)	3	0	0	0
2	2	0	4	0
3	7	1	10	1
4	12	2	8	3
5	7	7	7	5
6	4	21	9	24
7 (expert)	2	6	0	5

As these activities were the first experience of students creating videos, the survey also looked for mapping which additional contents related to it, they could have learned. Thus, Table VII shows answers considering how many students considered to have a good learning in relation to the following topics: storyboard, screen capture, video and audio editing. For both groups, more than 80% of the students confirmed to have learned at least one of these topics mentioned. In addition, group 1 had more people learning these topics than group 2. Analyzing more deeply the comments offered by students and analyzing the profile of each group, teachers identified that the second group had more people with some previous experience related to video creation. Thus, it probably influenced the answers collected.

TABLE VII. Number of students that agreed to have had a good learning related to some topics from the activity.

Themes	Group 1	Group 2
Storyboarding	3	3
Screen capture	24	12
Video edition	20	17
Audio edition	17	14

Following the idea of mapping other topics learned by students during the activity, an additional open question was offered to them. Thus, as the answer to that question students could share if they had learned something else. The results showed improvements related to development topics (e.g., object oriented programming [16], architecture and modularization [17][18]), beyond improvements in communicating to an audience. That was the soft-skill that was the most mentioned by the students (more than 20% per group).

The next question was more related to the learning methodology applied in the program the students were participating in. It looked to understanding what influence CBL had on the video classes created according to the students' perspective. Table VIII shows that a good part of the students considered the impact of the learning methodology minor (equal or less than 3): 23 students of the first group and 14 students of the second group. Aiming to better understand these answers, an additional area in the survey was offered requesting explanations.

TABLE VIII. CBL INFLUENCING VIDEO CREATION.

Scales	Group 1	Group 2
1 (strongly not influenced)	7	2
2	10	7
3	6	5
4	4	8
5	6	6
6	3	6
7 (strongly influenced)	1	4

After analyzing these answers, it was possible to achieve some important conclusions and learned lessons, as follows.

- According to some students from group 1, CBL would be present if some document describing the learning process was created. In all previous challenges offered to group 1 such document was requested, which could have influenced their mindsets. From that feedback, teachers realized they needed to improve how they presented the idea of the methodology instead of sharing a view that CBL depends on a formal document to be delivered during the learning process.
- In all challenges offered previously to the students of both groups, CBL vocabulary was used intensively. However, when the activity to create video classes began, these terms were not used as often by students and teachers. That approach should be improved.
- The activity was offered to the first group as a challenge. However, after talking with students and analyzing their experience, teachers realized that some students did not follow the CBL steps, such as deep research (Investigate phase) during that work. To consider an activity as a challenge, it is important to perform extensive research to help support some solution proposal. From that, teachers decided to no longer present the activity as a challenge to the second group, but simply as an activity.
- Some students, who had previous experience with other active learning/teaching approaches (e.g., project based learning [15], design thinking etc.), sometimes did not connect the steps of the CBL to the actions that they were taking, such as to answer the identified guiding questions. Only after talks with teachers, students realized this. That was an alert to improve CBL understanding.

Lastly, the survey requested the opinion of the students if the activity offered was useful to their learning. Table IX shows that group 2 thought it was more useful than group 1. However, almost 50% of the students (18 people) from the first group thought it was useful (answered from 5 to 7).

TABLE IX. OPINION OF THE STUDENTS CONSIDERING THE VIDEO ACTIVITY AS USEFUL TO THEIR LEARNING EXPERIENCE.

Scales	Group 1	Group 2
1 (strongly disagree)	3	1
2	4	1
3	6	0
4	6	8
5	7	8
6	4	8
7 (strongly agree)	7	12

After the activities performed by both groups, more than 120 videos were made available on the YouTube channel. Besides, the channel got more than 2 thousand subscribers, and became an additional reference to new editions of the educational program performed in Rio de Janeiro. When some video of the channel becomes outdated, teachers are looking to motivate the creators or new students to produce a new version of the video.

An interesting situation that happened with some students who made videos was to be recognized at national and international events of development from people, who were subscribers of the YouTube channel. Some videos achieved more than 10 thousand views in a few months, being a resource that the community has been interacting a lot with through questions and feedback.

After the participation in the program, teachers mapped on social media students who continued creating contents for the community (e.g., videos, papers etc.) or participating in events related to development (conferences, symposiums, hackathons etc.). From group 1, at least 15 people, and from group 2, at least 22 students participated in these activities.

Having students interested in producing contents and sharing experiences with other people, it is a way of contributing to the learning of more people and making the knowledge wheel spin even more.

V. CONCLUSION AND FUTURE WORKS

Aiming to contribute to the Brazilian community interested to learn more about mobile development, this paper described the learning experience of an activity related to video class creation applied in two multidisciplinary students' groups. The videos produced are available on a YouTube channel and focus on different themes related to iOS development.

Considering that such activity was offered in an educational program that applied CBL, it was important to understand how students looked for the methodology and how teachers could improve the approach to use it.

One future work intended is to propose a translation of the CBL vocabulary, which is currently in English, into Portuguese. Thus, many students who do not master English will be able to learn from a CBL version using their native language. When an immediate translation to Portuguese is made, some of the CBL terms can be ambiguous or misleading, as some participants of the program report. Thus, performing a study that can gather feedback from beginners or more advanced learners that use CBL it a possible approach to be followed.

Another work that teachers are thinking to adopt in the program is to identify from the very beginning which students are interested to produce content in Portuguese. Thus, a possible more personalized learning track related to production of new contents could be introduced to students. Hence, offering personalized tracks is a possible approach to engage students to learn more contents and maybe contribute to the learning of other people.

ACKNOWLEDGMENT

This work was supported by PPI Softex Convênio 01250.048578/2019-86.

REFERENCES

[1] A. Kybartaite, J. Nousiainen , V. Marozas, and R. Jurkonis, "WP4: Final report: Development and testing of new e-learning and e-teaching practices and technologies". N.p., European Virtual Campus for Biomedical Engineering (EVICAB), pp. e1584-e1593, 2007.

[2] Educationcorner, *The Learning Pyramid*. [Online]. Available from: https://www.educationcorner.com/the-learning-pyramid.html [retrieved: September, 2020]..

[3] M. Nichols, K. Cator, and M. Torres, "Challenge Based Learner User Guide". Redwood City, CA: Digital Promise. [Online]. Available from: https://cbl.digitalpromise.org/wp-content/uploads/sites/7/2016/10/CBL_Guide2016.pdf [retrieved: September, 2020].

[4] W. Hung, D. H. Jonassen, and R. Liu, "Problem-based learning". In the Handbook of research on educational communications and technology (3rd ed.), Routledge, 485-506, 2008

[5] P. K. Jha, "Modern Methods of Teaching and Learning". Rajat Publications, 2006.

[6] The Challenge Institute, *CBL*. [Online]. Available from https://www.challengebasedlearning.org [retrieved: September, 2020].

[7] B. Council, *Learning English in Brazil: Understanding the aims and expectations of the Brazilian emerging middle classes*. [Online.] Available from https://www.britishcouncil.org.br/sites/default/files/learning_english_in_brazil.pdf [retrieved: September, 2020].

[8] Apple Inc, *iOS Overview*. [Online]. Available from https://developer.apple.com/ios/ [retrieved: September, 2020].

[9] PUC-Rio, *DEV PUC-Rio channel*. [Online]. Available from https://www.youtube.com/channel/UCWb9EHguiXaEvLcGZiydIqA [retrieved: September, 2020].

[10] Apple Inc, *Swift Language*. [Online]. Available from https://www.apple.com/ swift/ [retrieved: September, 2020].

[11] Apple Inc, *UIKit Framework*. [Online]. Available from https://developer.apple.com/documentation/uikit [retrieved: September, 2020].

[12] Apple Inc, *Vision Framework*. [Online]. Available from https://developer.apple.com/documentation/vision [retrieved: September, 2020].

[13] Apple Inc, *Augmented Reality*. [Online]. Available from https://developer.apple.com/augmented-reality/ [retrieved: September, 2020].

[14] Apple Inc, *tvOS*. [Online]. Available from: https://www.apple.com/tvos [retrieved: September, 2020].

[15] J. S. Krajcik and P. C. Blumenfeld, "Project-based learning". In R. Sawyer (Ed.), The Cambridge Handbook of the Learning Sciences, pp. 317-334, 2006.

[16] B. D. McLaughlin, G. Pollice, and D. West, "Head First Object-Oriented Analysis and Design". 1st edition, O'Reilly Media, December 2006.

[17] E. Gamma, R. Helm, R. Johnson, and J. Vlissides, "Design Patterns: Elements of Reusable Object- Oriented Software", Addison-Wesley Professional Computing Series, 1994.

[18] J. Greene and J. Strawn, *Design Patterns by Tutorials. First Edition*. [Online]. Available from https://store.raywenderlich.com/products/design-patterns-by-tutorials [retrieved: September, 2020].

[19] M. Michalko, "Thinkertoys: A Handbook of Creative-Thinking Techniques". Ten Speed Press, 2nd ed, June 2006.

Performance Comparison of Two Deep Learning Algorithms in Detecting Similarities Between Manual Integration Test Cases

Cristina Landin*‡, Leo Hatvani§, Sahar Tahvili†§, Hugo Haggren†, Martin Längkvist‡, Amy Loutfi‡, Anne Håkansson¶
* Product Development Unit Radio, Production Test Development, Ericsson AB, Kumla, Sweden
cristina.landin@ericsson.com
†Global Artificial Intelligence Accelerator (GAIA), Ericsson AB, Stockholm, Sweden
{sahar.tahvili, hugo.haggren}@ericsson.com
‡School of Science and Technology, Örebro University, Örebro, Sweden
{cristina.landin, martin.langkvist, amy.loutfi}@oru.se
§School of Innovation, Design and Engineering, Mälardalen University, Västerås, Sweden
leo.hatvani@mdh.se
¶School of Electrical Engineering and Computer Science, KTH Royal Institute of Technology, Stockholm, Sweden
annehak@kth.se

Abstract—**Software testing is still heavily dependent on human judgment since a large portion of testing artifacts, such as requirements and test cases are written in a natural text by experts. Identifying and classifying relevant test cases in large test suites is a challenging and also time-consuming task. Moreover, to optimize the testing process test cases should be distinguished based on their properties, such as their dependencies and similarities. Knowing the mentioned properties at an early stage of the testing process can be utilized for several test optimization purposes, such as test case selection, prioritization, scheduling, and also parallel test execution. In this paper, we apply, evaluate, and compare the performance of two deep learning algorithms to detect the similarities between manual integration test cases. The feasibility of the mentioned algorithms is later examined in a Telecom domain by analyzing the test specifications of five different products in the product development unit at Ericsson AB in Sweden. The empirical evaluation indicates that utilizing deep learning algorithms for finding the similarities between manual integration test cases can lead to outstanding results.**

Keywords–Natural Language Processing; Deep Learning; Software Testing; Semantic Analysis; Test Optimization

I. Introduction

Employing Artificial Intelligence (AI) techniques for test optimization purposes in the industry is regarded to be beneficial due to their ability to analyze the complex software model and a large amount of generated test data [1]. One of the principal ideas behind test optimization is to test a subset of the test cases (in any form of test case selection, prioritization, and test suite minimization) while still covering the requirements [2]–[5]. Parallel test execution [6] and test execution scheduling [7] can be also considered as promising approaches to optimizing the testing process [8]. However, while employing the aforementioned approaches, manual work, domain knowledge, and human judgment are still required. Due to utilizing AI technologies, such as Natural Language Processing (NLP), machine learning and deep learning can help to reduce human effort and improve the performance of the optimization approaches. Additionally, test optimization has been considered as a multi-criteria optimization problem [3], where several criteria, such as dependency and similarity between test cases, execution time, and requirement coverage are recognized as critical elements for selecting, ranking, scheduling, or removing any test case in the testing cycle. As stated earlier, in manual test execution, test cases are designed and created manually, which may result in having similar test cases that are just designed or written differently. Finding the similarities between test cases opens the possibility to apply the aforementioned optimization approaches, such as parallel test execution. In fact, similar test cases can be clustered together and executed at the same time, in parallel with other test cases. Knowing the similarities between test cases at an early stage of a testing process can help us execute test cases more efficiently and directly, thus reducing costs and time [6] [9]. In this paper, we apply two deep learning algorithms for finding the similarities between manual integration test cases that are designed for testing five different products at Ericsson AB. Later, similar test cases are clustered and proposed for execution in parallel. This paper makes the following contribution:

- Applying and comparing the performance of two deep learning algorithms, finding the similarities between manual integration test cases against labeled data conducted from the so-called subject matter experts (SME).
- Clustering similar test cases and scheduling them for parallel test execution.

Moreover, the proposed approach in this paper is utilized to develop our previous work [6], for the similarity threshold calculation. The organization of this paper is as follows: Section II provides a background and problem statement. Section III presents an overview of research on NLP in the testing domain. Section IV describes the proposed approach in this paper. An industrial case study laid out in Section V. Section VI analyzes the performance between the utilized deep learning algorithms is compared against the labeled data. Threats to validity and delimitations are discussed in Section VII. Section VIII clarifies some points of future directions of the present work and finally, Section IX concludes the paper.

TABLE I. TWO EXAMPLES OF SIMILAR AND NON-SIMILAR TEST CASES. $TC_{i,j}$, WHERE TC STANDS FOR A TEST CASE, *i* IS THE TEST CASE NUMBER AND *j* IS THE PRODUCT NAME. THE HIGHLIGHTED WORDS ARE IMPORTANT WORDS FOR COMPARISON BETWEEN TEXTS.

Annotation	Test case specification
Similar	$TC_{1,A}$: This test case will **measure** the **current** value of **LED 1**. Start by **supplying 2.4 V** into **Pin** 2 to the FPGA G1 and **read** the output of **Pin 5**. **Pass** criteria is **10 mA**. **Save** the **result** in **database** 1.
	$TC_{2,B}$: **Measure** the **current** across **LED 2**. **Supply 2.4 V** into **Pin 2** to the FPGA G2 and **read** the output of **Pin 5**. **Pass** criteria is **15 mA**. **Save** the **result** in **db** 2.
Non-Similar	$TC_{1,A}$: This test case will **measure** the **current** value of **LED 1**. Start by **supplying 2.4 V** into **Pin** 2 to the FPGA G1 and **read** the output of **Pin 5**. **Pass** criteria is **10 mA**. **Save** the **result** in **database** 1.
	$TC_{3,B}$: This test case will **measure** the **voltage** of **LED 1**. **Supply 10 V** to the **input T1** and **measure** the **voltage** in **T2**. **Compare** the **results** with the **calculated** and **save** the **result** in **database** 1.

II. BACKGROUND

Ericsson AB is one of the leading providers of Information and Communication Technology (ICT) and has, among many units, a business unit network, which produces the latest technology in Radio Base Stations (RBS). An RBS is a radio transceiver used in wireless communication. Figure 1 shows a block diagram of an RBS, where the transmitter and receiver are the radio parts and the digital control supplies and receives the digital signals to both transmitter and receiver.

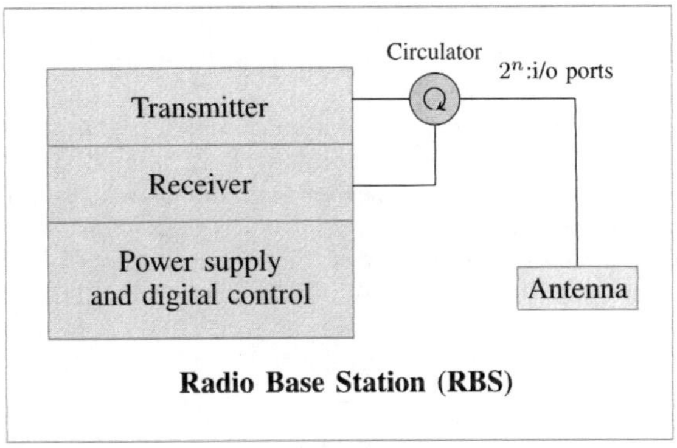

Figure 1. A block diagram of a simplified version of a Radio Base Station 2^n is the number of ports.

The power supply powers the RBS and its specification depends on the target market (e.g., USA, Europe, and Asia). Because both receiver and transmitter contain analog devices, these parts must be calibrated and tested at the device level and unit level together with the antenna. The number of ports to be tested in production is $2^n, (n = 1, 2, 3, ...)$ and each port may be tested separately. A circulator is a simplified version of the design, which only allows the signal to go one direction and not vice versa to protect the internal components. Among all faced challenges the new generation of RBSs are bringing into test and production, the test capacity and the long run-time of each test process can be considered as the main two challenges. The increase in functionality and the number of features (e.g., emerging technologies) that the new generation of products needs to cover aggravate the complexity of the RBS design. Although the design is more complex, the RBS still has to be tested to follow international standards, e.g., 3GPP, FCC, IEC, UL. These standards specify the technical protocols and requirements for mobile communication systems. The above-mentioned factors have resulted in the more complex testing process which increases the required number of test cases that need to be tested. Executing all generated test cases for testing an RBS without any specific order could lead to the waste of testing resources and time. Equation (1) indicates the total testing time, T, when the test cases are executed sequentially. Because of the RBS complex design, such as the number of ports, 2^n, and the number of technologies to cover, h, the total test time increases exponentially and linearly respectively. t_i represents the test time to run each test case and m is the total number of test cases.

$$T = h * 2^n * \sum_{i=1}^{m} t_i \tag{1}$$

Hereof parallel test execution has been considered as a potential solution to optimize the integration testing process at Ericsson. Moreover, the saving time (ST) using parallel test execution for similar test cases can be calculated as:

$$ST = \frac{(np - 1)}{np} \times 100 \tag{2}$$

where np is the number of test cases with the same system setup. We define the concept of two similar test cases in this paper as:

Definition 1. *Test case TC_1 and TC_2 are similar if only if they are designed to test the same functionality or they have the same preconditions, execution requirements (installation), system setup.*

In other words, if two or more test cases are semantically similar, they might be designed to test the same functionality or require the same system setup or pre-condition. Examples of similar and non-similar test cases are shown in Table I, where LED is Light Emitting Diode and FPGA stands for Field-Programmable Gate Array. They give a glimpse of how the test cases are described in natural language and their pre-requisites. Although parallel test execution is a promising approach for time and resource-saving, however, there are some assumptions that need to be satisfied. For instance, there are no dependencies between test cases and there are enough available test stations to execute test cases simultaneously. In fact, utilizing (2) (in one example scenario) means that the system setup or installation effort needs to be performed once for product A where $np - 1$ products can be executed after product A on the same test station. Since the designed test cases for testing RBSs are written in a non-formal language, employing NLP techniques for semantic analysis might provide some clues to detecting the similarities between test cases. Furthermore, similar test cases can be grouped into several clusters based on their semantic text similarities. On the other hand, finding the similarities between text cases manually requires human work where the testers need to go through the test case descriptions and comparing them with each other. However, analyzing a large number of test cases manually is a time-consuming process and suffers from ambiguity and uncertainty. Consequently, employing AI algorithms with a combination of human supervision can be considered as a promising approach, where the knowledge of the testers can be captured during the learning process. In addition, the use of NLP techniques can help test engineers to extract relevant information in a large document automatically and thereby distinguishing test cases from each other. Usually, test engineers use different terminologies and the quality of a test case specification is dependent on the test engineers' knowledge, experience, and skill. Therefore, it is crucial to find a proper NLP algorithm to meet the goal. In this regard, we decide to compare the performance of two deep learning algorithms to detect the similarities between test cases and comparing the performance of them against the labeled data conducted by SMEs at Ericsson. Deep learning algorithms for NLP have a high tolerance to noisy data and they are able to classify patterns on which they have not been trained [10], [11].

III. Related Work

There have been several techniques proposed for the crucial step of test optimization. The proposed strategies vary depending on the industrial product, development method, complexity of the models, and data availability and reliability [12]. The overall aim of test optimization is to minimize the required testing time by detecting failed test cases as early as possible. Since the duration and relevancy vary between test cases, the testing time can be reduced by test case selection, prioritization, minimization, and test execution scheduling. The proposed test case prioritization by Nardo et al. [13] uses a coverage-based method that prioritizes test cases with the most recent code changes. This strategy is suitable for software development practice, such as Continuous Integration (CI) [14] [15] [9] where the components are regularly implemented and tested during the development process. Fowler and Foemmel [16] propose an information retrieval approach for detecting code changes that are used for regression test prioritization. For full system testing [17] or when tracking of code changes is unavailable, history-based test prioritization has been proposed by several researchers [18], [19] for prioritizing test cases that have failed more frequently in the past. Spieker et al. [20] propose an adaptive reinforcement learning approach for history-based test case prioritization and selection that learns to rank test cases based on their duration, previous last execution, and failure history. One of the disadvantages of learning-based approaches is that it requires a history of executed test cases and the learning process needs to be repeated for any new product. Test case selection and prioritization based on human-designed test cases have the advantage of evaluating the test cases before they are even executed. Previously [6] used the Levenshtein distance to detect the similarity between each pair of test cases (which were designed to test five different products at Ericsson AB) to detect the similarities between them. The test case pairs were clustered into four groups (identical, very similar, similar, and partially similar) ranked for parallel test execution. The threshold for each of the mentioned groups in [6] is assigned manually using the subject matter expert (SME) experience. The NLP technique that was used in [6] did not take into account the order of the words in a test specification, which can be a disadvantage, considering how specific a procedure of each test case must be implemented. Using NLP techniques has received a great deal of attention in different domains, such as social network analysis [21]. NLP has also been studied to find sentiment analysis [22] and to find semantic and syntactic similarities in large context [23], where the training complexity can be considered as an important aspect. Moreover, using deep learning for natural language analysis has been a focus since the year 2000. Young et.al [24] discuss the recent trends in deep learning on NLP tasks. For learning word representations, Le and Mikolov [25] introduced a new method called Word2vec that finds semantic similarities between paragraphs taking into account the order and semantic context of the vectors (not only limited to a sentence or a fixed length of text), in order to predict words based on the content of the paragraphs. Patil et al. [26] use the Word2vec algorithm as inputs to the Convolutional Neural Network (CNN) to classify binary and multi-class document categorization. Although CNN is effective in finding semantic similarities, it has problems to preserve sequential order and model long-distance dependencies. Moreover, Tahvili et al. [27] [28] employed the Doc2vec algorithm (which is an extension of Word2vec) for finding the functional dependencies between manual integration test cases at Bombardier transportation.

In the present study, we aim to compare the performance of two well-known deep learning algorithms, Doc2vec and Sentence Bidirectional Encoder Representations from Transformers (SBERT), in a set of labeled data from five RBSs from Ericsson AB. Moreover, the similarity threshold which has been assumed manually in [6] can now be automatically computed though comparing the utilized edit distance approach with the deep learning algorithms.

IV. Proposed Approach

The proposed approach in this paper is mirrored in Figure 2. The manual test cases are the input to our model. In step 1 (**Similarity Analysis**) in Figure 2, the similarities between test cases are detected by employing deep learning algorithms, such as Doc2vec and SBERT. Applying deep learning models for semantic analysis provides a set of high dimensional vectors, where each vector represents a test case. To split test cases (step 2 in Figure 2) a clustering algorithm needs to be utilized which can handle high dimensional data points. Finally, since the main application of the proposed approach in Figure 2 is to test efficiency, similar test cases can be scheduled for test execution, e.g., parallel test execution. We need to consider that, the proposed approach in Figure 2 is not just limited to the mentioned algorithms, where other approaches, such as edit distance, string matching, and text classification can be utilized as well. Later in this paper, we provide more information regarding employing other techniques for both **Similarity Analysis** and **Splitting Test Cases** steps in Figure 2. Furthermore, in the upcoming subsections, more details are provided for the utilized algorithms for each step.

A. *Doc2vec*

Deep learning algorithms use representation learning to learn the data representation instead of using manually handcrafted features [29]. Doc2vec is a deep neural networks-based

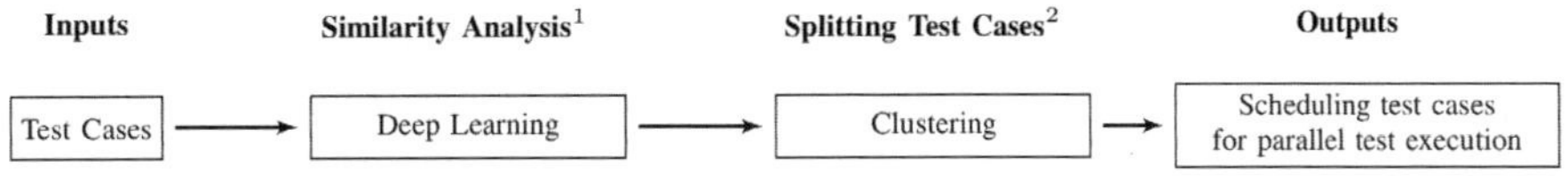

Figure 2. The block diagram of the proposed approach.

algorithm that generates a vector representation for a word, paragraph, or document [25]. Doc2vec represents a non-fixed length document into a vector. Besides, it concatenates each word of the document. Figure 3 shows a representation of the structure of the Doc2vec algorithm to predict the next word. For instance, $W3$ based on the sentence $[W1+W2]$. Producing in this way two vectors, one vector for the document, called D and one vector for the words called W. One important facility of this algorithm is to keep the words' properties and the relations between words and semantics of the whole document.

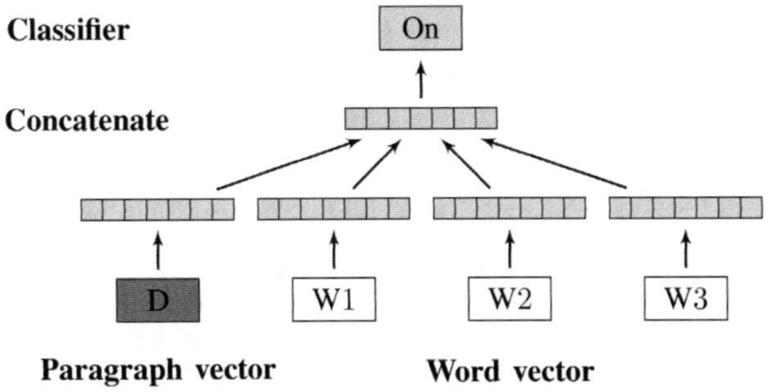

Figure 3. A representation of the Doc2vec algorithm to predict a word, based on the semantics of the sentence.

In fact, each paragraph will have an ID represented in paragraph vector D, and the words are represented in the word vector W. They will concatenate to predict the next word of the sentence.

B. SBERT

SBERT is an algorithm in the domain of NLP, which is designed to pre-train deep bidirectional representations from an unlabeled text [30]. SBERT is a modified version of BERT [31] that jointly conditions on both left and right context in all the layers. Reimers and Gurevych [32] developed sentence embedding based on Euclidian distance which allows finding semantic similarities in sentences and is suitable for clustering and information retrieval purposes. Furthermore, SBERT is computationally more efficient than the heavy and complex BERT. Figure 4 shows the structure of SBERT to compute similarity scores. SBERT adds a pooling operation to the output of BERT and computes the cosine-similarity between sentence embeddings u and v. The pooling operation is to derive a fixed-sized sentence embedding.

The pooling operation is added after BERT to give the same size to the sentence embeddings, u, and v. After this step, the similarities are computed using cosine-distance.

C. HDBSCAN

For the clustering part of the proposed approach in this paper, we propose to use the Hierarchical Density-Based Spatial

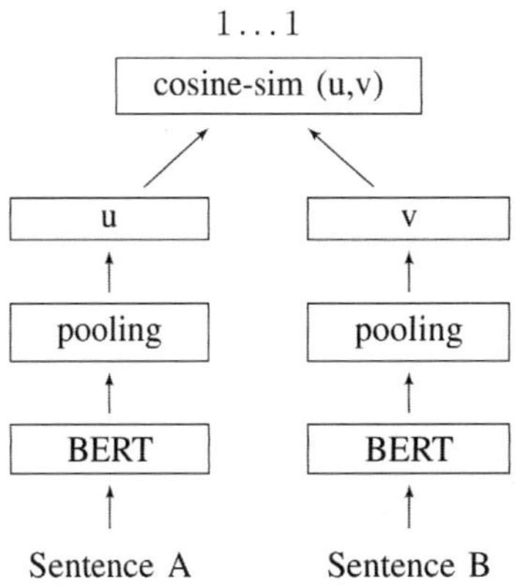

Figure 4. The architecture of the SBERT algorithm which is designed to compute similarity scores between sentences.

Clustering of Applications with Noise (HDBSCAN), which is a density-based clustering algorithm based on a hierarchical density estimate [33]. HDBSCAN generates a simplified hierarchy and extracts the most significant clusters. Using HDBSCAN has two main advantages: 1-HDBSCAN is able to clusters the high dimensional data point without employing any dimension reduction technique (e.g., Principal Component Analysis (PCA)), 2-HDBSCAN provides a cluster of non-clusterable data points which can be interpreted as noises, outliers or anomalies. In this paper, the non-clusterable data points are considered as non-similar test cases. However, if the high dimensional data is projected onto a lower dimension space (using a technique like PCA), other standard clustering techniques can be employed instead of HDBSCAN.

V. Industrial Case Study

The provided industrial case study in this work follows the proposed guidelines for conducting and reporting case study research in software engineering by Runeson and Höst [34] and specifically the way guidelines are followed in [35] and [3], [36]. Hereof, five multi-standard RBSs compatible with their respective number of test cases are utilized as a case under study.

A. Unit of analysis and procedure

The test specifications of five products of the 4th Generation (4G) RBS are our dataset, which includes 444 test cases in total. The utilized test cases are written in natural language text and by the SME at Ericsson. As illustrated in Figure 2 our approach aims to cluster similar test cases and also provide a cluster of non-similar test cases. Table I provides two real industrial examples of similar and non-similar test cases. However, using human knowledge and judgment for the similarity analysis is a time and resource-consuming process

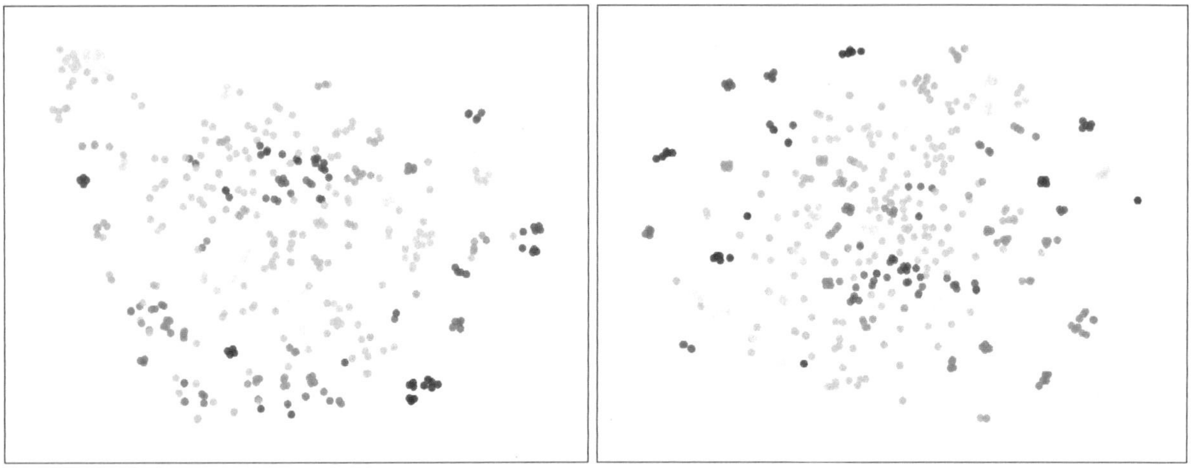

(a) The clustered test case using the generated vectors by the SBERT. (b) The clustered test case using the generated vectors by the Doc2vec.

Figure 5. The clustered test cases using HDBSCAN algorithm on the generated vectors by two deep learning algorithms. There are 75 and 76 clusters plotted in different colors for SBERT and Doc2vec respectively. The outliers are shown in gray.

and it might suffer from ambiguity and uncertainty. Therefore, employing AI techniques for similarity analysis and thereby clustering purposes is critical in large industries.

B. *Experimental Setup*

SBERT provides the option to train a new model or to use a pre-trained model to convert test cases to feature vectors. As our dataset is rather small and built out of test cases written in English, we are able to use a pre-made BERT-base model with mean-tokens pooling, *bert-base-nli-mean-tokens*, obtainable from the SBERT repository [37]. We have not made any customizations to the code and thus the result is a feature vector with 768 features for each of the 444 observed test cases. The employed implementation of the SBERT produces consistent results between different runs. For the Doc2vec approach to feature vector generation, we have used the Gensim [38] implementation. For this approach, we have used the following parameters: feature vector size of 100, min word count for dictionary inclusion of 1, and 100 training epochs. Gensim approach is based on training a new neural network every iteration and thus can produce various results depending on the input parameters and a random initial value. To estimate the impact of these parameters, we varied them within reasonable ranges across 150 iterations and found that the largest standard deviation from the results presented in this paper is 0.08 across all of the measures presented in Table III.

The generated feature vectors are then clustered using the standard implementation of the HDBSCAN algorithm using the default clustering values with distances being computed as cosine distances between feature vectors. Pairs of test cases from the labeled data are then compared against the clusters to obtain the confusion matrix from which precision, recall, and F1 score are calculated. Further details about the implementation of the HDBSCAN algorithm are available at [39].

VI. RESULT

Figure 5 shows the clustered test cases using the HDBSCAN, each color represents a unique cluster of test cases which are being considered as semantic similar by Doc2vec and SBERT algorithms. Figure 5a illustrates the obtained clusters using the provided vectors by SBERT, where the number of obtained clusters is equal to 75. Figure 5b shows the clusters where HDBSCAN used the generated vectors provided by Doc2vec, the number of obtained clusters is equal to 76. The t-SNE is used to plot the results after the clustering done by HDBSCAN. Both results are expected due to the properties of the dataset and resemble the SME's criteria. We need to consider that the size of each cluster is different for the Doc2vec and SBERT. Moreover, using HDBSCAN can help us to have a cluster of non-clusterable data points, which indicates to non-similar test cases in this study.

A. *Model Performance Evaluation*

Table II summarizes the cluster size and the obtained non-clusterable data points. The entire results and implementation source are available at [40]. In order to compare the performance of the employed deep learning algorithms against the labeled data, 402 out of 444 test cases manually labeled by the SME at Ericsson, wherein in total we received labels for 211 similar and 191 non-similar test cases. Test cases similarity detection might suffer the class imbalance problem when the class distributions (similar and non-similar) are imbalanced. Therefore, selecting a suitable performance metrics is critical and also influences the measured performance of a model [41]. To evaluate the performance of the proposed approach in this paper, precision, recall, and F1 score are measured instead of accuracy. F1 score conveys the balance between the precision and the recall, which is a suitable metric for the imbalance problems, shown in (3).

$$F1 \quad score = 2 \times \frac{Precision \times Recall}{Precision + Recall} \tag{3}$$

TABLE II. THE NUMBER OF CLUSTERS, CLUSTER SIZE, AND THE NUMBER OF NON-CLUSTERABLE DATA POINTS USING DOC2VEC, SBERT, AND HDBSCAN.

	Cluster Size	
Cluster Number	Doc2vec	SBERT
Cluster 1	5	3
Cluster 2	5	5
Cluster 3	7	3
⋮		
Cluster 75	3	2
Cluster 76	5	0
Non-clusterable	132	133

Table III summarizes the evaluation of the obtained results, using precision, recall, and F1 score.

TABLE III. THE PERFORMANCE COMPARISON OF DOC2VEC AND SBERT AGAINST THE LABELED DATA PROVIDED BY THE SME.

	Similar			Non-similar		
Algorithm	Precision	Recall	F1 score	Precision	Recall	F1 score
Doc2vec	0.952	0.943	**0.947**	0.937	0.947	**0.942**
SBERT	0.946	0.834	0.886	0.837	0.947	0.889

As can be seen in Table III, the F1 score for Doc2vec is 0.947 and 0.942 for similar and non-similar, respectively. The obtained F1 score for SBERT is about 0.89, which indicates a good overall performance as well but not as good as that of Doc2vec. Moreover, the presented clusters in Figure 5 and Table II can be utilized for parallel test execution and also test suite reduction. For parallel test execution, each cluster (which contains several test cases) can be scheduled for execution simultaneously. As mentioned before, if two test cases are similar in their test specifications they might be designed for testing the same functionality or they required the same precondition, i.e. in system setup. Using the presented results in Table II for instance for the Doc2vec algorithm, we have 5 test cases (distributed between five different products) which are grouped into cluster 1. There are two different scenarios in this case. 1-The mentioned five test cases are designed to test a common function between five different products. In this scenario, executing all five mentioned test cases leads to this function will be tested fully before we are scheduling another function for the testing. All other presented clusters in Table II can be executed parallel on the other test stations, while cluster 1 is executed completely. 2-The mentioned five test cases in cluster 1 are required the same installation effort. Thus the testing environment needs to be configured once for just one test case inside of cluster 1 and all other four test cases can be executed after each other on the same test station. Using 2 can help us to measure the saving time for this scenario. On the other hand, selecting just one test candidate from each cluster for execution can be utilized for the test suite reduction purposes. Furthermore, the non-clusterable data points presented in Table II indicate the non-similar test cases which can be executed sequentially before or after other similar test cases.

B. The Similarity Threshold Calculation

Previously [6], the test cases were classified into several classes (e.g., identical, very similar, similar) based on their Levenshtein distance and the similarity threshold, which was set manually using the SME's experience. In this regard, the similarity threshold is selected as $0.8 \leqslant \text{LD} \leqslant 1$, where 0.8 is the desired lower limit for the similarity of two test cases. Moreover, a Levenshtein distance equal to 1 represents two identical test cases and a Levenshtein distance lower than 0.8 represents non-similar test cases. Finding an optimal similarity threshold is beneficial in terms of reducing human judgment. It can also be utilized for identifying the first distance that test cases are started to be similar to each other. In this study, an automatic threshold detection approach (see **Threshold Detection**$^{2'}$ in Figure 6) is applied through measuring the Levenshtein distance between the vectors (which belong to the same cluster) generated by the deep learning models. The second contribution of this paper is to find the similarity threshold to delimit between similar and non-similar test cases using The Levenshtein distance in our previous work [6]. The Levenshtein distance is measured between all test cases that have been clustered as similar by HDBSCAN. Table IV presents The sum of the averages Levenshtein distance per cluster. In fact, the Levenshtein distance between each test case, which ended up into the same clustered, is measured. As can be seen, the mean value of the Levenshtein distances is equal to 0.69 and 0.64 for Doc2vec and SBERT respectively.

TABLE IV. THE SIMILARITY THRESHOLD CALCULATION USING DEEP LEARNING ALGORITHMS (DOC2VEC AND SBERT) AND CLUSTERED RESULTS (HDBSCAN) BASED ON LEVENSHTEIN DISTANCE.

Algorithm	Doc2vec	SBERT
Number of clusters	76	75
The sum of the averages Levenshtein distance per cluster	**0.69**	**0.64**

This result indicates that test cases can already be considered similar if their Levenshtein distance is equal or greater than 0.64 for SBERT and 0.68 for Doc2vec respectively. This improves the results found in [6], where the lowest boundary of similarity was assumed 0.8 in close consultation with SMEs at Ericsson. Moreover, these performance measures in this study are an improvement to the edit distance approach which used by us previously [6]. The F1 score of 0.61 using Levenshtein distance obtained utilizing the same dataset. According to the presented result in Table III, Doc2vec has a better performance compared to both SBERT and significantly better than Levenshtein distance on this application.

VII. THREATS TO VALIDITY

There are some risks in applying the proposed approaches in this paper. Infrastructure, enough available testing stations, and resource limitation can be considered as the major construct validity threat to the parallel test execution. For applying the proposed approach in this study, we need to have several available test stations for testing each product parallel with others. The coming technologies as 5G will only enlarge those challenges due to the increase in the number of elements i.e. the number of ports, making this solution a necessity. Using the test specifications for finding the similarities between test

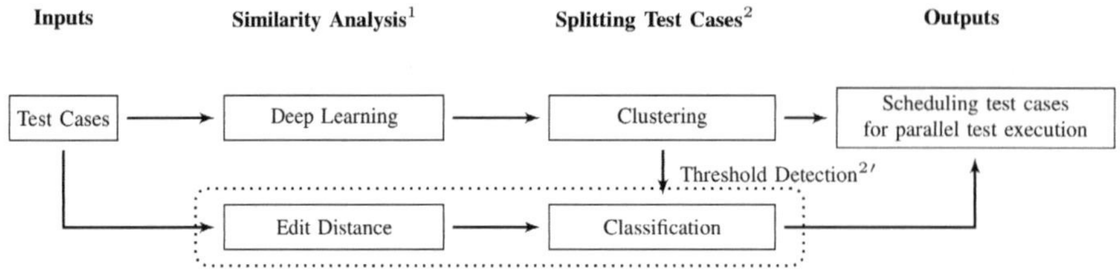

Figure 6. The similarity threshold calculation for the Edit distance approach using the clustering results. The lower part of the diagram shows the approach used previously in [6].

cases might be sensitive in terms of changing a single character in the test. For instance, $TC_{1,A}$ in Table I, the change of only one character in the pass criteria from $10mA$ to $100mA$ could affect much in the measurement results of a LED, which could result in a broken component. However, deep learning algorithms are more stable to the character changing compare to the edit distance and string matching approaches. The proposed approach in this paper has been applied on just one industrial testing project in the Telecom domain, however, it should be applicable to other similar contexts in other testing domains. Nevertheless, we cannot claim that the proposed approach in this paper works well in all fields where precision is a very important variable, e.g., medicine, chemistry, and electronics. Furthermore, the labeled data, which has been used for the performance evaluation was conducted manually by the testing expert at Ericsson and it might suffer from uncertainty. Therefore, another type of ground truth needs to be conducted in order to generalize the proposed approach in this study. Finally despite deep learning and word embedding approaches being interesting, one cannot exclude that traditional rule-based methods may also be applicable and sometimes result in better performance than the latest deep learning methods, which depend on the application. In our case, rules are given by the specialist in the area which could give more importance to specific sections on the test case description to find better insights and extract relevant features before clustering.

VIII. Discussion and Future Work

The main goal of this study is to compare the performance of two deep learning algorithms on an industrial case study. To this end, we make the following contributions: 1-Doc2vec and SBERT have been employed to detect the similarities between manual integration test cases automatically. The similarities have been extracted by analyzing test case specifications written in a non-formal natural language. 2-The evaluation of the proposed algorithms was performed by conducting an industrial testing project in the Telecom domain at Ericsson in Sweden. 3-The performance of the Doc2vec and SBERT was compared against the labeled data using SME knowledge at Ericsson. The obtained results show the outstanding performance of the mentioned deep learning algorithms on the conducted industrial case study. 4-The performance of the Doc2vec and SBERT was compared against our previous work [6] where the Levenshtein distance was utilized for the similarity detection on the same dataset. The obtained results indicate that the lowest boundary of similarity using Levenshtein distance can go down to 0.64 compared to 0.8, which was the empirical value used previously in [6] by the SME.

A. Future Work

The main future direction of this paper is employing other text analysis approaches such as edit distance and string matching for similarity detection. In fact, the mentioned approaches in Figure 6 can be extended to all existing text mining methods. Other clustering and classification algorithms can be adopted to Figure 6. As stated earlier, using data dimensionality reduction techniques, e.g., random forests, PCA and thereby applying other standard clustering techniques (e.g., k-means) might provide better results compared to HDBSCAN. Moreover, conducting a larger case study and comparing the performance of all text mining methods, which are applicable for similarity analysis, can provide a clue for finding the best method in terms of accuracy and execution time. Generally, running a deep learning or neural network algorithm requires more time compared to the other text-mining algorithm, which has a less complex structure. Developing the utilized algorithms of this study as a tool that can handle even larger sets of test specifications is one of the future directions. Despite the fact that the results found in this paper using deep learning algorithms are promising, they are entirely based on one dataset within a specific domain i.e. five fourth-generation (4G) RBSs. We aim to test this approach in other datasets and domains thus, in this way it can be generalized and transfer to other products, e.g., fifth-generation (5G) RBSs or even future generations of RBSs. Furthermore, we are aiming to verify the robustness of the tool. For this purpose, a long time study is needed within production, which will secure this tool to be scalable and compatible with different platforms proper of old and new technologies. A question left to answer is whether these deep learning approaches are better than the traditional rule-based methods for this application. Usually, the traditional rule-based methods are hand-crafted and require field knowledge, which may not be a disadvantage in very complicated industrial applications. Although we can see many potential improvements to the traditional rule-based methods, a formal comparison of those methods and deep learning methods is worth investigating.

IX. Conclusion

Parallel test execution plays a vital role in test optimization and can lead to saving time and cost in a testing process. In this paper, two deep learning algorithms (Doc2vec and SBERT) are applied and evaluated to find the semantic similarities between manual integration test cases for test optimization. The obtained results indicate that Doc2vec shows better performance (F1 score=0.947 for the similar test cases and F1 score=0.942 for non-similar test cases) compare to SBERT (F1 score=0.886

for the similar test cases and F1 score=0.889) when it evaluated against the labeled data. This conclusion opens possibilities to use the method for parallel testing and test suite minimization.

ACKNOWLEDGMENT

This work has been supported by the Swedish Knowledge Foundation (KKS) and VINNOVA through CoAIRob industrial research school and the TESTOMAT project respectively.

REFERENCES

[1] S. Khan and T. Yairi, "A review on the application of deep learning in system health management," *Mechanical Systems and Signal Processing*, vol. 107, pp. 241–265, 2018.

[2] R. Ducloux, L. Fourment, S. Marie, and D. Monnereau, "Automatic optimization techniques applied to a large range of industrial test cases," *Int. Journal of Material Forming*, vol. 3, no. 1, pp. 53–56, 2010.

[3] S. Tahvili, "Multi-criteria optimization of system integration testing," Ph.D. dissertation, Mälardalen University, December 2018.

[4] S. Tahvili et al., "Dynamic Integration Test Selection Based on Test Case Dependencies," in *The 11th Workshop on Testing: Academia-Industry Collaboration, Practice and Research Techniques*, 2016.

[5] S. Tahvili et al., "Towards earlier fault detection by value-driven prioritization of test cases using fuzzy topsis," in *The 13th Int. Conf. on Information Technology: New Generations*, 2016, pp. 745–759.

[6] C. Landin et al., "Cluster-based parallel testing using semantic analysis," in *2020 IEEE International Conference on Artificial Intelligence Testing (AITest)*, 2020, pp. 99–106.

[7] S. Tahvili et al., "sortes: A supportive tool for stochastic scheduling of manual integration test cases," *Journal of IEEE Access*, pp. 1–19, 2019.

[8] G. Rothermel, R. Untch, C. Chu, and M. Harrold, "Test case prioritization: An empirical study," in *Proceedings IEEE International Conference on Software Maintenance-1999 (ICSM'99).'Software Maintenance for Business Change'(Cat. No. 99CB36360)*. IEEE, 1999, pp. 179–188.

[9] S. Tahvili et al., "Cost-benefit analysis of using dependency knowledge at integration testing," in *The 17th Int. Conf. On Product Focused Software Process Improvement*, 2016, pp. 268–284.

[10] T. Khuat and B. Gabrys, "A comparative study of general fuzzy min-max neural networks for pattern classification problems," *Neurocomputing*, vol. 386, pp. 110 – 125, 2020.

[11] O. Engström, S. Tahvili, A. Muhammad, F. Yaghoubi, and L. Pellaco, "Performance analysis of deep anomaly detection algorithms for commercial microwave link attenuation," in *The 2020 International Conference on Advanced Computer Science and Information Systems*, October 2020.

[12] A. Petrenko, A. Dury, S. Ramesh, and S. Mohalik, "A method and tool for test optimization for automotive controllers," in *2013 IEEE Sixth International Conference on Software Testing, Verification and Validation Workshops*, 2013, pp. 198–207.

[13] D. Nardo, N. Alshahwan, L. Briand, and Y. Labiche, "Coverage-based regression test case selection, minimization and prioritization: A case study on an industrial system," *Software Testing, Verification and Reliability*, vol. 25, no. 4, pp. 371–396, 2015.

[14] P. Duvall, S. Matyas, and A. Glover, *Continuous integration: improving software quality and reducing risk*. Pearson Education, 2007.

[15] M. Fowler and M. Foemmel, "Continuous integration," 2006, [Online]. Available from: https://martinfowler.com/articles/continuousIntegration/ 2020.09.02.

[16] R. Saha, L. Zhang, S. Khurshid, and D. Perry, "An information retrieval approach for regression test prioritization based on program changes," in *IEEE/ACM 37th IEEE International Conference on Software Engineering*, vol. 1, 2015, pp. 268–279.

[17] A. Dias, R. Subramanyan, M. Vieira, and G. Travassos, "A survey on model-based testing approaches: a systematic review," in *Proceedings of the int. work. on Empirical assessment of software engineering languages and technologies*, 2007, p. 31–36.

[18] J. Kim and A. Porter, "A history-based test prioritization technique for regression testing in resource constrained environments," in *Proceedings of Int. Conf. on Software Engineering*, 2002, pp. 119–129.

[19] D. Marijan, A. Gotlieb, and S. Sen, "Test case prioritization for continuous regression testing: An industrial case study," in *Int. Conf. on Software Maintenance*, 2013.

[20] H. Spieker, A. Gotlieb, D. Marijan, and M. Mossige, "Reinforcement learning for automatic test case prioritization and selection in continuous integration," in *Proceedings of Int. Symp. on Software Testing and Analysis*, 2017.

[21] A. Sarlan, C. Nadam, and S. Basri, "Twitter sentiment analysis," in *Int. conf. on Information Technology and Multimedia*, 2014.

[22] P. Sanguansat, "Paragraph2vec-based sentiment analysis on social media for business in thailand," in *Int. Conf. on Knowledge and Smart Technology (KST)*, 2016.

[23] T. Mikolov, K. Chen, G. Corrado, and J. Dean, "Efficient estimation of word representations in vector space," 2013.

[24] T. Young, D. Hazarika, S. Poria, and E. Cambria, "Recent trends in deep learning based natural language processing," 2017.

[25] Q. Le and T. Mikolov, "Distributed representations of sentences and documents," in *Int. conf. on machine learning*, 2014.

[26] S. Patil, A. Gune, and M. Nene, "Convolutional neural networks for text categorization with latent semantic analysis," in *Int. Conf. on Energy, Communication, Data Analytics and Soft Computing*, 2017.

[27] S. Tahvili, L. Hatvani, M. Felderer, W. Afzal, and M. Bohlin, "Automated functional dependency detection between test cases using doc2vec and clustering," in *Int. Conf. On Artificial Intelligence Testing*, 2019.

[28] S. Tahvili et al., "Cluster-based test scheduling strategies using semantic relationships between test specifications," in *Int. Work. on Requirements Engineering and Testing*, 2018.

[29] D. Erhan et al., "Why does unsupervised pre-training help deep learning?" *J. Mach. Learn. Res.*, vol. 11, p. 625–660, 2010.

[30] J. Lee et al., "BioBERT: a pre-trained biomedical language representation model for biomedical text mining," *Bioinformatics*, no. 4, pp. 1234–1240, 2019.

[31] J. Devlin, M. Chang, K. Lee, and K. Toutanova, "BERT: Pre-training of deep bidirectional transformers for language understanding," in *Conf. of the North American Chapter of the Association for Computational Linguistics: Human Language Technologies*, 2019.

[32] N. Reimers and I. Gurevych, "Sentence-bert: Sentence embeddings using siamese bert-networks," in *Conf. on Empirical Methods in Natural Language Processing*, 2019.

[33] R. Campello, D. Moulavi, and J. Sander, "Density-based clustering based on hierarchical density estimates," in *Advances in Knowledge Discovery and Data Mining*, 2013.

[34] P. Runeson and M. Höst, "Guidelines for conducting and reporting case study research in software engineering," *Empirical Software Engineering*, vol. 14, no. 2, pp. 131–164, 2009.

[35] E. Engström and P. Runeson, "Decision support for test management and scope selection in a software product line context," in *Int. Conf. on Software Testing, Verification and Validation Workshops*, 2011.

[36] S. Tahvili, L. Hatvani, E. Ramentol, R. Pimentel, W. Afzal, and F. Herrera, "A novel methodology to classify test cases using natural language processing and imbalanced learning," *Engineering Applications of Artificial Intelligence*, vol. 95, pp. 1–13, August 2020.

[37] "Sbert source code and model repository," [Online]. Available from: http://github.com/UKPLab/sentence-transformers/ 2020.09.01.

[38] R. Rehurek and P. Sojka, "Software Framework for Topic Modelling with Large Corpora," in *LREC Work. on New Challenges for NLP Frameworks*, 2010.

[39] "Hdbscan source code and model repository," [Online]. Available from github.com/scikit-learn-contrib/hdbscan/ 2020.09.01.

[40] "Model performance evaluation," [Online]. Available from: http://github.com/leohatvani/landin-performance-comparison/ 2020.09.01.

[41] Z. Lipton, C. Elkan, and B. Naryanaswamy, "Optimal thresholding of classifiers to maximize f1 measure," in *Machine Learning and Knowledge Discovery in Databases*, 2014.

UML-based Model-Driven Code Generation of Error Detection Mechanisms

Lars Huning
Institute of Computer Science
University of Osnabrück
49069 Osnabrück, Germany
Email: lhuning@uos.de

Padma Iyenghar
Institute of Computer Science
University of Osnabrück
49069 Osnabrück, Germany
Email: piyengha@uos.de

Elke Pulvermüller
Institute of Computer Science
University of Osnabrück
49069 Osnabrück, Germany
Email: epulverm@uos.de

***Abstract*—The complexity of safety-critical embedded systems increases as more and more functions are realized in software. In order to deal with this rising complexity and still achieve a high-level of software quality, Model-Driven Development (MDD) is increasingly adopted in the industry. This paper proposes an MDD approach based on the Unified Modeling Language (UML) in order to automatically generate code for selected error detection mechanisms recommended by the safety standard IEC-61508. Thereby, we provide developers with a generative and automated approach for the software design and implementation of these error detection mechanisms. We demonstrate the application of our approach in the context of a safety-critical fire detection system.**

Keywords*–*Automatic Code Generation; Embedded Systems; Error Detection; Functional Safety; Model-Driven Development.

I. INTRODUCTION

Software quality is concerned with how well a piece of software conforms to a set of functional and non-functional requirements. It is especially important in safety-critical domains, where deviation from the requirements specification may result in serious harm for the environment or people, e.g., severe injuries or even loss of life [1]. A recent example is the crash of two aircraft of type Boeing 737 MAX, leading to the loss of life of everyone on board. The source for this crash has been traced to the malfunction of sensor equipment which led to an erroneous activation of a software module responsible for the crash [2]. Further accidents have occurred in several other safety-critical domains, such as railways, spacecraft or nuclear energy [3].

Safety standards, such as IEC-61508 [1], aim to decrease the risk of such accidents by proposing a set of software safety mechanisms that increase software quality. Several approaches in the literature have been suggested for providing support for some phases of the lifecycle of a safety-critical system defined in IEC-61508 (cf. Section V). However, step ten of the safety lifecycle of IEC-61508, which is the actual realization of the system and its safety mechanisms, has received little attention in the literature. Thus, the realization of the system is often left to the individual developers, i.e., realizing the safety mechanisms via handwritten code. This process has the usual drawbacks of manually implemented code compared to automatic code generation, e.g., bugs introduced by the developer.

This paper addresses this research gap for a subset of safety mechanisms recommended by IEC-61508, as proposed in [4]. For this, we present a Model-Driven Development (MDD) approach based on the Unified Modeling Language (UML) [5]. This approach enables developers to specify a set of error detection mechanisms in an application model via UML stereotypes. Subsequently, these error detection mechanisms may be automatically generated into source code without requiring any other manual changes to the application model. Thus, our approach automates the design and implementation of error detection mechanisms by leveraging generative programming in the form of MDD.

Error detection is a crucial element of safety-critical embedded systems for detecting and reacting to faults in the system during runtime. For example, the output of a sensor may be monitored for values that are outside the expected range, indicating an error in the sensor. Such an error may occur due to natural degradation processes in the sensor hardware. Alternatively, it may be the result of environment influences, such as cosmic rays or alpha particles that lead to spontaneous bit flips in the software of the sensor (also known as a *soft error*) [6].

In order to realize the vision of automatically generated error detection mechanisms via MDD, we extend a model representation for error detection mechanisms [7] and provide the following, novel contributions:

1) A generic software architecture based on wrapper classes that enables error detection via checksums, replica voting and sanity checking.
2) Model transformations that enable the automatic generation of these error detection mechanisms without requiring manual developer actions.
3) A prototype of our approach for the MDD tool IBM Rational Rhapsody.
4) A use case demonstration of our approach for a safety-critical fire detection system.

The remainder of this paper is organized as follows: In Section II, we present a model representation of error detection mechanisms that is the basis for the subsequent code generation. The code generation itself, as well as the design choices that shaped the process, are described in Section III. We apply these concepts in a use case, which is presented in Section IV. Section V presents existing literature related to our work, before we conclude this paper in Section VI.

II. MODEL REPRESENTATION

This section describes the first part of our approach, the model representation for error detection mechanisms. This

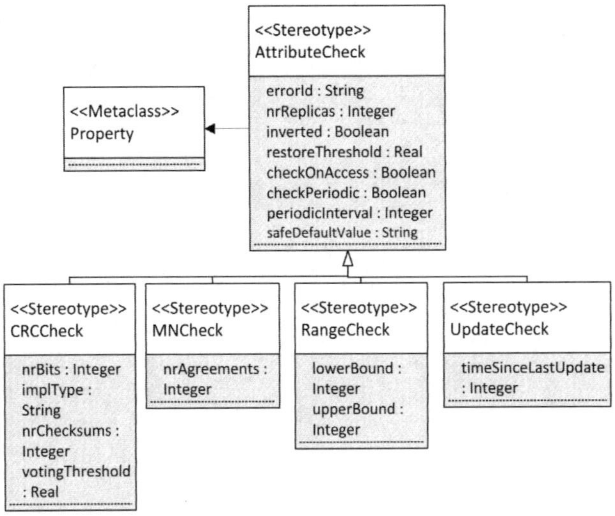

Figure 1. UML 2.5 profile for error detection mechanisms. Adapted and extended from [7].

model representation, in the form of a UML profile, is used in Section III to automatically generate source code for these mechanisms. Initial concepts of this profile have already been proposed for the purpose of memory protection in [7]. In this paper, the profile has been refined and extended to not only cover memory protection mechanisms, but also general error detection mechanisms. This entails a re-purposing of the <<CRCCheck>>, <<MNCheck>>, <<RangeCheck>> stereotypes, as well as the introduction of an additional stereotype, the <<UpdateCheck>>. Furthermore, as there are now more usage scenarios, the tagged values of the <<AttributeCheck>> stereotype have been extended. The extended profile is shown in Figure 1.

Each error detection mechanism is represented by its own stereotype that may be applied to any variable appearing in a UML model. However, the main targets are member variables (attributes) inside UML classes, as local variables are often not modeled in UML diagrams. Furthermore, due to their longer lifetime than local variables, it is more likely that attributes are the subject of an error.

At the center of the profile is a top-level stereotype, <<AttributeCheck>>. It contains all those tagged values, which are common among different types of attribute checks. Several concrete attribute checks inherit from this stereotype and provide additional modeling information relevant to the respective attribute check. For the scope of this paper, it is sufficient to know, that each attribute check contains several configuration parameters and that some of these parameters may be shared among several attribute checks applied to the same attribute. For example, the "nrReplicas" tagged value represents the number of replicas of the attribute to which the attribute checks are applied. If two or more attribute checks are applied to an attribute, then this value must be consistent among all modeled attribute checks, lest there may be conflicting modeling information.

Currently, the profile models the following error detection mechanisms:

- <<CRCCheck>>, which models a cycling redundancy checksum (CRC) for the protected attribute. The checksum may be used to detect that the variable has been changed in an unauthorized fashion, e.g., due to spontaneous bit flips caused by environmental circumstances [6].
- <<RangeCheck>>, which models a numeric lower and upper bound for the protected attribute. The bounds may be used to detect erroneous values delivered by sensors outside their specification range, as well as implementation errors, e.g., in case of a typographical error in a mathematical formula.
- <<MNCheck>>, which realizes an *M-out-of-N* check. It creates a total of N replicas of the attribute. Of these, at least M must agree with each other for the check to be passed. A well known example for this is *triple-modular-redundancy*, where there are a total three replicas, of which at least two must agree with each other. This enables error detection, e.g., in case one replica contains another value than the other two. It also enables error correction, i.e., in case two replicas still contain the same value, the third replica may be set to the value of the two others.
- <<UpdateCheck>>, which defines a duration t. In order to pass the check on access, the variable has to have been updated within the previous t. For example, the variable has to be updated within the previous 500ms before the variable was accessed. This type of check may be used to detect that the module responsible for updating the protected variable is still running, as well as observing its timing constraints.

III. CODE GENERATION

This section describes how a software architecture may be automatically generated from the UML profile described in Section II. The approach consists of two steps. In the first step, the UML application model designed by the developer is transformed via model-to-model transformations to generate model elements for the error detection mechanisms. This results in an intermediate model that contains the error detection mechanisms, as well as the original application model. In the second step, model-to-text transformations are performed that generate source code from the intermediate model.

A. Basic Concept

A key challenge for our approach is how to generate the error detection mechanisms in the model without manual developer actions. We term such transformations without any developer interactions *transparent*. In order to solve this design challenge, we employ the concept of a wrapper class that replaces the stereotyped protected variable. The transformation from the primitive variable to the wrapper class is shown in Figure 2. This wrapper class contains the variable that should be protected and replaces the original variable inside the containing class. We use the term *containing class* to refer to the class in which the variable that should be protected originally resides.

In order to achieve transparency for the replacement of the original protected variable (`var` in Figure 2), the wrapper class (`ProtectedAttribute` in Figure 2) contains a getter and a setter by which the protected variable may be accessed or

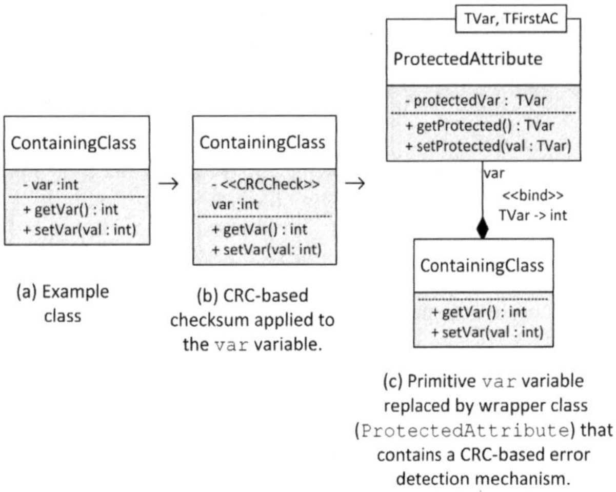

(a) Example class

(b) CRC-based checksum applied to the var variable.

(c) Primitive var variable replaced by wrapper class (ProtectedAttribute) that contains a CRC-based error detection mechanism.

Figure 2. Basic concept for the transparent generation of error detection mechanisms via MDD.

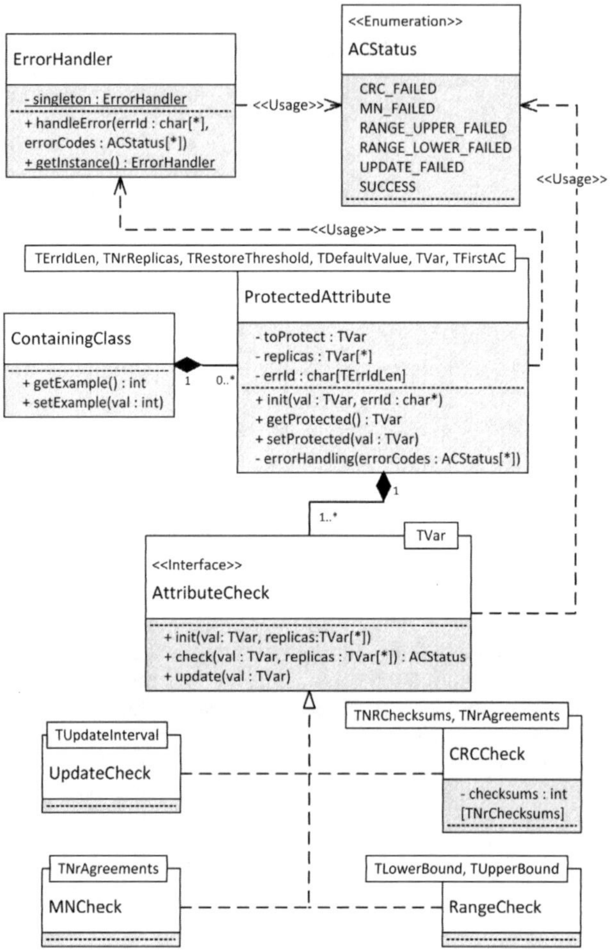

Figure 3. Generic software architecture for error detection at the variable level.

updated. Transparency may be achieved if the containing class (ContainingClass in Figure 2) observes the information encapsulation principle, i.e., var is only accessible through dedicated getter and setter methods in ContainingClass. If this is the case, then the getter or setter for var in ContainingClass may transparently call the getter or setter of ProtectedAttribute and pass along the return values of the getProtected() and setProtected() methods respectively.

The actual error detection check is performed when the method getProtected() is called. In case there is no error and the check is passed, the value of the protected variable (protectedVar in Figure 2) is returned. In case there is an error, specific error handling is performed to restore the system to a safe state. This is described further in Section III-D. The method setProtected() is used to update the value of protectedVar. During this update, depending on the specific error mechanism, additional operations may be carried out. For example, a new CRC checksum may be calculated for the updated value.

B. Software Architecture

This section describes the software architecture that may be automatically generated from the stereotypes shown in Figure 1. Reasons for certain design choices are explained in Section III-C. The software architecture is shown in Figure 3.

We use the class ProtectedAttribute as the wrapper class that contains the protected variable. It contains one or more instances of the AttributeCheck interface, which presents the previously mentioned abstraction of error detection mechanisms. Besides an initialization method, it provides two methods: check(), which performs the error detection, and update(), which may be used to update internal redundant values required to perform the error detection. As part of a prototype, we also implemented four realizations of these interfaces, corresponding to the mechanisms described in Section II (CRCCheck, MNCheck, RangeCheck, UpdateCheck). New error detection mechanisms may easily be introduced by constructing a corresponding class that realizes the AttributeCheck interface.

The enumeration ACStatus and the singleton class ErrorHandler are used to handle errors in case an error detection mechanism has detected an error. The template parameters TRestoreThreshold and TDefaultValue of ProtectedAttribute are also used for error handling. These error handling concepts are discussed separately in section III-D. The template TFirstAC in ProtectedAttribute refers to the template parameter employed to specify the types of error detection mechanisms used by ProtectedAttribute. Figure 3 shows the variant for a single error detection mechanism. Variants of ProtectedAttribute that include more error detection mechanisms would employ more template parameters that specify the type of one error detection mechanism each. In that case there may be a TSecondAC or even a TThirdAC as additional template parameters for the ProtectedAttribute class.

The remaining template parameters of ProtectedAttribute specify an error identifier string (TErrIdLen), the data type of the protected variable

(TVar), as well as the length of the array used to store replicas of the protected variable (TNrReplicas). These replicas may either be used as part of an error detection check, e.g., as part of an M-out-of-N check (<<MNCheck>>), or they may be used as additional copies of the protected variable for error correction in case the original fails the error detection check. For example, the <<CRCCheck>>, which uses a CRC checksum, does not require any replicas of the protected variable for error detection. However, such a replica may still be included within the wrapper class (ProtectedAttribute), as the replica may be used for error correction by restoring the value of the protected variable to the value of the replica [8].

C. Discussion of Design Choices

This section describes some design choices made in the development of the software architecture described in Section III-B. The basic concept presented in Section III-A shows the use of a CRC-based checksum in Figure 2 to protect a variable. While this is sufficient to explain the concept of transparency, safety standards recommend a wide variety of error detection mechanisms, which is also captured in the UML profile presented in Section II. Thus, it is necessary that the wrapper class introduced in Section III-A is part of an architecture that enables the use of different error detection mechanisms.

In order to enable the usage of different error detection mechanisms, we introduce an interface (AttributeCheck in Figure 3). This interface must contain methods for performing the error detection check and for updating any mechanism-specific redundancy (check() and update() methods in AttributeCheck). For example, a CRC-based checksum mechanism realizes this interface by providing a method that calculates a new checksum whenever the protected variable is updated, as well as a method that checks the current checksum for correctness whenever the protected variable is accessed. Several versions of the wrapper class may be implemented, each instantiating a different number of interface realizations. This way, there is no unnecessary memory overhead for instantiating more interface realizations than required. In order to still provide transparency, the specific types of the interface realizations may be passed as template parameters to the wrapper class (cf. template parameters of ProtectedAttribute in Figure 3). Due to the use of template parameters, the source code of the wrapper class is independent of any specific error detection mechanism. Furthermore, as the specific types are known at compile-time, no dynamic memory allocation is required. This is an important requirement in safety-critical embedded systems [9].

There is another design challenge that is due to the possibility of using several error detection mechanisms for the same variable. Different error detection mechanisms may require the same type of information, e.g., the value of the protected variable (cf. variable toProtect in class ProtectedAttribute in Figure 3), or the values of any replicas of the protected variable (cf. variable replicas in class ProtectedAttribute in Figure 3). Thus, values that may be used by several error detection mechanisms should be located inside the wrapper class in order to avoid unnecessary memory redundancy. Other values, that are specific to a certain error detection mechanism, should be located in the interface realizations of AttributeCheck in order to maintain the independence of the wrapper class of any specific mechanism. Examples for this are the template parameters of the AttributeCheck interface realizations in Figure 3. A specific example is the location of the checksum variable within the CRCCheck class, as no other error detection mechanism in our architecture employs CRC checksums.

D. Error Handling

The main purpose of this paper is to introduce an approach for the automatic generation of error detection mechanisms via MDD. However, once an error has been detected, the next step is to determine how such an error should be handled. We identify two categories for the error handling alternatives: those that are application independent (e.g., restoring from replicas) and those that are application specific (cf. Section IV for an example). Within the context of our approach, the main challenge is how such error handling mechanisms may be executed transparently during runtime.

Our approach detects errors when a protected variable is accessed. Therefore, a transparent approach requires that the protected variable is returned in any case, regardless whether an error has been detected. Thus, it is paramount that the system is in a safe state when the protected variable is returned. For this, our approach provides an iterative recovery process.

In the first stage, application independent recovery mechanisms are executed. For example, in case the error detection mechanism specifies replicas of the protected variable, these may be used to restore the protected variable to a safe value. Alternatively, the protected variable may be restored to a safe default value. The specific usage of these application independent recovery mechanisms is given via the tagged values shown in the profile described in Section II. The <<AttributeCheck>> stereotype contains the "nrReplicas" tagged value, that allow developers to include a number of replicas of the protected variable within the wrapper class ProtectedAttribute. The "restoreThreshold" tagged value may be used to specify how many of these replicas need to agree with each other in case of an error to restore the protected variable to the value of these replicas. A common example is that there are a total of three replicas. In case at least two of these replicas agree with each other, then the protected variable is restored to this value. The "safeDefaultValue" tagged value may be used to specify a safe default value for the protected variable.

At the code level, these tagged values are used to set the values for the template parameters of the ProtectedAttribute class (cf. Figure 3 in Section III-C). The "nrReplicas" and "restoreThreshold" tagged values correspond to the TNrReplicas and TRestoreThreshold template parameters, whereas the "safeDefaultValue" tagged value corresponds to the TDefaultValue template parameter. In case the application independent recovery mechanisms are not desired, developers may prevent their automatic code generation by not specifying any value for the relevant tagged values.

In case the application independent recovery mechanisms are not specified or their execution was unsuccessful, the ErrorHandler singleton (cf. Figure 3) is called. It is provided the information of the error identifier and the ACStatus enumeration value of the

`ProtectedAttribute` instance that failed the check (cf. Figure 3). Our approach assumes that this code, manually written by developers, returns the system to a safe state and returns a valid value for the protected variable in `ProtectedAttribute`. In a worst-case scenario the system may need to be shut-down in systems where fail-stop behavior is acceptable.

E. Transparent Model Transformations

Section III-A describes the basic concept for the model transformations that generate error detection mechanisms in a transparent way. For this, a primitive variable is replaced with a wrapper class that contains the required error detection mechanisms. This section describes the required model transformations for this approach in more detail. The class names used in this section refer to the elements from Figure 3.

- *Action 1*: At the beginning of the model transformations, each attribute in a UML class diagram is checked regarding whether a stereotype from the profile presented in Section II is applied. For each attribute where this is the case, the information of the tagged values of these stereotypes are parsed and stored temporarily.
- *Action 2*: After parsing the stereotype information, a getter and setter with default method declaration for the respective attribute are created in the containing class.
- *Action 3*: Besides adding getters and setters, it is also necessary to include the dependencies to the utilized classes, such as to the wrapper class (`ProtectedAttribute`). Furthermore, `ContainingClass` must contain a constructor for initializing the value of the protected variable inside the instance of the wrapper class.
- *Action 4*: In this step, the stereotyped attribute is deleted from the containing class. The information from the tagged values of the stereotype is still accessible due to action 1.
- *Action 5*: An instance of the wrapper class is added to the containing class, with the same name as the attribute that was deleted in action 4. The template parameters of the instance declaration may be inferred from the tagged values of the stereotype stored in action 1.
- *Action 6*: The constructor of the containing class is updated by calling the `init()` method of the created `ProtectedAttribute` instance. Here, the initial value of the protected variable is set, as well as the error identifier. The call of the `init()` method is prepended to the method body of the constructor. For this, we assume that the behavior of the method is supplied in textual form within the model. This may be achieved by employing the opaque behavior property of operations in UML.
- *Action 7*: The opaque behavior of the getter and setter created in action 2 is modified to return the results of `getProtected()` and `setProtected()` of the `ProtectedAttribute` instance created in action 5 respectively.

We implemented the automatic execution of these model-to-model transformations within the MDD tool IBM Rational Rhapsody [10], as well as the open source tool Papyrus [11]. Due to space constraints we do not discuss implementation details. However, we illustrate the application of these model transformations within Rhaposdy in Section IV.

IV. USE CASE

This section shows how our approach may be applied in the development of a safety-critical fire detection system. This system is conceptually similar to smoke detectors that are used in private households. However, in contrast to smoke detectors, fire detection systems employ multiple types of sensor information to determine whether a fire has been detected. In this specific application, we use temperature, humidity and infrared sensors besides the usual carbon monoxide sensors. This variety of sensors decreases the likelihood for a false alarm (e.g., due to smoke from burnt cooking), and also provides intentional redundancy, so that the fire detector remains partially operational in case a sensor malfunctions.

A. Safety Requirements

This section presents some selected safety requirements of the fire detection system which we will use to demonstrate our approach. The safety standard IEC-61508 [1] defines four Safety Integrity Levels (SIL), which mandate an increasing number of safety measures for each level. These measures aim to ensure the availability and reliability constraints associated with each SIL. According to [12], [13] a fire detection system may be classified as a SIL 2 system. For SIL 2 systems, IEC-61508 part 3, table A.2 recommends fault detection and diagnosis for software and hardware faults (e.g., a malfunctioning sensor).

This fault detection, among others, may be performed in the value and time domain. These fault detection checks correspond to the <<RangeCheck>> and <<UpdateCheck>> described in Section II. The fault detection may also be performed in the logical domain via error detecting codes, e.g., to detect soft errors (spontaneous bit flips). This corresponds to the <<CRCCheck>> described in Section II. While the complete fire detection system has to satisfy further safety requirements, the above requirements are sufficient to demonstrate our approach.

B. Hardware Level

This section presents the hardware elements used for our realization of the fire detection system. A Raspberry Pi 4B is used as the basis of the system and to process the sensor information. While the use of a Raspberry Pi may not be a cost-efficient solution for commercial fire detection systems, the application of our concept remains the same when applied to a lower-priced microcontroller. The Raspberry Pi is connected to several sensors: a gas sensor to detect carbon monoxide, an infrared sensor that may detect flames and a humidity and temperature sensor, that measure the respective values. Furthermore, the Raspberry Pi is connected to a buzzer that sounds an alarm when a fire has been detected. A button element deactivates the alarm when it is pressed.

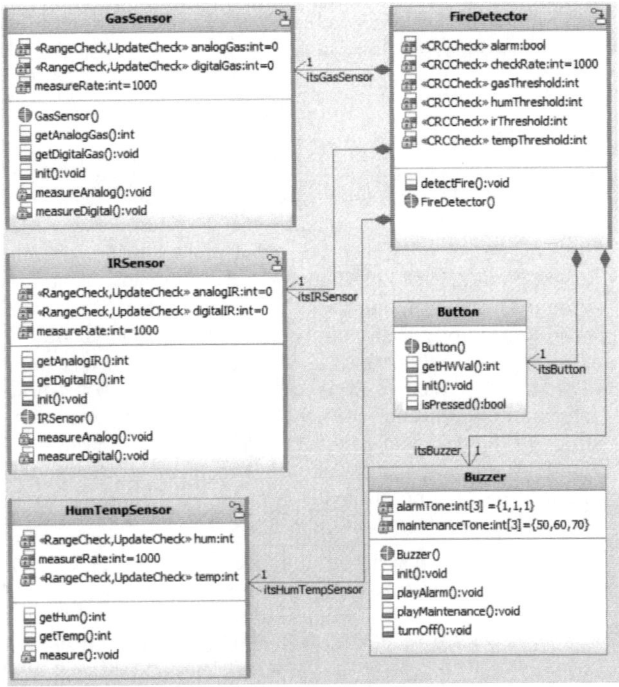

Figure 4. UML 2.5 class diagram showing the classes of the fire detection application that are relevant for the demonstration of the approach presented in this paper.

C. Functional Model of the Software

This section describes the software implementation of the fire detection system. From a high-level perspective, the implementation is a single program that runs as a background task on the Raspberry Pi that is automatically started when the Pi is booted. The program checks the measured values of the sensors every second. These values are each compared to a predefined threshold. If two or more sensor values are above the threshold for five seconds or more, the buzzer is used to sound an alarm.

Figure 4 shows a UML class diagram of the most important classes of the application. It is a screenshot from the MDD tool IBM Rational Rhapsody [10], i.e., the class diagram also contains implementation details from which the code for the application is generated automatically. The classes `GasSensor`, `IRSensor` and `HumTempSensor` represent the hardware sensors and contain methods that return the currently measured value of the sensors. Instances of these classes execute concurrently and update the member variables with the last measured value. The update frequency is one second (1000ms). These instances are created by the `FireDetector` class, which concurrently checks the member variables representing the sensor values (method `detectFire()`). These values are compared to their respective thresholds, which are also defined in the `FireDetector` class. If two or more sensor values exceed their respective threshold for five seconds in a row, an instance of the `Buzzer` class is used to activate the acoustic alarm (method `playAlarm()`). During each call of `detectFire()` the status of the `Button` instance is checked. In case the button is pressed, the alarm is turned off.

D. Applying Safety Stereotypes to the Functional Model

This section describes how the approach presented in Section III is applied to the functional application model presented in Section IV-C to fulfill the safety requirements described in Section IV-A. The approach is applied to a number of member variables within Figure 4. To each member variable that represents a measured sensor value, the <<RangeCheck>> and <<UpdateCheck>> stereotypes are applied.

The tagged values of the <<RangeCheck>> correspond to the upper and lower limit of the sensors' range, i.e., the check is failed in case a sensor returns a value outside of its specification range. The <<UpdateCheck>> is configured to report an error in case the sensor value has not been updated within the last minute when the variable is accessed. Both check types indicate that there is some kind of sensor malfunction. The `measureRate` variable in each sensor is not protected, as any errors related to this variable will be detected by the respective <<UpdateCheck>> for the sensor.

A number of member variables contain the stereotype <<CRCCheck>>. This stereotype is used to protect the variables from soft errors (i.e., spontaneous bit flips) that may occur in long lasting applications [6]. The protected variables are chosen, because they represent safety-critical values (e.g., the threshold for raising an alarm). Some variables, like the current sensor values, do not contain this sort of memory protection, as they are frequently overwritten and the likelihood for a soft error is small. Other variables, like the `alarmTone` variable in the `Buzzer` class, do not contain memory protection, as they are not strictly safety-critical. In this case `alarmTone` is not safety-critical, as it only contains the specific tone played during an alarm - a bit flip that changes this tone slightly is only a very minor issue from a safety perspective. Only protecting those variables that require memory protection from a safety perspective reduces the overhead of the safety mechanisms on the whole application.

In case any of the `ProtectedAttribute` instances (cf. Figure 2) report an error, the `ErrorHandler` singleton (not shown in Figure 4, cf. Figure 3) is used to log the detected error. Furthermore the singleton activates a maintenance tone (method `playMaintenance()` in class `Buzzer`). This is an acoustic warning, that the fire detection system provides only a limited protection and should be checked by a professional.

E. Code Generation

The UML class diagram presented in Section IV-C was created with the MDD tool IBM Rational Rhapsody [10]. It allows to specify the source code of the operations within the model and therefore enables code generation of the complete source code. We modified this code generation process by implementing a plugin that executes the model transformations described in Section III-E automatically. The plugin executes the model transformations each time source code is generated from the class diagram. The developer model (the class diagram shown in Figure 4) is not changed by the transformations. Instead, the plugin creates an intermediate model with the transformed model. In this transformed model, the member variables that contain a stereotype from the profile shown in Figure 1 have been replaced with a corresponding instance of `ProtectedAttribute` (cf. Section III for details). After the model transformations, the default code generation of

Rhapsody is applied to the intermediate model. For debugging purposes, developers have access to the intermediate model within Rhapsody.

F. Discussion

This section discusses the application of our approach to the use case presented in Section IV. As described in Section IV-C and Section IV-D, our approach enables developers to initially create a functional model of the application and apply a number of safety mechanisms in a following step. This approach has a number of advantages. First, developers do not require specific knowledge of how a error detection mechanism is implemented. The implementation is generated automatically by the model transformations described in Section III. Despite this automatic implementation, the tagged values of the stereotypes still allow to change important configuration parameters of the mechanisms. Another advantage of our approach is the increase in developer productivity. The implementation of the error detection mechanisms and the model transformations is only required once. Afterwards, both are reusable similar to an application programming interface (API). The automatic code generation of the error detection mechanisms also reduces the likelihood of bugs that may be produced by developers during manual implementation of the mechanisms. Additionally, our approach models the error detection mechanisms clearly visible within the UML model of the application, instead of hiding it in between other source code or sub-layers of the models.

While our approach enables these advantages, it also faces some limitations. These include the higher runtime and memory overhead associated with generic approaches, as opposed to implementations created explicitly for a specific application and hardware platform. Care is also required when our approach is used in systems with hard real-time requirements. While the runtime overhead of the error detection mechanisms is constant, it still has to be taken into account during timing analysis of the system.

The approach presented in this paper is extensible, i.e., other error detection mechanisms that work at the variable level may be included. For this, three steps are required:

1) A UML stereotype has to be designed that contains all the configuration parameters of the error detection mechanism as tagged values. This stereotype should inherit from <<AttributeCheck>> (cf. Figure 1 in Section II).
2) A dedicated class for the error detection mechanism needs to be implemented. This class has to realize the `AttributeCheck` interface (cf. Figure 3 in Section III-C).
3) Model transformations that parse the information from the stereotypes and create the required instance declarations for the class that implements the error detection mechanism. The specific steps for this have been described in Section III-E. These model transformations may be applied to a number of MDD tools. The only requirements are, that they allow developers to create class diagrams and that these diagrams may be modified via a tool specific API, e.g., IBM Rational Rhapsody [10], or via dedicated model-to-model transformations languages, e.g., Papyrus [11] in combination with the Epsilon framework [14].

V. Related Work

This section describes approaches that are related to ours. The automatic generation of error detection mechanisms has been proposed in a number of research approaches. However, they either do not consider the integration in an MDD context [8], or they depend on domain-specific modeling languages instead of building atop a wide-spread, standardized modeling language, such as UML [15], [16]. This makes integration into a wide variety of MDD tools more difficult, as these often only support UML. Our approach, in contrast, is entirely specified in UML on the modeling level. Another category of approaches enables the model-driven generation of structural model elements that represent safety features [17]. However, they depend on manual refinements of the model to produce the dynamic behavior of the safety feature. Thus, this approach is only semi-automatic.

UML-based approaches to model-driven code generation for safety mechanisms have been presented in [4], [7], [18], [19], [20]. The model representation presented in [7] is the basis for the UML profile presented in Section II. The approach in [4], on the other hand, describes a generic high-level workflow for generating code from UML safety stereotypes. We adopted this approach in this paper to derive our results. The approaches presented in [18], [19] describes model-driven code generation for an error handling mechanism. Their approaches may be used to automatically generate code for dealing with the errors, that the approach presented in this paper is able to detect. A model representation of selected safety design patterns for the use of code generation has been proposed in [20]. However, they provide only a model representation and leave the actual code generation for future work. Our approach may contribute to fill this gap.

Several other approaches combine selected safety aspects with MDD [21], [22], [23]. However, they target other phases of the development lifecycle rather than the actual realization step of the system which is the focus of our approach. As these phases are mostly located prior to the realization step, their approaches may be used in a complimentary fashion to ours.

The issue of error detection has also been targeted for specific application scenarios. The issue of software-based memory protection, which has been used as an example for an application scenario in this paper, has also received research attention, e.g., [8], [24]. However, they employ other techniques than MDD for code generation. Additionally, they only consider memory protection, while our approach is explicitly designed to incorporate other error detection mechanisms, such as sanity checking.

There is also some theoretical research regarding the automatic generation of fault-tolerance mechanisms, e.g., [25], [26]. As these approaches take all possible system states for the addition of fault tolerant mechanisms into consideration, they are limited to small and medium-scale systems.

VI. Conclusion and Future Work

In this paper, we propose an extensible, generic software architecture that enables the use of error detection mechanisms for primitive variables in safety-critical systems. We use a set of UML stereotypes that model the desired error detection mechanisms. These stereotypes may be applied to safety critical variables inside the UML class diagram of the application. By parsing these stereotypes and performing model-to-model transformations, we replace the stereotyped variable with a suitable wrapper class that performs the error detection checks during runtime before every access of the stereotyped variable. The generation result is transparent with respect to the rest of the application, i.e., no other parts of the application need to be changed by the developer when our code generation is used. The effectiveness of the approach is demonstrated by applying it to the development of a safety-critical fire detection system.

For future work, we will evaluate the runtime and memory overhead that the generated error detection mechanisms incur, as well as the overhead of performing the model transformations during code generation. Furthermore, we aim to extend our approach to a wide variety of safety mechanisms, thereby creating a model-driven code generation framework for safety mechanisms. We also aim to combine this approach with the concept of safety assurance cases, in order to improve validation and traceability of the specific assurance cases. Besides safety, we also aim to generalize our approach to include runtime monitoring of other non-functional properties, such as timing and energy. Finally, we want to extend the concept of model-driven code generation for embedded systems to other development issues, e.g., generating code for the low-level hardware initialization of heterogeneous microcontrollers from suitable model representations.

ACKNOWLEDGMENT

This work was partially funded by the German Federal Ministry of Economics and Technology (Bundesministeriums fuer Wirtschaft und Technologie BMWi) within the project "Holistic Model Driven Development for embedded systems in consideration of diverse hardware architectures" (HolMES).

REFERENCES

[1] IEC 61508 Edition 2.0. Functional safety for electrical/electronic/programmable electronic safety-related systems, International Electrotechnical Commission Std., 2010.

[2] P. Johnston and R. Harris, "The Boeing 737 MAX saga: Lessons for software organizations," Software Quality Professional Magazine, vol. 21, 2019, pp. 4–12.

[3] P. G. Neumann, Computer Related Risks. New York, NY, USA: ACM Press/Addison-Wesley Publishing Co., 1995.

[4] L. Huning, P. Iyenghar, and E. Pulvermueller, "A workflow for automatically generating application-level safety mechanisms from UML stereotype model representations," in Proceedings of the 15th International Conference on Evaluation of Novel Approaches to Software Engineering - Volume 1: ENASE, INSTICC. SciTePress, 2020, pp. 216–228.

[5] "OMG Unified Modeling Language Version 2.5.1," Object Management Group, Tech. Rep., 2017.

[6] R. C. Baumann, "Radiation-induced soft errors in advanced semiconductor technologies," IEEE Transactions on Device and Materials Reliability, vol. 5, no. 3, 2005, pp. 305 – 316.

[7] L. Huning, P. Iyenghar, and E. Pulvermueller, "UML specification and transformation of safety features for memory protection," in Proceedings of the 14th International Conference on Evaluation of Novel Approaches to Software Engineering, INSTICC. Heraklion, Crete, Greece: SciTePress, May 2019, p. 281–288.

[8] C. Borchert, H. Schirmeier, and O. Spinczyk, "Generative software-based memory error detection and correction for operating system data structures," in Proceedings of the 2013 43rd Annual IEEE/IFIP International Conference on Dependable Systems and Networks (DSN). Washington, DC, USA: IEEE Computer Society, 2013, pp. 1–12.

[9] MISRA C++2008 Guidelines for the use of the C++ language in critical systems, The Motor Industry Software Reliability Assessment Std., Jun. 2008.

[10] "IBM. Rational Rhapsody Developer. https://www.ibm.com/us-en/marketplace/uml-tools (accessed 20th August 2020)," 2020.

[11] "The Eclipse Foundation. Eclipse Papyrus Modeling Environment. https://www.eclipse.org/papyrus (accessed: 20th August 2020)," 2020.

[12] R. M. Robinson and K. J. Anderson, "Sil rating fire protection equipment," in Proceedings of the 8th Australian Workshop on Safety Critical Systems and Software - Volume 33, ser. SCS '03. AUS: Australian Computer Society, Inc., 2003, p. 89–97.

[13] S. Kim and Y. Kim, "A case study on an evaluation procedure of hardware sil for fire detection system," International Journal of Applied Engineering Research, vol. 12, 01 2017, pp. 359–364.

[14] "Epsilon family of languages. https://www.eclipse.org/epsilon/ (accessed 20th August 2020)."

[15] R. Trindade, L. Bulwahn, and C. Ainhauser, "Automatically generated safety mechanisms from semi-formal software safety requirements," in Computer Safety, Reliability, and Security, A. Bondavalli and F. Di Giandomenico, Eds. Cham: Springer International Publishing, 2014, pp. 278–293.

[16] M. Pezzé and J. Wuttke, "Model-driven generation of runtime checks for system properties," International Journal on Software Tools for Technology Transfer, vol. 18, no. 1, Feb 2016, pp. 1–19.

[17] R. Mader, G. Grießnig, E. Armengaud, A. Leitner, C. Kreiner, Q. Bourrouilh, C. Steger, and R. Weiß, "A bridge from system to software development for safety-critical automotive embedded systems," in 2012 38th Euromicro Conference on Software Engineering and Advanced Applications, Sep. 2012, pp. 75–79.

[18] L. Huning, P. Iyenghar, and E. Pulvermueller, "A UML profile for automatic code generation of optimistic graceful degradation features at the application level," in Proceedings of the 8th International Conference on Model-Driven Engineering and Software Development - Volume 1: MODELSWARD, INSTICC. SciTePress, 2020, pp. 336–343.

[19] D. Penha, G. Weiss, and A. Stante, "Pattern-based approach for designing fail-operational safety-critical embedded systems," in 2015 IEEE 13th International Conference on Embedded and Ubiquitous Computing, Oct 2015, pp. 52–59.

[20] P. O. Antonino, T. Keuler, and E. Y. Nakagawa, "Towards an approach to represent safety patterns," in Proceedings of the Seventh International Conference on Software Engineering Advances, Lisbon, Portugal, Nov. 2012, pp. 228–237.

[21] T. J. Tanzi, R. Textoris, and L. Apvrille, "Safety properties modelling," in 2014 7th International Conference on Human System Interactions (HSI). IEEE Computer Society, June 2014, pp. 198–202.

[22] K. Beckers, I. Côté, T. Frese, D. Hatebur, and M. Heisel, "Systematic derivation of functional safety requirements for automotive systems," in Computer Safety, Reliability, and Security, A. Bondavalli and F. Di Giandomenico, Eds. Cham: Springer International Publishing, 2014, pp. 65–80.

[23] N. Yakymets, M. Perin, and A. Lanusse, "Model-driven multi-level safety analysis of critical systems," in 9th Annual IEEE International Systems Conference. IEEE Computer Society, 06 2015, pp. 570–577.

[24] K. Pattabiraman, V. Grover, and Zorn, B. G., "Samurai: Protecting critical data in unsafe languages," in Proceedings of the 3rd ACM SIGOPS/EuroSys European Conference on Computer Systems 2008. New York, NY, USA: ACM, 2008, pp. 219–232.

[25] A. Arora and S. Kulkarni, "Detectors and correctors: A theory of fault-tolerance components," in Proceedings of the 18th International Conference on Distributed Computing Systems, ser. ICDCS '98. Washington, DC, USA: IEEE Computer Society, 1998, pp. 436–443.

[26] Y. Lin, S. Kulkarni, and A. Jhumka, "Automation of fault-tolerant graceful degradation," Distributed Computing, vol. 32, no. 1, Feb 2019, pp. 1–25.

MARKA: A Microservice Architecture-Based Application Performance Comparison Between Docker Swarm and Kubernetes

Tuğba Günaydın
Yıldız Technical University
Computer Engineering
İstanbul, Turkey
E-mail: tugba.gunaydin@std.yildiz.edu.tr

Göker Cebeci
Yıldız Technical University
Computer Engineering
İstanbul, Turkey
E-mail: goker.cebeci@std.yildiz.edu.tr

Özgün Subaşı
Integrated Finance
London, United Kingdom
E-mail: ozgun.subasi@integrated.finance

***Abstract*—Container-based distributed programming techniques are used to make applications effective and scalable. Microservice architecture is an approach that has been on the rise among software developers in recent years. This paper presents a case study comparing the performance of two commonly used container orchestrators, Docker Swarm and Kubernetes, over a Web application developed by using the microservices architecture. We compare the performances of Docker Swarm and Kubernetes under load by increasing the number of users. The aim of this study is to give an idea to researchers and practitioners about the performances of Docker Swarm and Kubernetes in applications developed in the proposed microservice architecture. The Web application developed by the authors is a kind of loyalty application, that is to say, it gives a free item in exchange for a certain number of purchased items. With this study, it was concluded that the Docker Swarm is more efficient as the number of users increases compared to Kubernetes.**

Keywords–Microservice Architecture; Performance Evaluation; Docker Swarm; Kubernetes; JMeter.

I. INTRODUCTION

With the microservice architecture, applications are developed that are very flexible and scalable. In the microservice architecture approach, the application is split up into its smallest functions; each function is dedicated for one job only, and it is called as microservice. Microservices are put in packages that are called containers that provide everything necessary for running [1]. Microservices are difficult to operate because they are distributed [2]. Container-based technologies are used to orchestrate microservices. Two technologies stand out in orchestrating microservices: Docker Swarm and Kubernetes [3].

The proposed prototype is a loyalty application. Today, it is very important to gain new customers and retain existing customers for restaurants and cafes. For this reason, loyalty applications are used. A product is offered to the customer free of charge for a certain amount of purchased product. With this study, the concept of loyalty application was realized with the microservice architecture approach.

This paper presents a performance comparison of Docker Swarm and Kubernetes on a microservice architecture-based Web application. As the number of users increased, the time to complete the test scenario of Docker Swarm and Kubernetes was compared. The study can be classified under three main titles: (1) Proposed Software Architecture and Application (software architecture, approaches and application used for implementation), (2) Test Scenario (scenario used to test the system, Docker Swarm and Kubernetes) and (3) Experimental Setup (load tests for orchestration tools). The rest of the paper is structured as follows. In Section II, we present the relevant studies in the literature. In Section III, our developed application and the microservice architecture used are discussed in detail. The test scenario simulating the operation of the application in real life is explained in Section IV. The experimental environment and parameters are shown in Section V. Finally, in Section IV, the results obtained are discussed and we conclude our work.

II. LITERATURE REVIEW

With the increasing importance of scalability in recent years, microservice architectures have become popular [4]. Microservices are used more effectively with container technology. There are different application approaches of container technology and performance evaluation studies of these approaches [5]. We compared performances of Docker Swarm and Kubernetes with an application using microservice architecture model.

Using scaling and microservice architecture approach studies of frequently used orchestrators, the appropriate orchestrator can be selected for a certain application [6]. In this comparison, the effect of more complex applications on the performance of orchestrators is clearly shown [7]. Studies have shown that cloud-based approaches are more performant and flexible than traditional approaches for developing increasingly complex applications [8]. We made a performance comparison by revealing the microservice architecture we use in our application.

There exist many studies focusing on designing and implementing traditional monolithic Web service based Service Oriented Architecture (SOA) systems with a focus on high performance [9]-[10]. However, in this particular study, our main focus is the use of microservices in creating SOA based systems with a focus on load balancing amongst the nodes. To enable the load balancing functionality, we utilize technologies like Docker Swarm and Kubernetes. In this study, the performance was compared by using the loyalty application MARKA in 3 scenarios: without an orchestrator, using Docker Swarm, and using Kubernetes.

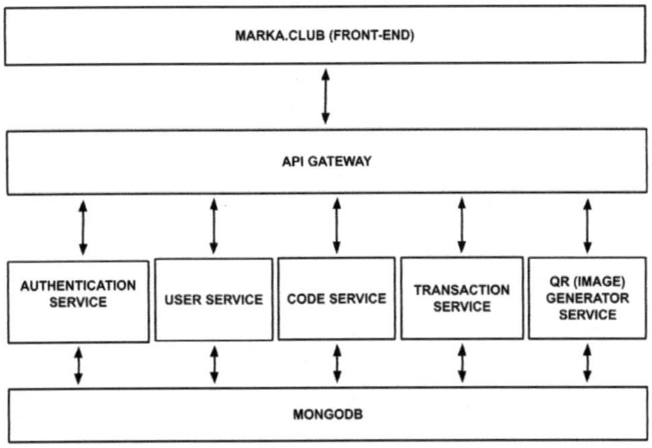

Figure 1. System Architecture Model and Network.

III. Proposed Software Architecture and Application

The Web application MARKA [11] has six microservices: API (Application Programming Interface) Gateway, Authentication Service, User Service, Code Service, Transaction Service, and QR (Quick Response) (Image) Generator Service. It also has a front-end for user control screen and a database for the management of data. The system architecture model can be seen in the Figure 1.

Microservices communicate with each other over the HTTP (Hyper-Text Transfer Protocol). For instance, in order to create a new transaction, the transaction service receives the information of the received code from the code service first, and then it gets the information of the user associated this code from the user service. If the user and the owner of the code are the same, it generates an error. This is because the user who created the code and the user using it cannot be the same. Then, the code service compares the company identification number associated with the code from the database and determines whether the code is a purchased item or a free item. When these jobs are completed, the transaction service creates the transaction. It calls the code service and updates the code as used. If the code is for the purchased item, it also receives the free item quantity information of the company from the user service (information on how many products will be given free of charge in sales). After getting the relevant company and the number of transactions, it calculates how many free items the user has won from the code service. From this, it calculates whether the user earns free items with the final purchased product(s). If the user has won free items, the code service generates as many codes as there are free items.

A. *Marka.Club (Front-End)*

Front-end (Marka.club) is a software provided for the end users to perform their operations. It enables the user to create an account, log into the system, create codes and use codes. End-user interactions are created here. An example of a company dashboard can be seen in Figure 2 and an example of a customer dashboard can be seen in Figure 3.

Customers buy the product and read the QR code produced by the restaurant. When they purchase the amount of product determined by the restaurant, they have the right to get one

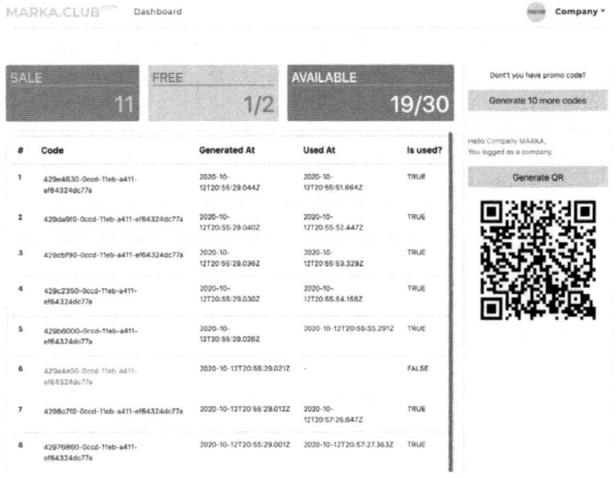

Figure 2. Marka.club Front-End Screen Company Dashboard

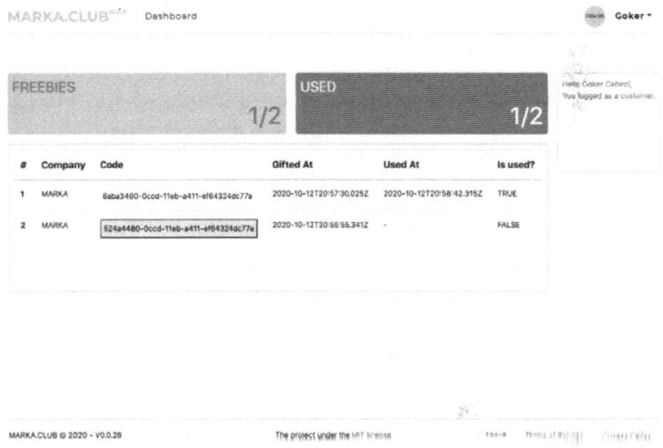

Figure 3. Marka.club Front-End Screen Customer Dashboard

free product, so they produce a QR code. The restaurant reads the QR code produced by the customer and gives one free product to the customer.

B. *API Gateway*

The API gateway is the microservice that ensures that the incoming request is directed to the responsible microservice.

C. *Authentication Service*

The authentication service is a login and register service. If a user is not yet registered in the system, first, they get registered into the system. There are two roles for registration: customer or company. After users register, they can log in.

D. *User Service*

The user service is the service that keeps the user information such as e-mail, first and last names, company-customer roles, etc.

E. *Code Service*

The code service is a microservice that generates the codes that the user will use in another role. For example, if the user's role is the company, it generates the codes that will be used by the customer when purchasing an item. If the user's role is the customer, he/she generates the codes that will be used by the company to get free items from the company. In other words, when the customer earns a free item, a code is generated for that free item and this code is used by the company. If it is a valid code, the company gives a free item to the customer.

F. Transaction Service

The transaction service keeps the code transaction information, such as which role produced the code, which role was used, and how many codes were produced and used.

G. QR (Image) Generator Service

The QR generator service converts the codes generated to the image file (QR) to be used on mobile devices. This feature will be used when the application is used on mobile devices.

H. Database

A database has been created in which all transactions and information are kept. MongoDB [12] was used as the database. A single database has been created for proof of concept, but each microservice uses its own collections that they are responsible for, and they do not interfere with other areas of responsibility.

IV. TEST SCENARIO

A test scenario was prepared to compare the container orchestration platforms' behavior under load. In this study, Docker Swarm and Kubernetes were used as container orchestration tools. Docker Swarm [13] is developed by Docker Engine. Kubernetes [14] is developed by Google. The responses of the platforms were measured according to the test scenario, depending on the request per unit time. The flow diagram of the test scenario is as shown in Figure 4.

The test scenario was created by simulating the real-time operation of the application: a company signs up for the system, then logs into the system. Anyone who does not exist in the system, be it a company or a customer, must sign up in order to log into the system. By signing into the system, a new user is created each time. The company generates codes for the items to sell. The codes generated by the company are saved into the database because the customers will use them automatically. The customer signs up for the system and then signs into the system. The customer will use all the unused codes stored in the database; we make the customers use all the codes generated to simulate a real-life load scenario for our load testing. The customer generates free codes in return for a certain number of codes used (as initially determined by the company). The unused codes generated by the customer are received and saved into the database. The company signs into the system and uses all of the unused free codes generated by the customer; with this, the customer takes the free items.

V. EXPERIMENTAL SETUP

The test procedure of the application was run in 3 different ways: test without orchestrator, which means without any container (except mongoDB); Docker Swarm test; and Kubernetes test. The application is run with Docker Swarm and Kubernetes on Docker Desktop.

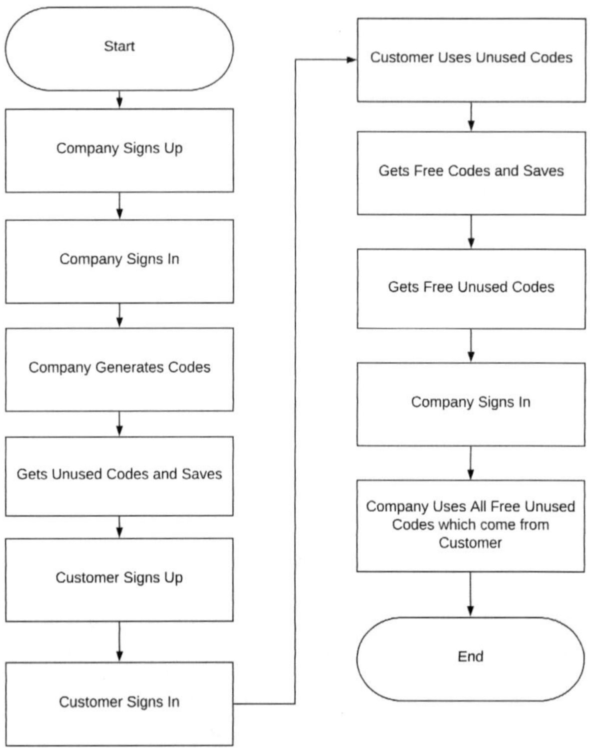

Figure 4. API Test Scenario Flow Chart

JMeter [15] is a tool for load testing. It is used to test the application against real-life situations. There are three basic parameters that should be in a JMeter test plan: Thread Group, Samplers and Listeners [16]. The thread group decides how many threads there will be and for how long each thread will be active. Samplers are for request types such as FTP (File Transfer Protocol) requests, HTTP requests, JDBC (Java Database Connectivity) requests etc. Listeners are used for the visualization of results in the form of a graph, table, etc.

There is a bar graph named "aggregate" in JMeter. The aggregate graph shows the average of the response time for each request in the test. We compared the average response times of requests by the number of users via aggregate graphs for each one of our tests.

Test Without Orchestrator, Docker Swarm and Kubernetes were compared with 10, 20 and 50 users as response times; Docker Swarm and Kubernetes were compared with 100, 200, 400 and 500 users as response times.

The letters on the charts are as follows:

- A: Company Sign Up,
- B: Company Sign In,
- C: Get user info,
- D: Generate codes,
- E: Get codes,
- F: Customer Sign Up,
- G: Customer Sign In,

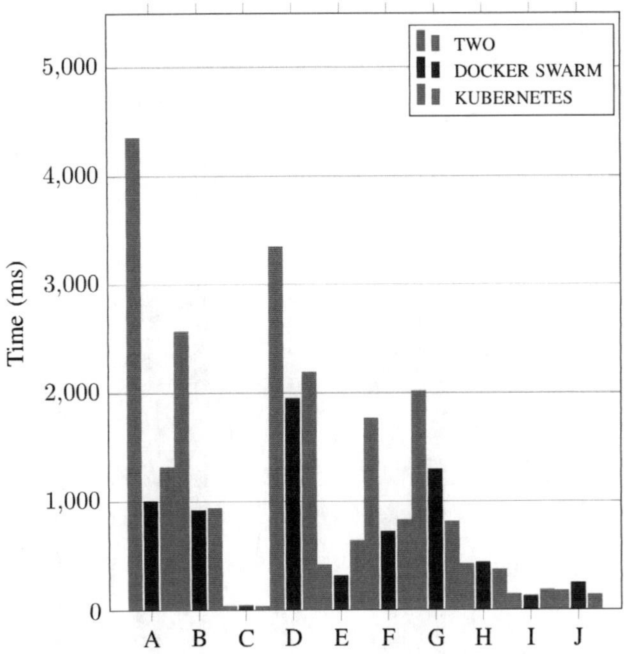

Figure 5. Comparison of Average Response Time with 10 threads

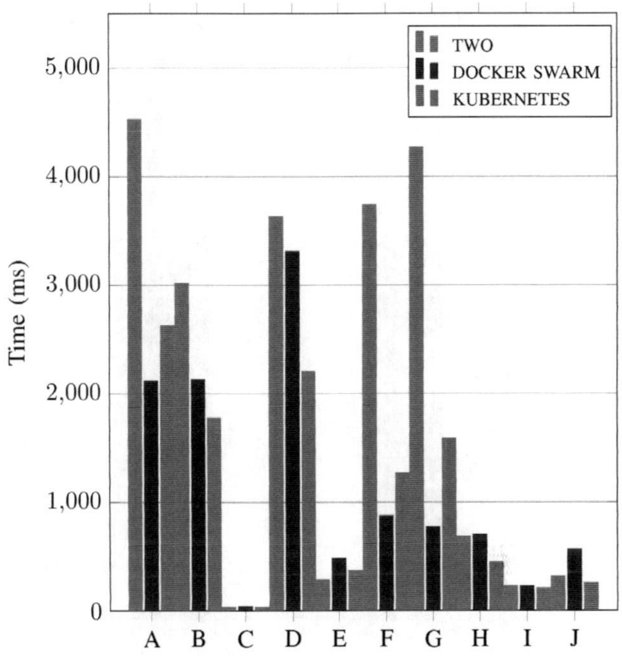

Figure 6. Comparison of Average Response Time with 20 threads

- H: Customer uses codes,
- I: Get gifts,
- J: Use gifts.

The average response times of each request in the test are shown on the aggregate graph with 10 users in Figure 5, 20 users in Figure 6, 50 users in Figure 7, 100 users in Figure 8, 200 users in Figure 9, 400 users in Figure 10 and, finally, 500 users in Figure 11.

A. *Test Without Orchestrator (TWO)*

For TWO, all services are used locally, without using any container or orchestration tool. The local system information is as follows: the Operating System is Windows 10 Home, the RAM is 8 GB, the Processor is Intel(R) Core(TM) i5-8250U CPU 1.60 GHz 1.80 GHz, and the System Type is 64-bit OS, x64-based processor. The JMeter settings for the number of threads (users) are 10, 20 and 50, the rump-up period (in seconds) is 0 and the loop count is 1.

Below are the times taken for each the test scenario to complete, based on the number of users:

- 10 users: 1 minute and 9 seconds,
- 20 users: 1 minute and 43 seconds,
- 50 users: 3 minutes and 40 seconds.

When we performed the test with 100 threads, some threads started timing out, so the test was not completed.

B. *Docker Swarm Test*

For Docker Swarm test, the application is using the Docker Desktop and Docker Swarm as orchestrator. Docker Swarm worked with 3 replicas. The local system information is the same as in the case of TWO. The JMeter settings for the

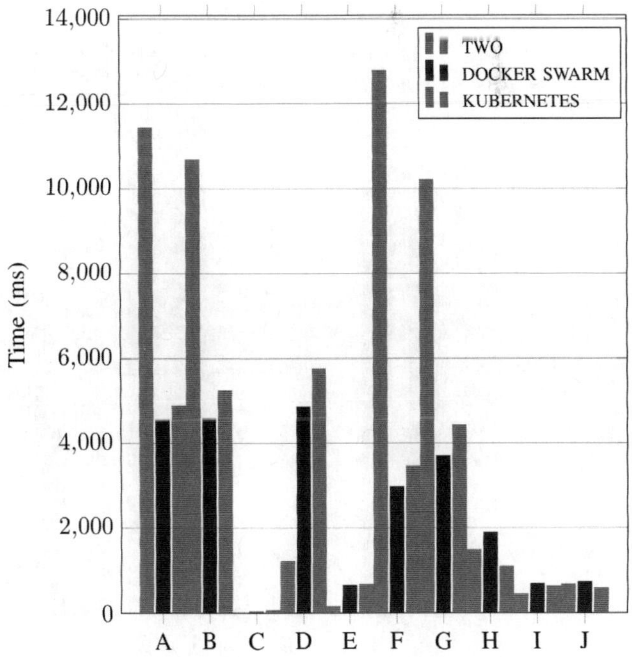

Figure 7. Comparison of Average Response Time with 50 threads

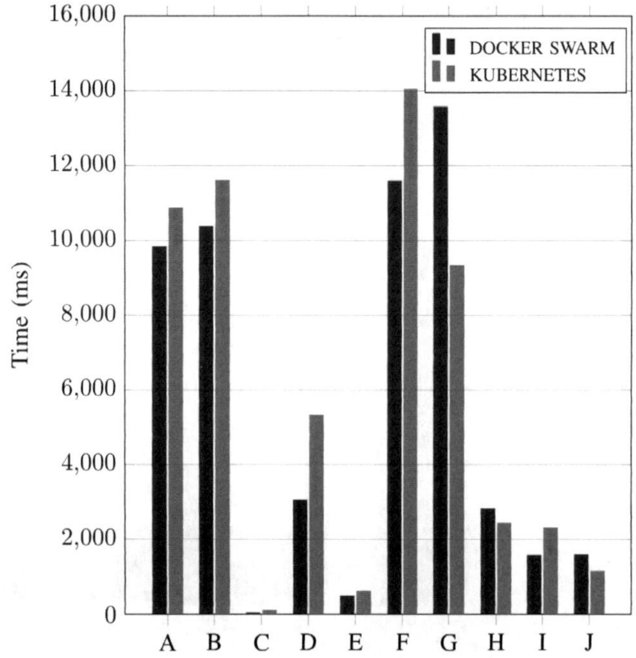

Figure 8. Comparison of Average Response Time with 100 threads

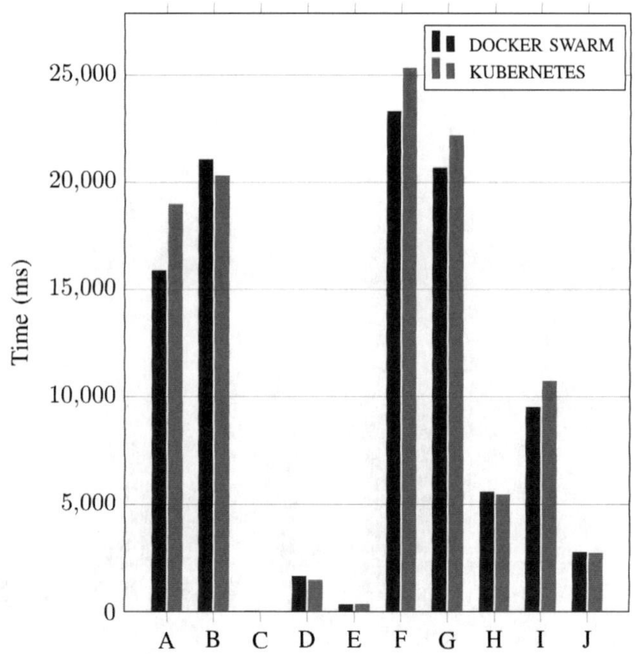

Figure 9. Comparison of Average Response Time with 200 threads

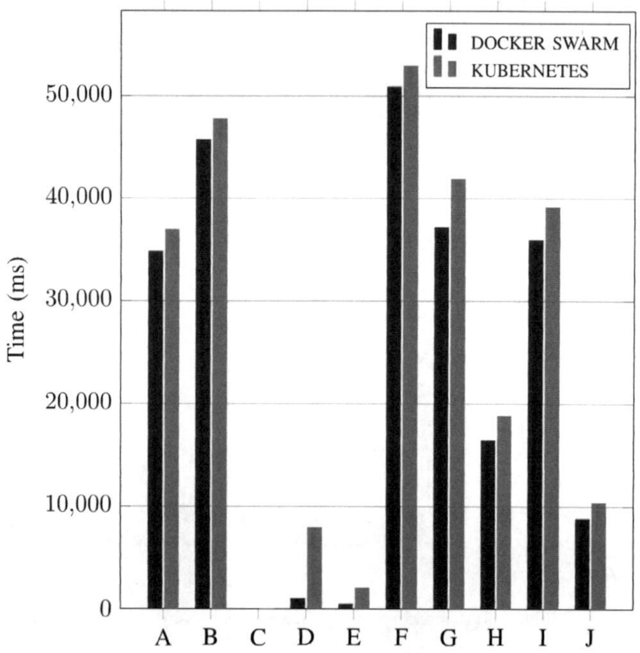

Figure 10. Comparison of Average Response Time with 400 threads

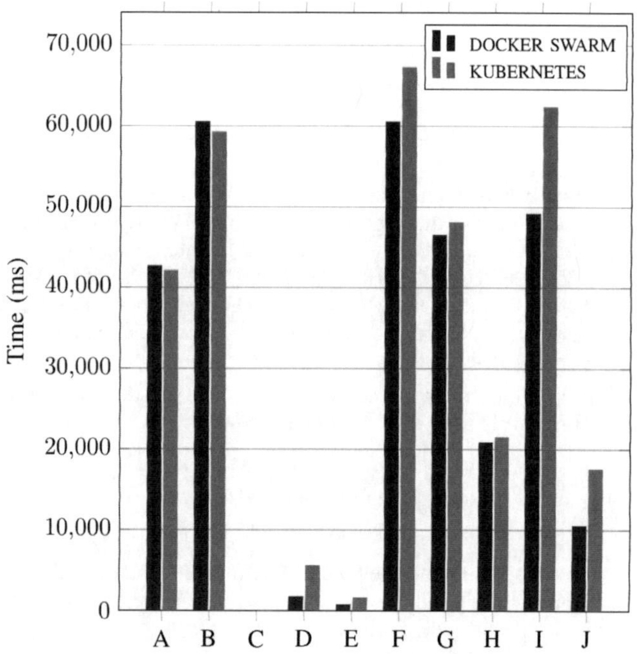

Figure 11. Comparison of Average Response Time with 500 threads

number of threads (users) are 10, 20, 50, 100, 200 and 400, the rump-up period (in seconds) is 0 and, finally, the loop count is 1.

Below are the times taken for each the test scenario to complete, based on the number of users:

- 10 users: 52 seconds,
- 20 users: 1 minute 42 seconds,
- 50 users: 4 minutes 7 seconds,
- 100 users: 6 minutes 53 seconds,
- 200 users: 12 minutes 18 seconds,
- 400 users: 34 minutes 51 seconds,
- 500 users: 44 minutes 16 seconds.

When we performed the test with 1000 threads, some threads started timing out, so the test was not completed.

C. Kubernetes Test

For Kubernetes Test, the application stand-up with using Docker Desktop and Kubernetes as orchestrator. Kubernetes worked with 3 replicas. Local system information is same with TWO. The JMeter settings for the number of threads (users) are 10, 20, 50, 100, 200 and 400, the rump-up period (in seconds) is 0 and, finally, the loop count is 1.

Below are the times taken for each the test scenario to complete, based on the number of users:

- 10 users: 51 seconds,
- 20 users: 1 minute 6 seconds,
- 50 users: 2 minutes 36 seconds,
- 100 users: 5 minutes 40 seconds,
- 200 users: 12 minutes 20 seconds,
- 400 users: 40 minutes 25 seconds,
- 500 users: 48 minutes 33 seconds.

When we performed the test with 1000 threads, some threads started timing out, so the test was not completed.

VI. Conclusion

The performances of Docker Swarm and Kubernetes under load were compared via an application. A conclusion has been reached regarding the performances of Docker Swarm and Kubernetes in the architecture described in this study.

The test we did without using an orchestrator (TWO) could not handle the load in more than 50 threads. Thus, it is clearly seen that it is not efficient as the load on the application increases. The application could not respond to high loads.

Although Docker Swarm takes longer time in tests with fewer users, when the number of users increased, it was completed in a shorter time than Kubernetes. The ability of Docker Swarm and Kubernetes to be scalable in load tests has not been tested in this study.

Considering the architecture of the application and the number of microservices, we can say that its complexity is low. For this reason, as the number of users increases, we see that the Docker Swarm test yields better results than Kubernetes and also completes in a shorter time.

In this study, 3 replicas were used in Kubernetes and Docker Swarm. As the number of incoming requests increases, the automated replica creation capabilities test will be discussed in a future study.

Acknowledgment

We would like to thank Associate Professor Mehmet Sıddık AKTAŞ (affiliation: Yıldız Technical University, Computer Engineering, İstanbul, TURKEY) for his valuable contributions and inspiring guidance.

References

[1] A. Modak, S. Chaudhary, P. Paygude, and S. Ldate, "Techniques to secure data on cloud: Docker swarm or kubernetes?" in 2018 Second International Conference on Inventive Communication and Computational Technologies (ICICCT). IEEE, 2018, pp. 7–12.

[2] R. Heinrich et al., "Performance engineering for microservices: research challenges and directions," in Proceedings of the 8th ACM/SPEC on International Conference on Performance Engineering Companion, 2017, pp. 223–226.

[3] N. Marathe, A. Gandhi, and J. M. Shah, "Docker swarm and kubernetes in cloud computing environment," in 2019 3rd International Conference on Trends in Electronics and Informatics (ICOEI). IEEE, 2019, pp. 179–184.

[4] N. Alshuqayran, N. Ali, and R. Evans, "A systematic mapping study in microservice architecture," in 2016 IEEE 9th International Conference on Service-Oriented Computing and Applications (SOCA), 2016, pp. 44–51.

[5] M. Amaral et al., "Performance evaluation of microservices architectures using containers," in 2015 IEEE 14th International Symposium on Network Computing and Applications, 2015, pp. 27–34.

[6] L. Mercl and J. Pavlik, "The comparison of container orchestrators," in Third International Congress on Information and Communication Technology, X.-S. Yang, S. Sherratt, N. Dey, and A. Joshi, Eds. Singapore: Springer Singapore, 2019, pp. 677–685.

[7] Y. Pan, I. Chen, F. Brasileiro, G. Jayaputera, and R. Sinnott, "A performance comparison of cloud-based container orchestration tools," in 2019 IEEE International Conference on Big Knowledge (ICBK), Nov 2019, pp. 191–198.

[8] W. Li and A. Kanso, "Comparing containers versus virtual machines for achieving high availability," in 2015 IEEE International Conference on Cloud Engineering, 2015, pp. 353–358.

[9] G. C. Fox et al., "Real time streaming data grid applications," in Distributed Cooperative Laboratories: Networking, Instrumentation, and Measurements. Springer, 2006, pp. 253–267.

[10] M. Aktas et al., "iservo: Implementing the international solid earth research virtual observatory by integrating computational grid and geographical information web services," in Computational Earthquake Physics: Simulations, Analysis and Infrastructure, Part II. Springer, 2006, pp. 2281–2296.

[11] Marka.club. [accessed Oct. 2020]. [Online]. Available: https://github.com/kodkafa/marka.club

[12] Mongodb. [accessed Oct. 2020]. [Online]. Available: https://www.mongodb.com/

[13] Docker swarm. [accessed Oct. 2020]. [Online]. Available: https://docs.docker.com/engine/swarm/

[14] Kubernetes. [accessed Oct. 2020]. [Online]. Available: https://kubernetes.io/

[15] Jmeter. [accessed Oct. 2020]. [Online]. Available: https://jmeter.apache.org/

[16] D. Nevedrov, "Using jmeter to performance test web services," Published on dev2dev, 2006, pp. 1–11.

A Model-Based Safe-by-Design Approach with IP Reuse for Automotive Applications

Morayo Adedjouma
Université Paris-Saclay, CEA, LIST
F-91120, Palaiseau, France
Email: morayo.adedjouma@cea.fr

Nataliya Yakymets
Université Paris-Saclay, CEA, LIST
F-91120, Palaiseau, France
Email: nataliya.yakymets@cea.fr

Abstract—**The paper presents an approach for design/safety co-engineering and reuse of safety IP Cores. The approach is based on a compositional development process coupling system development and safety processes from a formalization of activities proposed in ISO26262. The co-engineering approach integrates reuse of safety and design artifacts to reduce development efforts. We illustrate the approach on the example of an Adaptive Cruise Control System within a tool called Sophia. We discuss the advantages and limitations that the approach brings for the development of safety critical systems.**

Keywords–automotive system; model-based; functional safety; IP Core reuse.

I. INTRODUCTION

With the growing complexity of systems in the automotive domain, vehicles become more and more safety-critical as failures or hazardous decisions about the environment may lead to accidents that cause human lives. Due to the safety-critical nature of such systems, system and safety engineers are prone to follow safety standards (e.g., ISO26262 [1]), best system development pratices and associated tools. In this context, Model-Based System Engineering (MBSE) and IP Core reuse are promising approaches. MBSE helps to integrate various methods and tools for safety analysis into the common system modeling environment, to customize this environment to the automotive domain and to provide extensive traceability links across the safety analysis process [2]. The IP Core reuse approach allows reducing the system development efforts by using libraries of pre-existing design artifacts [3]. We also integrate the reuse of safety artifacts like libraries of failures modes, hazards, etc. to reduce the safety activities effort [4]. In practice, however, the tool support of the aforementioned approaches is not well integrated.

In this paper, we present an approach based on MBSE, Model-Based Safety Assessment (MBSA) and reuse concepts. Our approach extends such approaches as [5][6] to the automotive domain based on ISO26262 standard, in particular, the recommendations of Part 4 about product development at the system level. Although ISO26262 provides generic recommendations on which safety related workproducts should be issued, it does not specify the particular processes on how to get those workproducts. There may exist dependencies between workproducts recommended by ISO26262, which can slow down the system development. Therefore, an efficient way to implement the standard recommendations is to turn to system and safety co-engineering and parallelize steps of both processes when possible. The advantage of such an approach is that the safety activities do not block the system development activities, and vice-versa.

In addition, we apply well-trusted design principles by exploiting the ability to reuse pre-modeled (and already pre-analyzed) IP Cores, as well as libraries of safety artifacts. As defined in Part 4 of ISO26262, by IP Cores we consider well-trusted designs for elements (including hardware and software components), as well as well-trusted or standardized interfaces. By safety artifacts we understand well-trusted technical safety concepts and mechanisms for the detection and the control of failures [1]. Although, pre-analyzed design elements and safety analysis results are context-dependent and cannot be reused as-is according to ISO26262, certain artifacts (e.g., definition of generic failure modes, risks and their causes) can be detached from the context and reused in the form of libraries.

We illustrate the approach on an Adaptive Cruise Control (ACC) system [7]. The ACC is an example of safety-critical system that requires engineers to adopt a safety standard. We conduct our analysis of the ACC system using Sophia [6], a modeling tool which offers a graphical development environment for system design and safety analysis. Sophia semi-automates the proposed methodology and improves the traceability of system and safety artifacts at the early phases of the system development lifecycle. Using this case study, we show how to obtain a safe-by-design automotive system and reduce the design and analysis efforts due to the co-engineering and libraries reuse approach.

The rest of the paper is organized as follows. Section I motivates our work. Section II presents the current practices and weaknesses for safe development of automotive systems. We present our approach in Section III and its tool support in Section IV. We outline the approach application on the ACC system in Section V and discuss our concluding remarks in Section VI.

II. STATE OF THE ART AND PRACTICE

The integration of any classical safety analysis method into an MBSE environment requires three main steps [5]: (1) system model creation, (2) safety annotation and modeling, (3) safety analysis and generation of results. Several initiatives, approaches and tools have evolved over time in the field of MBSA. In these approaches, the system model can be created using languages, such as UML (Unified Modeling Language) [8], SysML (System Modeling Language) [9], or domain specific languages like EAST-ADL [10]. Then the system model is extended with the safety concepts and relations either by using safety profiles like [6][11]-[12] or by translating the system model into formal or safety languages for further analysis [13][14]. Some of these approaches come with a methodology to comply with standards, e.g., ISO26262 [10][12]. Once the model has been annotated with safety data, it can be analyzed using MBSA tools that offer one or a few methods for safety analysis. The latter case needs additional efforts to study the semantics of the languages and to implement the bridges between tools. Examples of analytical and simulation tools are xSAP [14] and AltaRica toolset [13]. Despite profound analysis provided by those tools, many of them require professional knowledge of modeling methods (e.g., Markov chains or Petri nets) and formal languages (e.g., AltaRica, SMV, etc.), which is a barrier for widespread utilization. Concerning reuse of pre-existing artifacts, these tools require reverse engineering to build system models. RiskWatch [15] or Pilar [16] are examples of tools implementing risk management methodologies. Those tools are exclusively qualitative, and based on various tabular structures filled by informal description methods. The running system is never explicitly modeled, hence there is no reuse capabilities of the IP Core provided. Some others research and model-based tools like Hip-Hops [17], Visual Figaro [18], CAFTA, Isograph Reliability Workbench [19], ConcertoFLA [20] and Medini Analyze [21] implement features to store and reuse some safety artifacts. Most of them provide libraries or databases of failure modes, their causes and effects, component failure patterns, etc. However, the lack of interoperability between the tools and/or closed data formats make it difficult to reuse and/or export the safety models, libraries and results.

There were also some initiatives and projects working on safety certification platforms, e.g., the European projects OPENCOSS [22] and AMASS [23]). These projects and their associated tools aim at safety certification according to different standards (including ISO26262) based on MBSA. As part of the AMASS platform, our work helps follow ISO26262 recommendations for the system development through a MBSE and MBSA approach in an unified environment. The work relies on open data and open languages (UML/SysML) and provides reusability features of IP Core and safety artifacts libraries.

III. Approach

Figure 1 presents the co-engineering methodology at a glance. The methodology shows how to conduct safety assessment based on the reference phase model for the development of a safety-related item at system level (Part 4) described in ISO26262. It allows conducting system development in parallel with safety assessment with respect to ISO26262 requirements. By parallelizing both concerns into a co-engineering process, the system development steps are not blocked by the safety steps. The reuse of pre-analyzed IP Cores and safety artifacts reduces development and analysis efforts.

The inputs for the proposed methodology are: 1) system description including requirements, functional and system architecture; and 2) safety analysis results from the FMEA (Failure Mode and Effects Analysis) [24], the FTA (Fault Tree Analysis) [25] and the HARA (Hazard Analysis and Risk Assessment), obtained at the prior phases of system development lifecycle, such as concept definition. To harmonize the methodology with ISO26262 reference model, we prefix its main steps with the appropriate clauses of the standard. The methodology includes the following steps:

- (4.5) Initiation of product development at the system level. We determine and plan the functional safety activities to perform during the development of Automotive System (AS).
- (4.6) Specification of the technical safety requirements synchronized with system requirements. The system requirements are specified and analyzed by the system engineer and safety expert to derive the technical safety requirements. At this stage, one can reuse existing safety mechanisms from the IP Core library for the requirements specification, e.g., fault detection measure, self-monitoring concept, warning concept.
- (4.7) System design synchronized with system safety analyses. The technical safety requirements as result of previous step help define the system design. If the library contains prior pre-modeled and analyzed components included in the system under analysis, they could be reused (with regard to appropriate impact analysis related to the new system context). Safety analyses are conducted on the defined architectural design to avoid systematic failures of the system. System safety analyses may include the HARA in the case of usage of reusable elements and if new hazards are introduced, the FMEA and the qualitative FTA. During safety assessment, various safety artifacts (hazards, failure modes, causes, effects, control mechanisms, etc.) could be reused from and added to the safety artifacts libraries. The newly analyzed elements are also stored into the libraries for their reuse during further iterations or for future usage in other projects.

IV. Tool support

The co-engineering methodology given in Section III is semi-automated in Sophia tool, a MBSE/MBSA framework [26]. Sophia includes a set of DSLs (Domain Specific Language) dedicated to several aspects of safety assessment methodology. Each DSL is a UML profile having its equivalent viewpoint [27]. As shown in Figure 1, each viewpoint could be used during one or several steps of the methodology. The Safety Requirement DSL describes a taxonomy and properties of safety requirements compliant with ISO26262 (Part 8). The Process Management DSL defines the evolution of system architecture through its lifecycle by introducing such concepts like system, function, hardware, software along with corresponding allocation relationships. The HARA, FMEA, FTA and property verification DSL describe the safety concepts related to these methods recommended in ISO26262.

Figure 2 shows an overview of Sophia architecture. The tool is implemented as Eclipse plugins on top of Papyrus tool, a customizable environment supporting modelling of systems using standardized languages (e.g., UML, SysML). The framework is modular so that dedicated analysis modules can be used either independently or conjointly in a given user-defined process. Sophia provides a fluent and integrated flow supported by ISO26262 Process package that interacts with the safety analyses. These packages 1) refer to the Safety and Reliability package providing generic definitions to dependability concepts; 2) provide a mechanism to save and reuse safety artifacts obtained during safety analyses in the form of annotated elements; 3) provide functionality to save and reuse pre-analyzed safe IP Cores in form of SysML models or SysML Blocks annotated with safety concepts. Sophia also provides bridges to other external tools for further safety analyses like NuSMV [28], AltaRica, FIDES [29]and

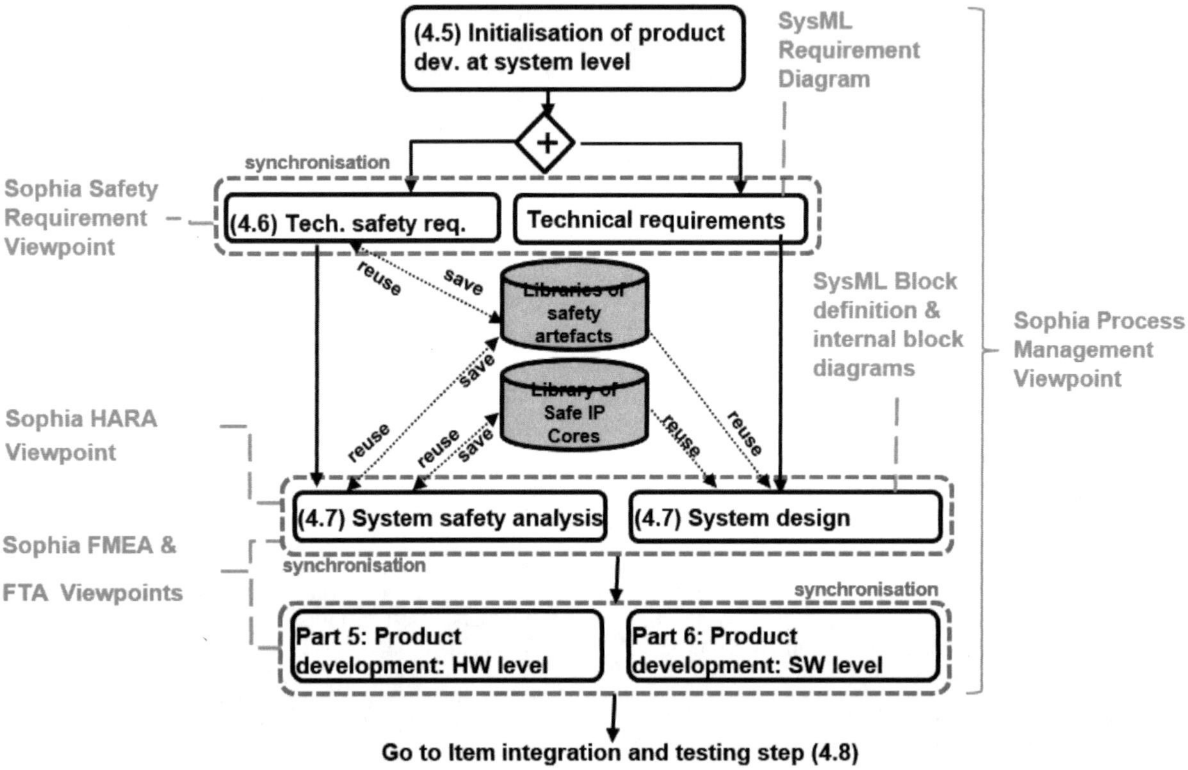

Figure 1. System/safety co-engineering methodology and safety viewpoints mapping

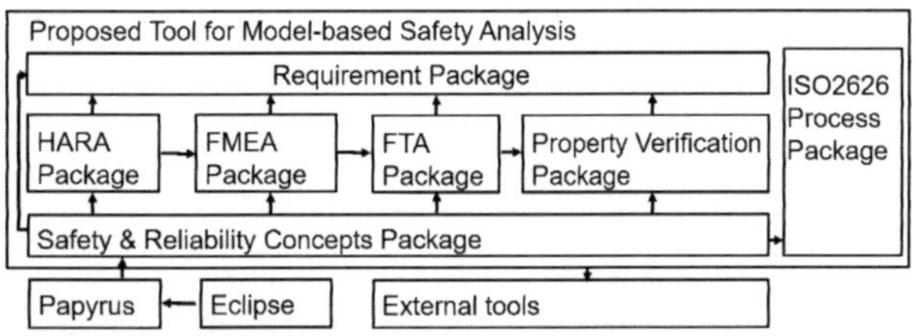

Figure 2. Sophia tool architecture to support ISO26262 recommendations

XFTA [13]. The analyses yield results that are propagated back through the design and display in the models using dedicated profiles, editors, tables, and Papyrus customization toolsets.

V. Case Study

We apply the proposed methodology (Figure 1) to design a safety-critical Adaptive Cruise Control (ACC) System. The ACC is a well-known automotive system that allows a vehicle's cruise control to adapt the vehicle's speed to the traffic environment. The ACC uses a radar attached to the front of the vehicle to detect whether preceding vehicles are moving in the path of the host car with the ACC. If there is no preceding vehicle, the ACC maintains the driver selected speed. When a preceding vehicle shows up, the system may automatically apply braking, control throttle or shift gear to adapt the vehicle speed and maintain the selected clearance without driver intervention.

A. *Initialization of Product Development at the System Level*

As we consider the reuse of various elements from IP Core and safety artifact libraries, we perform an impact analysis to assess the effects of the reused artifacts in our context and to determine the applicable safety activities that we will need to conduct for the ACC system development.

B. *Specification of the Technical Safety Requirements*

We capture and model the system requirements of the ACC system. Hereafter, we consider the requirement REQ_ACC_03 given in Figure 3. This requirement is satisfied by the component ACC module (Figure 4), and its refinement in several sub-requirements REQ_ACC_03a, REQ_ACC_03b, REQ_ACC_03c, are satisfied by the system function Increment speed, Decrement speed and Shift gear, respectively. These requirements are enriched with safety requirements (prefixed by Safety_REQ_ACC) specifying the safety measures/mechanisms identified as we performed the safety analyses of the system (see Section V-D). We store the technical safety requirements into the appropriate library for later usage.

C. *System Design*

Figure 4 shows the top level design of the ACC system with the interconnecting interfaces between its components. The core part of the ACC system is the ACC module. It processes data information from the Radar.

The ACC module sends a signal to Brake Control in case of braking. The Engine Control and Electronic Throttle Control control the vehicle speed by increasing or decreasing

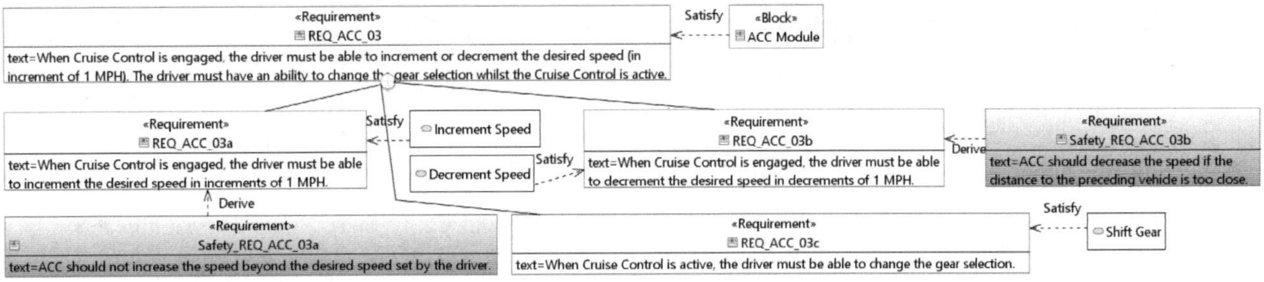

Figure 3. Excerpt of functional (shown in white) and safety (shown in red) requirements of the ACC system.

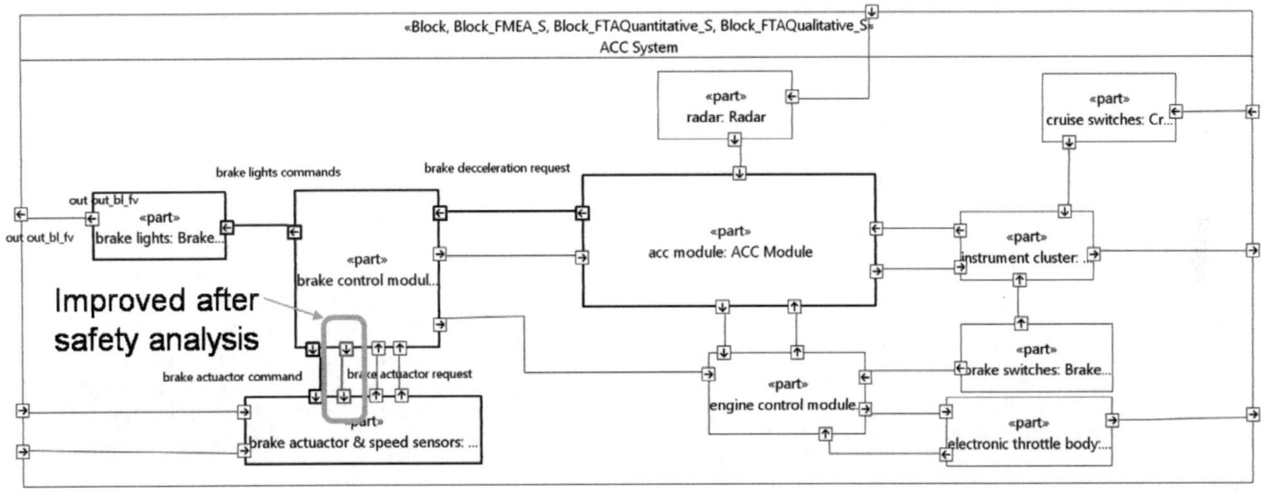

Figure 4. Top level architecture of the ACC system shown in Internal Block Diagram. The ACC architecture was modified (shown in green) to satisfy safety requirements

the throttle injection. The Cruise Switches component allows the driver to command the ACC functionalities and to set the selected speed and clearance. The Instrument Cluster is a panel in front of the driver that processes the Cruise Switches and sends them to the ACC and Engine Control modules. The Instrument Cluster also displays information regarding the ACC system state. The Brake Switches can deactivate the Cruise Control operation. The Brake Lights component allows illumination of the stop lamps during automatic braking from the ACC module request. The Brake Actuators & Speed Sensors component includes the sensors and devices, such as the brake pedal, the accelerator pedal, etc. The communication bus and the Controller Area Network (CAN) transmit all the signals between the components. We link the technical safety requirements to appropriate system components. The requirement REQ_ACC_03 given in Figure 3 is satisfied by the component ACC module (Figure 4). The sub-requirements REQ_ACC_03a, REQ_ACC_03b, REQ_ACC_03c, are satisfied by the system functions Increment speed, Decrement speed and Shift gear, respectively. Those system functions are realized by components that we reuse from the IP Core libraries, namely the Brake Lights, Brake Switches and Cruise Switches.

D. System Safety Analysis

Hereby, we focus on performing the HARA and FMEA analyses with Sophia tool [26] to illustrate the proposed concept of IP Cores and safety artifacts reuse.

HARA. We perform the HARA on the system design to determine new hazards and effects that may arise as we reuse some libraries elements in a new context. The HARA is based on the usage scenarios and the main functionalities of the ACC system. It takes into account requirement and architecture models defined in the Safety Requirements and Process Management viewpoints. Some HARA artifacts are defined in a specific library as model elements reusable from one viewpoint to another, e.g., the set of operating conditions are derived from the vehicle states and the malfunctions are specified for all functions that satisfied the functional requirements of the system. The hazards, nature of injuries are also coming from a predefined list corresponding to the injury category described in the ISO26262 standard. During the analysis, we reused the HARA results for the Brake Lights, Brake Switches and Cruise Switches that improved analysis time.

Hereafter, we analyze the following operational situation: the ACC system being active when the vehicle is driving on highway at medium speed, following a preceding vehicle. We

Component	Failure Mode	Customer Effects	Effect Severity	Final Severity	Detectability	Causes	Initial Cause Occurence	Initial Criticality	Preventions	Final Cause Occurence	Final Criticality
ACC Module	loss	crash	Level10	Level10	Level6	Missing input signal, CAN fault	Level6, Level6	Critical	Prevent activation of cruise mode when braking system fails	Level2, Level2	Moderate

Figure 5. Excerpt of the FMEA results for the ACC system. Columns 5, 9 and 12 are calculated automatically according rules given ISO26262

analyze the ACC function Increment speed (Figure 4) used to maintain the desired distance with the preceding vehicle. Some malfunctions associated with this function are the ACC system increases vehicle speed when it is too close to preceding vehicle and the ACC system increases vehicle speed beyond desired speed set by driver. The generic hazard Unintended acceleration is associated with these malfunctions. The resulting hazardous event, as defined by ISO26262, is a combination of the hazard and the operational situation, i.e., the ACC module requests an unintended acceleration when preceding vehicles are too close. In our example, the hazardous event is evaluated at the Automotive Safety Integrity Level (ASIL) C, with Exposure=E4, Controllability=C2, Severity=S3. Finally, we determine the safety goals for the hazardous events to prevent an unacceptable risk level from those events or reduce their impact. The safety goals refine/extend the ACC requirements defined in the Safety Requirement Engineering viewpoint (Figure 3). For our example of hazardous event, we define two safety goals, Safety_REQ_ACC_03a: ACC should not increase the speed beyond the desired speed set by the driver, and Safety_REQ_ACC_03b: ACC should decrease the speed if the distance to the preceding vehicle is too close. The newly analyzed ACC components and safety artifacts are stored into the IP Core and safety artifacts libraries (as shown in Figure 1).

FMEA. The FMEA complements the HARA by determining the corrective actions to be implemented to meet previously defined safety objectives. This analysis uses as inputs the usage scenarios, the ACC system architecture, as well as the results of the HARA model elements (libraries of accidents, malfunctions, hazardous events, accidents, etc.) and their properties (severity, ASIL, etc.). The analysis helps determine the effects and the criticality of single basic causes of failure modes at the component level until the system level.

With the help of the safe IP Core libraries, the tool traces the FMEA artifacts to the hazardous events and accidents previously identified in the HARA. Figure 5 shows the FMEA table generated for the ACC module component. The malfunctions found during the HARA are stored into the safety artifacts library and then reused for failure mode identification. As an example, we specify the failure mode Loss of the ACC module, its causes (missing input signal, CAN fault) and effects (loss). This failure mode can lead to different effects until the crash of the vehicle at customer level referring to the accident identified during the HARA. We found that the ACC module changes its criticality level from critical to moderate after application of recommended and well-trusted preventive actions (already existing in the libraries). The list of safety requirements is derived from the specified preventive actions: for our example, it is prevent activation of cruise module when braking system fails. These new safety requirements are traced by the tool to the safety goals elicited during the HARA. As during the HARA, the analyzed components with the FMEA results are stored to safe IP Core library (as shown in Figure 1). We reused existing results of the analysis for the Brake Lights, Brake Switches and Cruise Switches that reduce efforts to perform the FMEA.

Figure 4 shows how the ACC architecture was modified to satisfy the safety requirements derived during the ACC development process. The improved scenario is that the ACC module should send a brake actuator request to a new added Actuator Controller in order to duplicate the brake actuator command from both the Brake Control and the Actuator Controller.

VI. Conclusion and Discussion

The ever growing complexity of modern automotive systems presents certain challenges in meeting time to market constraints. To address this issue, we suggest a methodology that helps in formalizing, synchronizing and semi-automating the system development and the safety analysis activities recommended in ISO26262. The methodology includes the ability to reuse libraries of already pre-modeled and pre-analyzed IP Cores as basic elements for building more complex automotive systems. In addition, we can reuse safety artifacts (e.g., hazards, failure modes, etc.) for analysis of other systems. It makes the design process more flexible and reduces the design time.

We implement the proposed methodology in Sophia tool. Sophia is a modeling tool offering a graphical development environment for system design and safety analyses. It relies on SysML and UML languages, so that the models and libraries can be imported and reused in different modeling environments. Beside, as both the development and safety activities are conducted in the same environment, we avoid interoperability and traceability issues that undermine the reuse capabilities of certain tools. Although we focus on the system development process to demonstrate the methodology, the proposed methodology is applicable to later development phases, in particular, to software and hardware development and testing activities. For example, we may refer to FIDES to refill our IP Core libraries, as it is a well-known and standardized database for reliability prediction of hardware components.

We apply the model-based safety analysis and IP Core reuse approach to an ACC system. During the case study, we model the ACC system architecture and conduct safety analyses according to the proposed methodology. As a result, we identify critical components of the ACC system and propose architectural changes to reduce the system overall criticality level. In the case study, we reuse pre-analyzed IP Cores (in particular, Brake Lights, Brake Switches and Cruise Switches), as well as various HARA and FMEA safety artifacts (e.g., hazards, malfunctions, failure modes, safety mechanisms, etc.) across the development process. This possibility helps us reduce the design and analysis effort.

The case study shows the important efforts for the deployment of the methodology the first time: it takes time to model the system and to fill in the libraries. However, this effort may be rapidly amortized during next iterations or in future projects by saving time and cost on the analyses thanks to the reusability inherent to the model-based and IP Core reuse paradigms.

From our case study, we also notice the lack of certain domain specific expertise about which safety artifacts can be reused in specific context. Another difficulty comes from maintenance of the libraries while IP Cores or safety artifacts must be accompanied with justifications about their application context. As future work, we might consider exploration of solutions based on Safety Element out of Context (SEooC) concept from ISO26262. We would also develop dedicated libraries per domain to be able to address other standards (e.g., aerospace, robotic, and medical).

REFERENCES

[1] ISO 26262: Road Vehicles : Functional Safety. International Organization for Standardization, 2018.

[2] D. Brugali, "Model-driven software engineering in robotics: Models are designed to use the relevant things, thereby reducing the complexity and cost in the field of robotics," Robotics & Automation Magazine, IEEE, vol. 22, no. 3, 09 2015, pp. 155–166.

[3] D. D. Gajski et al., "Essential issues for ip reuse," in Proceedings 2000. Design Automation Conference. (IEEE Cat. No.00CH37106), 02 2000, pp. 37 – 42.

[4] I. Sljivo, B. Gallina, J. Carlson, H. Hansson, and S. Puri, Tool-Supported Safety-Relevant Component Reuse: From Specification to Argumentation. Cham: Springer International Publishing, 01 2018, pp. 19–33.

[5] N. Yakymets, S. Dhouib, H. Jaber, and A. Lanusse, "Model-driven safety assessment of robotic systems," in 2013 IEEE/RSJ International Conference on Intelligent Robots and Systems, 2013, pp. 1137–1142.

[6] N. Yakymets, M. Perin, and A. Lanusse, "Model-driven multi-level safety analysis of critical systems," in 2015 Annual IEEE Systems Conference (SysCon) Proceedings, 2015, pp. 570–577.

[7] W. Pananurak, S. Thanok, and M. Parnichkun, "Adaptive cruise control for an intelligent vehicle," in 2008 IEEE International Conference on Robotics and Biomimetics, 2009, pp. 1794–1799.

[8] The Unified Modeling Language Specification Version 2.5, 2015. Object Management Group, retrieved: September, 2020. [Online]. Available: https://www.omg.org/spec/UML/2.5/

[9] System Modeling Language Specification Version 1.5, 2017. Object Management Group, retrieved: September, 2020. [Online]. Available: https://www.omg.org/spec/SysML/

[10] P. Cuenot, C. Ainhauser, N. Adler, S. Otten, and F. Meurville, "Applying model based techniques for early safety evaluation of an automotive architecture in compliance with the ISO 26262 standard," in Embedded Real Time Software and Systems (ERTS2014), Toulouse, France, 02 2014.

[11] G. Biggs, T. Juknevicius, A. Armonas, and K. Post, "Integrating safety and reliability analysis into mbse: overview of the new proposed OMG standard," INCOSE International Symposium, vol. 28, no. 1, 07 2018, pp. 1322–1336.

[12] P. Feth et al., "Multi-aspect safety engineering for highly automated driving," in Computer Safety, Reliability, and Security, B. Gallina, A. Skavhaug, and F. Bitsch, Eds. Cham: Springer International Publishing, 2018, pp. 59–72.

[13] Altarica. Alatarica Association, retrieved: September, 2020. [Online]. Available: https://altarica.labri.fr/

[14] G. Biggs, T. Juknevicius, A. Armonas, and K. Post, "The xsap safety analysis platform," in Tools and Algorithms for the Construction and Analysis of Systems, M. Chechik and J.-F. Raskin, Eds. Berlin, Heidelberg: Springer Berlin Heidelberg, 04 2015.

[15] RiskWatch. Risk Watch International, retrieved: September, 2020. [Online]. Available: http://www.riskwatch.com/

[16] Pilar. EAR, retrieved: September, 2020. [Online]. Available: www.pilar-tools.com/en/tools/pilar/

[17] Hip-Hops. Hull University, retrieved: September, 2020. [Online]. Available: http://hip-hops.eu/

[18] Visual Figaro. Electricite De France, retrieved: September, 2020. [Online]. Available: https://sourceforge.net/projects/visualfigaro/

[19] Isograph Reliability Workbench, retrieved: September, 2020. [Online]. Available: https://www.isograph.com/software/reliability-workbench/

[20] B. Gallina, Z. Haider, and A. Carlsson, "Towards generating ECSS-compliant fault tree analysis results via ConcertoFLA," IOP Conference Series: Materials Science and Engineering, vol. 351, 05 2018, p. 012001.

[21] Ansys, Medini Analyzer. Ansys, retrieved: September, 2020. [Online]. Available: https://www.ansys.com/products/systems/ansys-medini-analyze

[22] OPENOCSS project. The OPENCOSS Consortium, retrieved: September, 2020. [Online]. Available: http://www.opencossproject.eu

[23] AMASS project. The AMASS Consortium, retrieved: September, 2020. [Online]. Available: https://www.amassecsel.eu

[24] IEC 60812: Analysis techniques for system reliability - Procedures for FMEA. International Electrotechnical Commission, 1985.

[25] NASA, "Fault tree handbook with aerospace applications," 2002.

[26] M. Adedjouma and N. Yakymets, "A framework for model-based dependability analysis of cyber-physical systems," in 2019 IEEE 19th International Symposium on High Assurance Systems Engineering (HASE), 2019, pp. 82–89.

[27] M. Mori et al., "Systems-of-systems modeling using a comprehensive viewpoint-based SysML profile," Journal of Software: Evolution and Process, vol. 30, no. 3, 2018, p. e1878, e1878 JSME-16-0093.R2.

[28] NuSMV. NuSMV Project, retrieved: September, 2020. [Online]. Available: http://nusmv.fbk.eu/

[29] FIDES. The Fides Consortium, retrieved: September, 2020. [Online]. Available: https://www.fides-reliability.org/

Effect of Data Science Teaching for Non-STEM Students A Systematic Literature Review

Luiz Barboza

CESAR School
Recife, Brazil 50030–390
Email: lcbj@cesar.school

Erico Souza Teixeira

CESAR School
Recife, Brazil 50030–390
Email: est@cesar.school

***Abstract*—The evolution of computing capacity allowed specialists in certain areas to benefit from this advance, although with little knowledge about data analysis technologies. In this way, our role as software scientists, more than increasing computational power, is to facilitate the access of people from other areas to these technologies and, with this combined effort, bring more relevant results to society. With this objective in mind, a systematic literature review was carried out to understand if (RQ1), how (RQ3) and why (RQ2) data science is being taught to students of non-STEM (Science, Technology, Engineering and Mathematics). The bases used in this research were ACM and IEEE, dismissing the articles that met the exclusion criteria. These criteria were: a) articles focused on the use of technology to improve the learning process in general; b) articles targeting different groups than the one prioritized here, non-STEM; c) educational improvements obtained with different proposals other than the introduction of data science.**

Keywords–Data Science; Non-STEM; Teaching.

I. INTRODUCTION

The popularity of data science courses has increased over the last five years (2015 to 2020), as we can see on the graph generated by Google Trends shown in Figure 1.

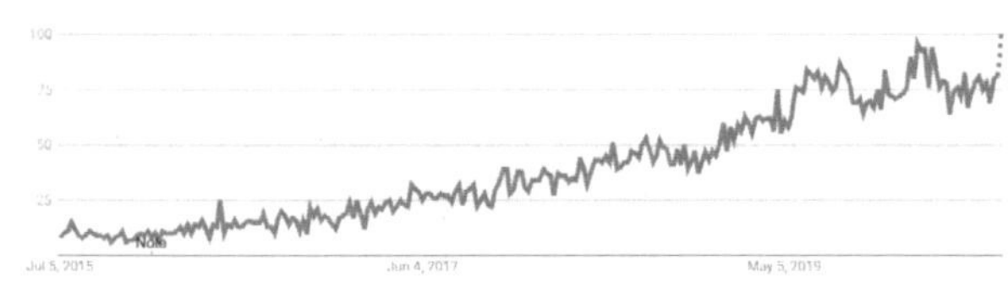

Figure 1. Worldwide search term, Data Science Course (source: Google Trends)

This is true for industry and academia, particularly in STEM courses, where this discipline has a solid base and even a reference curriculum [1] as the main guide. On the other hand, this type of knowledge is still not widespread in non-STEM areas. In fact, data science applied in different domain areas, is one of three data science pillars, as seen in Figure 2.

Bearing this in mind, a systematic review of the literature is presented based on the current state of the art of *if*, *how* and *why* data science is being offered in non-STEM courses. In the next sections, the method for research, selection, extraction and synthesization will be detailed to answer the three research questions.

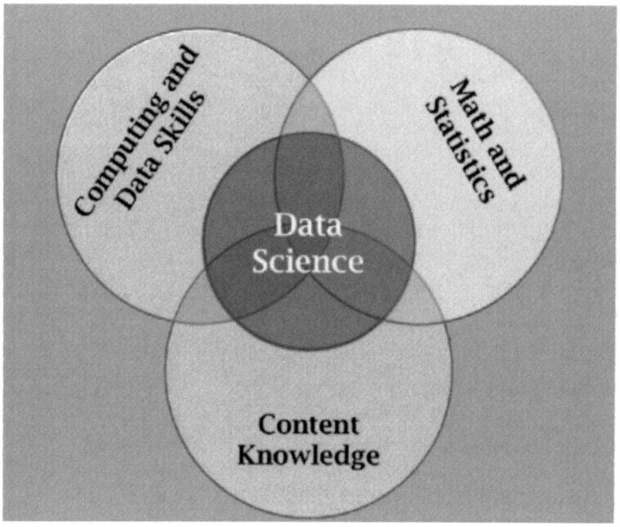

Figure 2. Data Science comprised of Computation, Domain Knowledge and Math/Statistics [2]

II. BACKGROUND

Since their emergence in the 1950s [3], machine learning algorithms have had limited applications, as they depended on computational power to process large volumes of data [4]. From the beginning of this century, the increase in computing power and the demand for understanding and relating the large mass of information available, machine learning solutions have become more sophisticated [5] and more popular in their use [6]. This popularization allowed machine learning to reach an important milestone, the possibility of access for people without specific training in science or data technology. Today, it is possible for people from different areas, such as Economics, Administration, Health, Philosophy, Architecture, among others, to be able to extract information from their data without the need for prior in-depth knowledge of data science. Even tough, this paper focuses on non-STEM students in general, we can consider economists as an example of it as the background context presented as follows. Like physicists, economists acquire non-experimental data generated by processes they want to understand. The mathematician John von Neumann defined a game [7] as: 1) a list of players; 2) a list of actions available to each player; 3) a list of how the accumulated winnings for each player depend on the actions of all players; and, 4) a time protocol that tells who chooses what and when. This definition corresponds to what economists call the economic system, a social understanding of who chooses what and when.

In addition, economists would like to conduct experiments to study how a hypothetical change in the rules of the game or in a pattern of behavior observed by some "players", for example, government regulators or a central bank, can affect the patterns of behavior of other players. Thus, the "structural model builders" in economics seek to infer, from historical patterns of behavior, a set of invariant parameters for hypothetical situations in which a government or regulatory body follows a new set of rules. "Structural models" look for invariant parameters to help regulators and market designers understand and predict data patterns in historically unprecedented situations.

Like physicists, economists use models and data to learn. These models are then used to explain new data. Then, new models are built as evolution of their predecessors. This allows us to learn from the depressions and financial crises of the past. Nowadays, with big data, faster computers and better algorithms, patterns can be seen where only noise was previously heard.

The work presented here proposes to evaluate how the study of data analysis, even if not in-depth, can better train students from different non-technical areas of study, such as Economics and Administration.

III. REVIEW METHOD

A. Research Questions

The research questions analysed here were: **RQ1)** How is knowledge in data science being taught to non-technical target audiences, particularly economics and business students? **RQ2)** What are the learning improvements that these students are experiencing with the use of data science in different areas of their studies? **RQ3)** What was the method used in teaching data science?

B. Search Protocol

Using IEEE and ACM as the main source of research without year of publication threshold, the work here will look for documents related to data science knowledge that are being introduced to either secondary or higher level education targeting non-technical audiences, such as students of economics or business administration, defined by the following research string:

("data science") AND (teaching OR education) AND (economics OR administration OR humanities OR non-technical)

The protocol applied here was comprised of four steps: 1) Apply the search string: apply the string according to the objectives; 2) Filter based on the criterion: Filter the articles by the inclusion and exclusion criteria by analyzing their abstracts; 3) Validate answers to the research questions: read the selected texts, checking if they answer the research questions. If so, extract them as a reference for the final article resulting from a systematic review; 4) Synthesize: apply the thematic synthesis method in order to summarize the research findings.

TABLE I. SELECTION PROTOCOL RESULTS

	IEEE	ACM
Initial set of papers	300	130
Passed inclusion criteria	11	18
Final list of papers	3	6

After the inclusion/exclusion criteria review, the article set was filtered if it answered one of the research questions. The results are summarized in Table I.

C. Selection

The criteria for the inclusion of the article are:

- The article should be written in the English language.

- The article should have its scope focusing on data science studies of non-technical target audiences.

The criteria for the exclusion of the article are:

- Articles focusing on the use of technology to improve the learning process.

- Articles targeting different groups other than the one prioritized here, namely, non-STEM.

- Educational improvements achieved through different proposals other than data science introduction.

- Data Science application without the explicit goal of educational purposes.

D. Extraction

At this step of the process, specific extracts of the analysed papers were identified as being a valid answer to any of the three research questions. As an example, [8] could be cited here, specially as the author starts beautifully with this sentence: *"Because no data exists in a vacuum, each Data Analytics major must choose an applied domain in which to specialize. The goal of this specialization is to understand the types of questions that data are used to answer in that discipline, and how data are collected and interpreted in this context. There are currently seven available domains: Anthropology and Sociology; Biology; Economics; Philosophy; Physics; Political Science; and Psychology"*

The domains mentioned by [8] adhered to the data science studies in different proportions, as depicted in Figure 3.

E. Synthesis

In order to answer the first research question, the following classification was applied: a) school level to which it was applied; b) location/scope; c) concepts taught; and d) target audience. The coding applied to analyze the answers of the second research question was: e) the achieved results; and f) how they were measured. Finally, the last research question had its own coding, g) the method used in teaching data science.

IV. RESULTS

A. RQ1) The IF

In order to answer this research question, the following aspects were analysed: education level, location/scope, concepts taught and target audience.

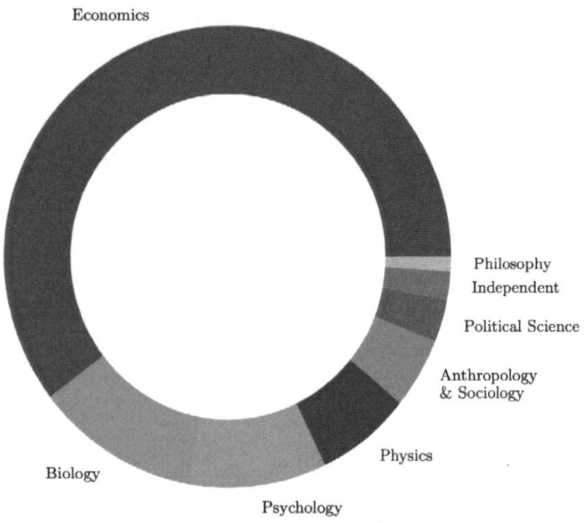

Figure 3. Proportion of courses applying data science on a particular study [8]

1) School Level: Junior High School (from 5th up to 9th graders): As seen in [9], Data Science is being taught to school kids, from 10 up to 15 years old. *"We organized a half-day long data science tutorial for kids in grades 5 through 9 (10-15 years old). Our aim was to expose them to the full cycle of a typical supervised learning approach - data collection, data entry, data visualization, feature engineering, model building, model testing and data permissions"*. The main goal of this experience is to expose young kids to data analysis reasoning and to an intuitive overview of the data science process. *Senior High School (from 10th up to 12th graders)*: A deeper approach can be observed in [10], in which programming (python), data analysis and problem solving are experienced by high school students. Serving as a bridge between programming intuition and logic to actual imperative coding, as stated by the author *"this course is a crucial component of the K-12 computational thinking pathways we are developing at our school district, which take students from block-based programming and computational thinking (elementary school) to text-based programming and applications of computer science (high school). Our mandatory 8th grade course serves as a bridge between these two components"*. *College/University level (undergraduate and graduate)*: At the college/university level is where we can see most of data science teaching. The most relevant aspect for the scope analysed here is *if* it is being taught to non-STEM students. This particular item will be reviewed under the target audience topic of this study. Anyhow, this kind of practice can be observed at undergraduate level by numerous authors [2][8][11][12][13][14]. To depict an example of it we can cite [12] *"data analysis and visualization techniques could be applied in an English literature class in order to help students better understand contextual information, analyze characters' social networks, and visualize literary techniques"*. At the graduate level, we can mention the experience reported by [15]: *"We are developing educational materials for data science to provide broad and practical training in data analytics non-CS students. This includes students majoring in science and engineering who want to acquire skills to analyze data, such as biology, chemistry, and geosciences. This also includes students in the humanities that would like to pursue data-driven research, such as journalism students interested in social media analysis"*.

2) Location/Scope: All the studies analysed report localized experiences, in the sense that none of the studies reported a broader experiment throughout a larger region rather than the local institution in which the study itself was used as base for the research. Most of the studies considered were based in the following states of the USA [14]: California [9][12][15], Washington DC [10] and Ohio [8]. The remaining of the studies were performed in Europe, in the following countries: Germany [2], Switzerland [13] and Finland [11].

3) Concepts Taught: The level of depth in which the concepts are being taught can be categorized in the following groups: Data Analysis, Programming, Big Data, Data Science and Machine Learning. *Data Analysis*: It can be defined [16] *"as a set of mathematical/statistical procedures, generally used as computer programs, embracing elementary but particularly multidimensional statistical techniques that require an iterative application in order to statistically process the data and extract information from the data set. This method involves the use of mathematical/statistical rules generally applicable and not subject dependent as procedures for the assessment of data and the acquisition of new information"*. With this definition in mind, some studies focused on analysing historical data and extracting knowledge from it, such as [2][9][11][12]. *Programming*: Constructing programs is recognized as a complex task, as mentioned by [17] over 30 years ago: *"All software construction involves essential tasks, the fashioning of the complex conceptual structures that compose the abstract software entity, and accidental tasks, the representation of these abstract entities in programming languages and the mapping of these onto machine languages within space and speed constraints"*. Nevertheless, it can present its intuition and rationale, in order to encourage early logical thinking, as [10] has been doing for high school students. *Big Data Engineering*: Parallel processing of large amounts of data has been disrupted by the iconic paper published by Google researchers about its now open source technology, MapReduce [18]: *"MapReduce is a programming model and an associated implementation for processing and generating large data sets"*. This is a key concept when talking about Data Engineering, which is also a discipline being taught as a foundation concept of Data Science Programs, as is being done by [15]. *Data Science*: According to [19], *"Data science updates the concept of data mining in the light of the availability of big data, that differ from data by their automatic generation through social networks, sensors and other data generating tools. In this sense, data science can be defined extending Giudici (2003), as an integrated process that consists of a series of activities that go from the definition of the objectives of the analysis, to the selection and processing of the data to be analysed, to the statistical modelling and summary such data and, finally, to the interpretation and evaluation of the obtained statistical measures'"*.In that sense, it comprises a more complete process, in which it processes large amounts of data in order to infer new knowledge for the business context. According to this view, some studies [14] offer a more complete program combining all previous concepts. *Machine Learning*: It is considered a subset of Data Science specialized in identifying patterns in data as described by [20] *"knowledge discovery process as the chain of accessing data from various sources, integrating and maintaining data in data warehouses, extracting patterns by machine learning methods"*. Some programs cover that important topic, including supervised, unsupervised methods and reinforced learning, as [8][13].

4) Target Audience: The last aspect, and probably the most important one, analysed in order to answer the research question RQ1, is to which target audience the data science content is being taught to, if to non-STEM or STEM only. On this topic we can observe different areas, from liberal arts, business and life sciences, that are being complemented with this kind of content. In [15], Journalist students use big data to understand social impact in a collaborative environment. [12] reports the use of data analysis to make social civic issues more tangible. Different areas such as: Anthropology and Sociology; Biology; Economics; Philosophy; Physics; Political Science; and Psychology were pointed in [8]. Besides humanities areas mentioned before, [14] presents evidences of data science being applied to to life science related courses, such as: Medical Statistics; Marine biology; Biostatistics; Genomics; Psychology; and Neuroscience. And lastly, [13] acknowledges a wide variation of courses being supported by data science studies: Physics; Biochemistry and physics; Environmental sciences; Earth sciences; Statistics; Mathematics; Biomedical engineering; Bioinformatics; Materials Architecture Management; and Social-Political Sciences.

B. RQ2) The WHY

The aspects analysed in order to answer this research question were the results achieved and how they were measured.

1) Results Achieved: Most of the success criteria adopted by the analyzed studies was the feedback of the students about the level of learning on the presented data science content [2][9][11][12][14][15]. In particular, we could mention [13] as an example *"The course has received so far two official evaluations by the students conducted on behalf of ETH Zurich. The general satisfaction has been 4.4/5.0 and the lecturers' evaluation 4.5/5.0 on the following aspects: understandable and clear explanation of the subject, learning goals, lecture significance, motivation to active participation, and material made available"*. In two other cases [8][10], since data science programs were being offered for the first time, what was mainly measured were the number of consecutive offerings and the popularity that of the courses, for example in [8]: *"Over the first four semesters of the program, we have offered 13 sections of Introduction to Data Analytics, enrolling approximately 240 students in total. At the end of the program's second academic year (2017–2018), there were already about 100 declared DA majors among the first year, sophomore, and junior classes. Overall, 37% of our majors are women, and this percentage has been rising with each class year. At the end of the 2018–2019 academic year, our first year with graduating seniors, we anticipate that we will enroll approximately 130 total declared majors, and that we will graduate 27"*. Besides the success level, based on student satisfaction or courses popularity, some studies collected lessons learned and improvements to be incorporated to the programs, as cited by [13]: *"This paper concludes that cross-disciplinary data science education is highly challenging and requires a very different approach in the design of study courses than data science education exclusively for computer scientists. However, this paper shows that cross-disciplinary data science education is feasible and highly rewarding for students"*.

2) Measurement Techniques: The achieved results mentioned in the previous section were measured in different ways. In some cases as a qualitative survey of students feedback, as in [11]: *"According to students feedback, the courses one and two went well. Both, the ADA as a subject, and the course structure were thanked. Most of all, the students appreciated the absence of a final exam"*. In some other cases, a more quantitative approach was made, even without the concern of being statistically validated, as in [13] and [9]. In comparison with cases that had this level of validation, as in [10]: *"We analyzed each construct using a repeated-measure ANOVA with a type 2 sum of squares, using time-of-survey (pre- or post-survey) as the within-subjects factor and gender, prior familiarity with Python, and the trimester they took the course in as between-subject factors. Post-hoc testing was done using a t-test (paired when the independent variable was time-of-survey), with the Bonferroni correction to address family-wise error rate"*. Lastly, for the course [8] that had popularity as its main success criterion, they simply performed an accrual offering after offering of the program.

C. RQ3) The HOW

1) Proprietary Methodologies: Most experiences apply proprietary methodologies [2][8][9][10][11][12][13][14][15] that are in some extent a variation of ACM Data Science Curricula [1], which originally was designed for technical undergraduate educational formation. As an example of a proprietary methodology we can mention [11]: *"To achieve a good learning atmosphere leading to effective learning, we use pedagogic methods, such as, collaborative learning, pair programming, and learning by doing. During the day, we are aloud to find something we haven't even planned. This approach draws us near to the ideology where data scientist is thought as 'part analyst, part artist'"*.

2) ACM Data Science Curricula: The ACM Data Science Curricula [1], comprises the following knowledge areas:

- Computing Fundamentals, including: Programming, Data Structures, Algorithms, and Software Engineering
- Data Acquirement and Governance
- Data Management, Storage, and Retrieval
- Data Privacy, Security, and Integrity
- Machine Learning
- Data Mining
- Big Data, including: Complexity, Distributed Systems, Parallel Computing, and High Performance Computing
- Analysis and Presentation, including: Human-Computer Interaction and Visualization
- Professionalism

V. LIMITATIONS AND THREATS TO VALIDITY

As a process to apply the techniques of a formal SLR, it was an interesting experience. Even if it were performed by applying a strict methodology, it relies only on technical research databases, ACM and IEEE. Some domain specific databases were used as reference, however no relevant studies were found. In that sense, this could be a threat to the validity of this study.

VI. CONCLUSION

In conclusion, teaching data science to different areas of knowledge other than the technical ones (non-STEM) is already collecting its fruits, and still has room for further growth. It is interesting to observe how it is being applied to different levels of students, from primary school and high school up to undergraduate and post-graduate courses. Another interesting point is that it is being offered to different target audiences, from economics, to medicine, social studies and so on. In terms of benefits, it is possible to see that the level of learning and interest on the subject are aspects that have being monitored by the providers of such courses. Not only that, but also the lessons learned in terms of how the teaching methodology could improve in order to present this kind of content to non-STEM students. Finally, the technique used to measure those results varies from practitioner to practitioner, ranging from no measurement at all up to statistically validated quantitative research.

VII. ACKNOWLEDGMENTS

This article was produced as the final activity of the first class, systematic literature review, of the doctorate program at CESAR School. Hence, we would like to thank the course professors, Cesar Franca and Paula Carvalho, as well as the course coordinator, Felipe Ferraz.

REFERENCES

[1] A. Clear, A. S. Parrish, J. Impagliazzo, and M. Zhang, "Computing Curricula 2020: Introduction and Community Engagement," in Proceedings of the 50th ACM Technical Symposium on Computer Science Education, ser. SIGCSE '19. New York, NY, USA: Association for Computing Machinery, 2019, pp. 653–654, event-place: Minneapolis, MN, USA. [Online]. Available: https://doi.org/10.1145/3287324.3287517

[2] J. Engel, "Statistical literacy for active citizenship: A call for data science education," Statistics Education Research Journal, vol. 16, no. 1, 2017, pp. 44–49.

[3] B. G. Buchanan, "A (very) brief history of artificial intelligence," Ai Magazine, vol. 26, no. 4, 2005, pp. 53–53.

[4] J. Dean and S. Ghemawat, "Mapreduce: Simplified data processing on large clusters," 2004.

[5] I. Mierswa, "May 9, 2017," library Catalog: ingomierswa.com. [Online]. Available: https://ingomierswa.com/2017/05/09/

[6] A. Ng, "What Artificial Intelligence Can and Can't Do Right Now," Harvard Business Review, Nov. 2016, section: Analytics. [Online]. Available: https://hbr.org/2016/11/what-artificial-intelligence-can-and-cant-do-right-now

[7] J. Von Neumann and O. Morgenstern, Theory of games and economic behavior (commemorative edition). Princeton university press, 2007.

[8] J. Havill, "Embracing the Liberal Arts in an Interdisciplinary Data Analytics Program," in Proceedings of the 50th ACM Technical Symposium on Computer Science Education, ser. SIGCSE '19. Minneapolis, MN, USA: Association for Computing Machinery, Feb. 2019, pp. 9–14. [Online]. Available: https://doi.org/10.1145/3287324.3287436

[9] S. Srikant and V. Aggarwal, "Introducing Data Science to School Kids," in Proceedings of the 2017 ACM SIGCSE Technical Symposium on Computer Science Education, ser. SIGCSE '17. Seattle, Washington, USA: Association for Computing Machinery, Mar. 2017, pp. 561–566. [Online]. Available: https://doi.org/10.1145/3017680.3017717

[10] "Pythons and Martians and Finches, Oh My! Lessons Learned from a Mandatory 8th Grade Python Class | Proceedings of the 51st ACM Technical Symposium on Computer Science Education." [Online]. Available: https://dl.acm.org/doi/abs/10.1145/3328778.3366906

[11] M. Marttila-Kontio, M. Kontio, and V. Hotti, "Advanced data analytics education for students and companies," in Proceedings of the 2014 conference on Innovation & technology in computer science education, ser. ITiCSE '14. Uppsala, Sweden: Association for Computing Machinery, Jun. 2014, pp. 249–254. [Online]. Available: https://doi.org/10.1145/2591708.2591746

[12] S. J. Van Wart, "Computer Science Meets Social Studies: Embedding CS in the Study of Locally Grounded Civic Issues," in Proceedings of the eleventh annual International Conference on International Computing Education Research, ser. ICER '15. Omaha, Nebraska, USA: Association for Computing Machinery, Aug. 2015, pp. 281–282. [Online]. Available: https://doi.org/10.1145/2787622.2787751

[13] E. Pournaras, "Cross-disciplinary higher education of data science - beyond the computer science student," Data Sci., vol. 1, 2017, pp. 101–117.

[14] S. Kross and P. J. Guo, "Practitioners Teaching Data Science in Industry and Academia: Expectations, Workflows, and Challenges," in Proceedings of the 2019 CHI Conference on Human Factors in Computing Systems, ser. CHI '19. Glasgow, Scotland Uk: Association for Computing Machinery, May 2019, pp. 1–14. [Online]. Available: https://doi.org/10.1145/3290605.3300493

[15] Y. Gil, "Teaching Parallelism without Programming: A Data Science Curriculum for Non-CS Students," in 2014 Workshop on Education for High Performance Computing, Nov. 2014, pp. 42–48.

[16] V. Vitali, "Formal methods for the analysis of archaeological data: Data analysis vs expert systems," Computer Applications and Quantitative Methods in Archaeology, 1990, pp. 207–209.

[17] F. P. Brooks, "No silver bullet essence and accidents of software engineering," Computer, vol. 20, no. 4, Apr. 1987, p. 10–19. [Online]. Available: https://doi.org/10.1109/MC.1987.1663532

[18] J. Dean and S. Ghemawat, "MapReduce: simplified data processing on large clusters," Communications of the ACM, vol. 51, no. 1, Jan. 2008, pp. 107–113. [Online]. Available: https://dl.acm.org/doi/10.1145/1327452.1327492

[19] P. Giudici, "Financial data science," Statistics and Probability Letters, vol. 136, may 2018, pp. 160–164.

[20] G. Kauermann and T. Seidl, "Data Science: a proposal for a curriculum," International Journal of Data Science and Analytics, vol. 6, no. 3, Nov. 2018, pp. 195–199. [Online]. Available: https://doi.org/10.1007/s41060-018-0113-2

Not Another Review on Computer Vision and Artificial Intelligence in Public Security

A Condensed Primer on Approaches and Techniques

Marcos Vinicius Pinto de Andrade
Software Engineering Department
Cesar School
Recife, Brazil
email:vinivdg@gmail.com

Ana Paula Cavalcanti Furtado
Computing Department
Pernambuco Federal University, UFRPE
Recife, Brazil
email: anapaula.furtado@ufrpe.br

Abstract— **The threats and attacks, perpetrated by criminals and terrorists in many cities around the world have made the use of automated tools for detecting violent acts via video feeds, an invaluable tool to law enforcement authorities. The use of surveillance cameras is widespread, becoming a *de facto* in the security of most cities and makes the use of such content in public security an obvious course of action. The major caveat is the enormous amount of footage that needs to be analyzed, making such tasks not suitable for human operators, and a great candidate for computer vision techniques. The present work aims to bring objective and synthetic information on the subject through a compilation of findings extracted from numerous articles on the subject, serving as a guide for those entering the area: what are the main strategies, approaches, techniques, and features of interest in the area. The paper, in comparison with older but more comprehensive reviews, boasts similar, even though not so comprehensive results, being a valuable starting point for newcomers to this dynamic research area.**

Keywords - artificial intelligence; computer vision; surveillance; public security.

I. INTRODUCTION

Security is among one of the major concerns in modern cities. To address this issue, authorities are using video surveillance on a scale never seen before. This context brings a problem: how to process video streams in a timely manner to avoid damages to people's health or property. The large number of cameras used for surveillance all over the world has created the necessity of streamlining the process of interpreting the large amount of visual data originated from such devices [1]. The obvious choice always leads to some sort of automation, because the amount of data originated from systems with hundreds of cameras will demand an extremely high number of operators, plus coordination and communication strategies in order to work properly, making such setups unpractical in real-world applications [2].

In this context, the advances in computer vision in the past years have made it the technology of choice in any system of automated or intelligent video processing. For this task, a plethora of methods have been developed for processing and analyzing different features or characteristics of video streams. The present research aims to find out what are the most used algorithms, strategies, and tools in computer vision with Artificial Intelligence (AI) for security and surveillance. Since this knowledge area has seen the number of works published grow each year, a study with objective information on how the knowledge in the area is evolving over the years, and what are the best practices used, gains importance serving as a guide for those arriving in the area, bringing guidelines on where to focus the time, resources and energy to make the contribution the most relevant possible.

The first readings in the area showed a myriad of works that, at first sight, seemed very heterogeneous. Further studies showed how many of the approaches are variations of similar algorithms or techniques. The idea for the study is to group all similar approaches, techniques, or algorithms in a way to make clear what are the so-called macro approaches in the area. This work intends to map, in a brief, but insightful way, what techniques of artificial intelligence are being coupled with computer vision techniques for processing security cameras feeds or recordings, aiming at automating violent events detection. Other works approach the same knowledge domain, but the main issue identified is that the search for comprehensiveness has generated works where the big picture, most of the time, is not clear enough for newcomers to the area addressed in this work.

The rest of the paper is structured as follows. Related work is presented in Section II, including the citation of some of the most interesting papers. The methodology is described in Section III and addresses how the papers were selected and the information extracted. The results of the findings are summarized in Section IV, and Section V is a conclusion that brings some observations on the analyzed material.

II. RELATED WORK PANORAMA

An interesting approach using dynamic images, namely a compression of series of video frames into a single bitmap, is presented by Imran et al. in [3]. These images are then fed into MobileNet a Convolutional Neural Network (CNN) for short-term spatio-temporal features extraction. These features are combined for a representation of the long-term dynamics of the video feed that is analyzed by a Recurrent Neural Network (RNN) that classifies a video content as violent or not. The method also implemented privacy protection layers and is said to have real-time performance capabilities.

Differently from [3], which uses the Optical Flow (OF) of the images, the work by Febin et al. [4] use a Scale-Invariant Feature Transform (SIFT) coupled with a Motion Bound Optical Flow, creating a method that is more robust when dealing with moving camera footage. The work brings results using both Random Forests (RF) and Support Vector Machines (SVM) as classifiers for performance comparison purposes.

In the field of Human Activity Recognition (HAR), [5] bring algorithms based on multi-features processing fed to a CNN for classification. The work claims the approach is reliable in complex real-world scenarios what should open possibilities for use in many areas like smart surveillance for children, elderly, and also uses for entertainment and human-machine interfaces. Interesting, yet simple, work is presented in [6]. A simple layout of a real-world alarm system based on smart surveillance, real word considerations like server topology and other technicalities are worth mentioning.

III. METHODOLOGY CONSIDERATIONS

For the search, the following databases were selected: IEEEexplore, Scopus, and Science Direct. The main motivation for this choice is based on the fact that this paper was written during the Covid-19 lockdown and these were the databases that could be accessed with no restrictions from outside the campus.

In a quick summarization, the present research consists of the following stages:

- Paper gathering and selection (including paper search, inclusion and exclusion criteria).
- A quick analysis of the approach used.
- Taxonomy definitions (a database structure with all information classes to be stored and how to do it).
- In-depth analysis of the tools used and/or created on papers.
- Findings compilation.
- Findings uniformization.
- Final synthesis.
- Comparison with similar studies previously selected.

In the selection of the final papers, four works were chosen to draw comparisons with the present work. They were more comprehensive, yet old works, and were used to analyze if the coverage and search quality of the research is acceptable [1]–[6].

The search was conducted initially in an automated way with posterior manual selection phases. Various search strings were tested until the searches began to bring more uniform results. The final search string defined was:

("computer vision" AND surveillance) AND ("computer vision" AND violence) OR ("computer vision" AND harassment)

Four exclusion passes were done after the search. They were based on exclusion criteria applied while title reading and then by abstract examination, and, finally, for the remaining papers, a complete reading was conducted for data extraction and posterior summarization. The first exclusion pass was based on a set of rules defined to maintain uniformity and usefulness of the gathered material, and also to reduce the total number of papers that would be read in full. They are listed below and the final results are depicted in

Figure 1 and **Error! Reference source not found.**. Below are the discriminated criteria.

- Keep a temporal range from 2012 - 2020: When technologies researched began to gain momentum, "the cat experiment" was used as a time mark.
- Eliminate health sciences related material.
- Eliminate other non-security-related material.
- Exclude all material related to Natural Language Processing (NLP).
- Exclude duplicates.
- Exclude non Artificial Intelligence (AI) material.
- Select reviews and surveys, but do not process them.

TABLE I. NUMBER OF PAPERS IN EACH STAGE

	FILTERS PASSES				
DATA BASE	AUTO SEARCH	INC/EXC CRITERIA	TITLE	ABSTRACT	CONTENT
IEEE	23	22	15	13	13
SCIENCE DIRECT	92	85	41	13	8
SCOPUS	35	34	32	18	16
TOTAL	150	141	88	44	37

All papers were gathered in Mendeley [22] for reading and extraction. The resulting data was compiled in an Excel spreadsheet. For databases that did not directly exported CSV files, JabRef [23] was used to do the conversion from RIS or BIB to CSV. The remaining papers were grouped in a single folder for reading and extraction.

The file structure described above permitted the free flow of documents up and down in the folder structure. If one needed to review a discarded document to reconsider a decision, it was instantaneous. All the time, it was possible to have access to all documents in full-text format, which proved to be useful in a small research team configuration, as was the case with the present work.

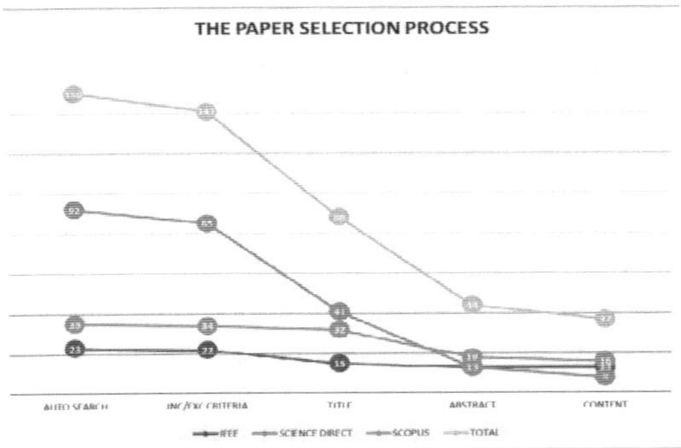

Figure 1. Overview of the selection process, with the amount of paper in each stage of the search/selection.

It was decided to take an approach similar to grounded theory, where a small portion of the material was read to establish a taxonomy of what was important to be extracted to answer the research question. Then, a search for specific pieces of information was conducted inside the papers. The data of interest in the case was:

- What is observed
- Feature identification strategy
- Feature extraction strategy
- Reasoning/classification strategy
- Solution statement by the researcher
- The computational cost of the proposed approach (if present).

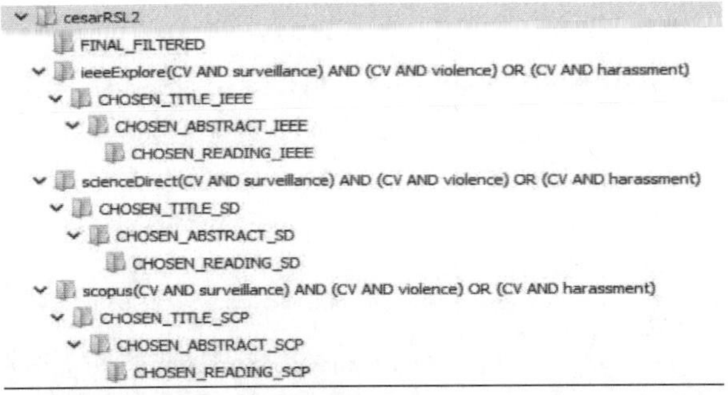

Figure 2. Folder structure inside Mendeley with all the selection stages.

Figure 2 shows a sample of the folder structure created inside Mendeley to process the files. The upper folder always will have all the files downstream, so it was possible to move papers up and down as they were selected or discarded in a given document search phase.

IV. RESULTS

The results can be divided into three main types of researches. First, there were the ones that used some algorithm of computer vision coupled with variants of a Machine Learning (ML) classifier, as in **Error! Reference source not found.**. This approach was found in the vast majority of the works with many variations using modified or enhanced solutions from prior works. A possible explanation may rely on the accuracy and speed of machine learning algorithms like SVM, Random Forests (RF), and their variants. Secondly,

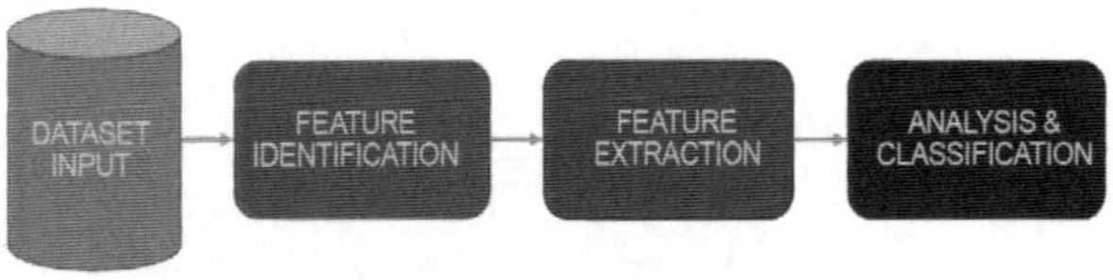

Figure 3. Topology of violence identification systems with Computer Vision and Machine Learning Classifier.

less common initiatives used computer vision algorithms and a kind of neural network for classification ranging from Recursive Neural Networks (RNN) to Deep Learning deployments. At the beginning of this research, there was an *a priori* idea that there will be an emergence of this approach that was not verified in the researched material, which leads to the third macro-approach, depicted in **Error! Reference source not found.**.

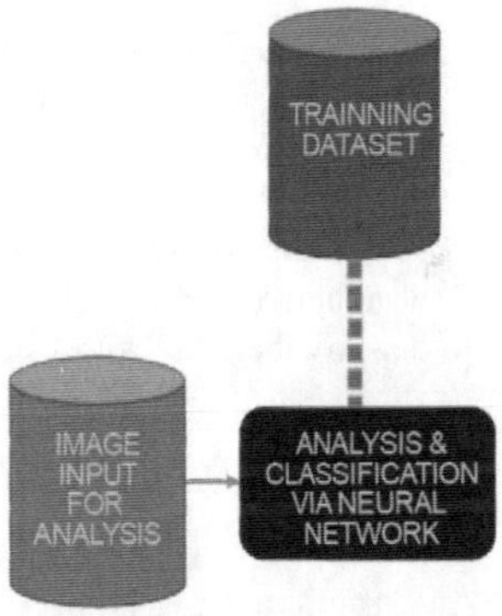

Figure 4. Topology of violence identifications systems with Neural Networks, were found custom trained and pre-trained model used via transfer learning.

The use of pre-trained, custom-trained networks, receiving the direct input of the image feed despite the lower number of occurrences was an approach more consistently identified in the search. The advent of transfer learning is making possible the use of pre-trained networks in many tasks without the burden of training that requires large datasets and more robust computing power. These things are not at easy reach for what was stated in the researched materials.

A. On what the algorithms process

Figure 5 summarizes the findings on what is processed in video feeds in the search of violent events. Most of the search features on images for things like edge and gradients and tracks them in the subsequent frames [3]. The other feature more commonly used was Optical Flow (OF), which is a measure of how the pixels of the image behave over time, which is an indicator of how abrupt the movements in the scene are. These are strong indicators of violent events taking place [7]–[9].

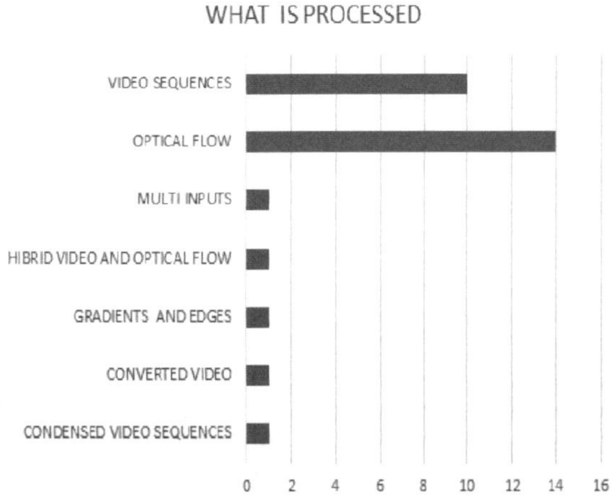

Figure 5. The distribution of findings on what the algorithms look at.

There were ingenious works, like [10], which uses image processing coupled with sensors placed in seats in a public transport vehicle informing when a passenger stands up. Also, it is worth mentioning the use of dynamic images [11][12]. Each approach has its own technicalities, but in general, these are the features the algorithms search within video sequences to classify them as violent or not.

B. The most used feature identifications and extraction strategies

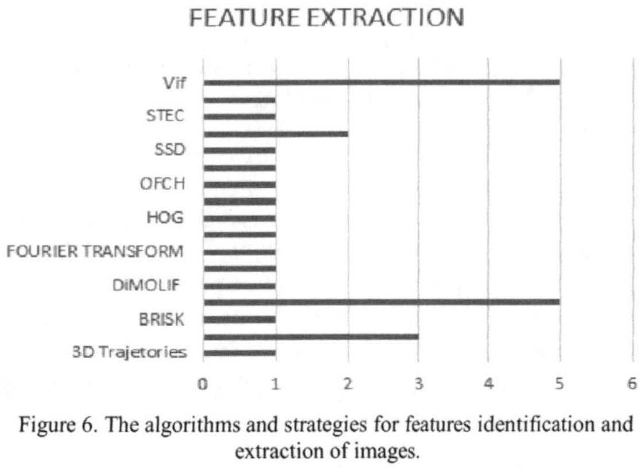

Figure 6. The algorithms and strategies for features identification and extraction of images.

The Violent Flow Descriptor (ViF) uses the variation of the OF magnitude in consecutive frames, being an indicator of abrupt events happening. This approach is present in many of the works. What differs is the subsequent classification model used, which ranges from extremely simple ML models like K Nearest Neighbor (KNN) [13] [14] to deep learning models [15][16].

The big lesson extracted from the material in **Error! Reference source not found.** is that approaches differ in detail, but all the papers used similar strategies with performance improvement modification both in accuracy and computational performance on training and recognition.

C. The main interpretation and classification techniques used and computational cost issues.

In the classification area still, ML techniques are prevalent (**Error! Reference source not found.**). SVM and its variations are by far the classifier implemented in almost half the studied solutions. Despite being used for a long time, SVM is a classifier with wide adoption mainly due to the fact that it is non computationally intensive in the training phase and generates models that perform very well near real-time for classifications.

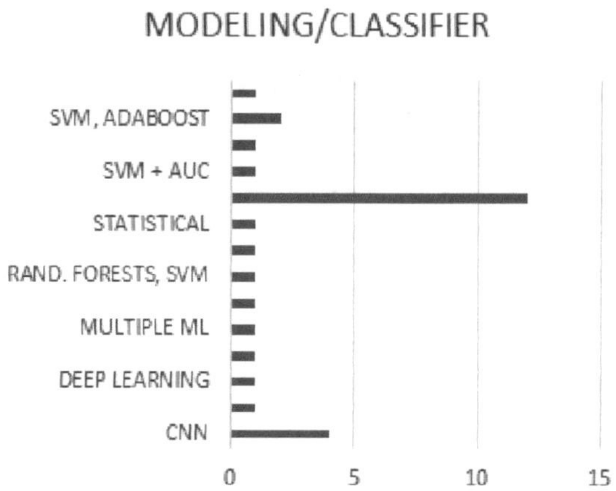

Figure 7. Classification strategies for violent or non-violent definitions.

Our findings raised the question on how are these technologies adoption evolving in time. Are SVM classifiers on their way to retirement? Is deep learning the next big thing in violence detection? For this matter, a short study was done with the evolution of publications on these technologies in the last ten to fifteen years that are presented below (Figure 8) giving a clear panorama on how techniques are evolving. The searches were conducted in Science Direct only, and give a clue on how things are evolving. As can be seen by the graphics, SVM classifiers are still a used choice, probably because of their capabilities and performance On the other hand, deep learning is now beginning to gain momentum on its adoption, being a promising new technology to build new approaches upon.

The use of an optical-flow-based descriptor seems to be reaching a plateau, but it is still relevant.

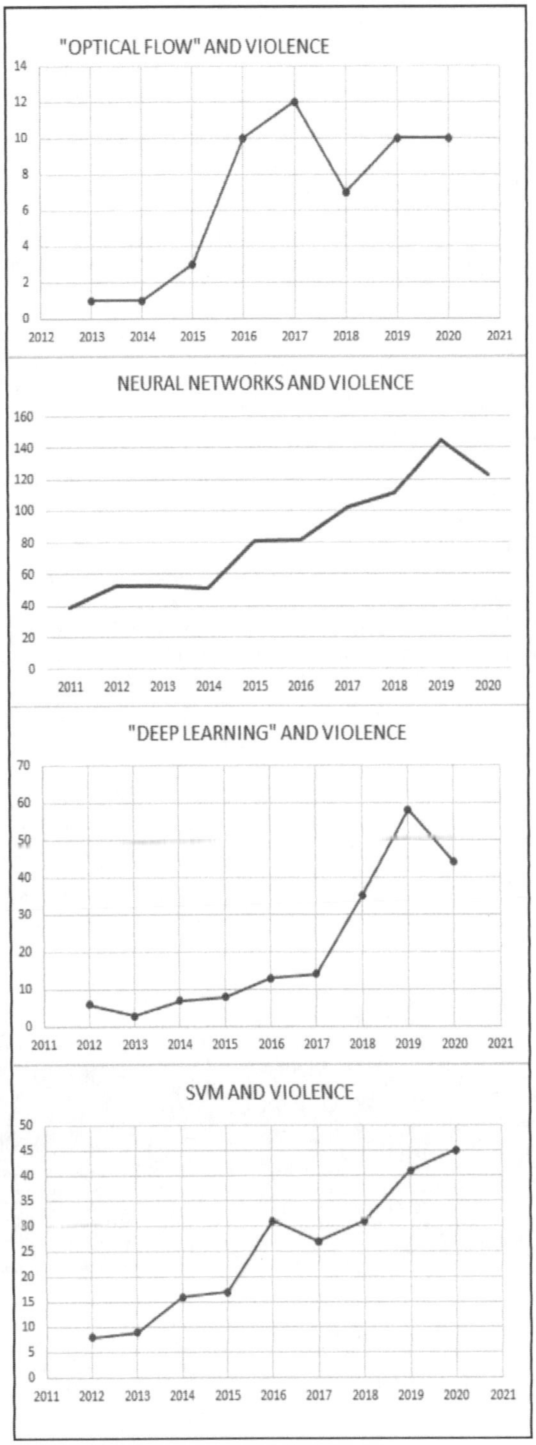

Figure 8: Evolution of the main technologies found in the work and their adoption evolution over time.

D. Comparison with other reviews

The scope of the present work was not to exhaust all techniques and approaches, but give a direction on how things are evolving in the academic area on automated surveillance with artificial intelligence and computer vision. Even though not having total comprehension ambitions, the study was able to spot all the main techniques and strategies found in larger and exhaustive studies, like [1]–[6].

V. CONCLUSION

Since the main goal of this research was to give a starting point for those entering the area, some observations on the big picture must be made by the research team. They are as follows:

- Despite being around for quite a while, SVM is still very used.
- The use of deep learning, although being much talked about, appears to be an interesting area to be explored.
- Neural network studies in these areas are being more streamlined by the use of pre-trained networks with good results (transfer learning).
- There was the occurrence of systems that worked in real-time, this being a crucial feature for any surveillance system aiming to prevent violence.
- Some experiments used reenacted scenes as datasets [11], which is an interesting way to supply training data.

TABLE II. ACRONYMS

ViF	Violent Flow Descriptor
STEC	Spatio Temporal Elastic Cuboid
SSD	Single Shot Detection
OFCH	Optical Flow Context Histogram
HOG	Histogram of Optical Gradients
DiMOLIF	Dist. of Magnitude and Orientation of Local Interest Frame
BRISK	Binary Robust Invariant Scalable Key-points
AUC	Area Under Curve
ML	Machine Learning

REFERENCES

[1] M. Ramzan *et al.*, "A Review on State-of-the-Art Violence Detection Techniques," *IEEE Access*, vol. 7, pp. 107560–107575, 2019.

[2] A. C. Nazare Jr. and W. R. Schwartz, "A scalable and flexible framework or smart video surveillance," *Comput. Vis. Image Underst.*, vol. 144, pp. 258–275, 2016.

[3] J. Imran, B. Raman, and A. S. Rajput, "Robust, efficient and privacy-preserving violent activity recognition in videos," in *Proceedings of the 35th Annual ACM Symposium on Applied Computing*, 2020, pp. 2081–2088.

[4] I. P. Febin, K. Jayasree, and P. T. Joy, "Violence detection in videos for an intelligent surveillance system using MoBSIFT and movement filtering algorithm," *Pattern Anal. Appl.*, vol. 23, no. 2, pp. 611–623, May 2020.

[5] A. Jalal, M. Mahmood, and A. S. Hasan, "Multi-features descriptors for Human Activity Tracking and Recognition in Indoor-Outdoor Environments," in *2019 16th International Bhurban Conference on Applied Sciences and Technology (IBCAST)*, 2019, pp. 371–376.

[6] A. Sangeerani Devi, S. Prakash, K. Laavanya, A. Shali, and D. Sathish Kumar, "Violence detection and target finding using computer vision," *Int. J. Eng. Adv. Technol.*, vol. 8, no. 5 Special Issue 3, pp. 235–238, Jul. 2019.

[7] A. Stergiou and R. Poppe, "Analyzing human–human interactions: A survey," *Comput. Vis. Image Underst.*, vol. 188, p. 102799, 2019.

[8] S. Roshan, G. Srivathsan, K. Deepak, and S. Chandrakala, "Chapter 11 - Violence Detection in Automated Video Surveillance: Recent Trends and Comparative Studies," in *Intelligent Data-Centric Systems*, D. Peter, A. H. Alavi, B. Javadi, and S. L. B. T.-T. C. A. in C. C. and I. of T. T. for S. T. S. Fernandes, Eds. Academic Press, 2020, pp. 157–171.

[9] P. Bour, E. Cribelier, and V. Argyriou, "Chapter 14 - Crowd behavior analysis from fixed and moving cameras," in *Computer Vision and Pattern Recognition*, X. Alameda-Pineda, E. Ricci, and N. B. T.-M. B. A. in the W. Sebe, Eds. Academic Press, 2019, pp. 289–322.

[10] A. Boukerche, A. J. Siddiqui, and A. Mammeri, "Automated vehicle detection and classification: Models, methods, and techniques," *ACM Comput. Surv.*, vol. 50, no. 5, 2017.

[11] R. K. Tripathi, A. S. Jalal, and S. C. Agrawal, "Suspicious human activity recognition: a review," *Artif. Intell. Rev.*, vol. 50, no. 2, pp. 283–339, Aug. 2018.

[12] S. Mohammadi, H. Kiani, A. Perina, and V. Murino, "Violence detection in crowded scenes using substantial derivative," in *2015 12th IEEE International Conference on Advanced Video and Signal Based Surveillance (AVSS)*, 2015, pp. 1–6.

[13] E. Y. Fu, H. Va Leong, G. Ngai, and S. Chan, "Automatic Fight Detection in Surveillance Videos," in *Proceedings of the 14th International Conference on Advances in Mobile Computing and Multi Media*, 2016, pp. 225–234.

[14] E. Y. Fu, H. V. Leong, G. Ngai, and S. Chan, "Automatic fight detection in surveillance videos," in *ACM International Conference Proceeding Series*, 2016, pp. 225–234.

[15] M. J. Santofimia *et al.*, "Hierarchical Task Network planning with common-sense reasoning for multiple-people behaviour analysis," *Expert Syst. Appl.*, vol. 69, pp. 118–134, Mar. 2017.

[16] Y. Fan, G. Wen, D. Li, S. Qiu, and M. D. Levine, "Early event detection based on dynamic images of surveillance videos," *J. Vis. Commun. Image Represent.*, vol. 51, pp. 70–75, Feb. 2018.

[17] I. Serrano, O. Deniz, J. L. Espinosa-Aranda, and G. Bueno, "Fight Recognition in Video Using Hough Forests and 2D Convolutional Neural Network," *IEEE Trans. Image Process.*, vol. 27, no. 10, pp. 4787–4797, Oct. 2018.

[18] X. Xu, S. Gong, and T. M. Hospedales, "Chapter 15 - Zero-Shot Crowd Behavior Recognition," V. Murino, M. Cristani, S. Shah, and S. B. T.-G. and C. B. for C. V. Savarese, Eds. Academic Press, 2017, pp. 341–369.

[19] A. Mumtaz, A. B. Sargano, and Z. Habib, "Violence Detection in Surveillance Videos with Deep Network Using Transfer Learning," in *2018 2nd European Conference on Electrical Engineering and Computer Science (EECS)*, 2018, pp. 558–563.

[20] C. James and D. Nettikadan, "Student Monitoring System for School Bus Using Facial Recognition," in *2019 3rd International Conference on Trends in Electronics and Informatics (ICOEI)*, 2019, pp. 659–663.

[21] I. Serrano, O. Deniz, G. Bueno, G. Garcia-Hernando, and T.-K. Kim, "Spatio-temporal elastic cuboid trajectories for efficient fight recognition using Hough forests," *Mach. Vis. Appl.*, vol. 29, no. 2, pp. 207–217, Feb. 2018.

[22] Elsevier Mendeley Tool. Available at https://www.mendeley.com/

[23] JabRef Tool. Available at https://www.jabref.org/

Requirements Validation Through Scenario Generation and Comparison

Radek Kočí

Brno University of Technology, Faculty of Information Technology,
IT4Innovations Centre of Excellence
Bozetechova 2, 612 66 Brno, Czech Republic
email: koci@fit.vutbr.cz

Abstract—**When designing systems, we must solve many problems associated with the correct definition of system requirements, the right understanding, and proper implementation. Finding that design or implementation contains an error or is incomplete, and identifying where a change needs to be made, are different issues that require different approaches. Models and diagrams, often diagrams from the Unified Modeling Language (UML), are used to capture the system's requirements and basic design. The basic ones include the domain model, use case diagram, activity diagram, and scenario models. Scenarios show the communication and cooperation of objects in solving the use case under specific conditions. If the system is implemented following the design, it is possible to generate scenarios at runtime (either actual implementations or using simulation models). Thus, we can have assumed scenarios of the investigated use case's behavior and real scenarios reflecting the performed design. In many cases, it is not useful to have a detailed view of the entire communication between objects. However, it is enough to focus on specific parts, such as messages or states of objects. In this paper, we will focus on detecting discrepancies between expected and actual behavior and quickly identifying the problem's location through scenarios.**

Keywords–Requirements modeling; simulation; scenarios.

I. INTRODUCTION

When designing systems, we have to solve many problems associated with the correct definition of system requirements, the right understanding, and proper implementation. There are many ways to approach these problems, but their common denominator is always verifying the correctness and correcting possible problems. Finding that design or implementation contains an error or is incomplete, and identifying where a change needs to be made, are different issues that require different approaches.

Models and diagrams, often diagrams from the UML language, are used to capture the system's requirements and basic design. The basic models include class diagrams, use case diagrams, and activity diagrams. The domain model (class diagram) depicts the basic concepts of the proposed system. The use case diagram summarizes the possibilities of using the system. The activity diagram captures the system's behavior in various conditions (it is a workflow defining individual use cases).

An integral part of the requirements and design analysis should be scenario modeling. Scenarios are an essential element, as they show the communication and cooperation of objects in solving the use case under specific conditions. Thus, one use case may have multiple scenarios, which may differ in certain parts. If the system is implemented (at least for verification purposes) following the design, it can generate scenarios at runtime (either actual implementations or using simulation models). Thus, we can have assumed scenarios of the investigated use case's behavior and current scenarios reflecting the created design. As already mentioned, one use case can have several different scenarios. However, the structure of the scenario is usually the same for the learned set of conditions. Therefore, it is possible to use scenarios to compare the expected and actual course of solving the use case.

Many tools allow you to set various conditional breakpoints and record the passage through set points. However, in many cases, it is necessary to reconstruct (or record) the entire path to the breakpoint (including information on the conditions achieved) at least from a specified point in time. A suitable means is to generate scenarios according to preset criteria. In many cases, it is not useful to have a detailed view of the entire communication between objects. Still, it is enough to focus on specific parts, messages, states of objects, etc. This paper will focus on how to detect differences between expected and actual behavior and quickly identify the problem's location through scenarios. We will focus only on selected problems of requirements and design validation through scenarios.

The paper is structure as follows. First, we introduce the basic principles of the work in Section III. The demonstration case study is described in Section IV. Then, problems of scenario modeling and validation are introduced in Sections V and VI.

II. RELATED WORK

This work is part of the *Simulation Driven Development* (SDD) approach [1][2], which combines basic models of the most used modeling language Unified Modeling Language (UML) [3][4] and the formalism of Object-Oriented Petri Nets (OOPN) [5].

One of the fundamental problems associated with software development is the specification and validation of the system requirements [6]. The use case diagram from UML is often used for requirements specification, which is then developed by other UML diagrams [7]. The disadvantage of such an approach is an inability to validate the specification models and it is usually necessary to develop a prototype, which is no longer used after fulfilling its purpose. Utilization of OOPN formalism enables the simulation (i.e., to execute models), which allows to generate and analyze scenarios from specification models. All changes enforced during the validation process are entered directly in the specification model, which means that it is not necessary to implement or transform models.

There are methods of working with modified UML models that can be transformed to the executable form automatically. Some examples are the Model Driven Architecture (MDA) methodology [8], Executable UML (xUML) [4] language, or

Foundational Subset for xUML [9]. These approaches are faced with a problem of model transformations. It is hard to transfer back to model all changes that result from validation process and the model becomes useless. Further similar work based on ideas of model-driven development deals with gaps between different development stages and focuses on the usage of conceptual models during the simulation model development process [10]. This approach is called *model continuity*. While it works with simulation models during design stages, the approach proposed in this paper focuses on *live models* that can be used in the deployed system.

III. Initial Assumptions

In this section, we will briefly describe the initial assumptions of the work. It consists of the basis of presented concepts and the way on how we will demonstrate their usage.

A. Basic Concepts

As already mentioned, we will deal only with selected possible uses of scenarios for requirements validation. Among the most important are in particular:

- During the development of requirements, scenarios of correct behavior under the given conditions were specified. Our goal is to verify this behavior on the created model or part of the implementation. In other words, verify that the messaging sequence matches the expected behavior.
- It is necessary to find out when and under what conditions a specific method is called.
- It is needed to verify whether a specific method is always called under certain conditions.

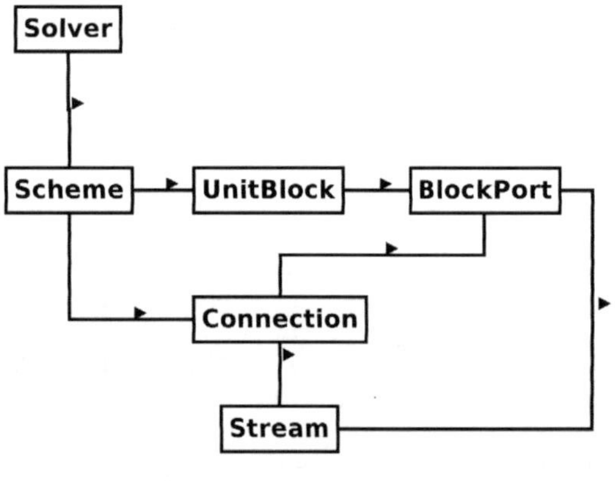

Figure 1. Domain model.

Because it is a simulation verification, it is always dependent on simulation (test) data. In our view, however, we are based on scenarios prepared in advance during the creation of requirements and design. Suppose the models are modified during the development process. In that case, these scenarios are modified (here we come across the MDE condition, namely that we always try to work at the model level).

B. Demonstration method

We will use the following procedure to demonstrate the possibilities of working with scenarios. We will present an example containing one simulation step in the balance calculation tool. We will design a domain model and a sequence diagram according to the standard procedure. We can create a workflow using Petri nets that allow us to generate scenarios. We then make a so-called scenario model based on these scenarios, which can be compared with scenarios generated under different conditions. In the next step, we will include a new request, which will be reflected in the addition of new calls to the scenarios. We modify the created scenario model and then compare it again with various generated scenarios.

IV. Case Study

In this section, we will present a simple example based on the part of the software solution of a tool for the simulation of balance calculations of technological processes. This part concerns the execution of one calculation step. We will present only the part of the calculation step that is essential for explaining the concept.

A. Domain Model

The basis of each design is a domain model that captures the basic concepts of the proposed system. These concepts, modeled mostly as classes, appear in other models describing objects' behavior or interaction. Technological processes are modeled by units (blocks) that work with input streams (e.g., water, air, gas) and generate output streams. During processing, the blocks recalculate the output streams' properties following the input streams and block settings.

```
Data:
simList : a list of blocks
forall b ∈ simList do
| initialize b
end
forall b ∈ simList do
    if b.hasChanged() then
        b.innerFunction()
        b.outFunction()
        foreach p ∈ b.ports do
            if p.hasChanged() then
                recalculate a stream
                copy a stream
                send a stream copy to the connection
            end
        end
    end
end
```

Figure 2. Description of the Balance calculation Use case.

The basic domain model is shown in Figure 1. It contains classes modeling the following concepts: blocks (`UnitBlock`), block ports (`BlockPort`), port connections (`Connection`) and streams (`Stream`). Each port stores information about the associated stream, streams are transmitted between blocks via a connection. The class `Scheme` models the schema containing blocks and joints. Balance calculations are then controlled by `Solver`.

B. Behavioral Model

A UML use case diagram is often used as the default model specifying individual use cases to capture system requirements. The behavior of use cases is then described in the text or modeled by other diagrams, such as the activity diagram. However, it is possible to use different formalisms, such as Petri nets. The chosen concept then defines in what detail the use case's behavior can be specified and how difficult it is to simulate the models created in this way due to requirements verification or transform into the selected source code. For our purposes, we will choose only one use case, namely performing a balance calculation. Its basic form is outlined in Figure 2.

Data:
b is a block
p ∈ b.ports is an output port of the b
s ∈ p is a steam associated to the port p
p.setAttr(value)
s.setValue(value)
p.setChanged()

Figure 3. Description of the attribute changing.

Each block models different technological units, and therefore the calculations are different too. However, the basic structure is the same, and from the simulation point of view, the critical question is whether or not any of the output streams have changed. Assume that each port has a flag set when any attribute of the associated stream from the output function changes. In this case, the behavior description could look like the one shown in Figure 3.

C. *Workflow Model*

To model behavior as workflow, the formalism of Petri Nets can be used. The model is conceived as a sequence of events, i.e., transitions, whether internal or external. The execution of an event may be conditional, and it is possible to define different branches and, thus, different specific use case execution scenarios. An event's execution may involve sending a message to another object, or the event may be executed in response to an incoming event. In the classical concept, it is necessary to map individual sent messages to specific methods of classes, which makes it difficult to read and understand the model. When using Petri nets, the scenario is clearly defined by a sequence of events (i.e., transitions), whether internal or external.

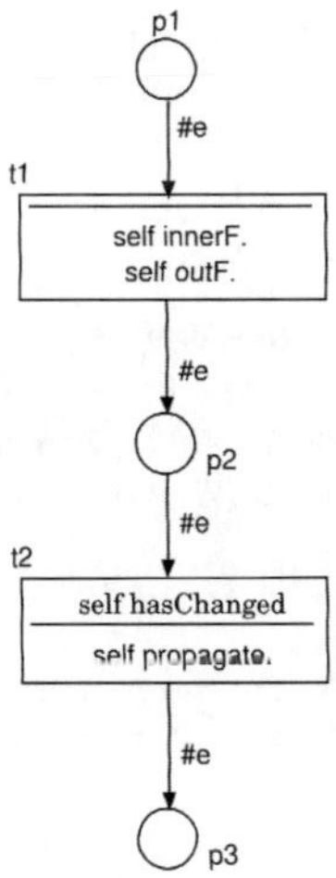

Figure 4. The *calculation* workflow.

Figure 4 shows the workflow modeling method for the Balance calculation use case from Figure 2. The workflow models the behavior for one specific calculation block. Figure 5 shows the workflow modeling method for the method *outF()*. The workflow models one possible scenario consisting of set one attribute of the port `@p` with value `10`.

V. Scenario Modeling

One scenario corresponds to a sequence of interactions between individual system objects or system objects and users. Interactions are often written in the form of a diagram, the most commonly used in this area being an activity diagram and a sequence diagram from UML. The activity diagram is suitable for modeling the whole use case's behavior, while the sequence diagram captures one specific use case scenario. This section will introduce the possibilities of using sequence diagrams as a base for scenario modeling.

A. *Predefined Scenarios*

Scenarios help to specify the correct, expected system behavior for a particular task. As already mentioned, scenarios are often modeled using sequence diagrams. The disadvantage is that the designer often creates these diagrams manually and must follow the rules for their creation, such as following the names defined by the domain model.

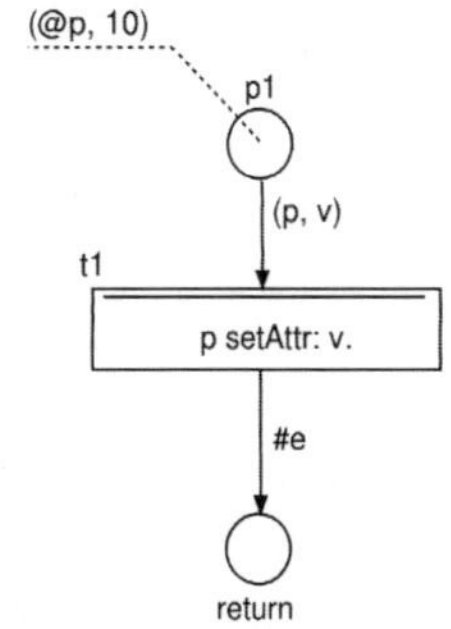

Figure 5. The *outF* workflow – one scenario.

However, if we have, in addition to the domain model, also created models of behavior as a workflow, it is possible to generate these scenarios and make our work easier. A small example of such a workflow, created using Petri nets, is shown in Figures 4 and 5. Figure 4 shows part of the method *calculate* of the *UnitBlock* concept (class), and Figure 5 shows part of the *outF* method's behavior.

The problem is that the outF method captures only one possible scenario, while the sequence diagram allows you to capture different variants of similar behavior. In this article, we will not deal with the possibilities of sequence diagrams. We will only outline this problem on a more complex diagram to capture the behavior caused by sending the method *calculate*, i.e., by performing the appropriate use case. The diagram is shown in Figure 6.

B. *Scenario Definition*

To define the scenario model, we start from the description of scenarios described in [11]. These scenarios work with Petri net models but can be easily adapted to messaging-defined scenarios. The scenario model is described as a messaging sequence, where messages can be grouped into blocks. These blocks represent one sub-scenario. There may be messages and sub-scenarios in the model, which may be repeated – it is possible to define their repetitions using regular expressions.

Each captured message is a pair of $\mathrm{msg} = (\mathrm{msg}^s, \mathrm{msg}^r)$ representing the sending of the message and its return (termination). Between msg^r and msg^r, there may be a sequence of additional messages that express the calculation to achieve the desired goal of the msg message.

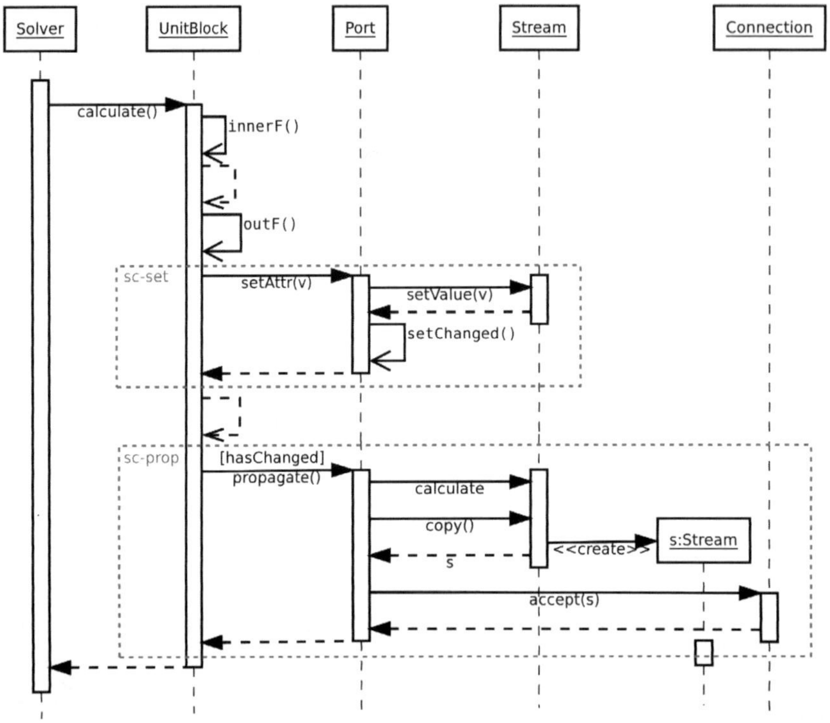

Figure 6. Sequence diagram of the balance calculation behavior.

The message $\mathrm{msg^s}$ is defined in the model as a parameterized tuple $\mathrm{msg^s} = (\mathrm{C_1\{o_1\}, C_2\{o_2\}, msg_n\{a_1, ..., a_n\}})$, where $\mathrm{C_1}$ is the classifier of the class whose instance sends the message $\mathrm{msg_n}$ ($\mathrm{msg_n}$ is the identifier of the sent message) of the object of class $\mathrm{C_2}$. Each of the listed elements can be parameterized; the parameters are given in curly braces. For the class classifier it is possible to mark (name) their instances ($\mathrm{o_1}$, $\mathrm{o_2}$), for the sent message its attributes can be defined ($\mathrm{a_1, ..., a_n}$). Attributes can have a form of specific values or just formal parameters.

The message $\mathrm{msg^r}$ is defined in the model as a parameterized tuple $\mathrm{msg^r} = (\mathrm{C_1\{o_1\}, C_2\{o_2\}, msg_n\{a_1, ..., a_n\}, ret})$, where the first three elements semantically correspond to the message $\mathrm{msg^s}$ and ret is the return value (object) of the message. This value can be a specific object, variable, or special symbol ε representing the information that the method returns nothing or the return value is not important from the scenario definition point of view.

We denote the scenario model by the symbol δ. The model consists of a sequence of symbols $\mathrm{msg^s}$, $\mathrm{msg^r}$, and δ, which can be repeated according to the given rules. The rules are simple. It is necessary to follow the pairing of $\mathrm{msg^s}$ and $\mathrm{msg^r}$, and the syntax of the notation. The rules can be described by a context-free grammar $\mathrm{G_M} = (\Sigma, \mathrm{N}, \mathrm{P}, \{\mathrm{S}\})$, where $\Sigma = \{\mathrm{msg^s}, \mathrm{msg^r}, \delta, *\}$ ($*$ represents the iteration symbol, i.e., the possibility of repetition), $\mathrm{N} = \{\mathrm{S}\}$ and P is a set of rewriting rules in the following form.

$$\mathrm{S} \Rightarrow \delta\,\mathrm{S}$$
$$\mathrm{S} \Rightarrow \delta *\,\mathrm{S}$$
$$\mathrm{S} \Rightarrow \mathrm{msg^s\ S\ msg^r}$$

When checking compliance with the rule, it is usually unnecessary to examine the parameters, only whether the correct syntax has been followed. This possibility can be expressed in grammar, either by engaging in the above context-free grammar or by creating a regular grammar.

The example scenario model from our example then looks like this. First, we define a sub-scenario $\delta_{\mathrm{sc\_set}}$ for setting the attributes corresponding to the red highlighted sequence *sc-set* in Figure 6.

$$\begin{aligned}\delta_{\mathrm{sc\_set}} = \ & (\mathrm{UnitBlock, Port, setAttr\{v\}}),\\ & (\mathrm{Port, Stream, setValue\{v\}}),\\ & (\mathrm{Port, Stream, setValue\{v\}}, \varepsilon),\\ & (\mathrm{Port\{p\}, Port\{p\}, setCahnged}),\\ & (\mathrm{Port\{p\}, Port\{p\}, setCahnged}, \varepsilon),\\ & (\mathrm{UnitBlock, Port, setAttr\{v\}}, \varepsilon)\end{aligned}$$

Another sequence that can be repeated is marked in red in Figure 6. Part of this sequence is captured as a sub-scenario $\delta_{\mathrm{sc\_prop}}$. The scenario captures only significant points for the idea; the whole scenario would be unnecessarily long in this listing.

$$\begin{aligned}\delta_{\mathrm{sc\_prop}} = \ & (\mathrm{UnitBlock, Port, propagate}),\\ & \ldots\\ & (\mathrm{Port, Stream, copy}),\\ & (\mathrm{Port, Stream, copy, s}),\\ & \ldots\\ & (\mathrm{Port, Connection, accept\{s\}}),\\ & \ldots\\ & (\mathrm{UnitBlock, Port, propagate}, \varepsilon)\end{aligned}$$

The resulting model scenario, which corresponds to Figure 6, is then captured by the scenario δ_{m}.

$$\begin{aligned}\delta_{\mathrm{m}} = \ & (\mathrm{Solver}, \mathrm{UnitBlock}, \mathrm{calculate}),\\ & (\mathrm{UnitBlock}\{\mathrm{b}\}, \mathrm{UnitBlock}\{\mathrm{b}\}, \mathrm{innerF}),\\ & (\mathrm{UnitBlock}\{\mathrm{b}\}, \mathrm{UnitBlock}\{\mathrm{b}\}, \mathrm{innerF}, \varepsilon),\\ & (\mathrm{UnitBlock}\{\mathrm{b}\}, \mathrm{UnitBlock}\{\mathrm{b}\}, \mathrm{outF}),\\ & \delta_{\mathrm{sc\_set}}*,\\ & (\mathrm{UnitBlock}\{\mathrm{b}\}, \mathrm{UnitBlock}\{\mathrm{b}\}, \mathrm{outF}, \varepsilon),\\ & \delta_{\mathrm{sc\_prop}}*,\\ & (\mathrm{Solver}, \mathrm{UnitBlock}, \mathrm{calculate}, \varepsilon)\end{aligned}$$

VI. SCENARIO VALIDATION

The validation is then performed by comparing the model scenario with the actual scenario, respecting the regular expression's control characters. A tool based on finite state machines can be used for evaluation. Evaluation can take place in several modes, depending on the type of authentication required.

- *Entire scenario validation.* We verify the whole sequence of the scenario. If we encounter a deviation, we record an error at this point. In this way, it is possible to verify that a method should not be called; that the method is not called in the correct place; or the method with the wrong parameters (attributes, object sending the message, the object receiving the message) is called.
- *Pass validation.* The model defines only the key aspects that must be followed in that order. If there are other calls outside these defined points, they are ignored for evaluation. It can be used, for example, if we are only interested in the question of whether a particular message is sent after another message has been executed.

A. Entire Scenario Validation

We will now introduce these verification concepts with our examples. Let us start with the whole sequence. We must first obtain a scenario of the actual models or implementations. We modify the original workflow to new conditions and then generate different scenarios, which, however, must structurally correspond to the model scenario. Such a workflow modification is shown in Figure 7 – in this case, the attribute is set more than once.

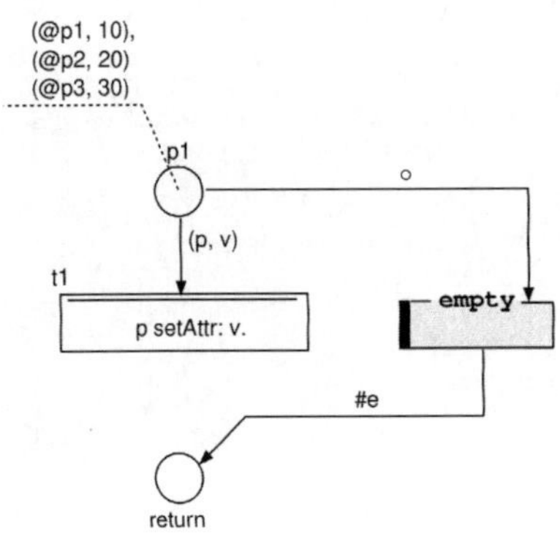

Figure 7. The *outF* workflow – second scenario.

The generated scenario δ_1 then corresponds to the original scenario from Figure 6, only the part marked *sc-set* is replaced by the sequence of calls from Figure 8. Sequence of calls $\delta_{\mathrm{sc-set1}}$ and $\delta_{\mathrm{sc-set2}}$ corresponding to marked blocks *sc-set1* and *sc-set2* in Figure 8 is as follows (only an example for *sc-set1* is presented).

$$\begin{aligned}\delta_{\mathrm{sc\_set1}} = \ & (\mathrm{UnitBlock}, \mathrm{Port}, \mathrm{setAttr}\{10\}),\\ & (\mathrm{Port}, \mathrm{Stream}, \mathrm{setValue}\{10\}),\\ & (\mathrm{Port}, \mathrm{Stream}, \mathrm{setValue}\{10\}, \varepsilon),\\ & (\mathrm{Port}\{\mathrm{p}\}, \mathrm{Port}\{\mathrm{p}\}, \mathrm{setChanged}),\\ & (\mathrm{Port}\{\mathrm{p}\}, \mathrm{Port}\{\mathrm{p}\}, \mathrm{setChanged}, \varepsilon),\\ & (\mathrm{UnitBlock}, \mathrm{Port}, \mathrm{setAttr}\{10\}, \varepsilon)\end{aligned}$$

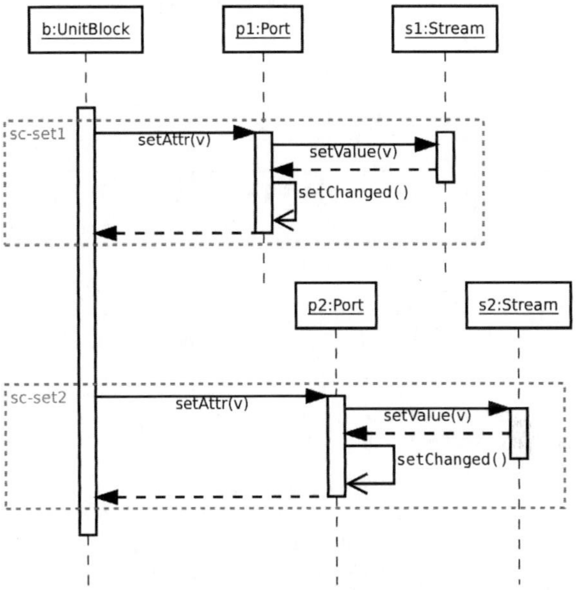

Figure 8. Sequence diagram of the extended *outF* workflow.

By comparing the sub-scenario $\delta_{\mathrm{sc\_set}}$ with the sequence of scenarios $\delta_{\mathrm{sc\_set1}}$ and $\delta_{\mathrm{sc\_set2}}$ we find that they are structurally identical, only substitutions $\{\mathrm{v}/10\}$ and $\{\mathrm{v}/20\}$ occur. Then, it can be concluded that $\delta_{\mathrm{sc_set}}* == \delta_{\mathrm{sc_set1}}, \delta_{\mathrm{sc_set2}}$ and then $\delta_{\mathrm{m}} == \delta_1$. The newly generated scenario thus corresponds to the scenario model.

B. Pass Validation

We will show a variant where we will not be interested in the whole scenario, but only the fulfillment of some condition. We will create/generate a model scenario containing only those calls that we consider crucial for validation. In our example, this can be the condition the propagate method must always be called after any call of the *setAttr* method. The model scenario can then look like this. The newly generated scenario thus corresponds to the scenario model.

$$\begin{aligned}\delta_{\mathrm{pass}} = \ & (\mathrm{UnitBlock}, \mathrm{Port}, \mathrm{setAttr}\{\mathrm{v}\}),\\ & (\mathrm{UnitBlock}, \mathrm{Port}, \mathrm{propagate})\end{aligned}$$

When comparing the model scenario with the generated one, we will only be interested in whether the above sequence is followed and other parts of the scenario will be uninteresting.

C. New Functionality Validation

The last example is the addition of new functionality to an existing requirements model and implementation. This functionality refers to a new type of attribute change propagated backward, i.e., through input streams back to input blocks. When setting the attribute, the given port must be set as changed, and at the end of the use case, the *backProp* method must be called, which will ensure data transfer in the correct direction. A possible scenario for this behavior is shown in Figure 9.

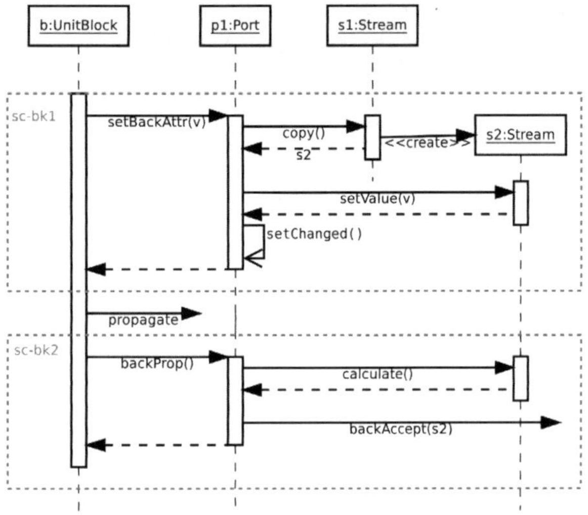

Figure 9. Scenario of the new functionality – backProp.

A model scenario δ_{back} verifying the correctness of the primary sequence of messages is shown in the following statement.

$$
\begin{aligned}
\delta_{\text{back}} = \; & (\text{UnitBlock}, \text{Port}, \text{setBackAttr}\{\text{v}\}), \\
& (\text{Port}, \text{Stream}, \text{copy}) \\
& (\text{Port}, \text{Stream}, \text{copy}, \text{s2}) \\
& (\text{UnitBlock}, \text{Port}, \text{backProp}) \\
& (\text{Port}, \text{Connection}, \text{backAccept}\{\text{s2}\})
\end{aligned}
$$

VII. CONCLUSION

In this paper, we introduced the basic concept of requirements validation and its implementation through scenarios. Scenarios can be described in various ways, such as sequence diagrams. However, workflows offer a more general description ability than a sequence diagram and allow the generation of specific scenarios or models, i.e., some patterns that can then be used for comparison. The workflow can be modeled, for example, by Petri nets, as briefly shown in this paper. Real scenarios can then be obtained either by modifying the workflow or directly from the implementation if a tool was available that captures essential information for generating sequence diagrams or their parts.

We currently have a tool for generating sequence diagrams from models described by Petri nets. The presented concept works only with a structural comparison. In the future, it seems to be an interesting possibility to parameterize the sequences themselves. This feature would make it possible, for verification purposes, to specify precisely which specific objects are involved in the communication, in what state, etc.

ACKNOWLEDGMENT

This work was supported by The Ministry of Education, Youth and Sports from the National Programme of Sustainability (NPU II) project IT4Innovations excellence in science - LQ1602.

REFERENCES

[1] R. Kočí and V. Janoušek, "Modeling and Simulation-Based Design Using Object-Oriented Petri Nets: A Case Study," in Proceeding of the International Workshop on Petri Nets and Software Engineering 2012, vol. 851. CEUR, 2012, pp. 253–266.

[2] R. Kočí and V. Janoušek, "Modeling System Requirements Using Use Cases and Petri Nets," in ThinkMind ICSEA 2016, The Eleventh International Conference on Software Engineering Advances. Xpert Publishing Services, 2016, pp. 160–165.

[3] J. Rumbaugh, I. Jacobson, and G. Booch, The Unified Modeling Language Reference Manual. Addison-Wesley, 1999.

[4] C. Raistrick, P. Francis, J. Wright, C. Carter, and I. Wilkie, Model Driven Architecture with Executable UML. Cambridge University Press, 2004.

[5] M. Češka, V. Janoušek, and T. Vojnar, "Modelling, Prototyping, and Verifying Concurrent and Distributed Applications Using Object-Oriented Petri Nets," Kybernetes: The International Journal of Systems and Cybernetics, vol. 31, no. 9/10, 2002, pp. 1289–1299.

[6] K. Wiegers and J. Beatty, Software Requirements. Microsoft Press, 2014.

[7] N. Daoust, Requirements Modeling for Bussiness Analysts. Technics Publications, LLC, 2012.

[8] R. France and B. Rumpe, "Model-driven development of complex software: A research roadmap," in International Conference on Software Engineering, FOSE, 2007, pp. 37–54.

[9] S. Mijatov, P. Langer, T. Mayerhofer, and G. Kappel, "A framework for testing uml activities based on fuml," in Proc. of 10th Int. Workshop on Model Driven Engineering, Verification, and Validation, vol. 1069, 2013, pp. 11–20.

[10] D. Cetinkaya, A. V. Dai, and M. D. Seck, "Model continuity in discrete event simulation: A framework for model-driven development of simulation models," ACM Transactions on Modeling and Computer Simulation, vol. 25, no. 3, 2015, pp. 17:1–17:24.

[11] R. Kočí and V. Janoušek, "Tracing and Reversing the Run of Software Systems Implemented by Petri Nets," in ThinkMind ICSEA 2018, The Thirteenth International Conference on Software Engineering Advances. Xpert Publishing Services, 2018, pp. 122–127.

Analyzing Challenges in Software Engineering Capstone Projects

Yvonne Sedelmaier, Dieter Landes
Faculty of Electrical Engineering and Informatics
Coburg University of Applied Sciences and Arts
96450 Coburg, Germany
e-mail: yvonne.sedelmaier@hs-coburg.de, dieter.landes@hs-coburg.de

Abstract—**Engineering complex software systems is a very delicate and challenging task, which involves a variety of technical, general non-technical, and context-specific non-technical challenges. Getting better insight into the nature of these challenges is of paramount importance for aligning intended learning outcomes and didactical setup in software engineering capstone projects that aim at exercising and extending these competences. In order to obtain a fine-grained understanding of perceived challenges in capstone projects, this work presents results of a qualitative analysis of self-reports which students wrote as post-mortem documents after being part of such a capstone project. As a main contribution, the qualitative analysis substantiates results in earlier work that technical issues tend to be less challenging than non-technical ones, e.g., collaboration within the team and beyond, issues of project management and organisation, and methodological issues related to requirements engineering and effort estimation. In addition, the paper reveals challenges that might have been overlooked so far, e.g., project organisation (and not just planning), individual motivation, and individual deficiencies in setting or adhering to deadlines.**

Keywords-capstone project; software engineering; challenges; qualitative analysis.

I. Introduction

Software is a core ingredient of nearly any part of our everyday life. Software, however, requires highly skilled developers. Consequently, software engineering education plays an important role in higher education in order to acquire and exercise these skills. Traditionally, universities emphasized technical skills, such as, e.g., programming or testing skills, in software engineering education. Undoubtedly, software development requires profound technical knowledge [1]. Evidently, technical proficiency is not the only thing that matters. In recent years, it has become increasingly clear that non-technical, or soft, skills are equally important as software is developed in teams of individuals which need to interact with each other and various stakeholders such as, e.g., customers or users of their software. Software engineers need to analyze and understand complex situations and use a creative and solution-oriented approach. Various researchers emphasize the importance of non-technical skills in software engineering [2]–[6].

Software engineering requires a specific profile of competences that combines technical, general non-technical, and context-specific non-technical skills [7].

Internal surveys we conducted over the years indicate that students tend to overestimate their level of technical and non-technical competences. Many software engineering projects fail due to at least one of the following reasons: scheduling, specifications and/or average manufacturing costs [8]. Button and Sharrock [8] also state that software engineers tend to distinguish between two basic types of problems: "First, those that are due to deficiencies in the state of general engineering practice, and second, those that arise from the state of the project they were engaged in. Engineering work on any particular development thus does not involve only the resolution of the problems arising from the specific circumstances of the project itself, but also contends with problems that are recognized as generic problems of engineering work per se" [8]. Students hardly believe these facts. In their opinion they would do much better and lead the project to success if they were the actors.

As soft skills are core competences of a software engineer, they should be a core ingredient of software engineering education at universities. Yet, soft skills should not be exercised in isolation, but rather in a typical professional setting and in conjunction with technical skills.

Project work is one approach to bring complexity and problem awareness into university education. Project work fosters many soft skills, such as communication skills and the ability to work together in a team. Interpersonal skills cannot be trained without other people around, and project work combines these competences with the context in which they are needed. Furthermore, project work offers students opportunities to understand inter-relationships between technical knowledge and soft skills. Project work in a university context gives students the chance to prove that they can really succeed while understanding the difficulties of project work and the reasons for failure.

This contribution investigates these issues in more detail. More specifically, the research question that drives this work is identifying the (major) challenges that students face in software engineering projects during their university education. To that end, we performed a qualitative analysis of post-mortem reports after finishing a capstone software engineering project.

The next section discusses related work before Section III provides some details on the setup of the capstone project and its underlying intended learning outcomes. Section IV outlines the research design before Section V presents and discusses the results of the qualitative analysis. A summary and outlook on future work concludes the paper.

II. Related Work

A better understanding of the inner workings of (capstone) projects in software engineering has been addressed in earlier work under various perspectives.

Brereton and Lees [9] investigate four factors that arguably have some impact on the outcomes of student projects. In particular, they focus on team size, range of abilities within the teams, the presence of female team members, and the mix of expertise beyond computing in the team. Their findings indicate that these factors do not have significant impact except for the gender mix – teams with two or more female members performed better than purely male teams.

Wikstrand and Börstler [10] identified various correlations between structural aspects of team projects. Most importantly, the type of the project, i.e., Web project, editors / generators, or other projects, plays a major role for project success. In addition, the authors identified project planning as a crucial, but often underestimated issue in student projects, particularly as students tend to not take planning and other process issues seriously.

Bastarrica et al. [11] investigated the role of four major aspects in capstone software engineering projects, namely technical challenges, teamwork, planning, and requirements clarification. For each of these four aspects, the authors tried to figure out if they changed between project initiation and closure with respect to their perceived value and difficulty. Most prominently, they perceived a decrease in the value of addressing technical issues properly and an increase of perceived difficulty of negotiating requirements with clients. On the other hand, in this study students seemed to have a realistic impression of difficulties associated to proper project planning, while they found teamworking harder than expected.

In a similar vein, Paasivara et al. [12] investigate 15 hypotheses with respect to a change in attitude over the duration of a capstone project. They also substantiated that technical issues lose importance, while non-technical issues, e.g., communication within the team and with stakeholders, understanding requirements, or following a defined process gained in terms of perceived importance and difficulty.

All the mentioned research provides valuable insights by substantiating of refuting hypotheses, based on a statistical analysis of data gained in surveys or interviews. Nevertheless, the origin of the formulated hypotheses remains unclear. For that reason, our research takes a step back in order to identify potential challenges, technical as well as non-technical, in capstone projects, based on a qualitative research design. In other words, our work tries to lay the foundation for formulating hypotheses on relevant success factors and challenges on a sound basis. This seems to be an important contribution to avoid overlooking crucial aspects due to premature formulation of hypotheses.

III. Structure and Goals of the Capstone Project

A. Educational Context

Students in our bachelor program in informatics can enroll in a Software Engineering project (SE project) in their final year. Participants acquired solid programming skills during courses in their first and second years, and they already took a compulsory introduction to software engineering and two elective courses focusing on software requirements, architecture, and testing in more detail. The SE project is intended as a means to tie together what has been learned on software engineering so far and gain hands-on experience in a self-directed mode. Students are supposed to learn from their own experiences, rather than getting rigid instructions from instructors. Generally, the main task in the project consists of devising and implementing a (Web-based) information system that supports and automates some business process (i.e., belongs to type "Web project" in Wikstrand's and Börstler's terminology [10]). In most cases, development is from scratch, i.e., no enhancement or reengineering of existing systems.

The SE project is offered as an elective course, which typically runs for 14 weeks with 6 European Credit Transfer System (ECTS) credits, i.e., puts a workload of approximately 180 hours on each participant. This workload includes 4 contact hours per week in which the project teams physically meet at the university. During these physical meetings, instructors are present, but act as observers in the background unless explicitly asked for support. Teams also meet virtually, using tools such as Skype or social media to make agreements. So far, we have had nine iterations of the SE project from 2011 to 2020.

Since the course is an elective, the number of participants varies from year to year, ranging from 10 to 25 students. Participants are split in project teams of 4 to 6 members. Typically, project topics are contributed by real customers and differ between teams. Customers typically do not have an IT background, which brings issues of multidisciplinarity into the projects.

Organizing a team, tailoring a process model, and developing a software system at the same time overstrained bachelor students. Therefore, we mixed bachelor and master students in the same project, starting with the third iteration of the SE project. Bachelor students focus on technical issues, constitute the development team, and experience project management in a more passive fashion. In contrast, the master students are in charge of leading the project and in particular of adapting the process model to the specific situation. Each team is free to choose a process model. In the more recent offerings of the project, teams regularly embarked on agile approaches, in particular Scrum [13]. The project teams decide on which deliverables and which project roles are really important and how they will implement the chosen process model.

To enable them to fulfill their roles, instructors offer on-demand coaching for master students to reflect and improve their leadership skills. This individual coaching establishes a forum to discuss challenges and problems they face in their teams and obtain help by the instructors to master these challenges.

B. Intended Learning Outcomes

The teaching goals of the capstone project differ for bachelor and master students. The focus for bachelor students lies on understanding and combining chunks of technical knowledge, which up to then have been isolated, into one big picture, and on integrating in a team, which includes fostering communication skills. Master students focus on organizing and leading a team. The difficulties for them are, e.g., communicating with team members, structuring tasks, and motivating team members for effective teamwork. Master students are responsible for the results and for meeting deadlines, as well as for assuring the quality of the software.

Intended learning outcomes are mainly competences and, consequently, assessment is competence-oriented as well. At least two instructors accompany/observe the project teams during the presence hours each week to get an idea of teamwork and individual contributions.

In particular, grading of the bachelor students is based on the following aspects:

- technical quality of results (completeness, complexity of the project topics) including artefacts, such as requirements specifications, software architecture documents, test specifications, etc.
- (customization of and) adherence to a process model,
- individual technical contribution,
- individual team-orientation,
- individual self-reflection, and
- final presentation.

Likewise, grading for the master students is based on

- adaptation of the process model including documentation of the tailored process,
- process quality and leadership,
- self-reflection, and
- final presentation.

A post-mortem reflection is conducted as an additional element to stimulate learning. To that end, students were asked to reflect on their own individual role in the project, as well as the performance of the entire team. Reflection and metacognition are advantages of project work and are didactical methods to foster soft skills and competences.

Self-reflection is stimulated in two steps. First, each of the students has to prepare a short individual self-report that addresses issues such as

- their roles and tasks in the project,
- their expectations with respect to the project and the degree to which these had been met,
- particular issues in the project that they personally would have handled differently and, from their personal point of view, more successfully,
- which role they would have liked in the project and what they would have done differently in that role, and
- how interaction and cooperation between team members evolved during the project, including their subjective explanation for these changes.

Secondly, one week after the project is complete, the project teams meet with instructors for a post-mortem analysis session of approximately two hours, which serves to reiterate any possible aspect that seems worth being discussed in the group.

The self-reports establish the data base that we analyze subsequently.

IV. Research Design

A. Qualitative Research Design

The research uses a mixed methods approach with focus on qualitative analyses applying the basic strategy of Grounded Theory (GT) [14] in combination with Mayring's content analysis [15] [16] . GT aims at developing middle range theories by generating codes in a multi-stage procedure [17]. One step of the analysis consists of going through the material carefully and assigning appropriate semantic codes to the text segments to which they apply. "Coding means categorizing of segments of data with a short name that simultaneously summarizes and accounts for each piece of data. Your codes show how you select, separate, and sort data to begin an analytic accounting of them" [18]. In particular, the generation of the code system is not accomplished up-front, but rather by inductive category formation while going through the material. Simultaneously, new or existing codes are added as tags to relevant portions of the material while reading, abstracting and interpreting the texts.

B. Research Questions

This paper focusses on the following research questions: What are the main challenges for students in SE projects? What are major issues they have to deal with?

C. Research Data

An SE project team consists of 5 members on average. The large majority of participants was male, with only four females taking part over the years. All females were enrolled in the bachelor program.

To get answers to the research question, we rely on students' post-mortem self-reports. Over nine years we collected 79 reports from 81 students in 13 teams. All teams were guided by a master student, so that 14 self-reports were written by master students. The reports have an average length of two pages of prose text. Self-reports were written anonymously.

The self-reports encompass lots of potentially interesting data, which may be analysed from various perspectives. At the current stage of our research, we focus on challenges in SE projects to answer our research questions.

D. Application of the Research Design

As outlined above, our approach develops a category system incrementally by first marking those text segments that refer to challenges that students had to face in SE projects. This was accomplished using the MAXQDA analysis tool [19]. In the first coding procedure, subcategories are developed by going through all self-reports and marking text passages. Doing so results in an initial category system with little structure, which possibly includes some duplications. In a second step, initial categories are merged, sorted, and grouped according to their meaning. In this way, an unambiguous and structured category system arises.

E. *Initial Results - Overview*

As a result, our research process yielded 1,379 codes in 19 categories. One of these categories is a main category "challenges", which is of particular interest for this paper.

The main category "challenges" encompasses 3 unambiguous subcategories (professional & technical issues, human factors, and organizational matters). Furthermore, we found 3 categories that collect complex challenges. Challenges in this category (internal communication, complexity, leadership) combine at least 2 challenges of the unambiguous categories. Challenges concerning internal communication, for example, may have human and organizational causes. In addition, a category "other challenges" was built to sum up marginal problems of working together.

Focussing on these relevant categories, 732 coded text segments from 72 self-reports were evaluated and showed the top three challenges in SE projects (see Table I and Figure 1): Human factors are the biggest challenges for students when working in a team, followed by organizational matters and professional & technical issues.

It is worth noting that the main categories "Internal communication", "Big picture / Complexity", and "Leadership (-)" are atomic in the sense that they do not have any subcategories.

TABLE I. STUDENTS' CHALLENGES IN SE CAPSTONE PROJECTS

	Students' Challenges in SE Capstone Projects		
	Percent (valid)	***Percent***	***Documents***
Human factors	87.5	79.75	63
Organizational Matters	75	68.35	54
Professional & Technical Issues	72.22	65.82	52
Internal Communication	50	45.57	36
Big Picture / Complexity	47.22	43.04	34
Other Challenges	40.28	36.71	29
Leadership (-)	25	22.78	18
DOCUMENTS with Code(s)	100	91.14	72
DOCUMENTS without Code(s)	-	8.86	7
ANALYSED DOCUMENTS	-	100	79

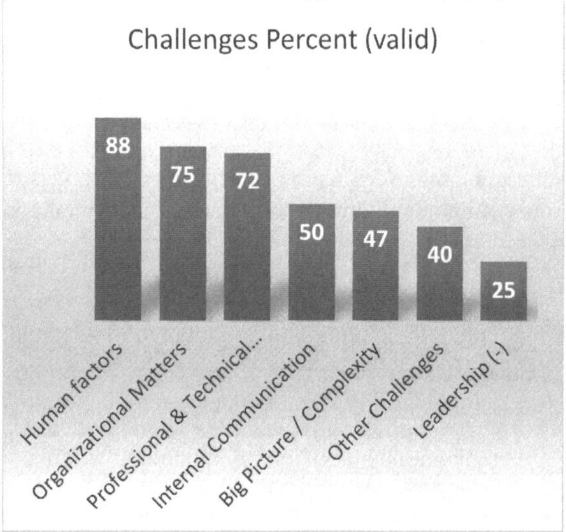

Figure 1. Students' Challenges in SE Capstone Projects (in percent)

F. *Most Prominent Issues in Main Categories*

A closer look at the main categories shows the following top issues within a specific category, as seen in Tables II, III, IV, and V.

TABLE II. TOP ISSUES IN HUMAN FACTORS

Top 4 Issues in Category "Human factors"		
Category	***Number of codes***	***Percent***
Collaboration bachelor and master students	32	10.49
Motivation	31	10.16
Collaboration	25	8.2
Communication with Third / Other Disciplines	20	6.56

The first subcategory refers to issues that relate to the interaction of bachelor and master students within a project team. The second subcategory reflects issues that are linked to a lack of individual motivation. The third subcategory refers to issues of how members of the project teams (excluding the master students) cooperated, while the last subcategory focusses on the communication with stakeholders outside the project team, possibly across disciplinary boundaries.

TABLE III. TOP ISSUES IN ORGANIZATIONAL MATTERS

Top 5 Issues in Category "Organizational Matters"		
Category	*Number of codes*	*Percent*
Time aspects / Timeliness	34	26.15
Management in general	33	25.38
Software Process Modell	16	12.31
Distribution of Tasks and Responsibilities	16	12.31
Communication	13	10.00

In terms of organisational matters, the first subcategory refers to issues related to stretching deadlines or skipping tasks due to time pressure or lack of time. The second subcategory collects issues related to organizing the project, e.g., developing a precise project plan, arrange meetings, facilitate meetings, etc. The third category refers to issues in the context of making the process model work properly. The fourth category addressed issues related to sharing the workload and assigning / accepting responsibilities in the project team, while the last one refers to (lack of) communication among team members.

TABLE IV. TOP ISSUES IN PROFESSIONAL & TECHNICAL ISSUES

Top 5 Issues in Category "Professional & Technical Issues"		
Category	*Number of codes*	*Percent*
Documentation	27	21.77
Software Requirements	25	20.16
Technical Knowledge	17	13.71
Effort Estimation	12	9.68
Tools	10	8.06

In the main category „Professional & Technical issues", the first subcategory deals with the deliverables beyond the actual code, e.g., requirements or architecture documents. The second subcategory refers to methodological issues related to clarifying requirements. The third and fifth subcategories deal with issues related to missing technical knowledge or tool deficiencies, while the fourth category refers to deficiencies related to time and effort estimations.

TABLE V. TOP ISSUES AMONG OTHER CHALLENGES

Top 3 Issues in Category "Other Challenges"		
Category	*Number of codes*	*Percent*
General Organisation	12	29.27
Shared Vision	9	21.95
Individual Situation	5	12.20

The main category „Other Challenges" relates to issues on a meta level, namely the organization of the project as a course and the individual situation of team members in the context of other subjects, but also a common understanding of priorities for the project, within the team or between team and instructors.

V. DISCUSSION

In contrast to the majority of earlier work on the subject, this work employs a well-founded qualitative approach to analysing educational data, in this case in the context of software engineering capstone projects.

Following this qualitative line of research, we arrived at 19 main categories of challenges that students face in capstone projects. These 19 main categories correspond to semantic clusters of issues raised in more than 70 textual post-mortem self-reports. Due to the chosen approach, categories and subcategories are subject to change whenever additional data become available.

The database of more than 70 textual self-reports is rich in the sense that it might provide insight from various diverse points of view. For now, we put a focus on identifying challenges students might face in a capstone project. Given that perspective, our result is closest in nature to the analysis by Paasivaara et al. [12]. Given our data, we can substantiate their findings that technical issues play only a minor role with respect to the "success" of a student project in comparison to other aspects, such as collaboration within the team and beyond, issues of project management and organisation, and methodological issues related to requirements engineering and effort estimation. In addition, we also found indications that, like stated by Wikstrand and Börstler [10], issues related to project planning are some challenge. Yet, our results are more fine-grained, thus allowing for more sophisticated hypotheses that might be tested subsequently. For instance, project organisation (and not just planning), individual motivation and individual deficiencies in setting or adhering to deadlines have not been mentioned as important issues in related research.

Furthermore, our findings are pretty well in line with the intended learning outcomes of the capstone project. As mentioned in Section III-B, developing problem-awareness with respect to issues related to a gross oversight and team formation and teamwork are among the most important goals of the capstone project. As these issues are mentioned frequently in the coded text segments (see Table I), students actually seem to realize that things look simpler as they are on closer inspection. As a consequence, we largely reached our intended learning outcomes.

VI. SUMMARY AND OUTLOOK

Providing students with an opportunity to tie together their knowledge on engineering (moderately) complex software systems and exercise and expand non-technical competences is paramount for well-educated graduates in software engineering. Capstone software engineering projects are very popular approach to that end. Yet, these capstone projects vary in terms of "success", both from the point of view of involved stakeholders and with respect to intended learning outcomes.

This paper aims at getting better insight into which challenges student face in software engineering capstone projects. To do so, self-reports of nine years were evaluated qualitatively with the MAXQDA analysis toolset. Our findings indicate that major challenges for students lie in human, organizational and professional. Furthermore, internal communication, complexity, and leadership are areas of potential difficulties in student projects.

As main results, our research identifies areas that pose difficulties of some sort or another to students when running a somewhat complex software engineering project. This establishes an opportunity to state more elaborate hypotheses on success or risk factors with respect to intended learning outcomes for software engineering outcomes.

In future studies, self-reports will be evaluated with other foci, e.g.: What are the learning outcomes from students` perspectives? What did students learn? Are there differences between bachelor and master students concerning the mentioned questions?

ACKNOWLEDGMENT

This work is funded by the German Federal Ministry of Education and Research (Bundesministerium für Bildung und Forschung) under grant number 01PL17022A as part of the EVELIN project. The authors are responsible for the content of this publication.

REFERENCES

[1] I. Sommerville, *Software Engineering,* 9th ed. Boston: Pearson, 2011.

[2] C. Gold-Veerkamp, *Erhebung von Soll-Kompetenzen im Software Engineering - Anforderungen an Hochschulabsolventen aus industrieller Perspektive*. Wiesbaden: Springer Vieweg, 2015.

[3] P. L. Li, A. J. Ko, and J. Zhu, "What Makes a Great Software Engineer?," in 37th International Conference on Software Engineering (ICSE), 2015, pp. 700–710.

[4] H.-K. Lu, C.-H. Lo, and P.-C. Lin, "Competence analysis of IT professionals involved in business services — Using a qualitative method," in 24th Conference on Software Engineering Education and Training (CSEE&T), 2011, pp. 61–70.

[5] I. Richardson, L. Reid, S. B. Seidman, B. Pattinson, and Y. Delaney, "Educating software engineers of the future: Software quality research through problem-based learning," in 24th Conference on Software Engineering Education and Training (CSEE&T), 2011, pp. 91–100.

[6] J. G. Rivera-Ibarra, J. Rodríguez-Jacobo, and M. A. Serrano-Vargas, "Competency Framework for Software Engineers," in 23rd Conference on Software Engineering Education and Training (CSEE&T), 2010, pp. 33–40.

[7] Y. Sedelmaier, *Basics of didactics for software engineering:* Research-based and application-oriented development and evaluation. Saarbrücken: LAP LAMBERT Academic Publishing, 2019.

[8] G. Button and W. Sharrock, "Project work: The organisation of collaborative design and development in software engineering," (en), *Comput Supported Coop Work*, vol. 5, no. 4, pp. 369–386, 1996.

[9] P. Brereton and S. Lees, "An Investigation of Factors Affecting Student Group Project Outcomes," in 18th Conference on Software Engineering Education & Training (CSEE&T), 2005, pp. 163–170.

[10] G. Wikstrand and J. Borstler, "Success Factors for Team Project Courses," in 19th Conference on Software Engineering Education & Training (CSEE&T), 2006, pp. 95–102.

[11] M. C. Bastarrica, D. Perovich, and M. M. Samary, "What Can Students Get from a Software Engineering Capstone Course?," in 2017 IEEE/ACM 39th International Conference on Software Engineering: Software Engineering Education and Training Track (ICSE-SEET), 2017, pp. 137–145.

[12] M. Paasivaara, D. Voda, V. T. Heikkilä, J. Vanhanen, and C. Lassenius, "How Does Participating in a Capstone Project with Industrial Customers Affect Student Attitudes?," in 2018 IEEE/ACM 40th International Conference on Software Engineering: Software Engineering Education and Training (ICSE-SEET), 2018, pp. 49–57.

[13] M. Klopp, C. Gold-Veerkamp, J. Abke, K. Borgeest, R. Reuter, S. Jahn, J. Mottok, Y. Sedelmaier, A. Lehmann, and D. Landes, "Totally Different and yet so Alike," in 4th European Conference on Software Engineering Education (ECSEE'20): ACM, 2020, pp. 12–21.

[14] B. G. Glaser and A. L. Strauss, *The Discovery of Grounded Theory: Strategies for Qualitative Research*. Chicago: Aldine Transaction, 2009.

[15] P. Mayring, *Qualitative Content Analysis*. Available: http://www.qualitative-research.net/index.php/fqs/article/view/1089/2385 (2020, Sep. 02).

[16] ____, *Qualitative Inhaltsanalyse:* Grundlagen und Techniken, 11th ed. Weinheim: Beltz, 2010.

[17] U. Kuckartz, *Qualitative Inhaltsanalyse. Methoden, Praxis, Computerunterstützung,* 4th ed. Weinheim, Basel: Beltz Juventa, 2018.

[18] K. Charmaz, *Constructing grounded theory,* 2nd ed. Los Angeles: SAGE, 2014.

[19] S. Rädiker and U. Kuckartz, *Analyse qualitativer Daten mit MAXQDA*. Wiesbaden: Springer Fachmedien Wiesbaden, 2019.

Code Quality Metrics Derived from Software Design

Omar Masmali
Department of Computer Science
The University of Texas
El Paso, Texas USA
email: oamasmali@miners.utep.edu

Omar Badreddin
Department of Computer Science
The University of Texas
El Paso, Texas USA
email: obbadreddin@utep.edu

Abstract-**Code smells are assumed to indicate bad design that can cause an unsustainable system. Many studies have tailored fixed threshold values for code smell metrics. However, these threshold values have ignored the fact that every system is unique, and it cannot be dynamically evolved throughout the codebase life cycle. This paper presents a novel approach that formulates dynamic code quality metrics with thresholds that are derived from software design. The first step in this approach is to measure the complexity of the design. Many researchers had developed many complexity metrics to measure the level of complexity in software models. Most of these metrics are limited and focus on counting the number of elements in each design, ignoring the unique characteristics of these elements and their interactions. In this study, we also propose a new methodology to measure the complexity of any software design. This measurement approach is based on evaluating each element in any class diagram by assigning a complexity rate. Finally, we propose a methodology to evaluate the effectiveness of this approach.**

Keywords - code quality; model-driven engineering; software quality metrics; UML class diagram; software design.

I. INTRODUCTION

An important goal of software engineering is to deliver software systems that can be sustainably maintained for an extended period of time. Software sustainability is a systematic challenge facing many communities, including professional software developers, open source communities and the research and scientific communities. It is estimated that half of software engineers' time and efforts are consumed performing avoidable maintenance activities. Current software code quality metrics that reply to code smells and technical debt suffer from key fundamental limitations. First, current methods are reactive in nature, as they are dependent on the emergence of adverse symptoms. Generally, such methods promote code refactoring to address deficiencies but provide little upfront guidance to avoid or minimize the emergence of such deficiencies. Moreover, current metrics are insensitive to diverse technologies, platforms and software contexts. This is a significant limitation, particularly at this period when software platforms, middlewares and contexts are in rapid flux. In addition, quality quantifications are not sufficiently fluid to adapt to changing software priorities and context throughout the software life cycle.

This paper presents a methodology to define code quality metrics with thresholds that are derived from software design. This ensures alignment between the intentional specification of software design characteristics and its implementation. This approach means that metrics can evolve as the codebase design evolves throughout the software lifecycle. Moreover, this approach means that each code module will have its own unique quality metrics that are tailored to its unique context. Also, in this paper, we introduce new complexity metrics for software designs. Many researchers had developed some complexity metrics to measure the level of complexity in software models [26]-[30]. Most of these metrics are limited in scope and focus on counting the number of elements in each design, overlooking the unique characteristics of these elements and their interactions. In this study, we propose a new methodology to measure the complexity of any software design. This measurement approach is based on evaluating each element in any class diagram by assigning a complexity rate.

The rest of the paper is structured as follows. In Section II, we describe the problem of current code quality metrics, then, we cover some related works. In Section IV, we present our proposed approach, and in Section V, we show the expected contribution of this work. In Section VI, we present the current status of our approach, and finally, we conclude our work in Section VII.

II. PROBLEM

Current code quality quantification methodologies adopt metrics with rigid thresholds. These methodologies do not adequately consider variations in development technologies and the architectural roles of various code and design elements. For example, one of the code quality metrics is large class code smell [1], defined as any class with more than 1000 lines of code. As software development platforms advance, managing a class with 1000 lines of code may no longer be detrimental to codebase quality. Similarly, high-performance computing platforms may require classes that are significantly larger in size to maximize performance. Moreover, long-living software systems may require significantly lower thresholds to accommodate the codebase as it evolves over an extended period of time.

To illustrate the current situation, consider the following simplified the Unified Modeling Language UML class diagram shown in Figure 1. The class diagram lists a data-heavy class (Class D), a computational heavy class (Class E) and some associations between classes. A software engineer who develops an implementation for this design, while following the design closely, will inevitably create code that suffers from significantly low sustainability quantification. For example, because Class D is data-heavy, its size, in terms of lines of code, will be very small, resulting in Lazy class code smell [14]. Similarly, Class C is designed to access many methods and attributes in other classes (it participates in five associations). The code analysis of Class C returns God class code smell [15].

Contemporary code analysis approaches that uncover code smells are agnostic to the intentions of the software designer, as demonstrated in the example above. Traditional analysis does not consider to what extent the implementation is aligned with the design. The identified code smells are frequently not an indication of unsustainable code but are, rather, a direct result of the intentional design specifications.

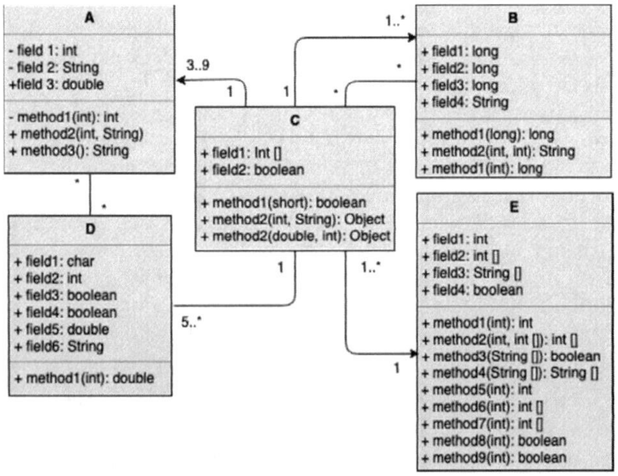

Figure 1. UML class diagram example.

Class D is Lazy because it is designed to host data and perform few computations. Class C is Large and has access to many external entities because it is designed as a root element in the design. Recommended code refactoring to remove the code smells will unavoidably suggest refactorings that are difficult to implement without violating the design specification. Therefore, we argue that such metrics with rigid thresholds are too rigid and are ineffective in characterizing codebase qualities.

III. RELATED WORK

This section will cover some related works in code quality metrics and design complexity metrics.

A. Code Quality Metrics

It has been argued that identifying appropriate code quality metrics and their thresholds is challenging, many have proposed using experience as a primary source for metric definition [21]- [23]. Code metrics are too sensitive to context and that metrics appropriate to one project are not adequate predictors for another. Aniche et al. investigated the effect of architecture on code metrics [4], proposing Software Architecture Tailored Thresholds (SATT), an approach that detects whether an architectural role is considerably different from others in the system in terms of code metrics and provides a specific threshold for that role. Our work presented in this paper is similar in the sense that it aims to improve the accuracy of code metric thresholds. However, while the SATT approach derives a unique threshold only if the architectural role of the module is deemed to be significantly different, our approach derives unique thresholds even in cases where the architectural role may only be slightly different. Gil and Lalouche demonstrated this phenomenon by applying both statistical and visual analyses of code metrics [2]. Fortunately, they demonstrate that context dependency can be neutralized by applying a Log Normal Standardization (LNS) technique. In a similar study, Zhang et al. showed that code metrics are dependent on six factors, namely, application domain, programming language, age, lifespan, the number of changes and the number of downloads [3].

Oliveria et al. proposed a method that extracts relative thresholds from benchmark data, and they evaluated their method in the Qualitas Corpus, finding that the extracted thresholds represent an interesting balance between real and idealized design rules [12]. Furthermore, Kapova et al. presented an initial set of code metrics to evaluate the maintainability that can be applied to different relational transformations, which play important roles when considering architecture refinement transformations [13]. The authors demonstrated the use of these metrics on a set of reference transformations to show their application in real-world settings and to help software architects judge the maintainability of their model transformations. Based on these judgments, software architects can take corrective actions (like refactorings or code-reviews) whenever they identify a decay in the maintainability of their transformations.

B. Design Complexity Metrics

Many different metrics for the class diagram has been developed to help software developers to analyze complexity and maintainability in the early phase of software lifecycle. One of them is developed by Peter, in [26], to analyze the complexity of architecture by using metric tree. He used UML diagram as an input to find some key indicators. He developed metrics to predict class's fault-proneness and to provide quality measurements. M. Genero discussed two groups of metrics to measure the complexity of class diagrams [30]. Kang et al. proposed weighted class dependence graphs to present a structure complexity measure for the UML class diagram by calculating classes and relationships between them [28]. They are using the entropy distance to measure the complexity of the class diagram. Use stochastic variables x and y to denote the output and input edges weight of each node. Doraisamy et al. proposed a model metric to be a guideline for software project managers in order to control and monitor software [25].

Moreover, a class diagram metrics proposed by Marchesi metrics to measure the complexity by balancing the responsibilities among packages and classes, and of cohesion and coupling among system entities [31]. The metrics are Design Size in Classes (DSC), Number of Hierarchies (NOH), Average Number of Ancestors (ANA), Direct Class Coupling (DCC), Cohesion Among Method of Class (CAM), and Measure of Aggregation (MOA). Chidamber and Kemerer proposed some metrics, only three of them for measuring the UML class diagram [27][29] which are Number of Children (NOC), Depth of Inheritance Tree (DIT), and Weighted methods per Class (WMC). Concas in his work focuses on investigating process complexity [5]. He defines process complexity as the degree to which a business process is difficult to analyze, understand or explain. claims that the only way to analyze the process complexity is by using the process control-flow complexity metrics. Ma et al. [32] proposed a hierarchical metrics set in terms of coupling and cohesion for large-scale Object-Oriented (OO) software systems. They analyzed the proposed approach on a sample of 13 open-source OO software systems to empirically validate the set. Fourati et al. [33] propose an approach that identifies anti-patterns in UML designs through the use of existing and newly defined quality metrics that examines the structural and behavioral information through the class and sequence diagrams. It is illustrated through five of some well-known anti-patterns: Blob, Lava Flow, Functional Decomposition, Poltergeists, and Swiss Army Knife. Kim and Boldyreff suggested a software metrics that can be applied to the elements of UML modelling [24]. The proposed UML metrics are based on the metamodel scheme and divided into four categories of metrics which are model, class, message, and use case metrics.

IV. PROPOSED SOLUTION

Our proposed approach derives code quality metrics and their dynamic threshold values from software designs. Beginning, our approach focuses on design elements pertaining to data types, their complexities, frequencies, and the estimated complexity of the operations of such data. Then, from the estimated class and method complexity, We quantified fuzzy quality metrics to measure two of the bad code smells, which are large class and long method.

A. Complexity Metrics

The approach involves assigning complexity rate [20] values to each attribute, method and association within the class as shown in TABLE I. We assign a complexity rate (Co_{Rate}) to an attribute's visibility ($V_{Att.}$) and type ($T_{Att.}$) to estimate the attribute's complexity (Att_{comp}). Each complexity rate (Co_{Rate}) can be primitive, simple, or complex. Then we estimate method complexity ($Method_{comp}$) by summing the complexity of the method's visibility ($V_{Meth.}$), the return type ($R_{Meth.}$) and the total parameters list ($P_{Meth.}$). Further, We estimate the association complexity ($Asso_{comp}$) by adding all incoming ($IN_{As.}$) and outgoing ($OUT_{As.}$) association links. Finally, by summing all attributes, methods and association complexities, we can estimate the class complexity ($Class_{comp}$), which we use to quantify code quality factors, such as expected lines of code for any class ($ELOC(Class)$).

The following formulas describe the proposed approach. Formula 1 estimates the complexity of the attributes, as derived from the UML class diagram shown above. Formula 2 estimates method complexity based on the complexity of the parameters and return types. Formula 3 estimates the complexity of the association for each class. Formula 4 uses the previous calculations to estimate the class complexity. The following describes the quantification approach in greater detail.

$$Att_{comp} = (V_{Att.} * Co_{Rate}) + (T_{Att.} * Co_{Rate}) \quad (1)$$

where (Att_{comp}) is attribute complexity, ($V_{Att.}$) attribute visibility, ($T_{Att.}$) attribute type and (Co_{Rate}) the complexity rate.

TABLE I. CLASSIFICATION OF THE COMPLEXITY RATE

Element	Scope	Name	Classification	Examples	Rating
Attributes	Visibility	Att_{Vis}	Primitive	Private	1
			Simple	Protected, Package	2
			Complex	Public	3
	Type	Att_{type}	Primitive	int, char, boolean	1
			Simple	float, long, double, str	2
			Complex	array, struct, tuple, date, time, list, map	3
			Derived	object, array of complex types	4
Methods	Parameters	$P_{Meth.}$	Primitive	int, char, boolean	1
			Simple	float, long, double, str	2
			Complex	array, struct, tuple, date, time, list	3
			Derived	object, array of complex types, map	4
	Return Type	$R_{Meth.}$	Primitive	int, char, boolean, void	1
			Simple	float, long, double, str	2
			Complex	array, struct, tuple, date, time, list	3
			Derived	object, array of complex types, map	4
	Visibility	$V_{Meth.}$	Primitive	Private	1
			Simple	Protected, Package	2
			Complex	Public	3
Association	Incoming	$IN_{As.}$	Primitive	1 to many	1
			Simple	many to many, 1 to 1	2
			Complex	all others (such as n .. m to many, etc..)	3
	Outgoing	$OUT_{As.}$	Primitive	1 to many	1
			Simple	many to many, 1 to 1	2
			Complex	all others	3

$$Method_{comp} = (V_{Meth.} * Co_{Rate}) + (R_{Meth.} * Co_{Rate}) + \left(\sum_{i=1}^{n} (P_{Meth.} * Co_{Rate})\right) \quad (2)$$

Here, $(Method_{comp})$ is method complexity, $(V_{Meth.})$ is method visibility, $(R_{Meth.})$ is method return type and $(\sum_{i=1}^{n}(P_{Meth.} * Co_{Rate}))$ is the complexity rate for all parameters in the method.

$$Asso_{comp} = \left(\sum_{i=1}^{n}(IN_{As.} * Co_{Rate})\right) + \left(\sum_{i=1}^{n}(OUT_{As.} * Co_{Rate})\right) \quad (3)$$

$(Asso_{comp})$ is the association complexity, $(\sum_{i=1}^{n}(IN_{As.} * Co_{Rate}))$ is the complexity for all incoming associations to the class and $(\sum_{i=1}^{n}(OUT_{As.} * Co_{Rate}))$ is the complexity for all outgoing associations.

$$Class_{comp} = \left(\sum_{i=1}^{n} Att_{comp}\right) + \left(\sum_{i=1}^{n} Method_{comp}\right) + Asso_{comp} \quad (4)$$

The class complexity $(Class_{comp})$ can be calculated by summing the complexity of all class attributes $\left(\sum_{i=1}^{n} Att_{comp}\right)$, the complexity of all methods in the class $\left(\sum_{i=1}^{n} Method_{comp}\right)$ *and* the class association complexity $(Asso_{comp})$.

Class complexity $(Class_{comp})$ and method complexity $(Method_{comp})$ can be used to estimate the expected lines of code for the class, or any method within the class, by multiplying them by the class factor (F_{Class}) or method factor (F_{Mehtod}). Both the class factor and method factor will be estimated empirically as part of the planned research activities.

B. Fuzzy Metrics

The fuzzy quality metrics are a new methodology to measure two of the bad code smells, which are large class and long method. This methodology is based on measuring the difference between the actual and expected values of the lines of code for the class and method. To demonstrate this concept, we illustrate a fuzzy metric for the large class and long method code metrics [20].

$$FuzzyMetric(Class) = LOC(class) - ELOC(class) \quad (5)$$

$$ELOC(Class) = Class_{comp} * Class(LOC_{factor}) \quad (6)$$

$$Class(LOC_{factor}) = \frac{LOC(Total) * LOC(Average)}{Class_{comp}(Total) * Class_{comp}(Average)} \quad (7)$$

Where $ELOC(class)$ is the expected size in terms of lines of code, $LOC(Total)$ is the total LOC for all classes, and $LOC(Average)$ is the average of LOC for all classes. Similarly, the fuzzy metric for method is defined as follows:

$$FuzzyMetric(Method) = LOC(Method) - ELOC(Method) \quad (8)$$

$$ELOC(Method) = Method_{comp} * Method(LOC_{factor}) \quad (9)$$

$$Method(LOC_{factor}) = Method_{comp}(Average) \quad (10)$$

V. EXPECTED CONTRIBUTIONS

The expected contribution of this work is to present a new methodology for estimating software code quality. We expect that design-driven code quality metrics will improve the maintainability and sustainability of software systems by considering the variations in development technologies and the architectural roles of various code and design elements. This ensures that the derived metrics are uniquely tailored to the software under development and the derived metrics can dynamically evolve throughout the codebase life cycle. Another contribution in this paper is to introduce new complexity metrics for software designs. The approach is based on evaluating every element in each software design by assigning a relative complexity rate. The complexity rate can be either primitive, simple, or complex. As such, the complexity of a system can be estimated by summing the complexity values of all elements within the system.

VI. CURRENT STATUS

This work has been formulated and submitted to different conferences. Overall, the plan came over the following phases. Phase 1: Define the complexity metrics for software design and evaluate it theoretically and empirically. Four conference papers have been submitted based on the first phase. One of those papers has been accepted at the 20th IEEE International Conference on Software Quality, Reliability, and Security. Two other papers were accepted at the Future Technologies Conference 2020 [34][35]. The fourth paper is under review at the Software Quality Days conference 2021. Phase 2: formulate and evaluate the fuzzy quality metrics. In this phase, three conference papers have been submitted to some venuses. The first one has been accepted and presented at the International Conference on Model-Driven Engineering and Software Development MODELSWARD 2020 [20]. The other two paper are under review at the International Conference on Computer Science and Software Engineering CASCON 2020, and 20th IEEE International Working Conference on Source Code Analysis and Manipulation SCAM 2020. Phase 3: Completing, submitting, and defending the dissertation.

The preliminary results pertaining to class-level complexity and code fuzzy smell are as follows. In class complexity we have applied the proposed approach on code repositories obtained from opensource projects. The selection criteria considered code repositories that are most active on GitHub [16]. We included, among others, codebases developed by Google [17], Microsoft [18] and the National Security Agency [19]. We compared the results from our quantification metrics to the actual metrics derived from the codebase analysis (Figure 2). High correlation with 84%, would suggest that our metrics accurately characterize codebase quality. In the near future, we plan to compare correlation values obtained from this approach to those obtained from applying traditional code quality metrics.

In fuzzy code smells we attempted an extensive empirical evaluation of fuzzy code smell approach using expert reviews of large corpuses [37] of smells in open source repositories by comparing our metics, and a wide range of static code analysis tools (PMD [38], infusion [39], JDeodorant [40], and JSpIRIT [41]), against the expert reviews data sets. The results for the precision and recall show that fuzzy smell method aligned significantly better with expert's data sets than contemporary code analysis tools as shown in Figure 3.

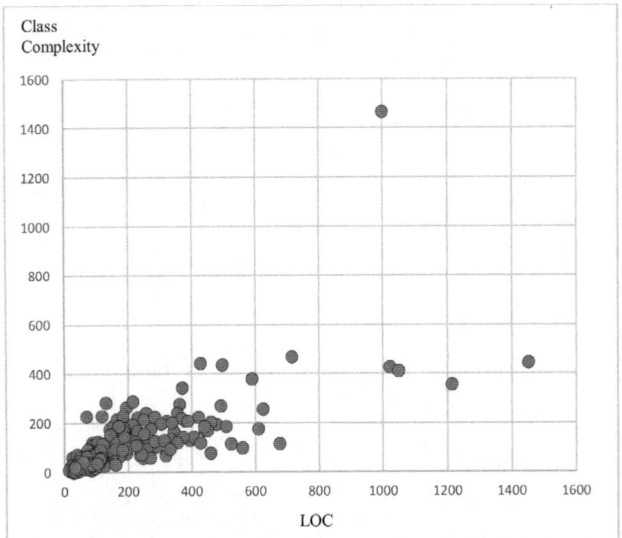

Figure 2. Correlation between class complexity and LOC.

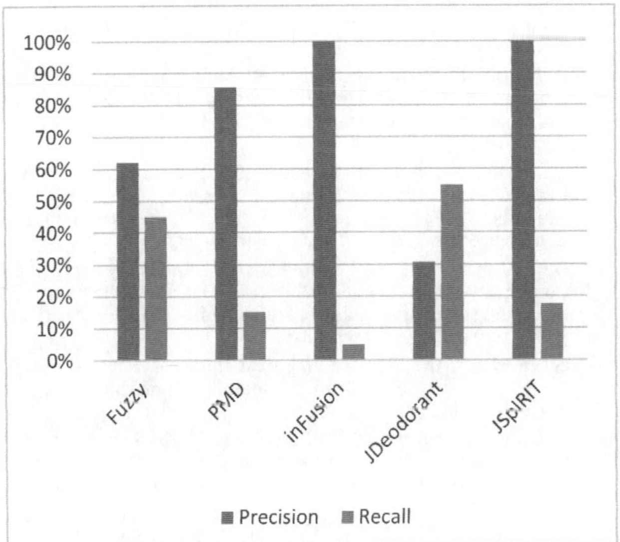

Figure 3. Precision and recall of large class code smell.

Finally, we calculated the F1 score, which is the harmonic mean of precision and recall. The F1 score is used because in many studies, the F-measure is the ultimate measure of performance of a classifier [36]. After calculating the F1 score for all the approaches, we found that the best performance for detecting a bad large class smell is our approach. Figure 4 shows that the accuracy of the fuzzy metric is the highest with 55%. The second highest is PMD with 39%, then JDeodorant with 33%, and after that JSpIRIT with 27%. The lowest accuracy is found for inFusion with only 7%. Moreover, for detecting a bad long method smell, we found that our approach is the best as well.

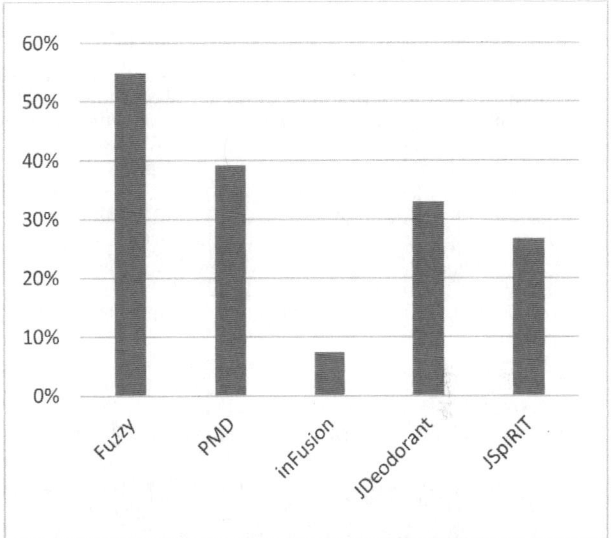

Figure 4. The total F1 score for classes of each tool.

VII. CONLUSION AND FUTURE WORK

In this paper, we presented a new approach that defines code quality metrics with thresholds that are derived from software design. This ensures alignment between the intentional specification of software design characteristics and their implementation. This approach means that metrics can evolves as the codebase design evolves throughout the software lifecycle. Moreover, this approach means that each code module will have its own unique quality metrics that are tailored to its unique context. Our approach started with measuring the complexity of each class and method in the system. We then estimated the expected size for each class and method by using the complexity measurement that we calculated from the first step. The last step is to calculate the fuzzy code smell based on the difference between the actual and expected size of each class and method.

The research plan in future work is to evaluate the proposed metrics theoretically and empirically by using the following methodologies: (1) Theoretical evaluation of the complexity metrics by using Weyuker's nine properties model. (2) Evaluate whether the metrics derived from software designs provide a better characterization of codebase quality and sustainability than alternate traditional metrics. (3) Quantify thresholds for the fuzzy code smells derived from the software design. (4) Compare our new fuzzy code smells with code smells resulting from code smells detection tools for different codebases.

REFERENCES

[1] R. Oliveira et al., "Identifying code smells with collaborative practices: A controlled experiment," presented at X Brazilian Symposium on Software Components, Architectures and Reuse (SBCARS). Brazil, 2016.

[2] J. Y. Gil and G. Lalouche, "When do software complexity metrics mean nothing? When examined out of context," Journal of Object Technology, vol. 15, no. 1, pp. 1-25. 2016.

[3] F. Zhang, A. Mockus, Y. Zou, F. Khomh and A. E. Hassan, "How does context affect the distribution of software maintainability metrics?" In 2013 IEEE International Conference on Software Maintenance, pp. 350-359.

[4] M. Aniche, C. Treude, A. Zaidman, A. van Deursen, and M. A. Gerosa, "SATT: Tailoring code metric thresholds for different software architectures," presented at IEEE 16th International Working Conference on Source Code Analysis and Manipulation (SCAM). Raleigh, NC, USA, 2016.

[5] G. Concas, M. Marchesi, S. Pinna and N. Serra, "Power-laws in a large object-oriented software system," IEEE Transactions on Software Engineering, vol. 33, no. 10, pp. 687-708, 2007.

[6] R. Wheeldon and S. Counsell, "Power law distributions in class relationships," In Proceedings Third IEEE International Workshop on Source Code Analysis and Manipulation, 2003, pp. 45-54.

[7] Y. Yao, S. Huang, Z. Ren and X. Liu. "Scale-free property in large scale object-oriented software and its significance on software engineering," In 2009 Second International Conference on Information and Computing Science, vol. 3, 2009, pp. 401-404.

[8] I. Herraiz, D. M. German and A. E. Hassan, "On the distribution of source code file sizes," In ICSOFT (2), 2011, pp. 5-14.

[9] M. Lanza and R. Marinescu, Object-oriented metrics in practice: using software metrics to characterize, evaluate, and improve the design of object-oriented systems. Springer Science & Business Media, 2007.

[10] D. Coleman, B. Lowther and P. Oman, "The application of software maintainability models in industrial software systems," Journal of Systems and Software, vol. 29, no. 1, pp. 3-16, 1995.

[11] B. A. Nejmeh, "Npath: A measure of execution path complexity and its applications," Communications of the ACM, vol. 31, no. 2, p. 188, 1988.

[12] P. Oliveira, M. T. Valente and F. P. Lima, "Extracting relative thresholds for source code metrics," IEEE Conference on Software Maintenance, Reengineering, and Reverse Engineering (CSMR-WCRE). Belgium, 2014.

[13] L. Kapova, T. Goldschmidt, S. Becker and J. Henss, "Evaluating maintainability with code metrics for model-to-model transformations," International Conference on the Quality of Software Architecture, 2010.

[14] D. Taibi, A. Janes, and V. Lenarduzzi, "How developers perceive smells in source code: A replicated study," Information and Software Technology Journal, Vol. 92, pp. 223-235, December 2017.

[15] F. A. Fontana, V. Ferme, and M. Zanoni, "Towards assessing software architecture quality by exploiting code smell relations," IEEE/ACM 2nd International Workshop on Software Architecture and Metrics. pp. 1-7, Italy, 2015.

[16] https://github.com/ , Accessed Feb. 2019

[17] https://github.com/google , Accessed Nov. 2019

[18] https://github.com/microsoft , Accessed Nov. 2019

[19] https://github.com/nationalsecurityagency , Accessed Nov. 2019

[20] O. Masmali and O. Badreddin. "Towards a Model-based Fuzzy Software Quality Metrics." In MODELSWARD, pp. 139-148. 2020.

[21] L. Michele, and R. Marinescu, Object-oriented metrics in practice: using software metrics to characterize, evaluate, and improve the design of object-oriented systems. Springer Science & Business Media, 2007.

[22] D. Coleman, B. Lowther, and P. Oman, "The application of software maintainability models in industrial software systems," Journal of Systems and Software, vol. 29, no. 1, 1995.

[23] B. A. Nejmeh, and W. Riddle, "The PERFECT approach to experience-based process evolution." In Advances in computers, vol. 66, pp. 173-238. Elsevier, 2006.

[24] H. Kim, and C. Boldyreff, "Developing software metrics applicable to UML models," Proc. of the 6th ECOOP Workshop on Quantitative Approaches in Object-oriented engineering, Malaga, Spain, June 2002.

[25] M. Doraisamy, S. bin Ibrahim, and M. N. Mahrin, "Metric based software project performance monitoring model", Proceedings of the IEEE International Conference on Open Systems (ICOS), August 2015.

[26] P. In, S. Kim, and M. Barry, "UML-based object-oriented metrics for architecture complexity analysis". Department of computer science, Texas A&M University, 2003.

[27] M. Manso, M. Genero, and M. Piattini, "No-redundant metrics for UML class diagram structural complexity". Lecture Notes on Computer Science, 2681, 2003, pp.127-142.

[28] D. Kang et al., "A structural complexity measure for UML class diagrams." In International Conference on Computational Science 2004 (ICCS 2004), Krakow Poland, June 2004, pp. 431-435, 2004.

[29] J. Bansiya, and C. G. Davis, "A Hierarchical Model for Object-Oriented Design Quality Assessment." IEEE Trans. on Software Engineering, 28, 1, 2002, pp. 4-17.

[30] M. Genero, M. Piattini, and C. Calero, "A survey of Metrics for UML Class Diagrams". Journal of Object Technology, 4 (9). p. 59-92. 2005.

[31] M. Marchesi, "OOA metrics for the unified modeling languages." In Proceedings of 2nd Euromicro Conference on Software Maintenance and Reengineering (CSMR'98), Palazzo degli Affari, Italy, March 1998, pp. 67-73, 1998.

[32] Ma, Yu-Tao, K. He, B. Li, J. Liu, and X. Zhou, "A hybrid set of complexity metrics for large-scale object-oriented software systems." Journal of Computer Science and Technology 25, no. 6, pp. 1184-1201, 2010.

[33] R. Fourati, N. Bouassida, and H. B. Abdallah. "A metric-based approach for anti-pattern detection in UML designs." In Computer and Information Science 2011, pp. 17-33. Springer, Berlin, Heidelberg, 2011.

[34] O. Masmali and O. Badreddin, "Code Complexity Metrics Derived from Software Design: Framework and Theoretical Evaluation", In Proceedings of the Future Technologies Conference (FTC 2020), Canada, Vancouver, 2020.

[35] O. Masmali and O. Badreddin, "Theoretically Validated Complexity Metrics for UML State Machines Diagram", In Proceedings of the Future Technologies Conference (FTC 2020), Canada, Vancouver, 2020.

[36] G. Forman, "An extensive empirical study of feature selection metrics for text classification." Journal of machine learning research 3, 2003, pp 1289-1305.

[37] T. Paiva, A. Damasceno, E. Figueiredo and C. Sant Anna, "On the evaluation of code smells and detection tools," Journal of Software Engineering Research and Development, Springer 2017.

[38] PMD. Accessed Feb. 2020. Avalibale at: https://pmd.github.io/

[39] inFuction. Accessed Feb. 2020. Avalibale at: http://loose.upt.ro/iplasma/

[40] JDeodorant. Accessed Feb. 2020. Avalibale at: https://github.com/tsantalis/JDeodorant

[41] JSpIRIT. Accessed Feb. 2020. Available at: https://sites.google.com/site/santiagoavidal/projects/jspirit

Automated Requirements Engineering Framework for Agile Development

Muhammad Aminu Umar
Department of Informatics, King's College London
Strand, London WC2R 2LS, United Kingdom
e-mail: aminu.umar@kcl.ac.uk

Abstract—**Requirements engineering has been established as a critical success factor for software projects. On the other hand, most requirements documents are often written in natural language; often prone to structure errors and inconsistent semantic, thereby, exposing the documents to misunderstanding arising from undue misinterpretations. This paper first proposes a framework to automate requirements engineering activities with focus on modelling while equally articulating the strategies and work plan for the implementation and evaluation.**

Keywords-Automation; Requirements engineering; NLP; Agile development.

I. INTRODUCTION

In software development, Requirements Engineering (RE) is a critical success factor as well as a complex process [1]. It is critical because the quality of the system depends largely on the quality of the requirements and, it is complex because it considers diverse product demands from a diverse set of stakeholders [2]. Inadequacies resulting from the RE process can have negative impact on the overall software development and lead to high costs for any organization involved [3]. Therefore, Requirements Engineering is highly significant to modern success of quality software development.

Software requirements are often specified in Natural Language (NL). Meanwhile, software requirements specified in natural language often suffer from ambiguity, incompleteness and inconsistency in the choice of syntax. Moreover, anything described in NL has the potential and tendency of being influenced by geographical, psychological and sociological factors in terms of understanding and interpretation [4]. It is therefore imperative that empirical studies are conducted to derive solutions to this challenge in software development with the emerging trends in human activities which must eventually be captured beyond NL. Consequently, addressing these problems through researches has paved the way for model-driven engineering and lately automated requirements engineering which have all improve the status of requirements written in natural language. These tools and technologies now facilitate software development generally. More specifically, these tools and technologies enable numerous RE activities such as requirements classification [5][6] requirements validation and review [7][8], inconsistency check in requirements [9], duplicate requirements detection [10], automated RE reuse [11], recommendation of omitted steps in requirements analysis [12] and RE security enhancement [13].

As part of the effort to support agile RE and the development of fast software in general, this work seeks to propose an automated RE framework that combines the Natural Language Processing (NLP) and the Artificial Intelligence techniques for more efficient agile software development. In agile development, rapid change and flexibility are very important and the development process is made as lightweight as possible. The essence of automated RE is to reduce software development time, effort, and cost of RE whilst still maintaining consistent, accurate and comprehensive requirements.

The remainder of this paper is structured as follows: Section 2 discusses automated requirements engineering. Section 3 discusses previous literature on automated requirements engineering. In Section 4, the techniques for the integration of NLP and Artificial Intelligence (AI) are highlighted. Section 5 summarizes the proposed work plan. Section 6 concludes the paper.

II. AUTOMATED REQUIREMENTS ENGINEERING

Requirements engineering is the lifecycle stage with the highest influence on the quality of a final product [14]. Traditional RE process continued to be applied to manage the knowledge generated in this field, and this has made it difficult to attain a quick and objective understanding of the diverse and continuous emerging needs of the interested stakeholders. Apart from the fact that automated RE development reduces cost, effort and time it enhances the quality of the final product. Requirements identification and requirements classification are two important activities supported by automated requirements elicitation from NL document [15]. Some of the successful techniques that have been employed to implement automated requirements elicitation are NLP and Information Retrieval [16]. Additionally, in recent times, text mining, which is an automated technique for generating requirements document have been employed [17].

Requirements engineering involves the process of finding out, analyzing, documenting and checking the services and constraints on a system [18]. The following are generic activities (phases) common to all RE process.

- Requirements elicitation. The process of identifying and collecting requirements from stakeholders and other sources. This includes both functional and non-functional requirements.
- Requirements analysis and specification. It is the logical breakdown and structuring of the proceeds from elicitation. It includes detailed understanding of the requirements and structuring such

information and other derived requirements as written documents and model diagrams.

- Requirements validation. Requires that the collected information is correct and well arranged to meet the system business objectives. This is done by making sure the documents and/or models with specified requirements are accurate, complete and correct.
- Requirements management. This step helps to keep track of possible changes in requirements and ensures that the changes are made to meet stakeholder's requirement.

Automated RE support has been successfully achieved in various activities (phases) of requirements engineering (see Table 1). The NLP plays a great role in achieving automated RE due to the fact that most requirements are written in natural language.

TABLE I. APPLICATION OF NLP IN RE ACTIVITIES

Ref	Elicitation	Analysis	Validation	Management
[12]			*	
[17]		*		
[19]			*	
[4]		*		
[20]	*			
[21]		*		
[22]		*		
[11]				*
[10]				*
[23]				*
[24]		*		
[25]	*			
[26]		*		
[27]	*			
[28]				*
[29]	*			
[30]		*		
[31]				*
[32]		*		

Accordingly, Lucassen et al. [30] have categorized the fundamental approach of all NLP and RE tools into four types based on their functions or what they can do:

1. Finding defects and deviations in natural language (NL) requirements document;
2. Generating models from NL requirements descriptions;
3. Inferring trace links between NL requirements descriptions and
4. Identifying the key abstractions from NL documents.

From the foregoing, the second category of tools forms the concern of this work.

III. RELATED WORK

Automated requirements engineering has attracted the attention of researchers over the years. Each work cited here has proposed an approach or a software tool to achieve the continuous effectiveness and efficient application of automated requirements engineering.

For instance, the UML model Generator from Analysis of Requirements (UMGAR) [4] is a domain independent tool which generates use case diagram, conceptual model, collaboration diagram, and designs class model. The tool follows the object-oriented analysis design approach while eliciting object from requirements described in Natural Language. It also uses the NLP techniques to process textual documents and XML import facility to visualize UML diagram.

Other works, such as [26], have proposed a framework that provides the requirements engineers with the capacity to automatically generate UML class diagram. The framework allows for reinterpretation of natural language requirements into models and has the possibility of specification reusability through reverse engineering process. The approach used the MIMB tool to transform the XML schema into a UML class diagram and vice versa.

In [33], the authors proposed a requirements model generation to support requirements elicitation from a lightweight textual document. However, the approach transforms requirements specification expressed in natural language into semi-structured specifications. The proposal was based on Cerno, which is a semantic annotation environment that uses high-speed context-free robust parsing combined with simple word search.

For [21], the Natural Language Processing technique was applied to automatically transform user stories into UML use case diagram. The approach uses TreeTagger parser to generate use case and Part of Speech (POS) tags allows for the categorization of term into various part of speech.

In [30], a Visual Narrator tool is described as a tool which automatically generates a conceptual model from a collection of user story requirements. This narrator tool was part of what the authors termed the 'Grimm method' – the method combines three Natural Language Processing and thereby enabling requirements tools to support conducting user story-based requirements engineering.

A system described in [22] is claimed to facilitate automatically the creation of conceptual model from functional requirements written in natural language. The tool allows for automatic identification of classes and relationships and subsequently renders the conceptual model with the Extended Entity Relationship (EER) diagram notations.

The use of Artificial Neural Network (ANN) for extracting actions and actors from requirement document by

[32] proposes an approach to automatically identify actors and actions in natural language-based requirements with the goal to overcome the challenges of manual extraction. This tool uses an NLP parser with a general architecture for text engineering, producing lexicons, syntaxes, and semantic analysis. This was achieved through the development of an ANN using five different use cases.

From the reviewed works, it is evident that automation of requirements engineering is a challenging area due to the nature of the diverse inputs to be processed i.e. natural languages. Therefore, this work proposes an alternative automation paradigm framework to automate RE. The proposed approach is an interactive tool support with dynamic model generation. This will be achieved through the integration of NLP and other artificial intelligence techniques.

IV. PROPOSED APPROACH

From our findings of the literature review, there is the need for research into a full and alternative automation paradigm and integration of more artificial intelligence techniques into automating requirements engineering. Therefore, this work proposes a framework that will facilitate automation of requirements engineering activities with specific focus on model generation (modelling) with traceability. The work intends to employ natural language processing techniques and artificial intelligence in the design and development of the framework.

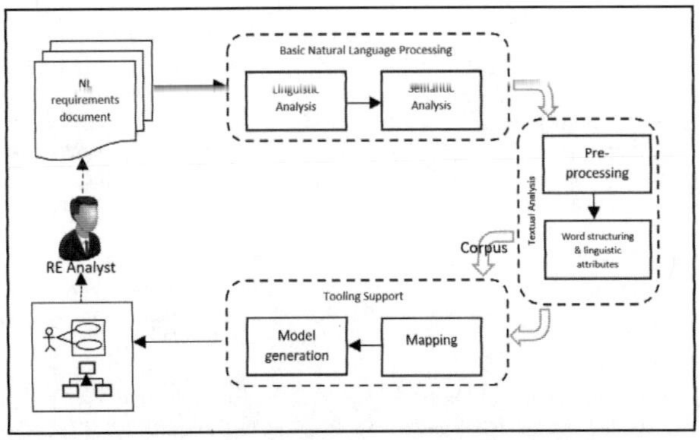

Figure 1. Overview of the proposed framework.

The proposed approach works as follows (see Figure 1). Initially, the analyst (requirements engineer) input a set of textual requirements written in natural language. These texts are analyzed by several natural language processing components with the target of gathering knowledge about the textual scenarios. Sentences, token boundaries, token properties, and semantic constituents are some of the information of the natural language processing components.

After the basic natural language processing is completed, the approach will carry out textual analysis through pre-processing, word structuring and linguistic attributes. The aim of pre-processing is to code the inputs required by the next processing step. A corpus which contains English words with their respective code will be used to compose requirements documents. These are words collected from several English natural language requirements texts from different domains.

Mapping linguistic tokens to the semantics specification is the next step in the approach. Token comprises of word/phrase from the corpus and the semantic attributes define in the previous step. The output of the approach is a set of UML models that will be subjected to review of human analyst. It is up to the analyst to corroborate the output of the approach and make an informed decision.

V. WORK PLAN

In order to accomplish this, we have defined a work programme. The work programme includes work on foundations, framework development and applications inform of case study evaluation.

- **Conceptualization** – this involves designing of the proposed framework and testing of the existing algorithms.
- **Tool development** – implementation of the tool support base on the proposed framework. Highlight of the development technique languages.
- **Applications** – this has to do with the evaluation through industrial case studies to establish the applicability of the proposed framework and generate useful feedbacks

VI. CONCLUSION

This paper proposes a new framework for automated requirements engineering using natural language processing and artificial intelligence techniques. The proposed framework herein will be implemented and evaluated using at least two institutions/organizations as case studies. This is to establish the applicability of the framework in order to serve as one of the several empirical evidences/sources for academic and corporate discourse and application.

ACKNOWLEDGMENT

This work is funded by the Petroleum Technology Development Fund (PTDF) of the Federal Government of Nigeria.

REFERENCES

[1] H. F. Hofmann and F. Lehner, "Requirements engineering as a success factor in software projects," *IEEE Software*, vol. 18, no. 4, pp. 58–66, 2001, doi: 10.1109/MS.2001.936219.

[2] T. Shah and S. Patel, "A Novel Approach for Specifying Functional and Non-functional Requirements Using RDS (Requirement Description Schema)," *Procedia Computer Science*, vol. 79, pp. 852–860, 2016, doi: 10.1016/j.procs.2016.03.083.

[3] H. Meth, M. Brhel, and A. Maedche, "The state of the art in automated requirements elicitation," *Information and Software Technology*, vol. 55, no. 10, pp. 1695–1709, Oct. 2013, doi: 10.1016/j.infsof.2013.03.008.

[4] D. K. Deeptimahanti and M. A. Babar, "An Automated Tool for Generating UML Models from Natural Language Requirements," in *2009 IEEE/ACM International Conference on Automated Software Engineering*, Auckland, New Zealand, Nov. 2009, pp. 680–682, doi: 10.1109/ASE.2009.48.

[5] E. Parra, C. Dimou, J. Llorens, V. Moreno, and A. Fraga, "A methodology for the classification of quality of requirements using machine learning techniques," *Information and Software Technology*, vol. 67, pp. 180–195, Nov. 2015, doi: 10.1016/j.infsof.2015.07.006.

[6] J. Cleland-Huang, R. Settimi, X. Zou, and P. Solc, "Automated classification of non-functional requirements," *Requirements Eng*, vol. 12, no. 2, pp. 103–120, May 2007, doi: 10.1007/s00766-007-0045-1.

[7] N. A. Moketar, M. Kamalrudin, S. Sidek, M. Robinson, and J. Grundy, "TestMEReq: generating abstract tests for requirements validation," in *Proceedings of the 3rd International Workshop on Software Engineering Research and Industrial Practice - SER&IP '16*, Austin, Texas, 2016, pp. 39–45, doi: 10.1145/2897022.2897031.

[8] W. Miao *et al.*, "Automated Requirements Validation for ATP Software via Specification Review and Testing," in *Formal Methods and Software Engineering*, vol. 10009, K. Ogata, M. Lawford, and S. Liu, Eds. Cham: Springer International Publishing, 2016, pp. 26–40.

[9] R. Sharma and K. K. Biswas, "A Semi-automated Approach towards Handling Inconsistencies in Software Requirements," in *Evaluation of Novel Approaches to Software Engineering*, vol. 410, L. A. Maciaszek and J. Filipe, Eds. Berlin, Heidelberg: Springer Berlin Heidelberg, 2013, pp. 142–156.

[10] A. Rago, C. Marcos, and J. A. Diaz-Pace, "Identifying duplicate functionality in textual use cases by aligning semantic actions," *Softw Syst Model*, vol. 15, no. 2, pp. 579–603, May 2016, doi: 10.1007/s10270-014-0431-3.

[11] Y. Li, T. Yue, S. Ali, and L. Zhang, "Enabling automated requirements reuse and configuration," *Softw Syst Model*, vol. 18, no. 3, pp. 2177–2211, Jun. 2019, doi: 10.1007/s10270-017-0641-6.

[12] D. Ko, S. Kim, and S. Park, "Automatic recommendation to omitted steps in use case specification," *Requirements Eng*, vol. 24, no. 4, pp. 431–458, Dec. 2019, doi: 10.1007/s00766-018-0288-z.

[13] N. Yusop, M. Kamalrudin, S. Sidek, and J. Grundy, "Automated Support to Capture and Validate Security Requirements for Mobile Apps," in *Requirements Engineering Toward Sustainable World*, vol. 671, S.-W. Lee and T. Nakatani, Eds. Singapore: Springer Singapore, 2016, pp. 97–112.

[14] S. M. Edgar, B. S. Oscar, and S. A. Alexei, "Knowledge meaning and management in requirements engineering," *International Journal of Information Management*, vol. 37, no. 3, pp. 155–161, Jun. 2017, doi: 10.1016/j.ijinfomgt.2017.01.005.

[15] H. Meth, A. Maedche, and M. Einoeder, "Is Knowledge Power? The Role of Knowledge in Automated Requirements Elicitation," in *CAiSE 2013, LNCS 7908*, Springer-Verlag Berlin Heidelberg, 2013, pp. 578–593.

[16] D. Berry, R. Gacitua, P. Sawyer, and S. F. Tjong, "The Case for Dumb Requirements Engineering Tools," in *REFSQ 2011. LNCS*, vol. 7195, Springer, Heidelberg, 2012, pp. 211–217.

[17] B. Aysolmaz, H. Leopold, H. A. Reijers, and O. Demirörs, "A semi-automated approach for generating natural language requirements documents based on business process models," *Information and Software Technology*, vol. 93, pp. 14–29, Jan. 2018, doi: 10.1016/j.infsof.2017.08.009.

[18] I. Summerville, *Software Engineering*, 9th ed. Person Education, Inc., 2011.

[19] N. A. Moketar, M. Kamalrudin, S. Sidek, M. Robinson, and J. Grundy, "An automated collaborative requirements engineering tool for better validation of requirements," in *Proceedings of the 31st IEEE/ACM International Conference on Automated Software Engineering - ASE 2016*, Singapore, Singapore, 2016, pp. 864–869, doi: 10.1145/2970276.2970295.

[20] Y. Li, E. Guzman, K. Tsiamoura, F. Schneider, and B. Bruegge, "Automated Requirements Extraction for Scientific Software," *Procedia Computer Science*, vol. 51, pp. 582–591, 2015, doi: 10.1016/j.procs.2015.05.326.

[21] M. Elallaoui, K. Nafil, and R. Touahni, "Automatic Transformation of User Stories into UML Use Case Diagrams using NLP Techniques," *Procedia Computer Science*, vol. 130, pp. 42–49, 2018, doi: 10.1016/j.procs.2018.04.010.

[22] V. B. R. Vidya Sagar and S. Abirami, "Conceptual modeling of natural language functional requirements," *Journal of Systems and Software*, vol. 88, pp. 25–41, Feb. 2014, doi: 10.1016/j.jss.2013.08.036.

[23] V. Antinyan and M. Staron, "Rendex: A method for automated reviews of textual requirements," *Journal of Systems and Software*, vol. 131, pp. 63–77, Sep. 2017, doi: 10.1016/j.jss.2017.05.079.

[24] V. Ambriola and V. Gervasi, "On the Systematic Analysis of Natural Language Requirements with CIRCE," *Autom Software Eng*, vol. 13, no. 1, pp. 107–167, Jan. 2006, doi: 10.1007/s10515-006-5468-2.

[25] R. Gacitua, P. Sawyer, and V. Gervasi, "Relevance-based abstraction identification: technique and evaluation," *Requirements Eng*, vol. 16, no. 3, pp. 251–265, Sep. 2011, doi: 10.1007/s00766-011-0122-3.

[26] Y. Alkhader, A. Hudaib, and B. Hammo, "Experimenting With Extracting Software Requirements Using NLP Approach," in *2006 International Conference on Information and Automation*, Colombo, Sri Lanka, Dec. 2006, pp. 349–354, doi: 10.1109/ICINFA.2006.374136.

[27] J. L. Cybulski and K. Reed, "Computer-assisted analysis and refinement of informal software requirements documents," in *Proceedings 1998 Asia Pacific Software Engineering Conference (Cat. No.98EX240)*, Taipei, Taiwan, 1998, pp. 128–135, doi: 10.1109/APSEC.1998.733606.

[28] J. Natt och Dag, T. Thelin, and B. Regnell, "An experiment on linguistic tool support for consolidation of requirements from multiple sources in market-driven product development," *Empir Software Eng*, vol. 11, no. 2, pp. 303–329, Jun. 2006, doi: 10.1007/s10664-006-6405-5.

[29] Q. A. Do, S. R. Chekuri, and T. Bhowmik, "Automated Support to Capture Creative Requirements via Requirements Reuse," in *Reuse in the Big Data Era*, vol. 11602, X. Peng, A. Ampatzoglou, and T. Bhowmik, Eds. Cham: Springer International Publishing, 2019, pp. 47–63.

[30] G. Lucassen, M. Robeer, F. Dalpiaz, J. M. E. M. van der Werf, and S. Brinkkemper, "Extracting conceptual models from user stories with Visual Narrator," *Requirements Eng*, vol. 22, no. 3, pp. 339–358, Sep. 2017, doi: 10.1007/s00766-017-0270-1.

[31] I. Reinhartz-Berger and M. Kemelman, "Extracting core requirements for software product lines," *Requirements Eng*, vol. 25, no. 1, pp. 47–65, Mar. 2020, doi: 10.1007/s00766-018-0307-0.

[32] A. Al-Hroob, A. T. Imam, and R. Al-Heisa, "The use of artificial neural networks for extracting actions and actors from requirements document," *Information and Software Technology*, vol. 101, pp. 1–15, Sep. 2018, doi: 10.1016/j.infsof.2018.04.010.

[33] N. Kiyavitskaya and N. Zannone, "Requirements model generation to support requirements elicitation: the Secure Tropos experience," *Autom Softw Eng*, vol. 15, no. 2, pp. 149–173, Jun. 2008, doi: 10.1007/s10515-008-0028-6.

A Prototype of Smart Navigation Service

Chia Hung Kao

Department of Applied Mathematics
National Taitung University
Taitung, Taiwan
Email: chkao@nttu.edu.tw

***Abstract*—Travelers may arrange tourist destinations, plan a travel route, book a hotel accommodation, and reserve a restaurant through different online services. However, the scattering of the above travel information hinders the efficient browse, search, and usage during the trip. Besides, the travel information is not leveraged well for timely and personalized assistance. In this work, a smart navigation service is proposed to provide efficient navigation for travelers. Based on travel planning and travel context of travelers, the smart navigation service can identify the purpose of travelers, and provide corresponding navigation through the information retrieved from transportation or news services proactively.**

Keywords–Navigation; travel navigation; cloud computing.

I. Introduction

Before a trip, travelers may arrange tourist destinations, plan a travel route, book a hotel accommodation, and reserve a restaurant through different online services [1]. During the trip, travelers can use smart devices to search for corresponding travel information preserved in different services [2]. For instance, travelers can log into online booking service (e.g., Booking.com [3], Agoda [4], Trivago [5], and so on) to retrieve the information of hotel accommodation, and then use navigation services to find the way to the hotel. Travelers can also log in to mail service to retrieve the message of transport ticket, find the way to the station, locate the correct platform, and take the corresponding vehicle to the tourist destinations. Moreover, travel planning preserved in the online calendar (e.g., Google Calendar) or note applications (e.g., Evernote [6], OneNote [7], and Google Keep [8]) provides navigation reference for travelers during the trip. However, it can be found that travelers need to manually perform several tasks through different services to achieve their purpose in the trip. Major obstacles are stated as follows.

- **The scattering of travel information:** One obstacle is that information associated with the trip could exist in several services, including online calendar, note applications, booking services, and mail services. Travelers need to browse and search for corresponding travel information from different services during the trip. The scattering of travel information hinders timely and efficient assistance to travelers [9][10].
- **The lack of personalized guidance:** The other obstacle is the lack of personalized guidance for travelers according to their travel plans. Based on the information (e.g., destination, transportation, reservation, and so on) preserved in the travel plan and the travel context of travelers (e.g., date, time, and location), corresponding navigation could be identified and provided proactively [11].

To overcome the obstacles identified above, a smart navigation service is proposed to provide timely and personalized navigation for travelers. The smart navigation service acquires travel information from different services under the authorization of travelers and derives a comprehensive travel plan. During the trip, the smart navigation service collects travel context of travelers from smart devices continuously, and identifies the purpose of travelers based on the identified travel plan. In addition, the smart navigation service collects information about transportation or emergency events continuously. According to the identified purpose of travelers and the collected transportation or emergency information, corresponding navigation can be provided for travelers proactively.

In the remainder of this work, Section 2 introduces the architecture of the smart navigation service. Section 3 describes an use case of the prototype of the smart navigation service. Finally, conclusion and future directions are given in Section 4.

II. Architecture

The overview of the smart navigation service is shown in Figure 1. Major components in the smart navigation service are stated as follows.

- **Smart devices:** The smart devices carried or wore by travelers acquire travel context (e.g., date, time, and location) and transmit the information to the travel navigation cloud continuously. The travel context will be used by the travel navigation cloud for identifying the travel status and purpose of travelers. Based on the purpose of travelers, the corresponding navigation can be displayed by the smart devices [12]. In the near future, augmented reality navigation can also be employed to achieve better assistance to travelers [13][14].
- **Travel navigation cloud:** The travel navigation cloud is responsible for three major functionalities in the smart navigation service. The first functionality of the travel navigation cloud is to construct a comprehensive travel plan based on the information preserved in different online services. Important information during a trip, including destination, transportation, accommodation, itinerary, restaurant, associated date and time, can be retrieved through Application Programming Interfaces (APIs) of different online services. The information can be further identified and recognized by

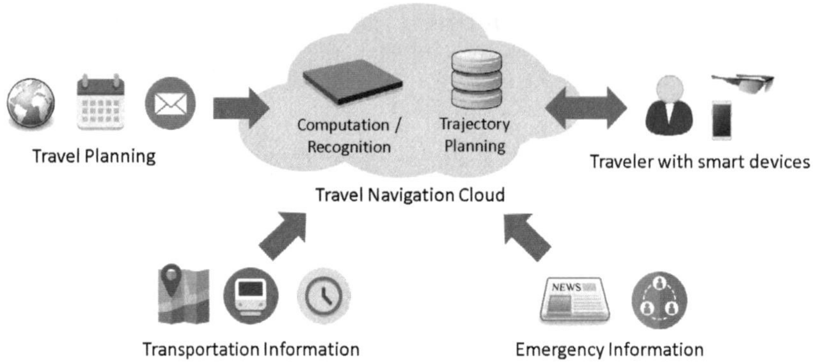

Figure 1. Overview of the smart navigation service.

natural language processing and named-entity recognition methods [15][16]. The second functionality of the travel navigation cloud is to collect current travel context (e.g., date, time, and location) of travelers through smart devices and identify the purpose of travelers based on the derived travel plan. The final functionality of the travel navigation cloud is to collect information from transportation services and news services continuously. Similarly, the collected information can be further identified and recognized by natural language processing and named-entity recognition methods. Based on the information recognized in the travel plan and the travel context of travelers, corresponding navigation according to the information provided by transportation services and news services could be identified and provided proactively.

- **Travel planning:** Travelers can arrange their travel plans through various online services nowadays. For instance, hotel accommodation can be reserved through online booking services. Transportation tickets can also be purchased online. In addition to the information preserved in different online services, corresponding reservation information might be provided for travelers through emails. Travelers can also use online calendar or note applications to manage their tourist destinations and associated itineraries. Thus, a travel plan can be extracted and identified from the above travel information existed in different services. Under the authorization of travelers, the travel navigation cloud acquires, analyzes, and identifies a comprehensive travel plan of travelers for proactive navigation during the trip.
- **Transportation information:** During a trip, travel from one place to another is one of the most important activities. However, travelers might need to forage for travel information scattered across different online services and make a right decision based on several transmit choices. The provision of personalized transportation information (e.g., timetable, route, vehicle status, travel time, and fare) will be highly beneficial to travelers [17]. Thus, detailed information of airport, rail service, ferry service, bus, and so on will be retrieved by the travel navigation cloud through APIs provided by service providers or government open data [18]. Based on the derived travel plan, identified travel context, and the transportation, proactive navigation can be provided for travelers for better travel experience.

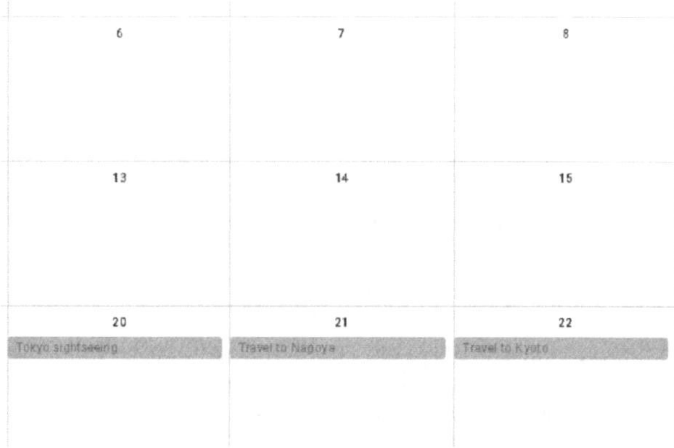

Figure 2. Travel plan in the online calendar.

- **Emergency information:** During a trip, emergency situations (e.g, disaster, traffic accident, strike, and so on) might happen and have influences on travelers. The travel navigation cloud retrieves news from different news services or social networks [19]. The location, occurrence time, and impact of specific emergency situations can be extracted by natural language processing and named-entity recognition methods. Based on the transportation information and the emergency information, the travel navigation cloud can identify and provide alternative travel choices for travelers to avoid emergency situations.

III. USE CASE

One use case is described to demonstrate the usage of the smart navigation service. As shown in Figure 2, a traveler arranges a list of cities (i.e., Tokyo, Nagoya, and Kyoto) on a journey and puts the information in the online calendar. On a specific day during the trip, the traveler arrives at the train station of the city (i.e., Tokyo). Through the travel context acquired by the smart device and the travel plan (destination city) retrieved from the online calendar, the travel navigation

Figure 3. Travel navigation for travelers.

cloud identifies the current travel status and the purpose of the traveler (i.e., travel to Nagoya). As shown in Figure 3, based on the identified purpose of the traveler and the transportation information retrieved from the government open data, train number, departure time, and arrival time of the appropriate train can be identified and provided by the smart navigation service. Thus, without manual operation, the traveler can get timely and personalized travel guidance efficiently. Better travel experience can be achieved.

IV. Conclusion and Future Work

A smart navigation service is proposed in this work to provide timely and personalized navigation for travelers. Based on travel planning and current travel context of travelers, the smart navigation service can identify the purpose of travelers, and provide corresponding navigation through the information retrieved from transportation services or news services proactively. The design of the smart navigation service is introduced, and the current prototype is demonstrated through a use case. Future work includes the integration of more online services, transportation services, and news services for comprehensive navigation for travelers.

Acknowledgment

This study is supported by the Ministry of Science and Technology of the Republic of China under grant MOST 108-2221-E-143-003-MY3.

References

[1] T. Stepan, J. M. Morawski, S. Dick, and J. Miller, "Incorporating spatial, temporal, and social context in recommendations for location-based social networks," IEEE Transactions on Computational Social Systems, vol. 3, no. 4, Dec 2016, pp. 164–175.

[2] K. Meehan, T. Lunney, K. Curran, and A. McCaughey, "Context-aware intelligent recommendation system for tourism," in 2013 IEEE International Conference on Pervasive Computing and Communications Workshops (PERCOM Workshops), March 2013, pp. 328–331.

[3] Booking.com, URL: https://www.booking.com/ [accessed: 2020-10-12].

[4] Agoda, URL: https://www.agoda.com/ [accessed: 2020-10-12].

[5] Trivago, URL: https://www.trivago.com [accessed: 2020-10-12].

[6] Evernote, URL: https://evernote.com/ [accessed: 2020-10-12].

[7] OneNote, URL: https://www.onenote.com/ [accessed: 2020-10-12].

[8] Google Keep, URL: https://keep.google.com/ [accessed: 2020-10-12].

[9] A.-C. Schering, M. Dueffer, A. Finger, and I. Bruder, "A mobile tourist assistance and recommendation system based on complex networks," in Proceedings of the 1st ACM International Workshop on Complex Networks Meet Information and Knowledge Management, 2009, pp. 81–84.

[10] R. Sood, "Intelligent mobile based tourist assistance system," in 2017 2nd International Conference for Convergence in Technology (I2CT), April 2017, pp. 655–658.

[11] P. Craig and Y. Liu, "A vision for pervasive information visualisation to support passenger navigation in public metro networks," in 2019 IEEE International Conference on Pervasive Computing and Communications Workshops (PerCom Workshops), 2019, pp. 202–207.

[12] M. K. Vichrova, P. Hájek, M. Kepka, L. Fiegler, W. Dorner, and M. Juha, "Peregrinus silva bohemica. a digital travel guide for navigation assistance," in 2019 9th International Conference on Advanced Computer Information Technologies (ACIT), 2019, pp. 492–495.

[13] A. Rácz and G. Zilizi, "Virtual reality aided tourism," in 2019 Smart City Symposium Prague (SCSP), 2019, pp. 1–5.

[14] S. M. C. Loureiro, J. Guerreiro, and F. Ali, "20 years of research on virtual reality and augmented reality in tourism context: A text-mining approach," Tourism Management, vol. 77, 2020, p. 104028.

[15] G. G. Chowdhury, "Natural language processing," Annual Review of Information Science and Technology, vol. 37, no. 1, 2003, pp. 51–89.

[16] R. S. Dudhabaware and M. S. Madankar, "Review on natural language processing tasks for text documents," in 2014 IEEE International Conference on Computational Intelligence and Computing Research, 2014, pp. 1–5.

[17] M. Handte, S. Foell, S. Wagner, G. Kortuem, and P. J. Marrón, "An internet-of-things enabled connected navigation system for urban bus riders," IEEE Internet of Things Journal, vol. 3, no. 5, 2016, pp. 735–744.

[18] P. Yochum, L. Chang, T. Gu, and M. Zhu, "Linked open data in location-based recommendation system on tourism domain: A survey," IEEE Access, vol. 8, 2020, pp. 16409–16439.

[19] N. Cassavia, P. Dicosta, E. Masciari, and D. Saccà, "Improving tourist experience by big data tools," in 2015 International Conference on High Performance Computing Simulation (HPCS), 2015, pp. 553–556.

The Technology Executive Role: A Study of the Main Competencies and Capabilities of the CIO / CTO

A Systematic Review

Carlos Sampaio
CESAR – Recife Center for Advanced Studies and Systems
Recife, Brazil
Email: ccbs@cesar.org.br

Felipe Silva Ferraz
CESAR – Recife Center for Advanced Studies and Systems
Recife, Brazil
Email: fsf@cesar.org.br

Abstract—**Emerging trends in technology bring about a fundamental career change for professionals and, consequently, for companies and businesses. The digital transformation and the introduction of new technologies are exerting a huge impact on the role and responsibilities of the Technology Executive to support the organization's goals. This study proposes to examine the skills and responsibilities associated with the role of the Technology Executive, systematically reviewing the literature and comparing patterns in the analysis of the profiles and skills for this role. The result shows that the competences of the Technology Executive have undergone a significant change to incorporate skills in different areas, apart from the traditional technical area, which can be categorized into five main groups: Technologist, Strategist, Enabler, Innovator, and Financial.**

Keywords* — *IT; Executive; CIO; CTO; Competency; Capability; Systematic Review; As a Service.

I. INTRODUCTION

The pace of technological development has reached such high rates that even the great discoveries of a few years ago already face challenges from the more recent competing technologies, before even being able to establish themselves in a competitive market like the one we live in. Emerging technologies, named by Gartner, Inc. as Nexus of Forces [1] [2], or the convergence and mutual reinforcement of trends, like: social, mobile, data analytics, cloud computing, and the Internet of Things, just to name a few, leads us to a reflection about what the professional of the future's work will be like. It is not difficult to be surprised by the pace of change that these technologies are exacting in today's professionals and businesses, but, at the same time, we see that this is exactly the fast pace that paves the opportunity paths for the entire reinvention of complicated business models, established decades, perhaps centuries ago [3]. These business models are replaced not only by creativity, innovation, or entrepreneurial vision but also by the simple competent application of those new technologies, promoting real revolutions in certain markets.

In view of these new innovative technologies, we observe a common trend, the "service-based" business models [4]. Initially associated with specific types of cloud computing and Big Data, the name came to be used by different offer opportunities, in markets with heavy user-centric services, as their main competitive distinctiveness. This trend is defined by the new jargon of Everything as a Service (XaaS) [4]. It is this type of offer that serves as a catalyst for several business initiatives with a focus on the global offer of services, and with accelerated growth, as is the case of some successful startups. These new business models are by nature extremely dynamic and flexible and benefit from the fact that they are not tied to long-term contracts or large investments in infrastructure, as with traditional models.

While emerging technologies and service-based business models are facilitators of innovation and a gateway to an excess of opportunities, it is not uncommon to be presented with excellent ideas for new products or services, that never left the drawing board. The failure to achieve a market-ready solution can be due to a simple lack of knowledge of the current technology state that would support this new venture, or to the unfamiliarity with the market for the supply of raw materials, support solutions, and information. The absence of the Technology Executive's proper knowledge and planning often results in innovative services offers that cannot scale to global demand, even local demand but with increased volume, because the technological platform has not been updated at the same speed as required, or due to the absence of a link to the next step of development [5]. All of these factors could pose as roadblocks and will terminate a project prior to even being started. In this scenario, the technology executive plays a fundamental role in the success or failure of a new idea or business model. However, the qualifications necessary for a good performance of this professional include, but are not limited to, in-depth technical knowledge, relationship with the market, leadership, negotiation skills, interpersonal skills, and strategic foresight of the future. This causes the recruitment and hiring of a professional with this skillset difficult and costly for the company [6]. Within this context, we observe opportunities and challenges to the mapping of the competencies and role of a Technology Executive, when submitted to the opportunity to offer these competencies in an "as a service" model.

This work intends to expand the knowledge about the role and competencies of the Technology Executive, evaluate the work that has already been done on the definition of this role, and how the responsibilities associated with this profile are categorized, to support future work that would allow for the development of a software abstraction with the ability to mimic the role of a Chief Information Officer (CIO) / Chief Technology Officer (CTO), even if partly.

The rest of the paper is structured as follows. In Section II, we present basic concepts related to the role of the Technology Executive and how its relevance and responsibilities to business success grew in importance over time. Next, in Section III, we introduce the methodology along with the objectives, the description of the methods, processes, and the protocol used in the systematic review of this study. In Section IV, we will detail the results associated with the research. Then, in the following section, we will interpret the results from the previous one and how they relate to the research questions. Finally, we conclude the work in Section VI, where some conclusions and future works will be depicted.

II. THE TECHNOLOGY EXECUTIVE ROLE

The preliminary applications, associated with computers and information systems, had simplified scopes of objectives and well-defined expectations for both the Information Technology departments and their managers. They were required to collect, store, and process financial and accounting data [7]. However, the responsibilities of this role evolved. The changes began with the need for hardware and software integration activities, in the 1970s, and continued with the design and implementation of networked platforms, in the 1990s. These changes continued with the analysis, selection, and acquisition of new software and services, in the 2000s. During the last decade, it became expected that the IT department produced a direct link with the companies' business model and results. The historical evolution for the responsibilities of the Technology Executive could be measured, in the history of companies, by the maturity and growth of their business model, from the basic use of technology in everyday processes to the exploration of emerging technologies to create a differential competitive in their business objectives.

III. APPLIED PROTOCOL

Based on the guidelines for performing Systematic Literature Reviews in Software Engineering proposed by Kitchenham [8], this work introduces the following methodology: (1) search strategy, (2) automatic search and selection, (3) identification of inclusion and exclusion criteria, (4) critical evaluation, (5) data extraction and (6) synthesis. This methodology is presented next in the order indicated above.

The principal goal of this review is to "identify studies that allow assessing the adoption of the concept of Everything as a Service, in the offering of technical, behavioral and business skills, associated with a technology executive". This study applied the aforementioned guidelines to systematically review the published research databases, looking for answers to three research questions:

- RQ1 - What studies on defining the technology executive role have previously been conducted?
- RQ2 - What are the responsibilities of the technology executive role?
- RQ3 - How are the competencies associated with the role of the technology executive categorized?

To properly define the scope of the principal goal of this review and allow for better structuring of the research questions, this study used the Population, Intervention, Comparison, Outcome, and Context (PICOC) criteria [8] in formulating the search strings, as will be presented on the following step.

A. Search Strategies

The research strategy underwent some modifications and trials before the use of the Population, Intervention, Comparison, Outcome, and Context (PICOC) criteria, due to the broad scope of our study, to better define the structure of the research questions. It was decided not to limit the findings by Context criterion to allow a larger universe of responses.

- Population: The technology executive (CIO / CTO);
- Intervention: Utilization of an "as a service" model;
- Comparison: Companies with a technology executive;
- Outcomes: Reduced dependence on technical, business, or behavioral skills.

B. Automatic Search and Selection

This work prioritized the search for results in the format of preliminary, academic, and industrial studies, which presented evidence about the objective of this work (PICOC), on the indicated research data sources. Research-Articles, Journals, Magazines, and studies presented at conferences, were used. Due to time constraints and better adherence to the methodology, only two selected data sources were used for this study. The IEEE Xplore and the ACM Digital Library are highly recommended and were chosen due to their recognized scope, content, and relevance. Both are data sources frequently used in reviews with the indexed scientific literature.

TABLE I. BUILDING OF SEARCH STRINGS

PICOC Criterion	Search String
Population	(("chief information officer" OR cio) OR ("chief technology officer" OR cto)) AND (challenges OR opportunities OR role OR attribution OR qualification OR competencies OR task OR survey)
Intervention	((("chief information officer" OR cio) OR ("chief technology officer" OR cto)) OR ((corporate OR enterprise) AND (it OR ("information technology")))) AND ("as a service")
Comparison	(("technology executive" OR "cto" OR "cio") OR (("c-level" OR "c level") AND ("it" OR "technology"))) AND ("enterprise" OR "enterprises" OR "company" OR "companies")
Outcome	(("it" OR "information technology") AND "as a service") AND ("cost reduction" OR "increased performance" OR ("return" AND "investment"))
Context	Not used

We chose to compose specific strings to match each Population, Intervention, Comparison, Outcome, and Context (PICOC) criteria. The detail of each criterion was used to form the basis for the building of each search string, as described in Table I.

These search strings were applied separately in each of the research databases, and later consolidated into a single reference file in the BibTeX format. The total number of results was 4,236. The initial results are shown in the Table II below, separated by data source and construction criteria for each search string.

TABLE II. INITIAL SEARCH RESULTS

PICOC Criterion	IEEE Xplore	ACM DL
Population	364	1476
Intervention	433	425
Comparison	194	902
Outcome	63	409
Context	Not used	Not used

The initial result, after consolidation, was assessed to exclude duplicated items. Next, the partial result was submitted to the inclusion and exclusion criteria presented in the next step of this study.

C. *Identification of Inclusion and Exclusion Criteria*

In this work, we admitted only studies related to the role of the Chief Information Officer (CIO) / Chief Technology Officer (CTO) as a technology executive. Results that did not highlight in their title any of the criteria for constructing the search terms were discarded. This review narrowed the studies examined to those published between 2017 and June 2020, as it is related to a more recent research area.

The studies that fit one or more of these following criteria were also excluded:

- Not written in the English language;
- Related to topics with similar acronyms, but different meanings from the desired;
- Call for works, prefaces, conference annals, handouts, summaries, panels, interviews, and news reports.

We will now describe the application of the inclusion and exclusion criteria presented above in the search and initial selection of research papers. This step started with an individual search per string, described in the previous stage, in each of the research sources. Each search result, associated with one PICOC criterion in one data source, was stored in a file in the BibTeX format. The result files were then concatenated and grouped by PICOC criteria, and then merged into a single result file to be imported into the Zotero software [9] for duplicates exclusion.

A total of 1,418 duplicate items were eliminated from the initial results after the consolidation. This activity produced 2,848 unique items that were submitted to the Inclusion and Exclusion Criteria.

Then, a list was generated with the results, in Comma-Separated Values (CSV) format, for importing into the Google spreadsheet tool (Google Sheets). Only articles of the types Conference Papers and Journal Articles were selected, using the Google Sheets filter tool and the "Item Type" column.

Additionally, it was established that the cut-off date required for consideration in this study would be works produced within the last 3 years at the most. We decided to consider only the results published from 2017 onwards as this study relates to new concepts and recent research areas. The Google Sheets filter tool was used again, and we selected all results with a value equal to, or greater than, 2017 in the column "Publication Year". This resulted in another 1,980 items excluded. After limiting the types of publications and applying the time cut-off criteria described above, the number of unique items was brought down to 869.

In the next step, we filtered the titles of the remaining articles to exclude items that do not highlight the relationship with the main purpose of this review or the alignment with any of the research questions. To do this, we used the Google Sheets filter function, with the syntax described below, to select articles using multiple criteria:

```
=FILTER('Sampaio-DPES_SLR'!A2:CI,
regexmatch('Sampaio-DPES_SLR'!E2:E ,
"CIO|CTO|Chief Information Officer|Chief
Technology Officer|Information Technology|as a
Service|Role|Technology Management|IT
Governance|Best Practices"))
```

A total of 238 works remained after this last step. We analyzed the title for each of these articles to determine its adherence to this systematic review. Several works that were not related to the main theme or research questions, but that met some of the terms used in the filter of the previous step were eliminated, as we can see from the details below.

Some works related to physics, performance analysis in software development, human resources, and deployment of cloud services, were included in the result due to the use of terms such as “role”, “software as a service”, “executive”, and the acronyms CIO / CTO. In such cases, papers whose titles did not comply with the scope of the review were eliminated. The works whose titles left uncertainties about their adherence to the main theme were also listed for review in the next step. At the end of this step, 193 entries were excluded, leaving 45 items for further analysis.

All abstracts of the remaining works from the previous stage were evaluated. We were able to perceive that they ranged greatly in content. Similar to the previous step, some works were eliminated because they did not have the desired adherence to the main object of this study. It was necessary to manually retrieve the summary field of some articles because they did not present this information as a result of the search and initial selection. Also included for later analysis were the articles in which the analysis of adherence with the scope of this work proved to be imprecise or left doubts. The reading of the abstract resulted in the exclusion of another 29 articles, leaving 16 for thorough critical analysis and data extraction.

Table III below shows the exclusion numbers for each step in this part of the study.

TABLE III. NUMBER OF STUDIES FILTERED IN EACH STEP OF THE SELECTION PROCESS

Selection process step	Number of articles selected
Data source search (after deduplication)	2848
Inclusion, exclusion, and time cut-off criteria	869
Title examination	45
Abstract analysis	16

D. Critical Evaluation

The studies that reached this critical evaluation step were submitted to a complete analysis. The studies were then analyzed in full, not just titles or abstracts. Six papers were discarded at the end of this stage since they did not exhibit adherence to the theme of the review nor answered any aspect of the leading questions. This resulted in a final set of 10 papers.

The final studies analyzed went on to the data extraction and synthesis stage, and the results obtained will be presented in the following section.

IV. Results

This study identified 10 primary studies [7][10]-[18] dealing with a wide range of research topics and exploration models for each different situation.

According to [13], it is possible to categorize the skills of the Technology Executive into four main groups, namely, Strategist, Innovator, Enabler, and Technologist. We were able to find agreement in the primary studies with all four above mentioned groups, including other groups of less expressiveness, such as Leadership, Processes, and Business. The Financial group also yield several references, similar in number to the main groups indicated above. Studies that did not fit into any of these groups were classified as General. These last groups of categories are valid because they register the tendency to be constituted in sub-categories or to facilitate the comprehension of the responsibilities associated with the Technology Executive, evaluated later in this work.

A. Quantitative Analysis

The proposed research process resulted in 10 primary studies, written by 34 authors, linked to 15 institutions, based in 10 different countries, spread over four continents, and were published between the years of 2017 and 2020. The combined keyword number from the studies assessed by this paper yield a total of 49 distinct entries.

In what concerns the country of origin, there was no highlight to be made. Chile, Indonesia, and China appear with a somewhat higher result than the others (all with two publications each). The remaining countries had one publication only. Despite the small general amount of publications found on the role of the Technology Executive and the responsibilities associated with that role, we note that the geographical distribution, which covers most continents, illustrates the global interest in this subject.

The most common keywords used in the studies, by order of frequency were CIO (4), CTO (3), IT Executive (2), Role (3), Chief Information Officer (2), Technology (2), Technology Management (2). All other items were cited only once. The first 4 keywords, namely: CIO, CTO, IT Executive, and Role, indicate precisely the research object sought by this work.

V. Discussion

First and foremost, it was possible to identify that the responsibilities associated with this role are constantly changing, which reflects in the need to constantly reconstruct the definition and attributions of that role. Secondly, we observed in many of the works, the statement that the fashion in which the profile for the Technology Executive is categorized is influenced by the type of exposure that the company has to Technology. The focus and performance of the executives vary, according to the company's orientation and exposure concerning technology, as well as its definition as a strategic asset or as an infrastructure base for operational efficiency. This comes to show that this research field is very extensive and that requires a continuous effort to contribute to its development.

The analysis also pointed to a shortage of supply capable of playing this role, associated with the need for specific training to accommodate the demand for Technology Executives. This is because there is still a misalignment between the expected performance of these Executives, by companies (demand), and the type of professional profile available to exercise this role (offer).

A. RQ1 – Assessment

We observed that most of the studies opted for the survey based on interviews (7 studies) when evaluating what types of studies have already been conducted to define the role of the Technology Executive. Some works opted for the use of forms or questionnaires, to qualify the moment of the interview, or in the selection of the interviewee (4 studies). The Literature Review was also used to qualify the interview step (3 studies). Other methods were used, to select the target audience and to analyze the profile characteristics, to define the role of the Technology Executive, and to answer this research question, but which were mentioned only once.

By grouping the types of automation used to select candidates for the interview and to effectively collect data for analysis, we found that most studies opted for some manual method of assessing requirements and profile characteristics. Another smaller group opted to use automated data selection and extraction techniques, with a highlight on the use of Natural Language Processing (NLP) [15] and on the analysis of public data sources in Social Networks [13].

To answer this research question, each work could contribute with more than one type of study, therefore, the total number of types of studies is not relevant when compared with the number of primary papers. Out of all primary papers selected for the final analysis, a single one failed to identify an acceptable answer to this research question.

B. RQ2 - Assessment

Only half of the studies analyzed indicated some type of formalization concerning the definition of responsibilities for the role of the Technology Executive. We understand that the interest in this area of study has taken a more accelerated pace over the past few years, when the attributions of this role were no longer restricted to the issues of the companies' operational infrastructure, and started to have an impact on strategic business objectives [7][13].

The concern with the alignment between the responsibilities of the Technology Executive and the strategic performance of companies, without neglecting traditional structuring, operational and support activities, became clear among the answers found. It was also possible to identify the growth in requirements for soft skills and negotiation, indicating that the main target audience for this role is increasingly closer to the top-level executives (C-Suite), and to the external client for the businesses.

> *"The Chief Technology Officer (CTO) is responsible for linking technology with strategy, market issues, and top management guidelines; it is also responsible for promoting innovation and facilitating the intersection among research, development, technology innovation, and leadership vision."* [18]

C. RQ3 – Assessment

An important highlight that arises as a result of this research is the finding, in the role of the Technology Executive, of many requirements commonly associated with the Business Executive. It is traditional to find technology profiles that play the role of the main executive; however, we find several positions occupied by professionals with first training in business [17].

This work found 43 different terms for category grouping of the Technology Executive profile. From these, the Technologist and the Strategist profiles (both with 7 citations each) stood out. The first profile can be traced back to the first moments of technology development. It is the technical role best known for its alignment with operational and structuring responsibilities. However, the latter describes a profile further aligned with the strategic business objectives, the Strategist profile. The other noticeable categories found in this work are gradually located between the first two described above. As they have a more technical or business tendency, they are the Innovator, Financial, and Enabler (each with 4 citations each). The last terms worth mentioning are Processes and Leadership (with 2 citations each), and 12 other categories that had only one citation each.

VI. Conclusion

According to the result of this literature review, the skills of the Technology Executive can be divided into five main groups, namely, Technologist, Strategist, Enabler, Financial, and Innovator. The purpose of this review was to identify previous studies on the role of the Technology Executive, which would allow us to categorize their main responsibilities and competencies. In the search phase, 2848 studies were found, of which 10 were classified as primary studies after applying the exclusion criteria.

Some limitations should be noted in the present study. First, the potential bias due to the design of the methodology using a single researcher only, with the task of deciding the selection criteria and analyzing the quality of the works by himself. Second, the absence of data sources outside the academic environment, such as social networks and specialized market research companies (Garter Inc. or McKinsey & Company as examples). The main focus of this work was to find patterns in how to assess the competencies and skills associated with the role of the Technology Executive to offer an overview of the current state of the art.

In future works, we intend to perform studies including other data sources, and the mapping of the specific duties of each profile from the Technologist to the Strategist can be outlined to support a proposal to develop a software abstraction of the most operational skills of the Technology Executive.

This work intended to provide an introductory overview of the difficulty related to mapping roles, competencies, and activities associated with the Technology Executive. The development of this research in future works will include and further explore other research databases to display these facts and points more palpably.

References

[1] Gartner Inc., "Nexus of Forces." [Online]. Available: https://www.gartner.com/en/information-technology/glossary/nexus-of-forces. [retrieved: December, 2019].

[2] M. Hwang, An assignment for the nexus of forces. In: AMCIS 2017 - America's Conference on Information Systems: A Tradition of Innovation, 2017.

[3] S. Ackx, "Emerging Technologies, Disrupt or be Disrupted," in ISSE 2014 Securing Electronic Business Processes, Springer Fachmedien Wiesbaden, 2014, pp. 177–187.

[4] Y. Duan et al., "Everything as a Service (XaaS) on the Cloud: Origins, Current and Future Trends," 2015 IEEE 8th International Conference on Cloud Computing, pp. 621–628, Jun. 2015.

[5] J. Pombinho, D. Aveiro, and J. Tribolet, "A Value-Oriented Approach to Business/IT Alignment – Towards Formalizing Purpose in System Engineering," Advanced Information Systems Engineering Workshops, pp. 555–566, 2012.

[6] A. Salim, "The c-suite is paralysed with fear, finds new report on digital transformation | The Drum," TheDrum, 2017. [Online]. Available: https://www.thedrum.com/news/2017/11/14/the-c-suite-paralysed-with-fear-finds-new-report-digital-transformation. [Retrieved: December, 2019].

[7] A. La Paz, J. Vasquez, and J. Miranda, "The CIO Gap and Mismatch," IT Prof., vol. 21, no. 2, pp. 66–72, Mar. 2019.

[8] P. Brereton, B. A. Kitchenham, D. Budgen, M. Turner, and M. Khalil, "Lessons from applying the systematic literature review process within the software engineering domain," Journal of Systems and Software, vol. 80, no. 4, pp. 571–583, Apr. 2007.

[9] H.T. Harish, "Zotero: Bibliographic Reference Management Software" Journal of Advanced Research in Library and Information Science 05, no. 01, February 19, 2018, pp. 42–49. doi:10.24321/2395.2288.201807.

[10] W. Noonpakdee, A. Phothichai, T. Khunkornsiri, and A. Nuntree, "CIO Competency in Digital Era: A Comparative Study between Government Organizations and Private Enterprises," 2020 IEEE 7th International Conference on Industrial Engineering and Applications (ICIEA), pp. 948–952, Apr. 2020.

[11] Y. Gong, M. Janssen, and V. Weerakkody, "Current and expected roles and capabilities of CIOS for the innovation and adoption of new technology," in ACM International Conference Proceeding Series, 2019, pp. 462–467.

[12] S. Kosasi, Vedyanto, and I. D. A. E. Yuliani, "Effectiveness of IT Governance of Online Businesses with Analytical Hierarchy Process Method," in 2018 6th International Conference on Cyber and IT Service Management, (CITSM), Aug. 2018.

[13] A. La Paz, "How to Become a Strategist CIO," IT Professional, vol. 19, no. 1, pp. 48–55, Jan. 2017.

[14] D. A. Saputra, I. Alif, R. A. Wijaya, Y. G. Sucahyo, and M. K. Hammi, "Role of IT in IT governance practices maturity perspective," International Conference on Advanced Computer Science and Information Systems, ICACSIS 2019, pp. 325–330

[15] A. Kumar, R. Mukundan, and K. Jain, "Technology Management Practices of CTOs in Emerging Economy India," 2017 Portland International Conference on Management of Engineering and Technology (PICMET), pp. 1–6, Jul. 2017.

[16] B. Lohmuller and A. Petrikhin, "The Growing Importance of Technology Executives / Hidden Chief Technology Officers and Their Organizational Roles," 2018 IEEE International Conference on Engineering, Technology and Innovation (ICE/ITMC), Jun. 2018.

[17] D. J. Mazzola, R. D. S. Louis, and M. R. Tanniru, "The path to the top," Communications of the ACM, vol. 60, no. 3, pp. 60–68, Feb. 2017.

[18] A. Farina et al., "The role of chief technology office (CTO) in a modern defense company," IEEE Aerospace and Electronic Systems Magazine, vol. 32, no. 3, pp. 52–56, Mar. 2017.

Teaching Agile Software Engineering Practices Using Scrum and a Low-Code Development Platform – A Case Study

José Carlos Metrôlho[1,2], Fernando Reinaldo Ribeiro[1,2], Pedro Passão[2]
[1]R&D Unit in Digital Services, Applications and Content
[2]Polytechnic Institute of Castelo Branco
Castelo Branco, Portugal
e-mail: metrolho@ipcb.pt, e-mail: fribeiro@ipcb.pt, e-mail: pedropassao@ipcb.pt

Abstract— **Following the recent trends in software engineering regarding the growing adoption of agile methodologies and low-code development platforms, and considering the results of surveys, we carried out on students, alumni and some IT companies, we adapted the software engineering teaching of a computer engineering course to the needs and new trends of the IT industry. The Scrum methodology and the OutSystems low-code development platform were used in a project-based learning approach for teaching agile software engineering practices. This approach was complemented with the presentation and discussion of several topics during the theoretical classes, lectures given by professionals from IT companies and study visits to an IT company that uses agile methodologies and low-code platforms. This approach aims to enhance the technical skills, namely development skills on a widely used low-code platform and other software engineering skills, but also to reinforce some non-technical skills of students like teamwork and communication, today highly valued by IT companies. The first results are quite positive.**

Keywords- agile methodologies; education; Low-code platforms; software engineering; Scrum; teaching.

I. INTRODUCTION

Several approaches have been used for teaching software engineering. The way they propose to do it differs. However, regardless of the proposed approach, there are some aspects that already seem to be well accepted and that seem to be a common trend for several approaches: there is an effort to make the teaching of software engineering as close as possible to what is done in IT companies; Most strategies try to provide students with practical experience in a software engineering project using methodologies and tools also used in IT companies; and there is a growing concern on empowering students with the non-technical skills required in a software project. To achieve this, it is important to be aware of the needs and trends of the market. It is important to understand how the main concepts of the software engineering subject are assimilated by the students and understand the point of view of the companies which employ and develop activities in this area.

Following the recent trends in software engineering, with regard to the growing adoption of agile methodologies and low-code development platforms, and considering the results of surveys carried out in some IT companies [1], we made some changes in the teaching of the software engineering subject. In this paper, we describe an experience in teaching software engineering. An agile development methodology and a low-code development platform were used in a project-based learning approach. This approach aims to enhance the technical and non-technical skills of students, today highly valued by IT companies, without, of course, neglecting other methodologies and topics related to software engineering.

The remainder of this paper will be as follows: Section II presents a brief review of related work; Section III presents a background about agile development and low-code development platforms; in Section IV, we present an overview of our methodology for teaching undergraduate software engineering using Scrum and a low-code development platform; Section V presents some lessons learned and challenges faced and finally, in Section VI we present some conclusions and we outline the future work.

II. RELATED WORK

Several approaches and strategies have been followed to provide students with the best training in software engineering. Some of them are more theoretical, more focused on the study of theory, concepts, methods and methodologies, while others are more practical, fostering practical experimentation to students, and often carried out in collaboration with companies. Some are more traditional, in the sense that they privilege traditionally used practices, others are more avant-garde and encourage contact with the most innovative practices and new market trends. All of them aim to give students the appropriate knowledge and skills for their professional activity in software engineering. However, the way they propose to do it differs.

Emulating the workplace using distributed software development projects, involving various courses or institutions, is an approach proposed by several authors (e.g., [2][3]). The Distributed and Outsourced Software Engineering course [2] proposed teaching software engineering using globally distributed projects. The projects were developed in collaboration with eleven universities in ten different countries providing students with the experience of working with different cultures, native languages and time zones. This approach also helped to alert students to the importance of understanding typical software engineering issues, such as the importance of software requirements for specifications, or the relevance of adequate system design. However, they also identify some time scheduling inconveniences, and difficulties in keeping teams committed to their peers. In [3], students work on real distributed open-source projects as full members of software development teams. Students use the same software development processes as regular team members and are provided with explicit mentorship from mentors from each project. With this approach students integrate and apply the skills they have learned in their courses and they develop and improve their technical communication skills in a real development setting.

The use of simulations and gamification to provide students with a variety of experiences that would not be possible in an academic environment, is an alternative proposed by other authors (e.g.,[4]–[6]). Usually, these approaches propose to gamify some phases of the software life cycle and some tasks associated to each of them. The goal is to increase the user's engagement, motivation and performance when carrying out specific tasks. However, these approaches also have some disadvantages. After two periods of teaching using Scrum with gamification to learn and train agile principles, Schäfer [5] identified some lessons learned. Gamification is motivating and helps to bring together participants with different experiences in project teams.

Several project-oriented approaches have been proposed in several software engineering training programmes (e.g., [7]–[10]. A project-based learning experience based on the formation of small heterogeneous teams was presented in [7]. Through a strategy of role rotation and documentation transfer, all students perform different tasks and face different challenges throughout the project. This is the case they decided not to include any external stakeholder. In [8], software engineering concepts are taught using the Scrum framework in real life projects. The requirements are discussed with external customers during a kick-off meeting. During the project, students work together as self-organized teams. They chose a project management and team coordination process and they are only asked to use some core tools that are needed to monitor the projects.

From a different perspective, the teaching of software engineering has been adapting to new developments and trends namely the agile methodologies. This topic has deserved the attention of many authors who have published several studies that address this subject. Usually, teaching agile methodologies has focused on teaching a specific method like Scrum (e.g., [11]–[13]) or XP (e.g., [14] [15]). A project-based learning approach using the Scrum framework in real life projects is presented in [11]. The module starts with a kick-off where external stakeholders introduce their topics, students apply for their preferred topics and the supervisors define the teams of 5–7 persons. After 3 weeks, the students must provide a project proposal which has to be presented and defended face-to-face against customer comments. The project proposal requires the definition of a clear aim of the project, as well as a backlog of requirements with an estimation and prioritization of the relevant user stories. The projects are run in sprints, with a final presentation and the hand-over of the results. An outline of the literature related to Scrum in software engineering courses [16] shows that providing students with practical experience is of vital importance when teaching Scrum in software engineering courses. It also states that most Scrum courses require students to work in teams in order to develop a non-trivial software project or practice simulation games. A study on the impact of using agile methods in software engineering education [17] concluded that using Agile practices would positively influence the teaching process and that they could stimulate communication, good relationships among students, active team participation, and motivation for present and future learning.

In fact, several approaches have been used for teaching software engineering. However, and as mentioned in [18], it is not clear which should be the best approach do follow because there are different perspectives on the different proposed approaches. Some of them propose to emulate the workplace using distributed projects or using simulations and games to simulate different scenarios. Others propose project-based learning where students can train the various stages of project development, following different methodologies, and develop non-technical skills. However, regardless of the approach followed, some aspects seem to already be well accepted and seem to be a common trend for several approaches. There is an attempt to bring teaching closer to business reality. Many of these strategies include providing students with hands-on experience in a software engineering project using methodologies and tools that are also used in IT companies. At the same time, many of these strategies have also focused on empowering students with the non-technical skills required in a software project. It is also true that more traditional approaches, in which students take on a more passive role and that place a higher priority on teaching students to follow instructions and rules, do not produce the intended results. Most current approaches, for teaching software engineering, try to help students develop their own ideas and strategies. They promote project-based learning and they try to engage students in the problem definition, design process and system thinking.

III. AGILE DEVELOPMENT AND LOW-CODE PLATFORMS

The growing spread of agile software development methodologies, the increasing attention they have attracted and their growing adoption by IT companies, seem to ensure that they will play an important role in the future. Some recent surveys demonstrate the importance and the high level of adoptions of these methodologies. A survey presented in the 14th annual state of agile report [19] shows that 95% of respondents report that their organizations practice agile development methods. Accelerating software delivery, enhancing ability to manage changing priorities, increasing productivity, and improving business alignment are the top reasons stated for adopting Agile. Scrum and related variants are the most common agile methodologies used by respondents' organizations (referred by 58% of the respondents). Another survey [20], which involved 3300 IT professionals, mentions an even higher percentage, stating that Scrum and related variants are used in 76% of companies. Additionally, some studies have demonstrated the greater satisfaction of companies and professionals who have adopted these methodologies. For individual professionals, they found that agile development seams to led to greater satisfaction mainly because of collaborative practices and business influences [21]. Another study [22] points out several benefits that were identified by companies that adopted agile methodologies namely: improving project monitoring and tracking, improving interaction and collaboration and fosters sharing knowledge.

Another trend that has been noted is the growing adoption of low-code development platforms by IT companies. The State of Application Development [20] refer that 41% of respondents said their organization was already using a low-code application platform and, a further 10% said they were about to start using one. This growing interest is also corroborated by the Low-Code Development Platform Market [23]. It reports that the global low-code development platform market size is projected to grow from USD 13.2 billion in 2020 to USD 45.5 billion by 2025, at a Compound Annual Growth Rate of 28.1% during the forecast period. The top reported reasons for adopting agile [20] are the ability to manage changing priorities, project visibility, business alignment, delivery speed/time to market and team morale. These reasons are in line with the advantages that are usually associated with the use of low-code development platforms: They comprise many of the same tools functionalities that developers and teams use to design, code, deploy and manage an application portfolio [24]; A significant part of the job can be done through a drag-and-drop interface and although developers may still need to do some coding this is just for specific tasks [25]; They are able to accelerate the delivery of new software and applications, allowing to update and deliver new features in short time periods, they allow build apps for multiple platforms simultaneously, and cross-platform support and data integration capabilities have already been built and can be customized easily [26]. In fact, these platforms have become quite popular and are currently spread across many companies around the world. A report from Forrester [27] evaluated the 13 most significant low-code platforms suppliers and identified Microsoft, OutSystems, Mendix, Kony and Salesforce as leaders.

Another important aspect is that low-code platforms have often been associated with agile development methodologies. The adoption of agile development methodologies, platforms and tools has been a way of improving the ease and speed at which applications can be developed. But, as referred in [28], there is still room for improvement and in particular when it comes to education and training, management commitment and staffing. There is also a need for greater involvement from the wider business, which agile and the use of tools such as low-code both encourage while, at the same time, enhancing developer productivity. The State of Application Development [20] revealed that companies that have adopted low-code have an 8% higher organizational agility score compared to those not using low-code. They also refer that this result seems to be related to the fact that a highly mature agile culture helps organizations maximize the benefits of low-code development platforms by combining the fast decision-making of agile with fast development speeds. However, to maximize agile teams' performance with a low-code platform, there are some aspects that must be followed with particular attention. Some of these aspects are identified in the document Adapting Agile to Build Products with Low-Code: Tips and Tricks [29] and are related to: the difficulty for teams in maintaining a sufficient backlog of user stories ready for development due to the faster development speed; the difficulty of new teams in low code to achieve the necessary quality from the beginning of the process; the significant difference in development velocity between co-dependent teams; the need for a strong product owner who is engaged, empowered and responsive; and the need for collaboration between developers and business analysts from the start of the development cycle, especially for complex user stories.

IV. Overview of our Approach

The software engineering subject is part of the second year of a computer science course (undergraduate course). It is a subject that has a semester load of 30 hours for theoretical classes and 45 hours for laboratory classes. The focus of our approach is to combine theory and practice and ensure that the topics covered remain appropriate to whatever the needs of employers and current trends in the area of software engineering are. A project-based approach is used in practical classes for teaching Software engineering.

The teacher of theoretical classes presents the concepts and methodologies and promotes discussion about them. In these classes, several aspects related to the software development cycle are taught and discussed. Students are provided with an introduction to several software development methodologies namely Waterfall, Extreme Programming, Scrum, Spiral, Rapid Application Development, Rational Unified Process, Feature Driven Development, Behaviour Driven Development, etc. Other topics analysed include quality and metrics in software engineering, requirements analysis, software design, implementation, testing, configuration management, among others. In addition to the presentation and discussion of several topics during the classes, other initiatives are organized and implemented, namely lectures given by professionals from software development companies and study visits to software development companies. These initiatives provide students with the contact and interaction with real software engineering projects with real stakeholders. They are carried out in the final weeks of the semester, so by that time the students have already acquired significant knowledge that will then allow them to get the most out of them.

In practical classes, students acquire some practice of software engineering through the process management, specification, design, implementation and validation of a software application, as a project for teams. Scrum is the adopted agile software development methodology. The teacher has experience with Agile methodologies and holds a professional certification in the adopted low-code platform. He was able to provide support during the initial learning phase of application development on the low-code platform, but also to support the various teams of students during the scrum sprints of development of their projects. The teacher acts as a product owner. Each team member has a specific role (e.g., Scrum Master, developer, etc.). Each team develops a different project. We have used Scrum because several employers of companies in the software development area, with whom we have had contact, use agile methodologies [1], namely Scrum and because our graduates have told us that it is clearly one of the methodologies they use most [30]. In addition, we also aim to improve students' teamwork, and this methodology is one that fits well with this goal. These skills of teamwork have been highly valued by employers and therefore they deserve to be worked on in this subject as well. We have been using Scrum in practical classes for years and the recent survey [1] only reinforced it and that is why we continue to use it.

In past editions of this subject, the projects were related to the development of games (using Unity) or even to continue work started earlier in other subjects of the course (developed in java). The new trends and the feedback we obtained in a survey [1] led us to, in the previous academic year, choose to introduce the development of projects in practical classes using a low-code platform. This is an area of great demand by our students' employers, so with this approach we also wanted to provide new skills at the level of coding competence. In other words, the survey we carried out [1] was clear as to the importance of coding skills, but also of other aspects such as requirements analysis and development methodologies. So, on the one hand, with this new approach we give students new coding skills using one of these development platforms widely used by several recruiting companies in the software development area. On the other hand, due to the characteristics of these low-code platforms, it allows us to emphasize and work with students on other different and important aspects of the development of software projects, such as requirements analysis, project design, project management project, development methodology, quality assurance, testing, planning, etc. When students complete the entire course, they obviously have much more comprehensive skills because in other subjects they learn to program in various other languages and paradigms (Java, PHP, Html, SQL, etc.). This subject of software engineering is not a programming subject but a subject in which the coding stage is only part of a whole. The whole concerns the cycle of software development and therefore it is also important to address and emphasize what is not so addressed in other subjects of the course. Namely the importance of development methodologies, planning, requirements analysis, software quality, testing, maintenance, documentation, etc. Considering this reality, it seemed to us that the use in this subject of a low-code platform in practical classes could bring advantages, and after having implemented it, we remain convinced.

To keep students motivated, the themes and objectives of the projects could be defined by the teams of students or alternatively by carrying out themes proposed by the teacher of the practical classes. With this new approach, projects include the development of web and mobile applications using a low-code platform. In practical classes Scrum is the development process used. The teacher of the practical classes monitors weekly the evolution of each of the projects. This monitoring allows for the assigning of grades between teams but also being able to differentiate the grades of each element of a team. Monitoring is weekly, during contact classes with students. The student teams, in addition to the weekly class time, also work outside of classes. Tasks are all registered in Trello, allowing the teacher and the whole team to have a permanent record of the progress of the respective project. Trello is used for project management and to track progress on tasks.

During the semester, the project evolves over several sprints (of two weeks), in which the teacher (acting as product owner) evaluates with the respective team what was achieved in the previous sprint and what should be the sprint backlog of the sprint that follows.

The final grade of the subject, in terms of the practical part, results from an intermediate evaluation of each student based on the work presented in the middle of the semester and from a second evaluation made at the end of the semester. In these two stages, a demo is made by each team, resulting in grades and feedback given by teachers to the various teams. The grades result from the application of parameters related to various aspects of the various phases of the project's development and the Scrum methodology. Some of the parameters are: Requirements analysis, software development process (e.g. roles, artefacts, timings, hits and misses), task scheduling, modelling (e.g. user stories, storyboards), implemented features, conclusions and future work, user interface, documentation, and final presentation and discussion. In the past academic year, due to Covid-19, classes were provided using video conferencing for teacher-student or teacher-team interaction. The fact that low-code platforms provide several online teaching materials (webinars, tutorials, examples, etc.) was also useful to successfully overcome the limitations mentioned above. This complementary material helped all teams to quickly and timely assimilate necessary knowledge about development in the adopted platform, in order to implement their projects.

We also noticed that the learning and adaptation to the use of low-code platform by students was overall very good. The developed projects resulted in applications with practically all user stories implemented and validated. The students in their final reports addressed aspects about the various stages and timings of the work developed, as far as software engineering is concerned. Some of the projects resulted in web applications with good user interfaces. Throughout the semester, we verified a high activity and motivation by practically all students. All projects resulted in functional applications, some of which reached quality close to the maximum score.

The low-code platform that we used in practical classes was the OutSystems. We choose this platform because it is a platform widely used by software development companies in Portugal and because we have had a collaboration protocol with that company for several years, under which we have accessible software licenses. Another important fact in the choice is that this platform can easily coexist with agile methodologies such as Scrum [31] and it is one of the leaders in the low-code market [27].

V. Lessons Learned and Challenges Faced

Even considering the entropy caused by the effects of Covid-19 (videoconference classes and student/team meetings also via videoconference), in the end it resulted in good results from both the theoretical and practical parts. The inclusion of the low-code platform in practical classes, allowed students to develop web applications, and to develop new skills in one of the low-code platforms widely used in software development companies. Additionally, and very importantly, this approach allowed us to meet the findings of the survey that was carried out on IT companies [1]. It allows to strengthening students with other skills related to software engineering like development methodologies, requirements analysis, project management, schedules, testing, etc. As mentioned before, this subject is not focused on coding, for that there are several others in the course where several programming skills are covered. We also believe that this approach contributes to the improvement of the non-technical skills of students, namely teamwork and communication.

It is also important to consider that Low-code platforms have some advantages and are suitable in the context of this subject of software engineering. However, they do not replace the need for the knowledge covered in other subjects to prepare our students for a wider range of knowledge, about other approaches and technologies that are also very useful and often necessary.

VI. Conclusion and Future Work

After listening to several stakeholders with the aim of keeping the themes and methodologies taught in the subject of Software engineering updated, we share in this paper an update done recently. This update consisted in making the projects developed in the practical classes using Scrum and a low-code platform. This decision was to reinforce students development skills (on a low-code platform currently highly used in the labour market) and lead students to a greater focus on other software engineering skills (teamwork, communication, requirements, software quality, schedules, documentation, among others). The results achieved were positive, and the feedback from the students was very rewarding. In a survey conducted at the end of the semester, on a scale of 0 to 6, students rated the overall satisfaction in relation to the subject with 5.4.

In the future, we will continue to be attentive to stakeholder feedback, to keep materials and methodologies updated in order to prepare students as best as possible and close to what is followed in the software development industry.

References

[1] J. C. Metrôlho and F. R. Ribeiro, "Holistic Analysis of the Effectiveness of a Software engineering Teaching Approach," *Int. J. Adv. Softw.*, vol. 12, no. 1 & 2, pp. 46–55, 2019.

[2] M. Nordio *et al.*, "Teaching Software engineering Using Globally Distributed Projects: The DOSE Course," in *Proceedings of the 2011 Community Building Workshop on Collaborative Teaching of Globally Distributed Software Development*, 2011, pp. 36–40, doi: 10.1145/1984665.1984673.

[3] R. Holmes, M. Craig, K. Reid, and E. Stroulia, "Lessons Learned Managing Distributed Software engineering Courses," in *Companion Proceedings of the 36th International Conference on Software engineering*, 2014, pp. 321–324, doi: 10.1145/2591062.2591160.

[4] M. Yampolsky and W. Scacchi, "Learning Game Design and Software engineering Through a Game Prototyping Experience: A Case Study," in *Proceedings of the 5th International Workshop on Games and Software engineering*, 2016, pp. 15–21, doi: 10.1145/2896958.2896965.

[5] U. Schäfer, "Training scrum with gamification: Lessons learned after two teaching periods," in *2017 IEEE Global Engineering Education Conference (EDUCON)*, 2017, pp. 754–761, doi: 10.1109/EDUCON.2017.7942932.

[6] W. Ren, S. Barrett, and S. Das, "Toward Gamification to Software engineering and Contribution of Software Engineer," in *Proceedings of the 2020 4th International Conference on Management Engineering, Software engineering and Service Sciences*, 2020, pp. 1–5, doi: 10.1145/3380625.3380628.

[7] B. Pérez and Á. L. Rubio, "A Project-Based Learning Approach for Enhancing Learning Skills and Motivation in Software engineering," in *Proceedings of the 51st ACM Technical Symposium on Computer Science Education*, 2020, pp. 309–315, doi: 10.1145/3328778.3366891.

[8] A. Heberle, R. Neumann, I. Stengel, and S. Regier, "Teaching agile principles and software engineering concepts through real-life projects," in *2018 IEEE Global Engineering Education Conference (EDUCON)*, 2018, pp. 1723–1728, doi: 10.1109/EDUCON.2018.8363442.

[9] M. L. Fioravanti *et al.*, "Integrating Project Based Learning and Project Management for Software engineering Teaching: An Experience Report," in

Proceedings of the 49th ACM Technical Symposium on Computer Science Education, 2018, pp. 806–811, doi: 10.1145/3159450.3159599.

[10] M. Gordenko and E. Beresneva, "A project-based learning approach to teaching software engineering through group dynamics and professional communication," in *Actual Problems of System and Software engineering. Proceedings of the 6th International Conference Actual Problems of System and Software engineering*, 2019, pp. 278-288.

[11] A. Heberle, R. Neumann, I. Stengel, and S. Regier, "Teaching agile principles and software engineering concepts through real-life projects," in *2018 IEEE Global Engineering Education Conference (EDUCON)*, 2018, pp. 1723–1728, doi: 10.1109/EDUCON.2018.8363442.

[12] G. Wedemann, "Scrum as a Method of Teaching Software Architecture," in *Proceedings of the 3rd European Conference of Software engineering Education*, 2018, pp. 108–112, doi: 10.1145/3209087.3209096.

[13] I. Bosnić, F. Ciccozzi, I. Čavrak, E. Di Nitto, J. Feljan, and R. Mirandola, "Introducing SCRUM into a Distributed Software Development Course," 2015, doi: 10.1145/2797433.2797469.

[14] J. J. Chen and M. M. Wu, "Integrating extreme programming with software engineering education," in *38th International Convention on Information and Communication Technology, Electronics and Microelectronics*, 2015, pp. 577–582, doi: 10.1109/MIPRO.2015.7160338.

[15] B. S. Akpolat and W. Slany, "Enhancing software engineering student team engagement in a high-intensity extreme programming course using gamification," in *27th Conference on Software engineering Education and Training*, 2014, pp. 149–153, doi: 10.1109/CSEET.2014.6816792.

[16] V. Mahnic, "Scrum in software engineering courses: An outline of the literature," *Glob. J. Eng. Educ.*, vol. 17, no. 2, pp. 77–83, 2015.

[17] S. Al-Ratrout, "Impact of using Agile Methods in Software engineering Education: A Case Study," in *2019 6th International Conference on Control, Decision and Information Technologies (CoDIT)*, 2019, pp. 1986–1991, doi: 10.1109/CoDIT.2019.8820377.

[18] S. Beecham, T. Clear, D. Damian, J. Barr, J. Noll, and W. Scacchi, "How Best to Teach Global Software engineering? Educators Are Divided," *IEEE Softw.*, vol. 34, no. 1, pp. 16–19, 2017, doi: 10.1109/MS.2017.12.

[19] Digital.ai, "14th annual state of agile report," 2020. https://stateofagile.com/ (accessed Aug. 20, 2020).

[20] OutSystems, "State of Application Development Report," 2019.

[21] M. Kropp, A. Meier, C. Anslow, and R. Biddle, "Satisfaction, Practices, and Influences in Agile Software Development," in *Proceedings of the 22nd International Conference on Evaluation and Assessment in Software engineering*, 2018, pp. 112–121, doi: 10.1145/3210459.3210470.

[22] F. Kamei, G. Pinto, B. Cartaxo, and A. Vasconcelos, "On the Benefits/Limitations of Agile Software Development: An Interview Study with Brazilian Companies," in *Proceedings of the 21st International Conference on Evaluation and Assessment in Software engineering*, 2017, pp. 154–159, doi: 10.1145/3084226.3084278.

[23] Marqual IT Solutions Pvt. Ltd (KBV Research), "Global Low-Code Development Platform Market By Component By Application By Deployment Type By End User By Region, Industry Analysis and Forecast, 2020 - 2026," Report, 2020. [Online]. Available: https://www.kbvresearch.com/low-code-development-platform-market/.

[24] OutSystems, "Low-Code Development Platforms," 2019. https://www.outsystems.com/low-code-platforms/ (accessed Jul. 30, 2020).

[25] C. Boulton, "What is low-code development? A Lego-like approach to building software," *CIO (13284045)*, 2019. http://search.ebscohost.com/login.aspx?direct=true&db=bth&AN=134645048&site=eds-live (accessed Aug. 07, 2020).

[26] J. Idle, "Low-Code rapid application development - So, what's it all about?," *Platinum Business Magazine*, pp 52–53, 2016.

[27] J. R. Rymer and R. Koplowitz, "The Forrester Wave™: Low-Code Development Platforms For AD&D Professionals, Q1 2019," 2019.

[28] I. Media, "Agile is as agile does. Understanding the role of agile development and low-code solutions in the delivery of digital transformation." Incisive Media, 2018.

[29] T. Huff, "Adapting Agile to Build Products with Low-Code: Tips and Tricks," 2019. https://www.outsystems.com/blog/posts/adapting-agile-to-low-code/ (accessed Jul. 28, 2020).

[30] J. Metrôlho and F. Ribeiro, "Software engineering Education: Sharing an approach, experiences, survey and lessons learned," in *Thirteenth International Conference on Software engineering Advances*, 2018, pp. 79–84.

[31] T. Huff, "Agile and Scrum: Understanding the Differences," 2019. https://www.outsystems.com/blog/posts/agile-and-scrum/ (accessed Jul. 12, 2020).

Integrating Two Metaprogramming Environments: An Explorative Case Study

Herwig Mannaert
University of Antwerp
Antwerp, Belgium
Email: herwig.mannaert@uantwerp.be

Chris McGroarty
U.S. Army Combat Capabilities Development Command Soldier Center (CCDC SC)
Orlando, Florida, USA
Email: christopher.j.mcgroarty.civ@mail.mil

Scott Gallant
Effective Applications Corporation
Orlando, Florida, USA
Email: Scott@EffectiveApplications.com

Koen De Cock
NSX BV
Niel, Belgium
Email: koen.de.cock@nsx.normalizedsystems.org

***Abstract*—The automated generation of source code, often referred to as metaprogramming, has been pursued for decades in computer programming. Though many such metaprogramming environments have been proposed and implemented, scalable collaboration within and between such environments remains challenging. It has been argued in previous work that a meta-circular metaprogramming architecture, where the the metaprogramming code (re)generates itself, enables a more scalable collaboration and easier integration. In this contribution, an explorative case study is performed to integrate this meta-circular architecture with another metaprogramming environment. Some preliminary results from applying this approach in practice are presented and discussed.**

***Index Terms*—Evolvability; Normalized Systems; Simulation Models; Automated programming; Case Study**

I. Introduction

The automated generation of source code, often referred to as automatic programming or metaprogramming, has been pursued for decades in computer programming. Though the increase of programming productivity has always been an important goal of automatic programming, its value is of course not limited to development productivity. Various disciplines like systems engineering, modeling, simulation, and business process design could reap significant benefits from metaprogramming techniques.

While many implementations of such automatic programming or metaprogramming exist, many people believe that automatic programming has yet to reach its full potential [1][2]. Moreover, where large-scale collaboration in a single metaprogramming environment is not straightforward, realizing such a scalable collaboration between different metaprogramming environments is definitely challenging.

In our previous work [3], we have presented a meta-circular implementation of a metaprogramming environment, and have argued that this architecture enables a scalable collaboration between various metaprogramming projects. In this contribution, we perform an explorative case study to perform a first integration with another metaprogramming environment. To remain generic, the two metaprogramming environments are aimed at generative programming for completely different types of software systems, and based on totally different meta-models. At the same time, they are suited for this study, as they both pursue a more horizontal integration architecture.

The remainder of this paper is structured as follows. In Section II, we briefly present some aspects and terminology with regard to metaprogramming, and argue the relevance of two related concepts: meta-circularity and systems integration. In Section III, we explain the need for collaborative metaprogramming and the issues that need to be solved. Section IV presents the architecture and meta-model of both metaprogramming environments whose integration is explored in this contribution. Section V elaborates on the possible integration of these metaprogramming environments, detailing the possibilities, progress, and remaining issues. Finally, we present some conclusions in Section VI.

II. Metaprogramming, Meta-Circularity, and Systems Integration

The automatic generation of source code is probably as old as software programming itself, and is in general referred to by various names. *Automatic programming*, stresses the act of automatically generating source code from a model or template, and has been called "a euphemism for programming in a higher-level language than was then available to the programmer" by David Parnas [4]. *Generative programming*, "to manufacture software components in an automated way" [5], emphasizes the manufacturing aspect and the similarity to production and the industrial revolution. *Metaprogramming*, sometimes described as a programming technique in which "computer programs have the ability to treat other programs as their data" [6], stresses the fact that this is an activity situated at the meta-level, i.e., writing software programs that write software programs.

Academic papers on metaprogramming based on intermediate representations or *Domain Specific Languages (DSLs)*, e.g., [7], focus in general on a specific implementation. Also related to metaprogramming are software development methodologies such as *Model-Driven Engineering (MDE)* and *Model-Driven Architecture (MDA)*, requiring and/or implying the availability of tools for the automatic generation of source code. Today, these model-driven code generation tools are often referred to as *Low-Code Development Platforms (LCDP)*, i.e., software that enables developers to create application software through configuration instead of traditional programming. This field is still evolving and facing criticisms, as some question whether these platforms are suitable for large-scale and mission-critical enterprise applications [1], while others even question whether these platforms actually make development cheaper or easier [2]. Moreover, defining an intermediate representation or reusing DSLs is still a subject of research today. We mention the contributions of Wortmann [8], presenting a novel conceptual model for the systematic reuse of DSLs, and Gusarov et. al. [9], proposing an intermediate representation to be used for code generation.

Concepts somewhat related to metaprogramming are homoiconicity and meta-circularity. Both concepts refer to some kind of circular behavior, and are also aimed at the increase of the abstraction level, and thereby the productivity of computer programming. Homoiconicity is specifically associated with a language that can be manipulated as data using that language, and traces back to the design of the language TRAC [10], and to similar concepts in an earlier paper from McIlroy [11]. Meta-circularity, first coined by Reynolds describing his meta-circular interpreter [12], expresses the fact that there is a connection or feedback loop between the meta-level, the internal model of the language, and the actual models or code expressed in the language. Such circular properties have the potential to be highly beneficial for metaprogramming, as they could enable a unified view on both the metaprogramming code and the generated source code, thereby reducing the complexity for the metaprogrammers.

Based on a generic engineering concept, systems integration in information technology refers to the process of linking together different computing systems and software applications, to act as a coordinated whole. Systems integration is becoming a pervasive concern, as more and more systems are designed to connect to other systems, both within and between organizations. Due to the many, often disparate, metaprogramming environments and tools in practice, we argue that systems integration should be explored and pursued more at the metaprogramming level. Just as traditional systems integration often focuses on increasing value to the customer [13], systems integration at the metaprogramming level could provide value to their customers, i.e., the software developers.

III. Toward Scalable Collaborative Metaprogramming

Something all implementations of automatic programming or metaprogramming have in common, is that they perform a transformation from domain models and/or intermediate models to code generators and programming code. In general,

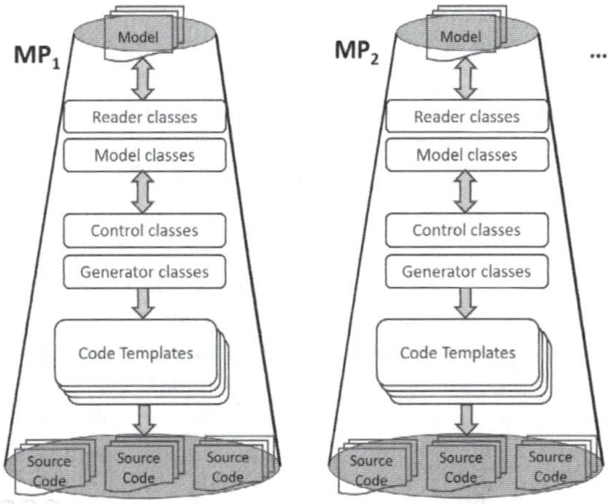

Fig. 1. Representation of the duplication of metaprogramming silos.

metaprogramming or code generation environments also exhibit a rather straightforward internal structure. This structure is schematically represented for a single metaprogramming environment at the left side of Figure 1, and consists of:

- *model files* containing the model parameters.
- *reader classes* to read the model files.
- *model classes* to represent the model parameters.
- *control classes* selecting and invoking the different generator classes.
- *generator classes* instantiating the source templates, and feeding the model parameters to the source templates.
- *source templates* containing the parameterised code.

Another metaprogramming environment will have a similar internal structure, as schematically represented at the right side of Figure 1. Such similar but duplicated architectures exhibit a *vertical integration* architecture. In this architecture, the functional entities are also referred to as *silos*, and metaprogramming silos entail several significant drawbacks. First, it is hard to collaborate between the different metaprogramming silos, as both the nature of the models and the code generators will be different. Second, contributing to the metaprogramming environment will require programmers to learn the internal structure of the model and control classes in the metaprogramming code. As metaprogamming code is intrinsically abstract, this is in general not a trivial task. And third, as contributions of individual programmers will be spread out across the models, readers, control classes, and actual coding templates, it will be a challenge to maintain a consistent decoupling between these different concerns.

We have argued in our previous work that in order to achieve productive and scalable adoption of automatic programming techniques, some fundamental issues need to be addressed [14][3]. First, to cope with the increasing complexity due to changes, we have proposed to combine automatic programming with the evolvability approach of *Normalized Systems Theory (NST)* providing (re)generation of the recurring structure and re-injection of the custom code [14]. Second, to avoid the growing burden of maintaining the often complex meta-code and continuously adapting it to new technologies, we have proposed a meta-circular architecture to regenerate the metaprogramming code itself as well [3]. We will go into some more detail on NST and the corresponding metaprogramming environment in the next section.

As this meta-circular architecture establishes a clear decoupling between the models and the code generation templates [3], it allows for the definition of programming interfaces at both ends of the transformation. This should remove the need for contributors to get acquainted with the internal structure of the metaprogramming environment. It also enables a more *horizontal integration* architecture, by allowing developers to collaborate on both sides of the interface. Modelers and designers are able to collaborate on models, gradually improving existing model versions and variants, and adding on a regular basis new functional modules. (Meta)programmers can collaborate on coding templates, gradually improving and integrating new insights and coding techniques, adding and improving implementations of cross-cutting concerns, and providing support for modified and/or new technologies and frameworks. Moreover, an horizontal integration architecture could facilitate collaboration between two metaprogramming environments. Exploring such a collaboration is the purpose of the case study in this paper.

IV. Structure of the Metaprogramming Environments

In this section, we present the architectures and meta-models of the two metaprogramming environments considered in this integration case study. The first metaprogramming environment is the NST meta-circular architecture, as it explicitly aims to realize horizontal integration and scalable collaboration. The second metaprogramming environment is concerned with a completely different application domain, i.e., models for simulation systems, and is based on a totally different meta-model. However, by clearly separating the modeling in the front-end from the generative programming in the back-end, it is also pursuing a more horizontal integration architecture.

A. Normalized Systems Elements Metaprogramming

Normalized Systems Theory (NST), theoretically founded on the concept of *stability* from systems theory, was proposed to provide an ex-ante proven approach to build evolvable software [14][15][16]. The theory prescribes a set of theorems (*Separation of Concerns*, *Action Version Transparency*, *Data Version Transparency*, and *Separation of States*) and formally proves that any violation of any of the preceding *theorems* will result in combinatorial effects thereby hampering evolvability. As the application of the theorems in practice has shown to result in very fine-grained modular structures, it is in general difficult to achieve by manual programming. Therefore, the theory also proposes a set of design patterns to generate the main building blocks of (web-based) information systems [14], called the *NS elements*: *data element*, *action element*, *workflow element*, *connector element*, and *trigger element*.

An information system is defined as a set of instances of these elements, and the NST metaprogramming environment instantiates for every element instance the corresponding design pattern. This generated or so-called *expanded* boiler plate code is in general complemented with custom code or *craftings* to add non-standard functionality, such as user screens and business logic. This custom code can be automatically *harvested* from within the anchors, and *re-injected* when the recurring element structures are regenerated.

While the NST metaprogramming environment was originally implemented in a traditional metaprogramming silo as represented in Figure 1, it has been evolved recently into a meta-circular architecture [3]. This meta-circular architecture, described in [3] and schematically represented in Figure 2, enables both the regeneration of the metaprogramming code

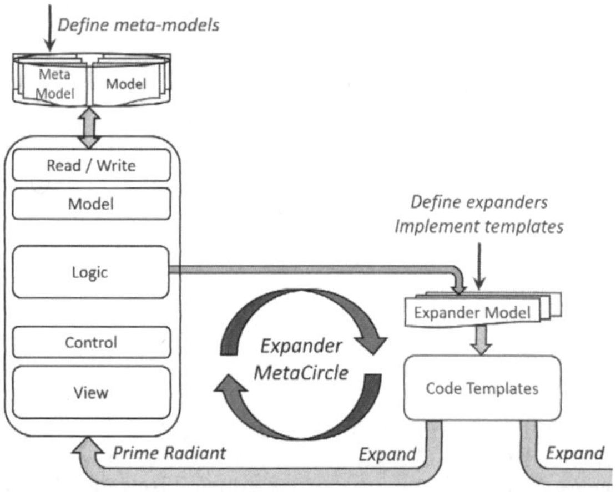

Fig. 2. Closing the meta-circle for expanders and meta-application.

itself, and allows for a structural decoupling between the two sides of the transformation, i.e., the domain models and the code generating templates.

The domain models for the web-based information systems are specified as sets of instances of the various types of NS elements. While these elements can be entered in a meta-application and/or graphical modeler, they are formally specified in XML files, whose structure is defined in a corresponding XML Schema.

As the NS meta-model is just another NS model [3], the various types of elements can be specified in XML files, just like any other instance of a data element. Aimed at the automatic programming of multi-tier *web-based information systems*, the meta-model of the NST metaprogramming environment is a model for web-based information systems.

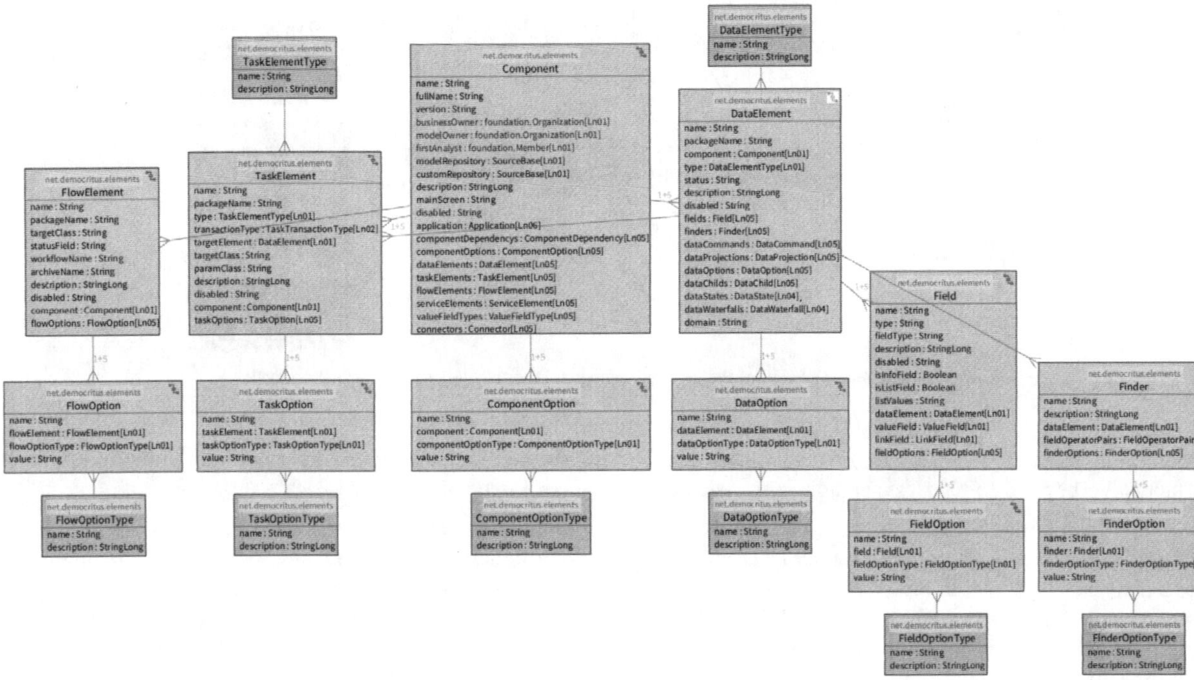

Fig. 3. A graphical representation of the core part the NS (data) meta-model.

The core data model of this metaprogramming environment is represented in Figure 3. This graphical representation, a screenshot from the *NST Modeler* tool, is similar to most *ERD (Entity Relationship Diagram)* visualizations, but uses colors to distinguish between different types of data entities [17]. The unit of an NS model is a *component*, and within such a component model, we distinguish the various types of NS elements [14], such as *Data elements*, *Task elements*, and *Flow elements*. These elements, colored light blue and located in the top row, can have options, e.g., *Task options*. Both the entities representing elements and their corresponding options, are characterized by a typing or taxonomy entity, e.g., *Task element type* or *Task option type*, represented in light red. The data elements contain a numer of attributes or *Fields*, where a field can be either a data attributes or a relationship link, and provide a number of *Finders*. Both fields and finders can have options characterized by corresponding option types.

Every individual code generator or *NS expander* is declared in an `Expander` XML file, specifying for instance the type of element it belongs to, and the various properties of the source artifact that it generates. For every such artifact expander, one needs to provide a coding `Template`, based on the *StringTemplate (ST)* engine library, and an XML expander `Mapping` file, specifying the various template parameters in terms of model parameters through *Object-Graph Navigation Language (OGNL)* expressions.

B. Generative Programming of Simulation Models

The United States Army has developed and documented hundreds of approved models for representing behaviors and systems, often separate from the simulation environments where they are to be implemented. The manual translation of these models into actual simulation environments by software developers, leads to implementation errors and verification difficulties, and is unable to avoid the workload of incorporating these models into other simulation environments.

In order to address these potential drawbacks, a generative programming approach is being examined, aiming to capture military-relevant models within an executable systems engineering format, and to facilitate authoritative models to operate within multiple platforms. The goal of this work is to be able to capture authoritative conceptual models and then to generate software to implement those representations/behaviors. This generated software can be quickly integrated into multiple simulations regardless of their programming language thereby saving development cost and improving the consistency across simulation systems.

The architecture of this metaprogramming environment, schematically represented in Figure 4, divides the problem into two domains, i.e., the front-end and the back-end. In the front-end, corresponding to the conceptual models at the left column, the *Subject Matter Experts (SME)*, scientists, and software model developers are able record the model definitions and behaviors or algorithms. In the back-end, represented in the three other columns, those model definitions and algorithms are transformed through templating and metaprogramming into executable code, targeted at specific architectures and implementations. To properly decouple these parts, an *Interchange Format (IF)* was created that allows one or more front-ends to be created to record models in a way that

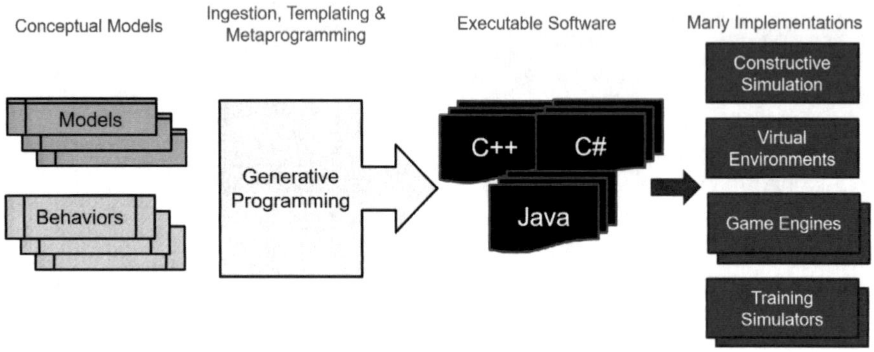

Fig. 4. Schematic representation of the generative programming architecture for simulation models.

suits the needs of the front-end user community, and to pass those models to be used for code generation in the back-end.

The interchange format between the front-end and the back-end is based on XML documents, whose structure is defined by an XML Schema or *XSD (XML Schema Definition Language)*. This interchange format structure, i.e., the XSD, is called the *Synthetic Training Environment (STE) Canonical Universal Format (SCUF)*.

This meta-model is not intended to support a full programming language, but rather to focus on the domain elements used within the U.S. Army's canonical descriptions of the simulation models. Nevertheless, it represents most concepts of a traditional procedural programming language. Specifically, these include the data type declarations, datastores, and various elements of algorithms, such as conditions, expressions and iterators. Figure 5 provides a class diagram of the SCUF meta-model, anew similar to most ERD visualizations.

To capture the human readable text of the canonical simulation model descriptions along with executable code in the front-end, the generative programming environment uses *PyFlow* [18], which is an open source project that is similar to other visual scripting frameworks including Unity's Bolt or Playmaker [19], and Unreal's Blueprints [20]. The U.S. Army added custom additions to PyFlow that includes both the ability to execute the models, as well as the capability to generate the *SCUF code*, the interchange format to transfer the model from the front-end to the back-end. The back-end code generator uses the *Apache Velocity* templating engine to create the output files in multiple programming languages (C#, C++, and Java currently).

V. Toward Integrating the Metaprogramming Environments

The two metaprogramming environments target the automatic programming of two different types of software systems: multi-tier web-based information systems, and executable (army) models for simulation systems. Consequently, the two metaprogramming environments have a completely different meta-model. Moreover, both the front-end technologies capturing the models, and the target programming languages —even the code templating engines— are different.

What both metaprogramming environments have in common is a structured decoupling between the definition of models and the generation of code. Moreover, the interchange format of the models is in both environments based on XML documents, whose structure is defined by an XML schema. This means that it is conceptually possible to map the generative programming environment for simulation models onto the collaboration architecture represented in Figure 2.

A. Embracing the SCUF Meta-Model

The NST meta-circular metaprogramming environment allows for the structural generation of all reader, writer, and model classes of any model —or meta-model— that can be expressed as a set of NST data elements. The SCUF meta-model, based on XML and defined by an XML Schema, satisfies this requirement. Based on the definition of the SCUF data entities (as represented in the class diagram of Figure 5, e.g., *TypeDefinition*, *DatastoreType*, *ConditionalBlock*, *Expression*, *Declare*, *Statement*, etcetera), NST data elements can be created. For instance, *Statement* needs to be defined as an NST data element with a *name* field which is a string, a *type* field that is a link to the *TypeDefinition* data element, and an *expression* field that is a link to the *Expression* data element. These data elements can be specified in XML, or in the user interface of the NST meta-application, or even directly generated from the XML Schema. For every data element, the various classes of the NST stack in the left part of Figure 2 can be generated. These include:

- Reader and writer classes to read and write the XML-based SCUF files, e.g., *StatementXmlReader* and *StatementXmlWriter*.
- Model classes to represent and transfer the various SCUF entities, and to make them available as an object graph, e.g., *StatementDetails* and *StatementComposite*.
- View and control classes to perform *CRUDS (create, retrieve, update, delete, search)* operations in a generated table-based user interface.

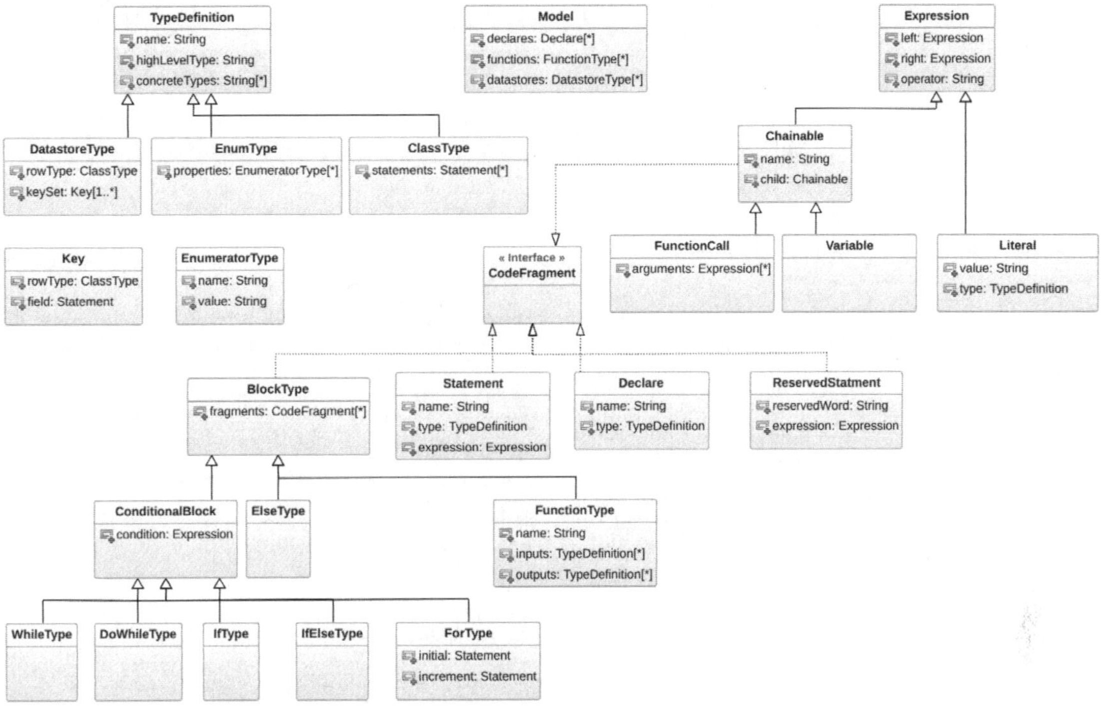

Fig. 5. A graphical representation of the core part the SCUF (data) meta-model.

This implies that the various existing SCUF models, representing instances of the SCUF data entities and therefore instances of the NST data elements, can be read and made available as an object graph, allowing to evaluate model parameters using *Object-Graph Navigation Language (OGNL)* expressions at the emplating engine. Moreover, an additional application with a table-based user interface is available to create, view, manipulate, and write SCUF models.

B. Supporting the Templating Engine

Having defined the SCUF data entities as NST data elements, the NST metaprogramming environment allows to evaluate SCUF model parameters through OGNL expressions in SCUF model graphs, and to make them available to coding templates. In order to simply activate the existing coding templates of the simulation models, and to use the NST metaprogramming environment as a piece of evolvable middleware to pass the SCUF models to the code templates for the simulation models, two tasks remain to be performed.

- Every coding template needs to be declared in a separate XML *Expander* definition.
- For every coding template, the appropriate OGNL expressions to evaluate the relevant model parameters, need to be defined in an XML *Mapping* file.

The fact that both metaprogramming environments use different templating engines causes a final integration issue. A first option would be to convert the *Velocity* templates of the simulation software to the *StringTemplate* format supported by the NST environment. In this scenario, the required effort would be proportional to the template base of the simulation models, and would need to be repeated for integration efforts with other environments using this templating engine. Moreover, *Velocity* templates allow more logic that would have to be ported to Java helper classes in the *StringTemplate* environment.

A second and preferable option is to include support in the NST metaprogramming environment for the *Velocity* templating engine. Considering the limited amount of templating engines being used by metaprogrammers, this scenario seems both manageable and worthwhile. Moreover, the effort would not be proportional to the size of the template base. And as there is virtually no logic in the current NST templates, i.e., all model parameters are combined and processed in the software that feeds the templating engine, it is reasonable to say that we expect no major blocking issues.

VI. Conclusion

The automated generation of source code, often referred to as metaprogramming, has been pursued for decades in computer programming, and is considered to entail significant benefits for various disciplines, including software development, systems engineering, modeling, simulation, and business process design. However, we have argued that metaprogramming is still facing several issues, including the fact that it is challenging to realize a scalable collaboration within and between different metaprogramming environments due, to the often vertical integration architecture.

In our previous work, we have presented a meta-circular implementation of a metaprogramming environment, and have argued that this architecture enables a scalable collaboration, both within this environment and possibly with other metaprogramming environments. In this paper, we have explored such a collaborative integration with another metaprogramming environment. This second environment for metaprogramming targets the generation of a different type of software systems, and is based on a different meta-model, but also exhibits a more horizontal integration architecture.

We have shown in this contribution how both metaprogramming environments can be integrated within the proposed meta-circular architecture, by extending the generation of the meta-code, i.e., the code that makes the actual parameter models available to the coding templates, to the second metaprogramming environement. We have explained that the only reason that the coding templates of this second metaprogramming environment cannot be seamlessly integrated yet, is that they use another templating engine. However, we have also indicated that it should be relatively straightforward to support this alternative templating engine.

This paper is believed to make some contributions. First, we show that it is possible to perform an horizontal integration of two metaprogramming environments, and to enable collaboration and re-use between these environments. Such integrations could significantly improve the collaboration and productivity at the metaprogramming level. Moreover, we show that this integration is possible between metaprogramming environments that are based on completely different meta-models. Second, we explain that the horizontal integration of a second metaprogramming environment with the meta-circular architecture, could largely remove the burden of maintaining the internal classes of this metaprogramming environment.

Next to these contributions, it is clear that this paper is also subject to a number of limitations. It consists of a single case of integrating a second metaprogramming environment with the meta-circular architecture. Moreover, the presented results are quite preliminary, and the second metaprogramming environment is not yet operational in the meta-circular architecture, as its templating engine is not yet supported in this architecture. Therefore, neither the complete horizontal integration, nor the productive collaboration between the two environments has actually been proven. However, this explorative case study can be seen as an architectural pathfinder, and we are planning to both broaden and deepen the collaboration on the horizontal integration of different metaprogramming environments.

REFERENCES

[1] J. R. Rymer and C. Richardson, "Low-code platforms deliver customer-facing apps fast, but will they scale up?" Forrester Research, Tech. Rep., 08 2015.

[2] B. Reselman, "Why the promise of low-code software platforms is deceiving," TechTarget, Tech. Rep., 05 2019.

[3] H. Mannaert, K. De Cock, and P. Uhnak, "On the realization of meta-circular code generation: The case of the normalized systems expanders," in Proceedings of the Fourteenth International Conference on Software Engineering Advances (ICSEA) 2019, 2019, pp. 171–176.

[4] D. Parnas, "Software aspects of strategic defense systems," Communications of the ACM, vol. 28, no. 12, 1985, pp. 1326–1335.

[5] P. Cointe, "Towards generative programming," Unconventional Programming Paradigms. Lecture Notes in Computer Science, vol. 3566, 2005, pp. 86–100.

[6] K. Czarnecki and U. W. Eisenecker, Generative programming: methods, tools, and applications. Reading, MA, USA: Addison-Wesley, 2000.

[7] L. Tratt, "Domain specific language implementation via compile-time meta-programming," ACM transactions on programming languages and system, vol. 30, no. 6, 2008, pp. 1–40.

[8] A. Wortmann, "Towards component-based development of textual domain-specific languages," in Proceedings of the Fourteenth International Conference on Software Engineering Advances (ICSEA) 2019, 2019, pp. 68–73.

[9] K. Gusarovs and O. Nikiforova, "An intermediate model for the code generation from the two-hemisphere model," in Proceedings of the Fourteenth International Conference on Software Engineering Advances (ICSEA) 2019, 2019, pp. 74–82.

[10] C. Mooers and L. Deutsch, "Trac, a text-handling language," in ACM '65 Proceedings of the 1965 20th National Conference, 1965, pp. 229–246.

[11] D. McIlroy, "Macro instruction extensions of compiler languages," Communications of the ACM, vol. 3, no. 4, 1960, pp. 214–220.

[12] J. Reynolds, "Definitional interpreters for higher-order programming languages," Higher-Order and Symbolic Computation, vol. 11, no. 4, 1998, pp. 363–397.

[13] M. Vonderembse, T. Raghunathan, and S. Rao, "A post-industrial paradigm: To integrate and automate manufacturing," International Journal of Production Research, vol. 35, no. 9, 1997, p. 2579–2600.

[14] H. Mannaert, J. Verelst, and P. De Bruyn, Normalized Systems Theory: From Foundations for Evolvable Software Toward a General Theory for Evolvable Design. Koppa, 2016.

[15] H. Mannaert, J. Verelst, and K. Ven, "The transformation of requirements into software primitives: Studying evolvability based on systems theoretic stability," Science of Computer Programming, vol. 76, no. 12, 2011, pp. 1210–1222, special Issue on Software Evolution, Adaptability and Variability.

[16] ——, "Towards evolvable software architectures based on systems theoretic stability," Software: Practice and Experience, vol. 42, no. 1, 2012, pp. 89–116.

[17] P. De Bruyn, H. Mannaert, J. Verelst, and P. Huysmans, "Enabling normalized systems in practice : exploring a modeling approach," Business & information systems engineering, vol. 60, no. 1, 2018, pp. 55–67.

[18] M. Senthilvel and J. Beetz, "A visual programming approach for validating linked building data." [Online]. Available: https://publications.rwth-aachen.de/record/795561/files/795561.pdf

[19] "How to make a video game without any coding experience." [Online]. Available: https://unity.com/how-to/make-games-without-programming

[20] B. Sewell, Blueprints Visual Scripting for Unreal Engine. Packt Publishing, 2015.

Computer-Project-Ontology

Construction, Validation and Choice of Knowledge Base

Raja Hanafi
National School of Computer Science
University of Manouba
Manouba, Tunisia
e-mail : rajarajahanafi@yahoo.com

Lassad Mejri
Faculty of Science of Bizerte
Carthage University
Bizerte, Tunisia
e-mail : Mejrilassad@gmail.com

Henda Hajjami Ben Ghezala
National School of Computer
University of Manouba,
Manouba, Tunisia
e-mail : hhbg.hhbg@gmail.com

Abstract—**The ontology design has developed within the framework of approaches of acquisition and capitalization of knowledge. In this case, we are talking about the design of the domain ontology which models the knowledge of a particular domain whose bounded terms are specified, mostly coming from controlled vocabularies. This ontology makes it possible not to encroach on another field of expertise. This has the advantage of being reused for applications designed within a defined domain. In this paper, we propose domain ontology(C-P-Onto: Computer-Project-Ontology) to represent knowledge in the field of computers projects. "Protégé" tool is the most popular and widely used tool for ontology development. Thus, we use this device for developing, validating and questioning the proposed ontology. In order to test it in a real field, the "HAL" will be applied as our knowledge base.**

Keywords-Computer project; Knowledge Capitalisation; Domain Ontology; Ontology Test; Ontology Validation.

I. INTRODUCTION

Recently, project management has been well established in companies, but the project's success in terms of quality, costs and deadlines is still difficult to reach. There are many failures, and one of them is the lack of capitalization of feedback during projects: learn lessons and reuse knowledge or acquired skills. The problem here is that these experiences are not always available in companies. This can be explained by the absence of the concept of capitalization, the lack of structuring of their experiments, or the outflow of experts [1].

During the realization of the projects, particularly the computer ones, project leader encountered many problems during the design phase. In the aim of solving these difficulties, designers either contact the old experts of the company or they look for similar projects in the market [2].

However, this process is not always efficient because it can be a waste of time, an exceeding of deadlines and a rise of cost.

In this context, we will propose a capitalization approach of memory knowledge of computer design projects. This approach presents a supporting decision in the project management phase of the design phase. Our decision-support process will not only help structure, formalize and capitalize knowledge, but also provide a dashboard in the form of indicators, information and a guide for the project leader.

In this paper, we will introduce our approach by focusing on its modeling part which is defined and explained by the proposition of domain ontology. This ontology describes all the concepts and relations associated to the computer project management term. After examining the coherence and the consistency of the proposed ontology, we will move to the process of creating a knowledge base in order to confirm our tests on a real level.

This paper is composed of four major sections. The first Section introduces the main works existing in the literature as well as a comparative study. Then, we describe our proposed approach architecture. The second Section involves the presentation the notion of ontology and the construction of the domain ontology. The third Section presents our analysis and reveals our knowledge base (HAL). The last and the four Section summarizes the main points mentioned in this article and open new horizons for future works.

II. PROPOSED APPROACH

We introduce in the following sub-section some of the most important contributions and capitalization models related to our research study.

A. Literature Review

1) Description Of The Models : In the literatures, various works addressed the project memory models which aim at the capitalization of knowledge and the construction of project memory.

IN [3] Ermine described the knowledge management processes. The proposed processes are based on a model that is called "margerite model". These processes can be internal or external. What interests us is the internal process of capitalization and sharing of knowledge within the company.

Harani [4] presents a design assistance tool whose main objective is the capitalization of knowledge involved in the design of a product for reuse.

Bekhti in [5] proposed a dynamic project definition and reuse process named DyPKM. This approach is based on a method that provides a structured trace of a project memory containing the context in which the design takes place and the logic resolution.

Zacklad [6] propose a groupware "MEMO-net" using the DIPA problem solving method for capitalization and knowledge management in design projects. This groupware is a tool that has two modules (design and diagnostic) that allows a project group to solve problems encountered during the design (capitalization of the design logic) and to preserve the characteristics related to such a product.

Serrano [7] proposed a global system of capitalization of knowledge allowing the actors of the company to exploit the important mass of information. This system also makes it possible to capitalize events in the field of Open Source Intelligence (OSI) based on the Web Lab platform.

2) Comparative Study Of The Studied Approaches : After we have studied these different approaches, we decided to propose our own classification (Table I). This comparative study is based on a set of criteria, namely:

- Simplicity of the method: This criteria means that the models must be used in an easy way and without the intervention of any other methods.
- Resource: Includes the data representing the constraints to be considered and the data of the project organization. The resource used in our contribution must be the memory project.
- Application domain: This criterion gives a global vision on the field of application. In our research study, we focus on the field of computer projects.
- Use of case based reasoning (CBR): We have introduced this criterion because we believe that it is crucial to use the CBR in the learning part.
- Capitalization level: This criterion is proposed in order to check the importance of the conception level. We try to determine, for each model, the level or the part concerned by the capitalization (context, design, realization, etc).

TABLE I. COMPARATIVE STUDY OF APPROACHES

Model	Simplicity of the method	Resource	Application domain	Use of (CBR)	Capitalization level
Ermine's process [3]	Complex (marguerite model)	Corporate memory	Area of economy	No	Design
Zacklad 's model [6]	Complex Collective Software (DIPA)	Diverse	For all design projects	No	Conception and context
Serrano [7]	Global + wave (weblab platform)	Open source (blog, internet, site,etc)	Field of defense	No	Event
Harani Model [4]	Simple help tool	Company knowledge	Computer, mechanical, industrial	No	Design + Feature
Bekhti model [5]	Simple process	Project memory	Design project (all areas)	No	Context + design rational

Based on our comparative study we will define in the next section our approach to capitalize knowledge of project memory. This approach aims to provide decision support in project management from the design phase to the implementation.

B. Towards a knowledge Capitalization Approach

Our goal is to present an approach that helps the leader to deal with its new project by referring to the experiences and knowledge which are stored in a project memory. This section introduces the architecture of our approach and in particular the modeling part which is composed of three models: the project class model, the project model and the rational design model. The architecture of our approach contained three main parts (Fig.1):

- The offline process: It is from modelization (models + ontology) to the project excavation. This part starts with the proposal of the models to identify and to classify projects.
- An online process: It is from the acquisition of new project until the project learning. This part presents CBR reasoning cycle, which are development, remembering, adaptation, revision, validation and learning.
- A base case: It contains all the instances of the ontology, projects, project classes, problems, solutions and suggestion.

In the following subsections we will start with the offline process description. We will explain the proposed models namely project model, project class model and rational design model, and then we will introduce the proposed ontology.

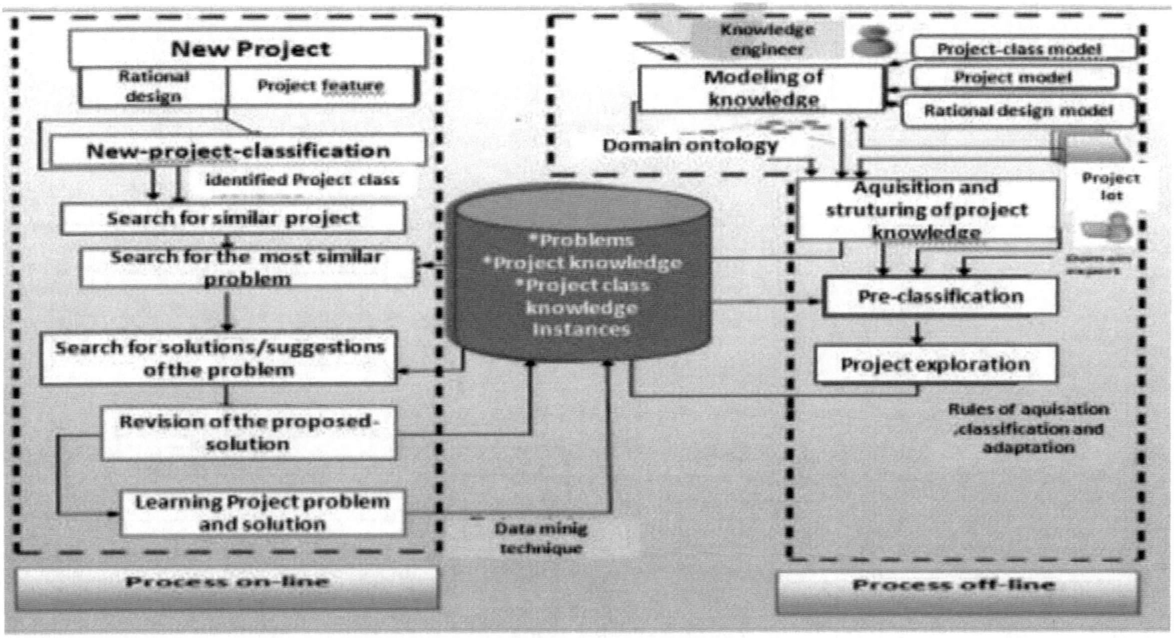

Figure 1. Architecture of the proposed approach.

1) The Project Class Model : In the same organization, we can distinguish different classes of computer project such as security, software engineering, imaging, data base, artificial intelligence, etc. It is in this context, that we propose this model to allow the leader to classify, from the beginning, the project. This process can be done by specifying the project knowledge, its resolution method such as Scrum [8] and Pert [9], its reasoning rule and its architecture.

The Project class model (Fig.2) is composed of three elements:

- Project class: This element is composed of two lists: a list of projects belonging to the same class, and a list of common denominators such as rules and keywords.
- Project class knowledge: All the knowledge related to the project class in question are associated to all the rules used in the reasoning phase for this type of project class.
- Point of view: This component presents the method of conducting project class and the type of architecture used.

2) The project model: We have proposed this model to identify the project itself. When the user is in front of a new project he will first determine the characteristics of each project. These will be used as indexes to select similar ones. The proposed project model (Fig. 2) has three dimensions. The choice of components of this model is inspired from the composition of the project memory:

- Project identifier: This pillar gives general information about the project. It includes the project name, abstract, project team.
- Project features: This component reflects all the characteristics that a project can have during its realization. Among these characteristics, we can quote the size, scope, cost, time, complexity, type, team project, scheduling, etc.
- Deliverable: This class is composed of two sub-classes:

-Type of deliverable: It can be a service, a product (software, hardware), etc.
-Rational design: Contains the list of problems, suggestions and solutions for each computer project.

3) Rational Design Model : Once the project has been identified, the user must see the logical design part to distinguish similar problems and select solutions. For the purpose of presenting this part, we have suggested the design logic model explained below.

The design rationale, in the project memory, consists of modeling the process of decision-making through all the elements characterizing this process. These elements are the problem objects, suggestions, and participants [10]. This model (Fig.2) is presented using three essential components:

- Problem list: Each problem is described by its name, its textual description and its attributes.

- Suggestion list: Before reaching the final solution the designers have proposed a set of suggestion.
- Solution list: For each problem there are one or more solutions that are defined (text) and argued (arguments).

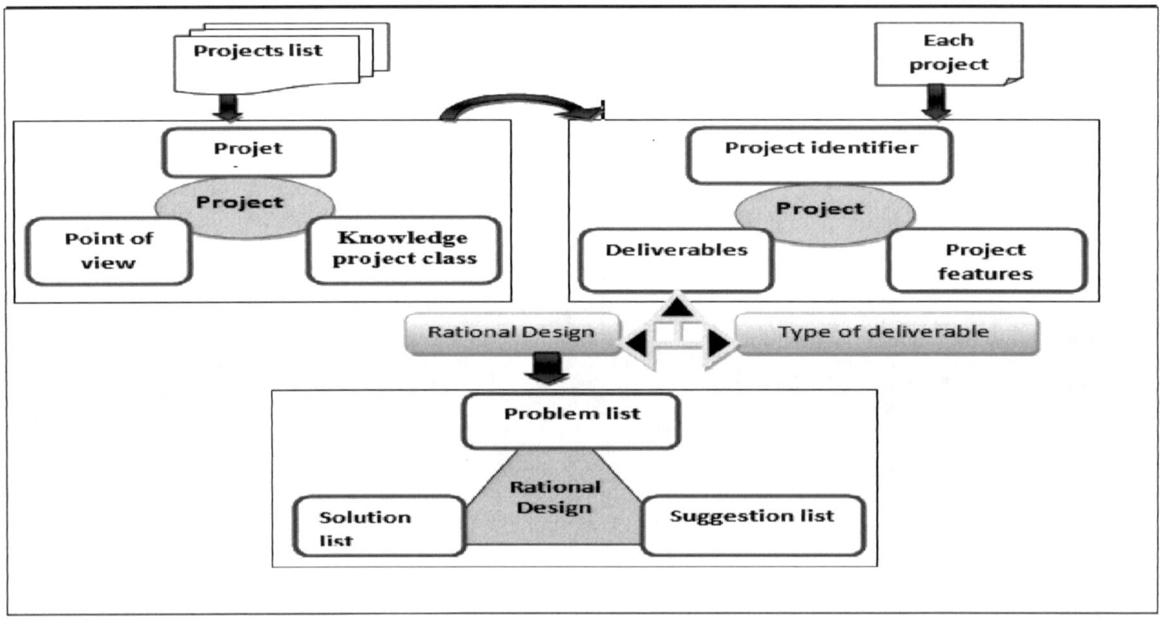

Figure 2. Knowledge Modelisation (Proposed Models)

By studying the components and elements of the proposed models we have noticed that the field of information projects contains a huge quantity of concepts and terms which relate to each other. It is in this context that we decided to present the important mass of this knowledge with one of the techniques of knowledge representation. In this research study, we will propose domain ontology relative to the notion "computer project" in order to present concepts composing this domain and relations between them.

III. Ontology

Using ontology and other related knowledge has also become very important for storing, and managing of huge amount of research data [11]. Ontology is essentially defined by a set of business concepts and relationships. The instantiation of these different concepts gives birth to a new case to study in the future (new project, new thesis).

A. Components Of Ontology

To describe a domain with ontology, knowledge of this domain should be defined by the following five components [13]:

- Concepts: (concepts also called class) representing the meaning of a field of information, whether by the metadata of a namespace or the elements of a given domain of knowledge.
- Relations also called properties: It translates the associations existing between the concepts. These relationships allow us to see the structuring of concepts, the ones compared to the others.
- Function: Presents special case of relations, of which an element of the relation can be defined according to the preceding elements.
- The axioms: Also called rules are used to describe assertions of the ontology in order to define the meaning of the components of the ontology.
- Instance or individual: Constituting the extensional definition of ontology; these objects convey knowledge about the domain of the problem.

A. The Methodology Of Ontology Construction

The construction of ontology is a difficult task requiring the implementation of an elaborate process to extract the knowledge of a domain, manipulated by computer systems and interpreted by human being. There are many methods of ontology construction. Different types of ontology construction approaches are distinguished according to the support on which they are based: from texts, dictionaries, knowledge bases, semi-structured diagrams, relational diagrams, etc. In what follows we present some methods of ontology construction.

- The Text To Into [14] methodology is an application for extracting ontologies from corpora or web documents and it also allows the reuse of existing ontologies.
- The Onto Builder methodology [15] allows us to build ontology from web resources.
- METHONTOLOGY [16] is a structured method to build ontologies from scratch. It is based on the experience acquired in developing ontology in a special domain.
- KACTUS [17] designed to be applied in more general settings. This methodology, which aims to reuse existing ontologies, is interesting since it avoids building an ontology from scratch.

By studying these four methods, we have proposed a new method for the construction of our ontology. Our methodology is based on METHONTOLOGY methodology. It is a method of building ontology from scratch which is related to computer projects domain experiences. To apply the proposed methodology, we will follow these three steps:

1. Choice of the relevant terms of the field, favoring the semantic normalization and specify the relations between the different terms.
2. Formalization of knowledge and the construction of a referential ontology.
3. Evaluation, testing, validation and documentation of the proposed domain ontology. In our situation, we used the ontology editor "Protégé" [18] to formalize our ontology.

C. Basic Steps For Building Ontologies

- Step 1 'classes and class hierarchy': The first step as illustrated in Fig. 3 gives the computer project and management project related classes or concepts. All the concepts shown in the figure are focusing on the project-concept, project-team-project-features and rational-design.
- Step 2 'object properties of ontology (Fig. 4) ': We define it according to relationship which we want to add between classes.
- Step 3 'data properties of ontology': In this step we display data properties of proposed ontology which show the relationship between individuals.
- Step 4: In this step we add the details of the instances, relations, classes and properties. These details present the definition, description and the type of each element.
- Step 5 'the axioms of ontology': Axioms are used to describe the relationship between classes, attributes and individuals.
- Step 6 'the instance of ontology': Defining the instance (individual), first one should select the right class, and then create its instances for the class. The final instantiation of this ontology (individuals + instances) is actually the new case on which our reasoning is based (Fig. 6). They help to establish a common vocabulary to describe the case, or the model knowledge needed to index and organize the event. We have advanced our thesis research topic to instantiate our proposed ontology.
- Step 7 'the reasoning of ontology': To have a consistent ontology and ready to be properly interrogated and without contraction we carried out a reasoning using the automatic reasoner of the "Protégé tool".

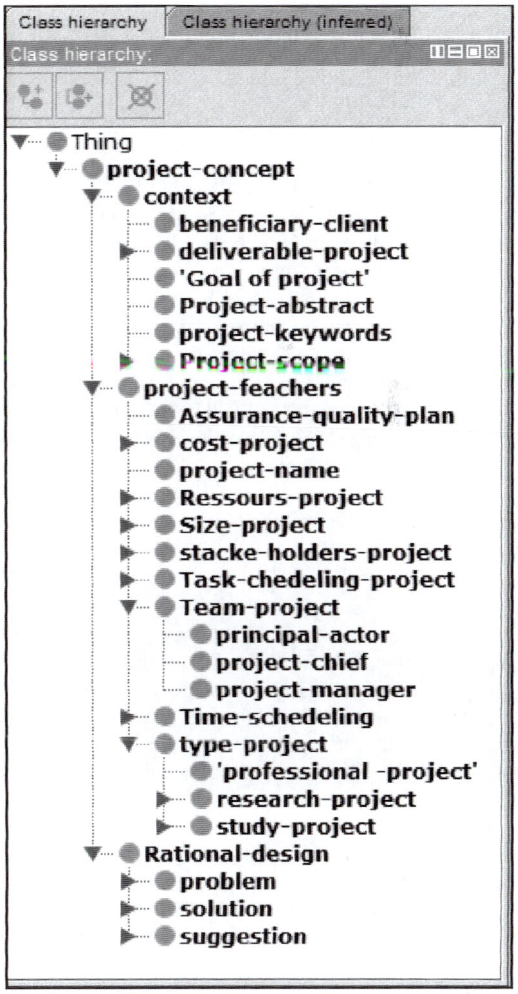

Figure 3. Classes of the Proposed Ontology.

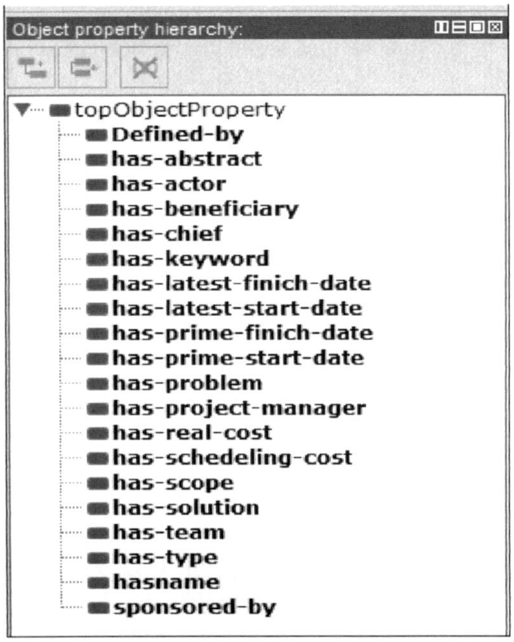

Figure 4. Property and Relationship.

IV. RESULT AND ANALYSIS

In order to validate our ontology (especially the choice of concepts and relations between concepts) we carried out two types of validations:

- A first validation made by a professional who is an expert in the computer field. He is a computer project manager in a company located in France.
- A second validation was made technically by the standard tool "Protégé"[18]. This validation is done using three tests: consistency test, coherence test and query test.

In this section, we will describe the main tests used to verify the coherence and the consistency of the proposed ontology.

A. Knowledge Base

The first goal in this part of the research study is to create a knowledge-base that contains all instances of the concept defined by the proposed ontology. To achieve this goal, we decided to work with real examples of computer research projects. It is in this context that we decided to test our ontology with the help of the dozen end-of-study projects that we have supervised.

The second objective is to be able to question our ontology. This step is also due to two other sub-phases: The validation of the coherence and the consistency of the created ontology. It is in this context that in the following sub-sections we will present our procedures to carry out these tests.

B. Coherence test :Reasoner tab

The great advantage of using Protégé is the possibility of checking whether the ontology created does not contain contradictory definitions. From the Reasoner menu, we can select FaCT++ or HermiT, then select Reasoner or Start Reasoner to classify the active ontology. We can also select Reasoner or Synchronize Reasoner to classify again at any time.

Once we validate that our ontology is classified by selecting the entities tab and then the "Class hierarchy (inferred)" tab that appears in the "Class hierarchy" view. It should contain classes that sub-class Thing. Once we have validated that our ontology is classified, you can execute a query using Dl-Query tab.

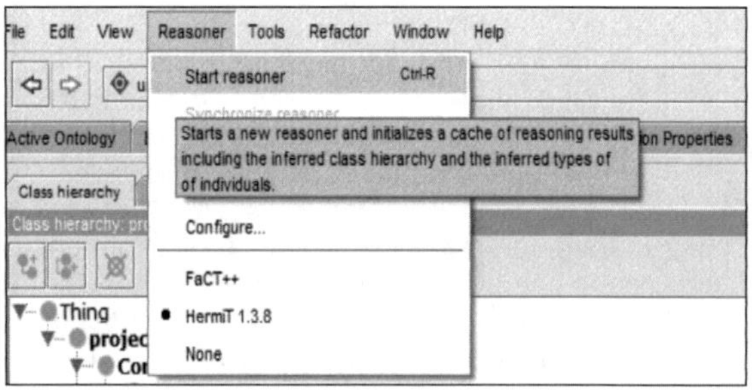

Figure 5. Coherence Test (Ontology ' s Reasoning)

C. Consistency test : Dl-Query tab

We have utilized the DL Query to check the consistency of the ontology hierarchy. The DL-Query tab provides a powerful and easy-to-use feature for searching a classified ontology. So we can only execute a query on a classified ontology. Before attempting to execute a query, we should run a classifier: Using the DL, we can have as a result a list of super classes, subclasses, instances or direct subclasses of a class expression. In our case we have to display all the projects (fig.6) which are instances of the class "project_name". The complete display (without failure) of the results of the query requested shows that our ontology is well classified.

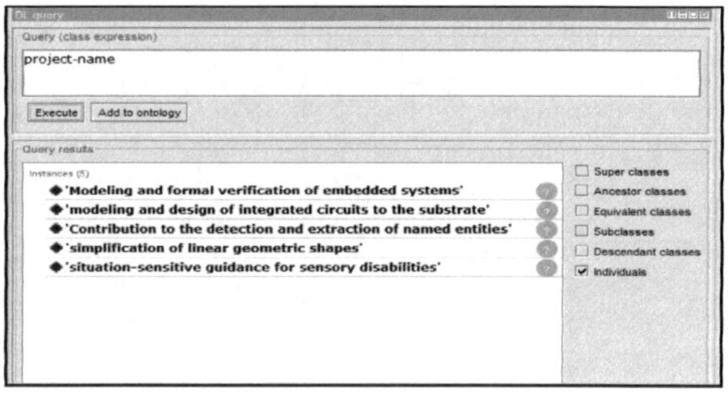

Figure 6. Example of Test With Dl-Query.

D. *Query an ontology via a sparql query Request:*

After we have tested our ontology we can now request it by several methods: either we load it into an RDF database like JENA [19], Sesame [20], Stardog [21], etc, or we can simply use the SPARQL-query (Fig.7) option automatically integrated in the "Protégé tools" [21].

Here we used the SPARQL-query to request our ontology. We have launched an example of a query in SPARQL-query that allows us to display all the classes and subclasses of the created ontology. The result is displayed on two columns "subject and project" as indicated in the request (Fig. 8).

These results are still modest and weak. The application of SPARQL-query does not allow us to display, for example, all individuals of such a class with a given condition. It is in this context that we are going to orient our future work on the interrogation of ontology using API such as JENA and Sesame. In addition, even if our ontology is consistent and well classified but the shortcomings of interrogation by SPARQL-query shows the weakness of inferences especially at the instances level.

SPARQL query:

```
PREFIX rdf: <http://www.w3.org/1999/02/22-rdf-syntax-ns#>
PREFIX owl: <http://www.w3.org/2002/07/owl#>
PREFIX xsd: <http://www.w3.org/2001/XMLSchema#>
PREFIX rdfs: <http://www.w3.org/2000/01/rdf-schema#>
SELECT ?subject ?object
        WHERE { ?subject rdfs:subClassOf ?object }
```

Figure 7. Example of a Sparql Query is Request).

subject	object
web-technologie	web
cost-project	project-feachers
mastere-project	study-project
data-base-system	Data-base
embedded-software	embded-system
type-projcct	project-feachers
context	project-concept
data-mining	Data-base
solution-name	solution
Small	Size-project
distributed-system	inteligent-system
programming-layers	software-ressource
knowledge-discovery	knowledge-management

Execute

Figure 8. Example of a Sparql Query result.

V. Conclusion and Futures Works

The main objective of this research study was to propose a domain ontology that helps to present a computer project field (concept and relation). Moreover, we described multiple methodologies in the construction of ontology and we ended this section by proposing a method of construction of a domain ontology based on METHONTOLOGY methodology.

Given the importance of the information and knowledge of the website of publication and archiving, we chose to apply it to feed our knowledge base. For future works, we will focus on interrogating by utilizing the API "JENA"[19]. Also, we will try to complete the on-line process of our approach to apply the concept of case-based reasoning (CBR).

References

[1] J.Stal-Le Cardinal, J.-L.Giordano and G.Turré," Les Retours d'expérience du Projet, Réduire les Risques, Augmenter les Performances Collectives (From The Project Reduce Risks, Increase Collective Performance)", https://hal.archives-ouvertes.fr/hal-01482335, 2014.

[2] B.Francois, " La Capitalisation Des Connaissances Dans un Contexte de Projet (The Capitalization of Knowledge in A Project Context)", Thesis submitted as part of the project management master's program, University of Quebec at Rimouski, 2014.

[3] J-LErmine, "Knowledge Management(Gestion de Connaissance)",HeLavoisier, p.166, https://hal.archives-ouvertes.fr/hal-00997696/file/. pdf,2003.

[4] Y.Harrani, "A Multi-model Approach For the Capitalization of Knowledge In The Field of Design",Thesis, specialty in Industrial Engineering, 1997.

[5] S.Bekhti, "A Dynamic Process For Defining And Routing Project Memories" ,University of Technology Troyes, France,2003.

[6] M.Lewkowicz and M.Zacklad, "Using Problem-Solving Models to Design Efficient Cooperative Knowledge-Management Systems Based on Formalization and Traceability of Argumentation", EKAW '00: Proceedings of the 12th European Workshop on Knowledge Acquisition, Modeling and Management, Pages 288–295, 2000.

[7] L.Serrano, "Vers Une Capitalisation Des Connaissances Orientée Utilisateur: Extraction et Structuration Automatiques d'informations à Partir de Sources Ouvertes": (Towards user-oriented knowledge capitalization: Automatic Extraction and Structuring of Information From Open Sources), Thesis, 2014.

[8] M. Sliger, "Agile Project Management with Scrum", paper presented at PMI® Global Congress2011—North America, Dallas, TX. Newtown Square, PA: Project Management Institute, 2011.

[9] N.Mahfouf and B.Ramdhani, "Planification et ordonnancement d'un projet avec des moyens limités au sein d'ENGTP", ("Planning and Scheduling of a Project with limited Means Within ENGTP"), thesis , 2014.

[10] S.I.Hyder, J.Ansari, M.S.Ramish and M.Y.T.Fasih, "Emerging Role of Ontology Based Repository in Business Management Research", Journal of Organizational Knowledge Management, p.17, 2017.

[11] B.Chabot,"Ontologies-Pourquoi-Quoi Comment(Ontologies:Why?What?How?), Published on October 26, 2017.

[12] J. Busse, B. Humm, C. Lubbert and F. Moelter, "Actually, What Does Ontology Mean? A Term Coined by Philosophy in the Light of Different Scientific Disciplines", Journal of Computing and Information Technology, vol. 1, no. CIT 23, p. 29–41, 2015.

[13] J.Chaumier, "Les Ontologies Antécédents, Aspects Techniques et Limites (Ontologies History, Technical Aspects And Limits)", Documentalist-Information Sciences », Vol. 44, pages 81 to 83 ISSN 0012-4508, 2007.

[14] A.Maedche, E.aedche, S.Staab, "The TEXT-TO-ONTO Ontology Learning Environment", a Software Demonstration at ICCS-2000 Eight International Conference on Conceptual Structures, 2000.

[15] H.Roitman, A.Gal, "OntoBuilder: Fully Automatic Extraction and Consolidation of Ontologies from Web Sources Using Sequence Semantics", Technion, Israel Institute of Technology Technion City, 2004.

[16] M.Fernandez,A.Gómez-Pérez,N.Juristo,"From Ontological Art Towards Ontological Engineering", Acte of AAAI, 1997.

[17] G.Schreiber, B-J.Wielinga, W.Jansweijer, "The kactus view of the 'o' word.", IJCAI'1995, Workshop on Basic Ontological Issues in Knowledge, 1995.

[18] V.Giudicelli, "Ontologies et l'éditeur Protégé - Application à la Formalisation des Concepts de Description d'IMGT-ONTOLOGY (Ontologies And The Protected Editor - Application To The Formalization Of IMGT-ONTOLOGY Description concepts)", 2010,

[19] https://jena.apache.org/documentation/ontology/accessed August 06, 2018.

[20] https://websemantique.developpez.com/tutoriels/francart/debuter-avec-sesame/, March 25, 2018.

[21] About: Stardog, http://dbpedia.org/page/Stardog, March 22, 2018.